TWISTED PATHS

Twisted Paths

Europe 1914–1945

Edited by
ROBERT GERWARTH

OXFORD
UNIVERSITY PRESS

OXFORD

UNIVERSITY PRESS

Great Clarendon Street, Oxford OX2 6DP

Oxford University Press is a department of the University of Oxford.
It furthers the University's objective of excellence in research, scholarship,
and education by publishing worldwide in

Oxford New York

Auckland Cape Town Dar es Salaam Hong Kong Karachi
Kuala Lumpur Madrid Melbourne Mexico City Nairobi
New Delhi Shanghai Taipei Toronto

With offices in

Argentina Austria Brazil Chile Czech Republic France Greece
Guatemala Hungary Italy Japan Poland Portugal Singapore
South Korea Switzerland Thailand Turkey Ukraine Vietnam

Oxford is a registered trade mark of Oxford University Press
in the UK and in certain other countries

Published in the United States
by Oxford University Press Inc., New York

© The Several Contributors 2007

The moral rights of the authors have been asserted
Database right Oxford University Press (maker)

First published 2007

British Library Cataloguing in Publication Data
Data available

Library of Congress Cataloging in Publication Data
Data available

Typeset by Laserwords Private Limited, Chennai, India
Printed in Great Britain
on acid-free paper by
Biddles Ltd., King's Lynn, Norfolk

ISBN 978–0–19–928185–5

1 3 5 7 9 10 8 6 4 2

Acknowledgements

The publication of this book would not have been possible without the assistance and support of many individuals who unsparingly gave their time to provide invaluable feedback and criticism. The editor is particularly indebted to Martin Conway and Robert Evans for their encouragement and support. Furthermore, Robert Aldrich, Markku Anttila, Pieter Briegel, Tom Buchanan, Sally Cove, Porscha Fermanis, Juliane Fürst, Robert Gildea, David Harvey, John Hiden, Emese Lafferton, Rana Mitter, Dirk Moses, Thomas Munch-Petersen, Phillip Morgan, Holger Nehring, David Priestland, Paul Readman, Jay Sexton, Zara Steiner, David Stevenson, Mary Vincent, Jonathan Wright, and several anonymous readers offered challenging feedback about individual chapters and the project as a whole.

For financial and logistical support, the editor is deeply indebted to the British Academy and Corpus Christi College, Oxford, whose generosity allowed for the time, space, and congenial environment to produce this volume. The editorial team at Oxford University Press provided invaluable help while the book was being produced. Finally, the editor would like to thank the many publishers and copyright holders for their permission to reprint illustrations.

Contents

List of Contributors

STEFAN BERGER is Professor of Modern German and Comparative European History at the University of Manchester. He is currently chairing a European Science Foundation Programme on 'Representations of the Past. The Writing of National Histories in 19th and 20th Century Europe' (2003–8). He is also completing a British Academy funded project on 'Britain and the GDR, 1949–1990'. He has published widely in the areas of comparative labour history, history of historiography, nationalism, and national identity. His most recent book is *Inventing Germany* (London, 2004).

R. J. B. BOSWORTH is Professor of Modern History at the University of Western Australia. Among his numerous publications are: *Nationalism* (Harlow, 2007) *Mussolini's Italy: Life under the Dictatorship 1915–1945* (London, 2005), *Mussolini* (London 2002), and *The Italian Dictatorship: Problems and Perspectives in the Interpretation of Mussolini and Fascism* (Oxford, 1998).

PATRICIA CLAVIN is Fellow and Tutor in Modern History at Jesus College, Oxford. She is currently working on a study of the Economic and Financial Organization of the League of Nations funded by the Arts and Humanities Research Council. In 2000, she published *The Great Depression in Europe, 1929–1939* (London, 2000). She is also the co-author (with Asa Briggs) of *Modern Europe, 1789–1989* (London and New York, 1997; 2nd edn. 2003).

MARTIN CONWAY is Fellow and Tutor in Modern European History at Balliol College, Oxford. He has written about the extreme right in Belgium during the inter-war years and the Second World War. He has also written more generally on the extreme right and Catholicism in twentieth-century Europe. He is currently working on a book on Belgium after the Second World War. Among his publications are: *Collaboration in Belgium: Léon Degrelle and the Rexist Movement 1940–1944* (New Haven and London, 1993) and *Catholic Politics in Europe 1918–1945* (London, 1997). He is also the co-editor (with T. C. Buchanan) of *Political Catholicism in Europe, 1918–1965* (Oxford, 1996) and (with J. Gotovitch), *Europe in Exile: European Exile Communities in Britain 1940–1945* (Oxford and New York, 2001).

R. J. CRAMPTON retired as Professor of Eastern European History at the University of Oxford in October 2006 and is now on Emeritus Fellow of St Edmund Hall. His research interests lie in the field of twentieth-century Balkan history. Among his main publications are: *The Hollow Détente: Anglo-German Relations in the Balkans, 1911–1914* (London and Atlantic Heights, NJ, 1981), *A Concise History of Bulgaria* (2nd edn., Cambridge, 2005), *Eastern Europe in the Twentieth Century—and After* (London and New York, 1996), *The Balkans since the Second World War* (London and New York, 2002), and *Bulgaria* (Oxford, 2007).

NICHOLAS DOUMANIS is Senior Lecturer in History at the University of New South Wales, Sydney. He is currently finishing a book dealing with the Greek *longue durée* and is preparing a study on the modern Mediterranean. He is also working on pluralism and social accommodation in the late Ottoman Empire. His main publications include *Myth and Memory in the Mediterranean* (London, 1997) and *Italy: Inventing the Nation* (London, 2001).

R. J. W. EVANS is Regius Professor of History at the University of Oxford. He is also a Fellow of Oriel College and a Fellow of the British Academy. His publications include: *The Making of the Habsburg Monarchy, 1550–1700: An Interpretation* (Oxford, 1991), *Great Britain and East-Central Europe, 1908–48: A Study in Perceptions* (London, 2002), and *Austria, Hungary, and the Habsburgs. Essays on Central Europe, c. 1683–1867* (Oxford, 2006). He is also co-editor (with H. J. Pogge von Strandmann) of *The Revolutions in Europe, 1848–9: From Reform to Reaction* (Oxford, 2000).

ROBERT GERWARTH is British Academy Postdoctoral Fellow at Corpus Christi College, Oxford, and Faculty Lecturer in Modern European History at the University of Oxford. He has also held visiting fellowships at Harvard University and the NIOD in Amsterdam. His publications include *The Bismarck Myth: Weimar Germany and the Legacy of the Iron Chancellor* (Oxford, 2005, paperback 2007) as well as scholarly articles in *Contemporary European History*, *German History*, and *Past and Present*.

MARY HILSON is Lecturer in Contemporary Scandinavian History at University College London. Her main research interests are in nineteenth- and twentieth-century Swedish and Scandinavian history, in particular comparative social history and popular politics. Her publications include *Political Change and the Rise of Labour in Comparative Perspective Britain and Sweden c. 1890–1920* (Lund, 2006). She is currently working on a general history of the Nordic countries since 1945 and on the history of the consumer co-operative movement in comparative perspective.

ALVIN JACKSON is Richard Lodge Professor of History at the University of Edinburgh. His research interests lie in the political relationship between Britain and Ireland in the nineteenth and twentieth centuries. He has written extensively on the Union, and on Irish Unionism. He has published numerous articles and five books, including *The Ulster Party, 1884–1911* (Oxford, 1989), *Ireland 1798–1998: Politics and War* (Oxford, 1999), and *Home Rule: An Irish History, 1800–2000* (London, 2003).

HUBERTUS F. JAHN is University Senior Lecturer in Russian History at Cambridge University and a Fellow of Clare College. His main publications include *Patriotic Culture in Russia during World War I* (Ithaca, NY, 1995) and (co-edited with James von Geldern) *Birches, Bolsheviks, and Balalaikas: Popular Culture in Russian History* (special issue of *Journal of Popular Culture*, 1998).

FRANCES LANNON is the Principal of Lady Margaret Hall, Oxford. She has published widely on Spanish social and political history in the nineteenth and twentieth centuries. Among her publications are *Privilege, Persecution, and Prophecy. The Catholic Church in Spain 1875–1975* (Oxford, 1987) and *The Spanish Civil War, 1936–1939* (Oxford, 2002). She is also the co-editor (with Paul Preston) of: *Elites and Power in Twentieth Century Spain* (Oxford, 1990).

ROSS MCKIBBIN is Emeritus Research Fellow at St John's College, Oxford, and a Fellow of the British Academy. He specializes in twentieth-century British history. At the moment he is working on the political structure of England between 1918 and 1951 which will be the subject of his forthcoming James Ford Lectures in British History at Oxford University. His publications include *Evolution of the Labour Party, 1910–1924* (Oxford, 1991), *Ideologies of Class: Social Relations in Britain, 1880–1950* (Oxford, 1991), and *Classes and Cultures: England 1918–1951* (Oxford, 1998).

PETER ROMIJN is Research Director of the Netherlands Institute for War Documentation (NIOD) in Amsterdam and Professor of Twentieth Century History at the University of Amsterdam. His principal publications include 'The War, 1940–1945' in J. C. H. Blom, R. Fuks-Mansveld, and I. Schöffer (eds.), *A History of the Jews in the Netherlands* (London, 2002), '"Restoration of Confidence": The Purge of Local Government in the Netherlands as a Problem of Postwar Reconstruction', in Istvàn Deàk, Jan T. Gross, and Tony Judt (eds.), *The Politics of Retribution in Europe: World War II and its Aftermath* (Princeton, 2000), 173–93, *Snel, streng en rechtvaardig: Politiek beleid inzake de bestraffing en reclassering van 'foute' Nederlanders 1945–1955* (Groningen, 1991; 2nd edn. Amsterdam, 2002), and *Burgemeesters in oorlogstijd. Besteren onder de Duitse bezetting.* (Amsterdam, 2006).

KRISTINA SPOHR READMAN is Lecturer in International History at the London School of Economics. Educated at the University of East Anglia, Sciences Po Paris, and Cambridge University, she has also held a Junior Research Fellowship at Christ's College, Cambridge. She specializes in twentieth-century German and Baltic history and is currently working on International Law and the Baltic question in the Cold War. Publications include *Germany and the Baltic Problem after the Cold War: The Development of a New Ostpolitik, 1989–2000* (London, 2004), and scholarly articles in *Historical Journal* and *Cold War History*.

JOAN TUMBLETY is Lecturer in Modern European History at the University of Southampton. Her research interests are focused on the cultural history of twentieth-century France, with special interests in gender, sport, and the radical right. Her publications include 'Responses to Women's Enfranchisement in France, 1944–1945', *Women's Studies International Forum*, 26 (2003), '"Civil Wars of the Mind": The Commemoration of the 1789 Revolution in the Parisian Press of the Radical Right', *European History Quarterly*, 30 (2000) and 'Revenge of the Fascist Knights: Masculine Identities in *Je suis partout*, 1940–1944', *Modern and Contemporary France*, 7 (1999).

List of Maps

List of Tables

List of Illustrations

Every effort has been made to trace copyright holders but this has not been possible in all cases. If notified, the publisher will be pleased to rectify any omissions at the earliest possibility.

1

Introduction

Robert Gerwarth

When the German photographer Albert Renger-Patzsch published his critically acclaimed book *The World is Beautiful* in 1928, many of the most prominent reviewers raised the question if it was possible to appreciate the beauty of the world in an age overshadowed by the legacies of the Great War, economic uncertainty, and widespread anxiety over the future of European civilization. Seventeen years later, after the experience of the unprecedented atrocities committed during the Second World War, the answer to this question seemed obvious. For many contemporary observers who had lived through the turmoil of the period, the entire era since 1914 resembled (in the words of Charles de Gaulle) a 'second', but more devastating, 'Thirty Years War', a time in which any fleeting moments of hope or optimism had at best been an expression of naivety.

Following this pattern, historical textbooks of early twentieth-century Europe have often tended to characterize the period as a crisis-ridden 'dark' interlude between two eras of economic prosperity and peace. Set against the 'golden age' of post-1945 (Western) European integration and economic growth, as well as the pre-war era of European global domination, the years between 1914 and the end of the Second World War are commonly described as an 'age of catastrophe' (Eric Hobsbawm), a 'period of terrible violence, instability and fragmentation' that can 'be seen merely as a nightmarish parenthesis between two eras of globalization and integration' (Julian Jackson).

Given the scope of the horrors which Europe experienced both within the period and its immediate aftermath, such verdicts seem more than justified. By 1945 much of Europe was in ruins. Since 1914, roughly eighty million people had been killed in the course of wars and civil wars, in the extermination camps of the Nazi regime, and in the forced labour camps of Stalinist Russia. In the First World War alone, the dead totalled more than eight million military casualties and, according to some estimates, a further five million civilians who perished as a result of war, civil war, and famine. In the Second World War, more than forty million people—two-thirds of them civilians—were killed. Apart from the two world wars, Europe witnessed the Russian and Spanish Civil Wars (resulting in up to three million deaths in the first case and about 500,000 in the second), the Russo-Polish War of 1919–21, and the war between Greece and Turkey of 1920–2, as well as major revolutionary and counter-revolutionary upheavals in Central and Eastern Europe. Between five and six million Jews and hundreds of thousands of Sinti and Roma were brutally murdered. A continent that had prided itself on being the 'cradle of civilization' had become the site of some of the most barbaric acts of mass murder in recorded history.

In the wake of war and the repeated reshuffling of borders, Europe also experienced unparalleled waves of forced migration: four to five million refugees in the years 1918–22, and as many as forty million 'displaced persons' between 1945 and 1950. Families were torn apart, communities destroyed, and economies exhausted. Europe's global predominance in cultural, economic, and political affairs was irrevocably lost. When viewed from the perspective of 1945 and compared with the situation in 1900, Europe's history in the first half of the century must have seemed very dark indeed.

The question remains as to whether European history between 1914 and 1945 should be judged retrospectively (that is, from the utter devastation caused from the late 1930s onwards) or whether we are hereby doing injustice to the numerous more positive elements of the period—from social reform, democratization, and the enfranchisement of women in many countries to mass-commodity consumption, an unusual degree of cultural productivity, the expansion of leisure time, and scientific innovation, as well as new forms of state action to counter the economic depression—that existed alongside ethnic, political, and socio-economic conflict. The sheer scale of war and genocide in the first half of the twentieth century doubtless makes it difficult to appreciate any of the seemingly short-lived achievements in inter-war European history, but they were, of course, as much part of that period's legacy as were the experiences of ultra-violence and economic crisis. It is indeed almost impossible to understand the success of European integration, social policies, and industrial practices in the post-1945 period without acknowledging their heavy debt to ideas and forms of policy-making developed before the Second World War. Even in the field of international relations, it seems questionable if a linear story of European 'decline' and 'failure' can adequately capture the pluralism and ambivalence of European history in the first half of the twentieth century. The League of Nations, for example, commonly charged with responsibility for failing to prevent rearmament and the outbreak of the Second World War, nevertheless made substantial contributions in the fields of healthcare, drug control, economic cooperation, labour legislation, and laws to prevent the illegal trafficking of women. Its work foreshadowed aspects of European and global cooperation that are usually described as emerging *after* the Second World War, for example, by creating the first genuinely international civil service (the Secretariat), many of whose members played an important role in post-war institutions such as the United Nations, the European Community, the World

Health Organization, the International Court of Justice, or the International Labour Organization.

Given the diversity of the period's legacy, it cannot be the aim of this volume to replace the narrative of Europe's linear decline between 1914 and 1945 with an alternative, univocal interpretation of the period. Instead, it offers a series of concise introductory essays on the often different (and sometimes similar) historical experiences of twelve European states and regions, as well as two chapters on the League of Nations and Europe's myriad connections with the 'wider world'. As a result, this volume differs from previous general histories on the period in two substantial ways. First, the book moves beyond the view that the history of early twentieth-century Europe can only be understood in terms of catastrophe. That history is composed of many different and often contradictory cross-currents is an insight that was articulated by two of inter-war Europe's numerous prominent intellectuals, Ernst Bloch and Siegfried Kracauer. What Bloch called 'non-synchronicity' and Kracauer the 'heterogeneity of the historical universe' acknowledges the multiple temporal strands that rarely, if ever, cohere in any historical period. This volume consequently aims to provide a more balanced synthesis of new historical research on the twisted paths of European states and regions in this period, presenting an account that refrains from depicting early twentieth-century European history as a one-way street into the abyss. While this collection certainly does not try to paint the period in rosy colours, it suggests that both 'darker' and 'lighter' elements in Europe's history were capable of evolving simultaneously, and that European societies followed twisted paths through the age of the two world wars. Without neglecting the more familiar stories of war, genocide, and economic depression, each chapter will demonstrate that political stability and regime collapse, social progress and mass poverty, the crisis of European civilization and remarkable cultural achievements could exist alongside each other, and that even for the belligerent European countries which participated in the wars after 1914 and 1939, the 1920s and early 1930s were a *post*-war period, not just a crisis-ridden prelude to the Second World War. This volume consequently addresses a wide canvas of events, ranging from the military struggles of the two world wars (and their manifold consequences), the intense political conflicts which resulted in the Bolshevik revolution of 1917, the challenges of political and cultural nation-building in East-Central Europe, the Fascist and Nazi seizures of power in Italy and Germany, and the Spanish Civil War of 1936–9 to the often neglected achievements of the period, such as innovations in social welfare, the introduction of far-reaching labour laws, and the breakthrough of parliamentary democracy and republicanism in countries previously ruled by autocratic or semi-autocratic governments. International history, both in terms of inner European affairs between 1914 and 1945 and Europe's multiple connections with the 'wider world', also features prominently. Despite the fact that the First World War brought Europe's global domination to an abrupt end, it continued to maintain multiple ties with the wider world. Apart from the continued existence of formal empires, and German and Italian attempts at empire-building, the volume addresses the beginnings of Europe's cultural and economic 'Americanization' and the enduring personal networks that resulted from international migration.

Secondly, in order to emphasize the extraordinary degree of diversity that characterized the period, this volume broadens the geographical focus by offering succinct interpretations of historical developments in nearly all areas within Europe's natural borders, from the Atlantic to the Arctic Ocean, from the Bosporus to the Urals and the Mediterranean. Starting with the often marginalized Scandinavian countries whose impact on inter- and post-war concepts of welfare, education, and social peace as well as on modern architecture and design was considerable, the volume covers developments in western, southern, and eastern Europe, as well as the successes and shortcomings of the League of Nations and Europe's close ties with the rest of the world. Some readers will no doubt be surprised to see that small countries such as the Scandinavian and Baltic states or Belgium and the Netherlands receive nearly as much space as Russia, Germany, France, and Britain. Yet one of the principles of this book is to avoid the temptation of homogenizing European history by focusing exclusively on the belligerent 'Great Powers' and to emphasize instead that the histories of smaller states can illuminate the diversity of Europe's experiences in the first half of the twentieth century. Although the larger states' particular weight and influence in inner and extra-European affairs is undoubted (and indeed reflected in the decision to devote separate chapters to their histories in the period), considerable attention is also given to countries and regions which are all too often lost from view behind the histories of larger states. Wherever possible, nation-states with similar political, social, or cultural agendas have been grouped together in one chapter to allow for fresh comparative, transnational, or transregional perspectives. In the cases of the Baltic and Scandinavian countries, the Iberian Peninsula, the Balkans, the Successor States, and the Low Countries, such an approach seemed particularly fruitful. For similar reasons, it has been decided to include a chapter on 'The Two Irelands' which suggests that the Irish Free State followed a very different path from Britain after 1922, while Northern Ireland, though remaining part of the United Kingdom, had a distinct political and religious life that may be seen as much in the context of Irish as of British history.

There are several challenges in writing a multi-authored general history along these lines. One of the challenges for any history textbook of this scale is the reconciliation of breadth and depth. Although it would be impossible for any one-volume study to cover every aspect of European history between 1914 and 1945, this book is unusually broad in its geographical and thematic scope. Without pretending (or desiring) to be a 'total history', or indeed a conclusive account of European history in the age of two world wars, this book attempts to encourage debate about the multifaceted nature of a period that is all too often approached as a pathological phenomenon in textbooks. We are acutely aware that in a book with such broad coverage, many important aspects of European history in this period can only be discussed in passing and that some geographical areas (most notably Switzerland) could not be included due to limitations of space. However, it is hoped that the survey-style nature of this volume will stimulate further general interest in (and debate about) one of the most dramatic periods in modern European history. Our readers are encouraged to use this book as a starting point for further explorations of this rich and diverse period, and to read it alongside both thematically ordered textbooks and case studies on individual aspects of early twentieth-century European history. For this purpose, readers will find a short list of further suggested reading at the end of each chapter.

A related challenging task was to ensure the greatest possible cohesion for this book while at the same time seeking to argue that there was no 'normative' European experience between 1914 and 1945. To be sure, Europe underwent many common processes, from economic change to social modernization and the transition to mass politics, but the ways in which these common processes were refracted through Europe's political cultures differed remarkably. A contemporary traveller, Patrick Leigh Fermor, who walked through Europe from the Netherlands to Turkey in 1933, accurately conveyed a sense of the irreducible diversity of European states and societies in the literary descriptions of his journey, during which he encountered a wealth of cultural diversity as well as highly divergent levels of living standards and urbanization.

Because of Europe's diversity, it is necessary to adopt an 'open' approach to the subject matter, rather than a 'hard' definition of European history which emphasizes its common experience and its distinctiveness from other areas of the world. Both before 1914 and again after 1945, it was relatively easy to decide on the borders of Europe. In the inter-war-period, however, there was little qualitative difference between Europe and states experiencing modernization beyond Europe's geographical borders such as Ataturk's 'Europeanizing' Turkey, or indeed Japan. In this respect, 'Europe' was not so much a clearly definable subject as a constellation.

A final point relates to periodization. Although this book starts in 1914 and ends in 1945, it should be emphasized that neither of these dates constituted decisive turning points in the histories of *all* European states. For the large number of countries that did not participate in the First World War—notably Denmark, the Netherlands, Norway, Spain, Sweden, and Switzerland—August 1914 did not mark the kind of caesura that it clearly did in the belligerent countries. The same applies to 1945. For a German Jew who had managed to survive the horrors of the Holocaust, 8 May 1945 obviously had a very different meaning than it did for the peoples of Spain, Portugal, Sweden, Ireland, and Switzerland, all of whom had remained neutral during the Second

World War. Similarly, for many Europeans, the end of the Second World War did not always divide violence and repression from post-war reconstruction and the dawn of the democratic age. For a substantial number of people, the years that followed the end of the Second World War were the worst of the twentieth century. Food shortages, high levels of violence against civilian populations, economic dislocation, and mass suffering continued after 1945, particularly, but not exclusively, in Eastern Europe. As the following chapters will demonstrate, there is indeed much to be said for interpreting the period of 1914–45 as Europe's 'age of catastrophe'. Yet it should not be forgotten that Europe's early twentieth century was *also* characterized by learning processes and often remarkable achievements and innovations that survived the devastations of the Second World War and shaped the second, 'happier' half of that century.

FURTHER READING

Berend, Ivan T., *Decades of Crisis: Central and Eastern Europe before World War II* (Berkeley, Calif., 1998).

Berghahn, Valler R., *Europe in the Era* of *Two World Wars: From Militarism and Genocide to Civil Society.* (Princeton, 2006).

Berman Sheri, *The Social Democratic Moment: Ideas and Politics in the Making of Interwar Europe* (Cambridge, Mass., 1998).

Bessel, Richard (ed.), *Fascist Italy and Nazi Germany: Comparisons and Contrasts* (Cambridge, 1996).

Borejsza, Jerzy W., and Klaus Ziemer (eds.), *Totalitarian and Authoritarian Regimes in Europe: Legacies and Lessons from the Twentieth Century* (New York, 2006).

Cambridge History of Christianity, ix. *World Christianities c.1914–c.2000*, ed. Hugh McLeod (Cambridge, 2006).

Clavin, Patricia, *The Great Depression in Europe, 1929–1939* (London, 2000).

Conrad, Peter, *Modern Times, Modern Places* (London, 1998).

Conway, Martin, *Catholic Politics in Europe 1918–1945* (London, 1997).

Donald, Moira, and Tim Rees (eds.), *Reinterpreting Revolution in Twentieth-Century Europe* (New York, 2001).

Hobsbawm, Eric, *Age of Extremes: The Short Twentieth Century 1914–1991* (London, 1994).

Jackson, Julian, *Europe 1900–1945* (Oxford, 2002).

Luebbert, Gregory M., *Liberalism, Fascism, or Social Democracy: Social Classes and the Political Origins of Regimes in Interwar Europe* (Oxford, 1991).

McCabe, Susan, *Cinematic Modernism: Modernist Poetry and Film* (Cambridge, 2005).

Mann, Michael, *Fascists* (New York, 2004).

Mazower, Mark, *Dark Continent: Europe in the Twentieth Century* (London, 1999).

Rees, Tim, and Andrew Thorpe (eds.), *International Communism and the Communist International 1919–1943* (New York, 1998).

Reynolds, Sian (ed.), *Women, State and Revolution: Essays on Power and Gender in Europe since 1789* (Amherst, Mass., 1987).

Steinberg, Gerald, *A World at Arms: A Global History of World War II* (Cambridge, 1994).

Steiner, Zara, *The Lights that Failed European International History, 1919–1933* (Oxford, 2005).

Stevenson, David, *Cataclysm: The First World War as Political Tragedy* (New York, 2004).

Timms, Edward, and Peter Collier (eds.), *Visions and Blueprints: Avant-Garde Culture and Radical Politics in Early Twentieth-Century Europe* (Manchester, 1988).

Vinen, Richard, *A History in Fragments: Europe in the Twentieth Century* (London, 2000).

2

Scandinavia

Mary Hilson

INTRODUCTION

For a sparsely populated and relatively peripheral area of Northern Europe, the three Scandinavian countries—Denmark, Norway, and Sweden—generated a considerable amount of international interest during the inter-war period. By 1939, Sweden in particular had gained an international reputation as a model state, which had responded successfully to the economic and political crisis of the 1930s. Particularly influential was a book by the American journalist Marquis Childs, *Sweden: The Middle Way* (1936), which helped to establish the idea of the Swedish and Scandinavian 'middle way' as a compromise between free-market capitalist democracy and fascist or communist totalitarianism. Writing in *The Spectator* in 1938, Anthony Blunt commented that, 'The Scandinavians are the very best sort of people, who seem to have all the advantages of being progressive without any of the unpleasantness. They have achieved real democracy of a kind, and one which is apparent at every step.' Childs's favourable impressions were echoed by a team of observers from the British Fabian Society, which visited Sweden in 1936 to investigate the impact of the recent social reforms. Swedish fame for innovation in social policy was strengthened by a matching reputation for extreme modernity in design and architecture, demonstrated to the world through the Exhibition of Arts, Crafts, and Home Industries held in Stockholm in 1930. In Denmark it was the agricultural co-operative societies and the Folk High Schools for adult education which attracted the admiration of international delegations. Sir E. D. Simon, in a book written for the Left Book Club in 1939, pointed to the Scandinavian countries and Switzerland as a model for the defence of democracy against the 'terrific challenge' of the dictators in 'these dark days'. Most enthusiastic of all was the British Labour politician Hugh Dalton, who wrote in 1936 that the Swedish recovery from the depression had been 'sensational' and nothing short of 'an economic miracle'. Swedish industrial output did indeed grow impressively, by 67 per cent between 1932 and 1937, though economic historians now agree that this was largely for structural reasons rather than a direct result of enlightened economic policy.

It may be noted that by the late 1930s the Scandinavian governments were also actively promoting this image of their region as egalitarian, peaceable, stable, democratic, and ultra-modern, in contrast to so much of the rest of Europe. One example of this was the publication of an English-language book entitled *The Northern Countries in World Economy* in 1937, the northern countries in this case including also Finland and Iceland. Published by a government-sponsored organization for the promotion of economic cooperation, the book was intended to be 'a manifestation of the spirit of cooperation among the northern Nations'. This was, however, a remarkably novel image of the region. Seen from the perspective of 1914, there was little to suggest that inter-war Scandinavian history would follow this course, and that the region would avoid the political and social upheavals which beset much of continental Europe during most of the period. Denmark, Norway, and Sweden were small, relatively poor, and strategically vulnerable countries. Rapid industrial development during the 1890s and 1900s had resulted in social polarization and conflict, especially in Sweden and Norway. In the century after 1830, almost three million Scandinavians emigrated to the New World and elsewhere, rates which measured in proportion to population were among the highest in Europe. Moreover, parliamentary democracy was a fragile phenomenon, established around the beginning of the period and no less vulnerable to political extremism than similar regimes elsewhere in Europe.

Despite mutually intelligible languages and a degree of shared history, the Scandinavian countries differed from one another in important ways. Norway was a young country, which had only gained independence from Sweden in 1905 and was strongly influenced by the liberal nationalist movements which had campaigned for this independence during the late nineteenth century. It lagged behind the other Scandinavian countries in its economic development, though it had gained a degree of parliamentary government in 1884. After independence was achieved, the thoughts of Norwegian nationalists turned towards national consolidation and economic development through the rapid expansion of hydroelectric power and the related electrochemical and metallurgical industries. Sweden, by contrast, had a well-developed and rapidly expanding industrial sector by the turn of the century, but it also had an unreformed political system and a monarchy and conservative establishment unwilling to accept the final demise of great power aspirations in 1905. Denmark retained its North Atlantic possessions, including Iceland, the Faeroe Islands, and Greenland, but for the last quarter of the nineteenth century its politicians had governed in acute consciousness of their vulnerability to their much larger neighbour Germany, following military defeat in 1864.

This chapter is concerned with the three Scandinavian countries: Denmark, Norway, and Sweden. As the example of the *The Northern Economies* discussed above makes clear, it would have been possible to include Finland here as well. Despite the different language there were strong historic and cultural ties between Finland and the rest of Scandinavia, since Finland had been part of Sweden until 1809, and still retained an influential Swedish-speaking minority. As Kristina Spohr Readman discusses in her chapter, however, there are also good reasons for considering Finland together with the other Baltic States that achieved independence from Russia at the end of the First World War. Moreover, it was only really from the second half of the 1930s that the idea of Scandinavia was expanded (as *Norden*, or the Nordic region) to include Finland. There is a danger here that one views the earlier part of the period through the prism of post-1945 Nordic cooperation, which is not necessarily appropriate.

There are two main questions for historians of Scandinavia during the inter-war period. The first concerns why the Scandinavian countries seemed to be able to overcome the problems of the era so much more successfully than many larger nations. The Scandinavian states were not immune to the major threats of the period: political extremism, dictatorship, social instability, violence, and war. How significant were these threats in Scandinavia and how successfully were they resisted? Secondly, to what extent is it possible to distinguish a common Scandinavian path in this period? The nineteenth-century aspiration to found a pan-Scandinavian state seemed a distant memory in 1905, when there was a real possibility that the break-up of the Swedish–Norwegian union would lead to war between the two countries. In its place, however, there was after 1917 an emerging sense of the need for Scandinavian solidarity among some small and vulnerable states. The response to this was a heightened commitment to internationalism, through participation in the League of Nations, and attempts to strengthen a sense of Nordic solidarity and cooperation. From the 1930s, this also included Finland, independent since 1917. Nordic histories seemed to converge with the Crisis Agreements of the early 1930s, and the broadly similar economic and social policies which followed. But this pan-Nordic solidarity was to be severely tested by the events of the Second World War: Finland fought two wars against the Soviet Union (see the chapter on Finland and the Baltic States), Norway and Denmark were invaded by the Nazis in April 1940, and the Swedish government emerged from the war with the purity of its neutrality severely compromised.

THE 1920s: PARLIAMENTARY DEMOCRACY UNDER THREAT?

Despite the tensions in intra-Scandinavian relations after 1905, the three states were able in 1912 to agree a joint declaration of neutrality in the event of a European war. This neutrality was maintained after August 1914, though none of the states was immune to the effects of the war. Like other neutral states, the Scandinavian countries experienced a beneficial increase in trade, though domestic prices rose very rapidly. By 1920 the cost of living index had risen to 262 for Denmark, 270 for Sweden, and 302 for Norway, where 1914 = 100 in each case. A turning point came in 1916, when submarine warfare began to cause serious disruption to international trade, and Norway in particular suffered heavy losses in its merchant marine. These difficulties also affected the food supply, so that by the winter of 1916–17 there were severe shortages of basic foodstuffs in all the Scandinavian countries, and widespread hunger demonstrations took place across Scandinavia during the spring of 1917. The situation threatened to generate grave social unrest and political instability, only exacerbated by the revolutions in Russia, and the civil war in Finland following that country's independence from Russia in December 1917.

The threat of revolution in 1917–18 was not unique to Scandinavia of course; indeed, events there were strongly influenced by developments in the rest of Europe, notably in Russia. Sweden's neutrality and geographical proximity to Russia meant that in the immediate aftermath of the February Revolution, Sweden was the main source for news on Russia, and events there were followed with great interest in the Swedish press. Lenin himself visited Stockholm in April 1917, though historians are divided on the extent to which the Swedish communists were influenced by the Bolsheviks or by other radical political currents. The syndicalist Central Organization of Swedish Workers (Sveriges Arbetarnes Centralorganisation, or SAC), founded in 1910, had over 30,000 members in 1920. At the end of the First World War there was very little evidence to suggest that liberalism, capitalism, and democracy were any more robust or unthreatened in Scandinavia than in the rest of Europe. Despite their non-belligerent status, the Scandinavian countries in 1918 were faced firstly with problems similar to those in other European countries. These included: the internal problem of minorities and the issue of national security; secondly, the need to make parliamentary democracy function effectively; and thirdly, post-war economic instability and resulting social conflict.

All three Scandinavian countries were signatories to the Covenant of the League of Nations in 1920 (newly independent Finland was admitted in December of that year). From 1923 they were treated as a distinctive block, with a rotating entitlement to one of the non-permanent seats on the League Council. Some Scandinavians, such as the Norwegian polar explorer Fridthiof Nansen and the Swedish labour politician Hjalmar Branting, played a leading role in seeking to establish the League in the forefront of post-war aspirations for international peace. Indeed, the League could claim as one of its early successes the peaceful resolution of a Scandinavian issue when, in 1921, it confirmed Finnish sovereignty over the Swedish-speaking inhabitants of the Åland islands, but with provisions for local autonomy and the demilitarization of the islands.

In fact, the question of national minorities was relatively straightforward for the Scandinavian countries when compared to the complex ethnic jigsaw of Eastern Europe. At first glance, Scandinavia seemed to lack the major ethnic, linguistic, and religious cleavages that the Versailles Treaty and Wilson's Fourteen Points were intended to tackle. There were ethnic and linguistic minorities in Scandinavia of course, including the Finnish-speaking Kvens of northern Norway, the Swedish-speaking minority in Finland, and a small gypsy or *tattare* population, but the existence of these groups lacked the potentially explosive implications of the existence of minorities elsewhere in Europe. The most significant minority group in Norway and Sweden was the Sami people (or Lapps as they were known to contemporaries), who lived a largely nomadic existence in the northern parts of Norway, Sweden, Finland, and north-western Russia. The prevailing attitude of the authorities to these people, strongly influenced by social Darwinism, was largely one of condescension: they were regarded as an inferior race which could be either safely ignored or left to the civilizing efforts of missionaries. Attempts to exploit the economic resources of the north in both Sweden and Norway had brought about encounters with the Sami, of course, but they were too few to offer any serious resistance.

There was more potential for problems of national unity in Denmark, since that country still had sovereignty over its north Atlantic islands. The indigenous people of Greenland were ruled directly as a colony, but both the Icelanders and the Faeroese were gradually distancing themselves from Copenhagen, aided by the growth of a commercial fishing industry. Iceland gained what amounted to almost full autonomy in 1918, while remaining under the auspices of the Danish crown. In the Faeroes there were moves towards greater cultural autonomy, including the adoption of a Faeroese flag and the widespread use of the Faeroese language, which were tolerated by Denmark. In fact, the one ethnic question in Scandinavia which did perhaps have the potential to become a problem arose not from the north Atlantic, but from Slesvig on the southern border of Denmark. German rule over the Danish-speakers of northern Slesvig had been a source of grievance to the Danish ruling elite since 1864, and there was disappointment that the matter was not mentioned in President Wilson's Fourteen Points. Nonetheless, the Danish government assumed that the Danish-speaking parts of Slesvig would be returned to Danish sovereignty following the defeat of Germany, while some ultra-nationalists argued for the Danish border to be extended as far south as Kiel. The peace treaty made provision for the matter to be settled by plebiscite, and for the purpose the region was divided into two zones: the northern, predominantly Danish-speaking zone voted as a whole in February 1920, while the southern zone voted by local government district a month later. The result of the plebiscites was a blow for Danish nationalists: the north produced a three-quarters majority in favour of reunification with Denmark, but in the south not a single district, including the major city of Flensburg, voted in favour. The Danish government had no choice but to accept the result, and on 10 July 1920 King Christian X rode across the border on a white horse to claim the new territory. The settlement proved to be effective, for it generated little of the ethnic tension seen in other parts of inter-war Europe.

Figure 2.1. King Christian X reclaims northern Slesvig as part of the Danish kingdom following the plebiscites, July 1920.

Despite the lack of important ethnic cleavages, the issue of nationalism had the potential to undermine fragile parliamentary democracy in both Sweden and Denmark. (In Norway, where liberalism had formed the backbone of the nationalist movement for independence, anti-democratic nationalism was much less prominent.) In Sweden, a suffrage reform enfranchising most men over 24 had been enacted in 1909, but the aspirations of democrats continued to be frustrated by the intransigence of the unreformed upper house of parliament, and the personal ambitions of the monarch, Gustav V. Following the end of the Swedish–Norwegian union in 1905, an emergent group of ultra-right-wing conservatives began to look to the monarchy as a focus for their ambition of reviving Swedish great power aspirations, expressed above all in demands for greater defence expenditure directed against Sweden's old enemy Russia. The Liberal government which took office in 1911 angered this group with its proposals to cut defence spending. In February 1914 the pro-defence campaign reached its climax when many thousands of demonstrators marched in Stockholm in support of increasing national defence (the so-called Farmers' March or *bondetåget*). King Gustav V, admiring the stance of his relative Kaiser Wilhelm, intervened and supported the pro-defence group's position in a speech to the demonstration in the palace courtyard. The Liberal government fell, and was replaced by a conservative, royally approved government under Hjalmar Hammarskjöld, which continued in office following two elections that same year. The political situation became calmer under the auspices of a wartime truce. In the spring of 1917, however, the Liberals and the Social Democrats defeated the government's defence proposals in parliament. This amounted to a vote of no confidence in the Hammarskjöld government, which duly fell, but following the intervention of the King was replaced by another conservative government under Carl Swartz. Against the background of the wartime hunger demonstrations the situation was now rather tense, but the leader of the reformist Social Democratic Party (SAP), Hjalmar Branting, was able to channel popular unrest into demands for constitutional reform and, following elections in September 1917, a new Liberal/SAP government took office on the basis of its parliamentary majority. The main aim of this government was to steer through a constitutional reform guaranteeing virtually universal and equal suffrage for both houses of parliament and for municipal elections, which was duly achieved.

In Denmark, the Social Democratic Party (SD) had worked in cooperation with the Liberals (RV) to secure universal suffrage, achieved through a constitutional reform in 1915. But here too parliamentary democracy faced a challenge from the nationalist right. As in pre-war Sweden, conservative nationalists turned to the monarchy as a channel for their dissatisfaction with the Liberal government's handling of the Slesvig issue. Tensions were heightened by a simultaneous major conflict in the labour market, in the early spring of 1920. In March, King Christian X took matters into his own hands by summoning the Liberal prime minister, C. T. Zahle, and demanding his resignation. When Zahle refused, the King simply dissolved his government and established a new, conservative one. The Social Democrats protested that the King had executed a *coup d'état* and managed to persuade the syndicalists to support their call for a general strike in defence of parliamentary democracy. The King was eventually persuaded to give in, let his government fall, and call a new parliamentary election. The so-called Easter Crisis (*Påskekrisen*) had been resolved peacefully, and shortly afterwards the labour market conflict was also settled.

There is broad consensus among historians that the years 1917–20 mark the final breakthrough for the principle of parliamentary democracy in Sweden and Denmark. In both cases the critical influence appears to have been the willingness of the majority of the labour movement to embrace parliamentary reformism as the main route to socialism, and to cooperate with bourgeois liberal parties in order to achieve that goal. This outcome was by no means inevitable, however. One concrete result of the hunger demonstrations and social unrest of the spring of 1917 was the institutionalization of a permanent split in the labour movement, with the founding of left-wing socialist parties in Denmark and Sweden. These new parties had their roots in the anti-defence socialist youth movements which had existed within the social democratic parties in both countries since the turn of the century, and were strongly influenced by events in Germany and Russia, though Bolshevism had perhaps less influence as an ideological force than anarcho-syndicalism. The situation remained tense throughout 1917–18. In Sweden, the Social Democrats were able to channel social unrest into support for parliamentary reform, secured through the election of a Social Democratic/Liberal government in the autumn of 1917, though there were further outbreaks of social unrest throughout 1918. In Denmark, where parliamentary reform was enacted in 1915, left-wing opposition to the Social Democrats' cooperation with the Liberals was growing throughout 1917, exacerbated by high levels of unemployment. There were strikes and disturbances throughout 1918, reaching a peak in November with several days of rioting in Copenhagen, sparked initially by demands for the release of left-wing political prisoners. That this did not escalate is perhaps explained by the strength of the reformist leadership of SD, like their counterparts in Sweden, and the party's declared willingness to defend parliamentary democracy. Indeed, on the same day as some of the most serious rioting, the SD congress adopted a comprehensive social reform policy.

By 1920, both SD and the SAP were explicitly committed to reformism under the influential leadership of Thorvald Stauning and Hjalmar Branting respectively. Stauning's 1923 pamphlet, 'Parliamentarism or Dictatorship', placed his party firmly within the democratic camp, and at its Odense congress the same year, the party adopted a new programme which broke with the past in that it amounted to a blueprint for government rather than an attack on the capitalist system. The following year, the social democrats were able to prove their commitment to the existing system when they formed their first minority government; it lasted two years before it fell over difficulties in getting its economic policy agreed in parliament. The SAP's 1920 programme, meanwhile, amounted to a fairly radical statement of socialist ideology with its demands 'to reform fundamentally the economic organization of bourgeois society'. That said, the party was also clear that this ambition was to be achieved through political means, and Branting demonstrated that he was prepared to give guarantees against radical action on either defence or nationalization when the party formed its first minority government in the same year. Some historians have suggested that revolution was against the innate character of the Scandinavian societies, the history of which had always been characterized by gradual, peaceful evolution. Opponents of this position argued (and have continued to argue) that the embrace of the institutions of liberal capitalism amounted to a betrayal of the true revolutionary aspirations of the working class. For the dominant groups in both social democratic parties, however, and indeed in the other mainstream parties as well, the battle for parliamentary democracy was over by the early 1920s. The problem that remained was how to make parliamentary democracy *work*, and in response to a succession of short-lived minority governments during the 1920s there were many critics, from both right and left, who advocated alternative means of achieving their preferred political goals.

Meanwhile in Norway, revolution might have seemed to some to be a real possibility during the 1920s. Here the major parliamentary reform had come in 1884, much against the wishes of the Swedish king. Perhaps because of this the Norwegian Labour Party (DNA) had never developed a tradition of cooperation with bourgeois liberalism to secure reforms. According to the historian and party activist Edvard Bull, writing in the 1920s, the decisive influence on the party was the rapidity of Norwegian industrialization after 1905, which radicalized the workforce. More recent research has cast doubt on this suggestion, arguing that more significant was the party's internal structure, which allowed radical groups from the Trondheim region in particular to gain a majority at the party's congress. The personality of the radical leader, Martin Tranmæl, was also thought to be influential, just as Branting and Stauning were equally important in steering their parties towards reformism. Whatever the cause, Tranmæl's radical Trade Union Opposition won a majority at the DNA's congress in the spring of 1918 and, declaring DNA to be a revolutionary party, subsequently applied to join the Communist International. Unlike Denmark or Sweden, in Norway it was the social democratic wing which split off from the main party to form a minority splinter group. The relationship with Comintern was not a happy one, especially following the publication of the so-called Twenty-One Theses, demanding complete allegiance to Moscow, and Tranmæl is known to have wanted to leave the organization as early as 1920. The labour movement was also weakened by high levels of unemployment and declining trade union membership. In the spring of 1923, the so-called Kristiania proposal to leave Comintern was adopted, and three labour parties contested the 1924 elections: DNA, the Social Democrats, and the Communist Party (NKP). In 1927, DNA reunited with the Social Democrats and made some significant gains in the election of that year, to the extent that they were invited by the king to form a minority government. This government, which survived for only fourteen days before it was defeated over its budget proposals, was perhaps the most extreme illustration of the difficulties of parliamentarianism. Wary of its experience, DNA returned to campaigning on an explicitly revolutionary platform in 1930.

It is difficult to judge the extent of genuine support for the stated revolutionary aims of the Norwegian Labour Party in the 1920s. Immediately after DNA left Comintern, approximately a quarter of its membership and half of its parliamentary representatives defected to the new Communist Party, though in many cases this was only temporary. Indeed, it was the growth of a strong parliamentary group around the moderate social democrat Johan Nygaardsvold which helped to outweigh the extra-parliamentary radical opposition centred on Tranmæl, and to push the party overall towards a more moderate position. Further, DNA's advance in municipal elections also strengthened the party's commitment to practical reform work. Nonetheless, support for communism remained strong within the trade union movement, particularly in the regions

Figure 2.2. The radicalization of the Norwegian Labour Party: 'Down with the War. Long live the Revolution.'

furthest from Kristiania (Oslo). Overall, however, it might be more accurate to suggest that *fear* of Bolshevism was always stronger than hopes or dreams of its success. Certainly the bourgeois parties were able to campaign effectively on an anti-Bolshevik platform, and this may go some way to explaining the greater coherence of the Norwegian far right compared with Sweden and Denmark. Nonetheless, it cannot be overlooked that one of the major political parties in Norway, claiming with some justification to speak for a majority of the organized working class, was committed on paper at least to overthrowing parliamentary democracy until the early 1930s.

In Norway, as in Denmark and Sweden, political tensions were exacerbated by severe economic difficulties and the social polarization and conflict resulting from chronically high levels of unemployment. Overall, the Scandinavian economies performed relatively well during the years 1918–39, even though rates of growth never matched the very spectacular development of the years before 1918, especially in Norway. As open economies relying heavily on exports, they were of course vulnerable to falling commodity prices and shrinking international trade after 1929, but this also aided their relatively speedy recovery from the Great Depression. Industrial expansion continued throughout the period, especially in Sweden where new technology was enthusiastically applied to developing new consumer goods industries by companies such as L. M. Ericsson, Electrolux, and Volvo. The concentration of capital and consolidation of smaller enterprises into larger ones was regarded favourably and the anti-trust legislation found in some countries was regarded with some scepticism. Fordist ideas about the rationalization of the production process made relatively little impact in Denmark and Norway during the 1920s, but Frederick Taylor's influential book on production methods had first appeared in a Swedish translation in 1913 and influenced attempts to rationalize production and improve efficiency throughout Swedish industry. The most famous—or perhaps notorious—example of Swedish trust capitalism was a vast international business founded on the production of matches. Swedish Match developed rapidly during the 1920s to the point that by 1928 it had control of more than half the world's match production and majority shares in match companies in thirty-three different countries. It collapsed as spectacularly as it had risen when its director Ivar Kreuger shot himself in March 1932, and the Stockholm stock exchange had to be closed for a week amid financial scandal and allegations of phoney profits.

Despite the overall trend of economic expansion, the Scandinavian economies followed the European inter-war pattern of instability and crisis, accompanied by persistently high levels of unemployment. Unemployment averaged around 20 per cent in Denmark and Norway for the period 1921–39; in Sweden, it was slightly lower at just under 15 per cent. All three countries followed the European wartime pattern of a speculative boom and high levels of inflation continuing to 1920, followed by depression and falling commodity prices. The consensus was that these difficulties were best tackled by orthodox economic policy, namely fiscal restraint, deflation, and the maintenance of the gold standard. All three countries were able to stabilize their currencies at pre-war parities: Sweden was back on gold by 1924, Denmark by 1926, and Norway by 1928. The cost of this policy was a relatively severe depression by the mid-1920s, especially in Norway and Denmark. Some unemployment relief was provided by municipal government, though those employed on emergency relief schemes were paid strictly below market wages. The shortcomings of these policies were recognized, but they were seen as a necessary evil, to which there was no viable alternative. Classical nineteenth-century liberalism seemed to have no answers to the economic problems, but nor, at least during the 1920s, did social democracy.

By the end of the 1920s, it was clear that the main political bone of contention had become the question of the extent to which governments should be prepared to intervene in the economy. Faced with falling agrarian prices and rising levels of farm indebtedness and bankruptcies, the non-socialist parties (or bourgeois parties as they are generally known in Scandinavia) did demonstrate that they were prepared to compromise the principles of economic liberalism to support the agrarian sector, through buying surplus produce and forming compulsory price cartels for some commodities. Farmers in all three countries felt deeply threatened by the post-war world. By 1930, one in ten Norwegian farmers was threatened with bankruptcy, and emigration to the New World no longer provided the escape route that it had during the second half of the nineteenth century. In addition there was a sense that the modern post-war world, with its enthusiasm for technology and industry, was a direct challenge to all that the farmers stood for. For this reason, the new farmers' parties which emerged in Sweden in 1921 and Norway in 1920 were initially defensive organizations above all, seeking to regain some of the political influence enjoyed by the Scandinavian farmers for much of the late nineteenth century. As the economic situation worsened, however, they played a more active role in advocating farmers' interests, in some cases through compulsory collective organization. In Norway and Denmark in particular, there was clearly the potential for the development of an agrarian proto-fascist movement. In Norway, this took the form of an organization called Country People's Crisis Aid (Bygdefolkets Krisehjelp), which eventually became absorbed into the fascist National Unity (Nasjonal Samling, or NS) party after 1933. In Denmark, the Farmers' Union (Landbrugernes Sammenslutning, or LS) took some votes and parliamentary seats off the traditional agrarian party; more significantly, it was also able to mobilize 40,000 farmers in a protest march to Copenhagen in the summer of 1935, in a demonstration that was clearly modelled on the Finnish Lapua movement (see Chapter 12 on Finland and the Baltic States).

That these movements ultimately failed was perhaps to do with the complexity of the rural society: it was never a question of a simple divide between town and country. The larger freeholders, who had formed the backbone of nineteenth-century liberalism and whose interests were represented in the three agrarian parties (Venstre in Denmark, Bondepartiet in Norway, Bondeförbundet in Sweden) formed a very different group to the smallholders (*husmænd, arbeiderbønder*) who were usually forced to seek waged employment to supplement the meagre living they could make from the land. This latter group were increasingly the target of social democratic campaigning, in the parties' aspirations to unite the 'little people' (*småfolk*) against capitalism. The Norwegian Forestry and Agricultural Labourers' Union, founded in 1927, was by 1930 the largest union in the trade union federation, accounting for 10 per cent of its members. This growth came during a period of considerable difficulty for the labour movement. Although the central trade union federations were able to consolidate their control over national wage bargaining in most industrial sectors, the wage negotiations were more likely to be about limiting cuts in wages than agreeing rises. High levels of chronic unemployment weakened the trade unions and led to falls in membership—of as much as 40 per cent in the Norwegian trade union federation between 1920 and 1927. It might be true that real wages continued to rise, as a result of the fall in commodity prices, and that those workers in employment at least could enjoy the benefits of a growing range of mass-produced consumer goods, but the experience of chronic unemployment had a profoundly demoralizing effect on the working class, in Scandinavia as elsewhere in Europe. And in the face of apparent social democratic impotence to tackle the problem, it was above all the communists—syndicalists in some areas—who had the best claim to speak for the working classes. This less compromising view of class conflict, together with a sense of desperation on the part of many unemployed workers, resulted in some violent confrontations between labour demonstrators and the authorities in some parts of Scandinavia towards the end of the 1920s. The most notorious incident took place in the Swedish district of Ådalen in 1931, when military personnel opened fire on a crowd demonstrating against the use of strike-breakers in the local sawmill and killed five people.

THE SCANDINAVIAN RESPONSE TO THE DEPRESSION:
THE CRISIS AGREEMENTS OF THE 1930s

The international depression began to affect the Scandinavian economies from the summer of 1930. Falling agricultural prices had a particularly devastating impact on Denmark. The 1931 abandonment of the gold standard by Britain, which provided the market for one-third of Danish agricultural exports, made a bad situation worse, followed by the equally worrying news in January 1932 that Germany was raising customs duties on butter, thus effectively cutting off another export market. Unemployment peaked in 1932 at 32 per cent in Denmark, at 31 per cent in Norway, and at 23 per cent in Sweden (in 1933).

There was little in the experience of the 1920s to suggest that Scandinavia was any less vulnerable to the political and social effects of the Depression than other countries. Parliamentary democracy was functioning but scarcely doing so effectively: there had been twelve different governments in Sweden between 1920 and 1932, and few governments throughout Scandinavia had been able to command a parliamentary majority. While liberal democracy seemed unable to offer a solution to the crisis, there were a number of voices arguing for a more extreme response. The Norwegian Labour Party was, as we have seen, committed to socialist revolution, while those on the right argued for the need for a 'strong man' to come to the rescue.

The crisis in Scandinavia did not, however, result in authoritarian government. Instead, in a development that was remarkably similar in all three countries—and that was also paralleled by the 'red–earth' coalition of 1937 in Finland, and the 'government of the working classes' formed between the Labour Party and the agrarian-liberal Progressive Party in Iceland in 1934—the social demo-cratic parties were able to negotiate a compromise agreement with the agrarian parties, which gave them the parliamentary majorities necessary to steer through some rather innovative economic crisis policies. These so-called 'red–green' coalitions are seen as important historically in that they marked the beginnings of social democratic political dominance in Scandinavia, and allowed the social democratic parties to embark on a programme of major social reform. Indeed, within the Swedish historiography in particular, the 1930s has generally been viewed as one of the main twentieth-century watersheds, perhaps more significant as a turning point than the Second World War.

The first of the Scandinavian crisis agreements was the so-called Kanslergade Agreement in Denmark in January 1933, named after the prime minister's residence where the negotiations took place. In fact, the agreement was less of a sudden breakthrough than the culmination of a series of compromises agreed between the social democrats and the bourgeois parties during the preceding years. The immediate trigger for the talks, however, was the need for consensus on the devaluation of the krona. Negotiations between representatives of the Social Democrats, the Liberals, and the Agrarian Party continued for eighteen hours before a deal was struck. In return for the SD concessions on devaluation and agrarian price support to help the farmers, the Agrarian Party agreed to support the social democrats' unemployment and welfare policies and to abstain in a parliamentary vote on an ongoing labour market conflict, which was settled immediately following the negotiations. The timing of the agreement appears symbolic with historical hindsight, for it was concluded just one day before Hitler came to power in Germany.

The Kanslergade Agreement was observed with great interest in Sweden. Here the SAP had formed its fourth minority government, under the leadership of Per Albin Hansson, following its electoral success in 1932. The party's aim, once in office, was to implement its new crisis programme, but in this it was opposed by the bourgeois parties. Influenced by events in Denmark, from April 1933 the SAP commenced negotiations with the Agrarian Party, and in May was able to make an agreement with them, the so-called crisis agreement, or Cow Deal (*kohandel*) as it became known. As in Denmark, this compromise was founded on SAP concessions on protectionist measures to help farmers, while the Agrarian Party for its part agreed to support the SAP crisis programme for public works paid at market wages and funded through a government budget deficit. The arrangement allowed the SAP to continue to rule as a minority government with Agrarian Party support until 1936, when after an election the two parties formed a true coalition government. The equivalent crisis agreement in Norway was perhaps more unexpected, given the previously uncompromising stand of DNA towards cooperation with the bourgeois parties. Not only this, but only a few months before the possibility of a red–green agreement was mooted, the Agrarian Party had been negotiating with the fascist National Unity party over the possibility of establishing a new national block. But these talks came to nothing, and the agreement which was eventually struck bore a strong resemblance to the crisis agreement in Sweden, which was very influential on the process. The Agrarian Party agreed to support DNA's new labour market policy, while DNA agreed to state support and protection for agriculture.

The significance of the crisis agreements was thus above all that they allowed the social democratic parties in all three Scandinavian countries to introduce radical economic policies to tackle unemployment and thus hasten the Scandinavian recovery from the Depression. In breaching the solidity of the bourgeois front against socialism, the social democratic parties had managed to challenge the dominance of orthodox economic liberalism. In doing so, they had also abandoned their traditional commitment to the socialization of the economy. Within the SAP in particular, the finance minister Ernst Wigforss had developed a proposal for a counter-cyclical economic policy to tackle unemployment, to be put into practice through a programme of public construction works paid at market wages. Wigforss's programme is sometimes described as 'Keynesian before Keynes'. It is true that the SAP's counter-cyclical policy was developed before the publication of Keynes's *General Theory* in 1936, but Wigforss was well aware of the debates within contemporary English liberalism and drew on these, as well as on the Marxist theory of under-consumption and the economic thinking of the so-called 'Stockholm school' group of economists—including the liberals Bertil Ohlin and Knut Wiksell, and the social democrat Gunnar Myrdal—in formulating his ideas. Practically, the forced abandonment of the gold standard in 1931 was also influential, in that it released Sweden from a serious constraint on economic policy. For DNA, the electoral setback of 1930, when the party had returned to its Marxist roots and campaigned on a radical socialist manifesto, had forced a fundamental rethinking of its ideology. Similar ideas to Wigforss's were expounded by Ole Colbjørnsen and Axel Sømme, influencing the DNA's 1933 programme 'Work for All' (*Hele folk i arbeid*). But as the title of their 1933 pamphlet, 'A Norwegian Three Year Plan' (*En norsk treårsplan*) suggests, the main influence here was less British liberalism than Stalinist economic planning, and indeed the Nazi crisis plan announced in 1932. None of Keynes's books ever appeared in a Norwegian translation, compared with the various editions that were available in Sweden and Denmark.

Economic historians have long debated the significance of the crisis programmes in helping the Scandinavian economies to recover from the Depression. Most studies have concluded that the crisis agreements and implementation of the programmes came too late to have any real impact, and that the public works policies merely helped to aid the recovery, rather than to start it. This was especially true for Norway where DNA was not able to introduce its policies until 1935. Instead the emphasis is placed on structural explanations, principally the early recovery of the main export markets for Scandinavian goods which benefited the most important industries, which was also stimulated by the 1931 devaluation. Nonetheless, with hindsight it would be hard not to see the crisis agreements of 1933 and 1935 as very important moments in the history of the three Scandinavian states. The agreements not only allowed the social democrats to introduce some innovative economic policies, based on ideas which were to form the bedrock of economic policy in many European states after the Second World War. The 'red–green' coalitions are also associated with the introduction of some significant welfare reforms, which laid the foundations for the post-war welfare state. The new spirit of compromise also pervaded the labour market, resulting in the famous Saltsjöbaden Agreement between trade unions and the employers' federation in Sweden in 1938, which established a system for the negotiation of labour movement conflicts free from government intervention.

One important question which has concerned Scandinavian historians is thus why it was possible to establish a peaceable and workable solution to the problems of the early 1930s. Why did democracy survive in Scandinavia when it succumbed to authoritarian governments in so many other parts of Europe? According to the Swedish political scientist Ulf Lindström, the crisis agreements were symptomatic of the flexibility of the Scandinavian political system, and the ability and determination of all the mainstream political parties—socialist and non-socialist alike—to combat the threat of fascism. For some historians the innate pragmatism and reformism of Scandinavian social democracy—even in Norway where the 1920s were seen as a temporary distraction—was seen as influential. Others have emphasized the strength of the farmers in holding the balance of power during the early 1930s: the pivotal role in negotiating the Swedish agreement, for example, is given not to the SAP leader Per Albin Hansson, but to the agrarian politician Axel Pehrsson of Bramstorp, who did much to develop his party as a modern interest organization. More recently, Bo Stråth and Eva Österberg among others have sought to understand the Scandinavian model in terms of its very deep historical roots, based on a Scandinavian penchant for democracy, consensus, and equality stretching back to the Enlightenment or even further. This approach can seem to be unhelpfully teleological, though it is certainly true that the 1933 and 1935 agreements did not merely arise on the spur of the moment but were rooted in earlier developments. Above all, perhaps, it is necessary to see the agreements as a Scandinavian phenomenon, where the Danish Kanslergade Agreement had a profound impact on the Swedish negotiations, and the Swedish agreement likewise on the Norwegian. In this sense, the crisis agreements could be seen as the partial achievement of the early twentieth-century attempts to foster pan-Scandinavian cooperation within the labour movement, in opposition to the contemporary hostility in intra-Scandinavian relations.

The crisis agreements were also significant in that they allowed the social democratic parties to introduce some long-awaited reforms in welfare policy. Even if the question of the future of capitalism was still an open one for the parties, they had accepted the need to act to ameliorate the effects of social inequality and especially unemployment. Under the influence of prominent party thinkers like Karl Steincke in Denmark and Gustav Möller in Sweden, this had developed into comprehensive proposals for social reform by the 1930s. What was most distinctive about this social reform was the emphasis on universality: social policies were to benefit not just the working class, but the whole of society. By the 1930s, even DNA had begun to present itself as a party of popular appeal rather than a narrowly working-class one, and the formation of coalitions within the agrarian parties merely consolidated this trend. Steincke stated his vision of a welfare system that was 'humane but not soft, democratic but not demagogic, a blend of radical and conservative so far as is necessary if we are not to end in reaction or Bolshevism. It would distinguish itself both from the bleeding-heart sentimentalism that is so nauseating and from the ice-cold rationality that is so chilling.' These ideas were encapsulated, most famously, in the Swedish concept of the 'people's home' (*folkhem*) introduced by Per Albin Hansson in a speech to parliament in 1928:

The foundation of the home is community and solidarity. The good home knows no privilege or neglect, no favourites and no stepchildren. There, no one looks down on another, no one strives to gain advantage at the expense of others, the strong do not repress and rob the weak. In the good home equality, thoughtfulness, cooperation and helpfulness prevail. Applied to the great people's and citizens' home this would mean the breakdown of all social and economic barriers that now divide citizens into privileged and deprived, into the rulers and the ruled, into rich and poor, the propertied and the destitute, the robbers and the robbed. Swedish society is not yet the good citizens' home . . . If [it] is to become [so] class differences must be banished, social care must be developed, there must be an economic levelling out, the workers must be accorded a share of economic administration, democracy must be introduced and applied to social and economic life.

For mainly linguistic reasons the term *folkhem* never entered popular usage in Norway or Denmark, but the ambitions behind the welfare reforms were very similar.

The *folkhem* concept also serves to illustrate that there were many different influences on Scandinavian welfare thinking during the inter-war period. The term first appeared in social democratic discourse during the mid-1920s, but it had its roots in turn of the century conservatism, when the provision of homes and smallholdings was seen as a means of tackling the problem of emigration. The welfare reforms introduced in the 1930s drew on conservative and liberal ideas, as well as social democracy. Social reformers from all political persuasions were influenced in particular by widespread fears about population decline, fears which were also found in other parts of Europe. Typically, this debate in Scandinavia was tinged with concerns about 'race hygiene' and eugenics. Steincke's major work on welfare reform, *Fremtidens forsørgelsesvæsen* (The Welfare System of the Future) devoted a whole chapter to the issue of race improvement. There was broad consensual support for the laws passed in 1934, in all the Scandinavian states, sanctioning compulsory sterilization for citizens with congenital learning difficulties or mental illness, 'sexual deviants' and those who had committed sexual crimes, alcoholics and drug abusers, and those suffering from conditions such as epilepsy. There was also legislation prohibiting marriage between people in these groups. Between 1934 and the 1970s, many thousands (nearly 63,000 in Sweden, for example) of sterilizations were carried out; about half of these were performed using indirect force, that is, the patient was persuaded to give their consent by the medical experts concerned, and a small proportion involved direct force. The matter provoked a prominent public debate during the 1990s and the Scandinavian governments were forced to compensate some of the surviving victims of forced sterilization. It must be pointed out, though, that with the exception of some individuals with extreme views, eugenics in Scandinavia never came under the influence of the racial pseudoscience which drove the racial experiments carried out by the Nazis. In Scandinavia, eugenicist practices were generally motivated by concerns for social efficiency and productivity rather than demands for racial purity: the goal was to promote a healthy and efficient society by stamping out social problems such as alcoholism, drug abuse, and mental illness.

For social democratic welfare reformers such as Steincke, forced sterilization and other coercive policies were intended to play only a minor role in improving the population. The main solution to the population problem was always seen as better social and healthcare legislation. The main architects of population policies in Sweden, the social democrats Gunnar and Alva Myrdal, whose book *Kris i befolkningsfrågan* (The Crisis in the Population Question) made a big impact when it appeared in 1934, insisted on the need for individuals to have free will in the rational planning of their families. Policies designed to ease the economic burden on young families were therefore to be accompanied by paid maternity leave and the recognition of the rights of mothers to return to their employment after childbirth, as well as the right to abortion and the free dissemination of contraceptive advice. Uniquely among European states, Sweden passed a law in 1939 prohibiting the marriage bar in women's employment. In Denmark, married women were prohibited from working in some municipalities, but their right to work was upheld in principle, and the 1935 Population Commission advocated reforms in childbirth and family life similar to the Swedish model as the best way to tackle declining birth rates. Norway was the exception here, since DNA's revolutionary period had tended to subjugate feminist demands to the class struggle, and a family model based on a gendered division of labour remained much stronger well into the post-1945 period. As a whole, though, Scandinavian population policies were in stark contrast to some of the more conservative pro-natalist programmes found in other parts of Europe.

Social democratic welfare policies in the inter-war period were therefore characterized by the following ideas. First, they stressed individual autonomy, and the onus on individuals to take responsibility for improving their own lives. The Scandinavian labour movements had traditionally emphasized self-improvement and auto-didacticism, but the idea was also rooted in the Lutheran beliefs in self-reliance and the value of work. The aim of welfare policy was not only to help citizens, but also to cultivate in them healthy and industrious habits. Secondly, welfare policies were to be prophylactic. The state was to play an active role in creating the good society, rather than merely responding to social problems. This rested on a deep-rooted faith in the ability of the state to act benignly in the best interests of society. Finally, social democratic welfare policies reflected a profound faith in the ability of technology, scientific enquiry, and rational planning to construct this new and better society. In this way, social democratic ideology was a powerful expression of modernity in inter-war Scandinavia. This was especially marked in Sweden, where modernizing nationalists, such as Gustav Sundbärg in an intervention in the early twentieth-century debate on how to prevent emigration, spoke of the wish to create a new 'great power' era for Sweden by reinventing the nation as the embodiment of the modern age. Thus, while during the 1920s it had been Denmark—especially its agriculture and education system—which was seen as the epitome of Scandinavian democracy and progress, by the 1930s most international interest was directed towards Sweden. Most of this came from the USA, influenced by publications such as Marquis Childs's *Sweden: The Middle Way*, where Swedish interventionist economic and social policies were cited approvingly as examples of how Roosevelt's New Deal might work in practice. But the cultural affinities between Scandinavia and the UK meant that first Danish and then Swedish social and economic reforms were studied with great interest there as well.

The Scandinavian reputation for modernity also found expression in the arts, specifically architecture and design. Influenced by Le Corbusier and also the architecture of Weimar Germany, Swedish architects in particular found that modernist ideas about the relation of form and function could be adapted to serve the need for mass-produced homes built rationally and cheaply. The functionalist concern with natural light and simple lines also corresponded with both traditional Swedish aesthetics and the contemporary obsession with hygiene. Functionalism became something of an official design doctrine in Sweden following the 1930 Stockholm Exhibition, and the co-option of many leading functionalist architects to the Social Democratic government's housing commission in 1933. During the same year, a leading group of architects, including Gunnar Asplund, Uno Åhrén, Gregor Paulsson, and others, published a functionalist manifesto, *acceptera* (to accept), outlining their vision of a modern aesthetic underpinned by democratic values. These ideas were also applied to town planning, with the rebuilding of many central parts of the major Scandinavian cities, and the design of furniture and household necessities.

The modernity of the Scandinavian countries certainly impressed many visitors to the region, but the advance of cultural modernism was by no means uncontroversial. The architecture and design presented at the Stockholm Exhibition was criticized for being un-Swedish: only later did it come to be seen as a fundamental expression of a distinctively Swedish aesthetic. Although the Social Democratic prime minister Per Albin Hansson made his home in a new functionalist house in the Stockholm suburb of Bromma, some within his party, such as the mayor of Stockholm, Carl Lindhagen, criticized the functionalist aesthetic as dreary and utilitarian. Against the brave new world of the modern nation there could also be found a sense of nostalgia for the vanishing rural past, expressed in Sweden, for example, in the enthusiasm for *hembygd* (local heritage) societies and museums during the 1920s and 1930s, most prominently the popular open-air Skansen museum in Stockholm, with its collection of traditional farm buildings from different parts of the country. Moreover, there was also some political support for those who wished to resist the forces of modernity politically. The Ådalen riots in 1931 (see above) and similar disturbances in Denmark and Norway, even if not quite as serious in terms of loss of life, had demonstrated that the possibility of political violence lay only just below the surface. The Social Democratic government elected in 1932 did its best to play down the significance of the events in Ådalen, attributing the disturbances to the work of a few communist agitators and therefore alien and out of place in a modern social democratic welfare state. But political violence and disorder did not disappear: to take just one example, there were also disturbances, involving over 2,000 people and directed largely against police officers, at an autumn fair in Eskilstuna, a city controlled by the SAP, in 1937. More worrying, seen against the background of international developments during the 1930s, was the potential for right-wing anti-democratic politics. Disenchantment among farmers had led to the foundation of proto-fascist agrarian organizations in Denmark and Norway, and although these never had the significance of the

Finnish Lapua movement, the Danish Farmers' Union was able to mobilize 40,000 farmers in a march to Copenhagen in 1935. Traditionally, fascism in Scandinavia has been regarded as an imported phenomenon, which failed because of its lack of sympathy with Scandinavian ideas and values. It was certainly the case that the Danish Nazi Party, the DNSAP, drew its strongest support from Slesvig in southern Jutland, clearly influenced by German Nazism just across the border. The Swedish right had traditionally shown much admiration for and affinity with German militarism, and Swedish Nazis were also attracted by the notion of a superior pan-Nordic Aryan race. But there was also the potential for home-grown varieties of fascism. Dissatisfaction with the parliamentary system in Norway made the idea of the 'strong man', who would override party divisions, attractive to some, and the name of the polar hero Fridthiof Nansen was canvassed as a suitable candidate for this role. Vidkun Quisling's National Unity party (NS), founded in 1933, was based on the clear ambition of staging a *coup d'état* and setting up Quisling as a kind of Norwegian Hitler. In Sweden and Denmark, sympathy for the Nazi cause was demonstrated by youth organizations allied to the conservative party in each country which also began to adopt Nazi organizational tactics such as the wearing of political uniforms, though they were not particularly anti-Semitic. In Sweden, the Nazi movement disintegrated following internal disputes between its leaders, and the extreme right never gained parliamentary representation either in Sweden or Norway. In Denmark, the Social Democratic Party achieved its best ever election success in 1935, campaigning on the slogan 'Stauning or Chaos', but the threat remained. Although the mainstream parties consolidated their position in the 1939 election, the radical parties won fourteen mandates (out of a total of 148) between them, of which three were won by the DNSAP.

In the event, the main threat posed by fascism to Scandinavian democracy turned out to be external rather than internal, and this experience has unsurprisingly been influential in shaping the historiography. The escalation in international tension during the 1930s strengthened the impetus for Nordic cooperation, and from 1932 regular meetings of the Scandinavian foreign ministers were resumed. Following the Abyssinia crisis in 1936, these talks gained a renewed urgency and the possibility of a Nordic defence pact was discussed, though it foundered over the different geopolitical outlooks of the Scandinavian states. For Denmark, the vulnerability of the southern border with Germany was always the prime consideration, whereas for Sweden the traditional enemy always had been, and remained, Russia, now the USSR. Norway, meanwhile, had undergone something of a reorientation towards the north Atlantic since the First World War. Its government clashed with the Danish one over Norwegian claims to eastern Greenland during the early 1930s, and trading and diplomatic links with Britain were strengthened. These differences were demonstrated after the outbreak of the Second World War. When the USSR invaded Finland in the autumn of 1939, the Swedish government was divided between those advocating non-intervention, and the Social Democratic foreign minister Rickard Sandler, who was in favour of sending troops to aid the Finnish war effort. The supporters of neutrality won the day, but approximately 8,000 Swedish volunteers went to fight in Finland and there was a strong sense that 'Finland's cause is our cause'. This stood in contrast to the passivity of the Swedish reaction to the invasion of Norway and Denmark by Germany on 9 April 1940.

The Second World War thus saw a divergence in the experiences of the Scandinavian countries. Denmark and Norway were invaded and occupied. In Denmark, the Germans governed with the cooperation of a coalition government consisting of all the major parties (with the obvious exception of the communists). There was relatively little resistance until the summer of 1943, when a campaign of strikes and sabotage initiated partly by the communists and stimulated also by Allied and SOE intervention obliged the Germans to introduce more direct rule. In Norway, the invasion was resisted militarily with the aid of Allied forces, and the delayed capitulation allowed the king and government to exile themselves to London for the duration of the war. This left Sweden alone to pursue the traditional Scandinavian position of neutrality, which its government did with the strong support of the population, though critics argued that the claim to neutrality was actually compromised by pragmatism, for example, in the concessions made to Germany in allowing the transit of troops through Sweden to Norway, and the restrictions on free speech and political expression domestically.

CONCLUSIONS

The three Scandinavian countries emerged from the Second World War relatively unscathed. Norway in particular had sustained some damage to its infrastructure, and both Denmark and Norway had lost citizens in the resistance fighting, but overall these losses (3,600 and 10,000) were extremely modest compared to the rest of Europe. Even the small Danish Jewish population was saved, thanks to an eleventh-hour evacuation to Sweden in 1943. Moreover, the political system had also survived intact in all three countries. The Danish Social Democrats, tarnished by their participation in the collaborative coalition government, lost some electoral support to the communists immediately after the war, but their Swedish and Norwegian counterparts were both strengthened by their experiences of the war. DNA's leaders returned from their London exile as popular heroes, and were able to use the strong feelings of national unity to continue the policies begun during the 1930s. The SAP also benefited from its association with a policy of neutrality that had been both popular and effective in keeping Sweden out of the war. For these reasons, it is perhaps tempting to see the Second World War as being merely a temporary interruption to the course of twentieth-century Scandinavian history, rather than the fundamental turning point it seemed to be in other parts in Europe. For Scandinavia, the crucial moment came in the 1930s, when the crisis agreements allowed the social democratic parties to overcome the problem of minority parliamentarianism and to embark on innovative programmes of economic and social reform. Much of the welfare legislation was actually enacted after 1945, but the fundamental principles—universalism and the emphasis on education (*uppfostran* in Swedish)—had been laid in the 1930s. The myth of Scandinavia as the 'middle way' undoubtedly gained much of its credence from the bi-polarization of the Cold War, but the roots of this too lay firmly in the 1930s.

So why were the Scandinavian countries so successful in overcoming the problems of the inter-war years and maintaining parliamentary democracy? Although it has become fashionable in recent years to denigrate the contribution of the social democratic parties to this process, in Scandinavia itself at least, the willingness of these parties to compromise, and their ability to produce forward-thinking, innovative thinkers in economic policy and social reform was certainly decisive in making Scandinavia less vulnerable to economic hardship and social conflict. The success of the inter-war Scandinavian democracies was, however, by no means inevitable. There was no Scandinavian *Sonderweg*, stretching back to the eighteenth century (or even earlier), which was characterized by an indigenous tradition of peasant democracy combined with a tendency towards social equality, and faith in the benign influence of the strong state as an instrument of social change. Political violence and disorder, and support for more authoritarian solutions to contemporary crises, were always possibilities.

Above all, though, the Scandinavian experience of the inter-war period was in many ways similar across the three countries. There were of course important differences between Denmark, Norway, and Sweden which could not be overcome by mutually intelligible languages or shared histories. During this period, however, despite some residual hostility between Sweden and Norway, the histories of the Scandinavian countries did appear to converge, culminating in the shared crisis agreements between social democrats and agrarian parties in 1933 and 1935. Structural similarities go some way towards explaining this convergence: all three countries had fairly similar social structures, with a large agrarian sector, and all three countries experienced similar economic difficulties as small, open economies producing raw materials for export. In addition, successive governments in all three states were acutely conscious of their military weakness and strategic vulnerability between the great powers. But to understand the similarities of the 1930s crisis agreements, we also have to look to the exchange of ideas within Scandinavia, and the legacy of earlier attempts to foster Scandinavian cooperation, mostly at the level of civic society. Once again the role of social democracy has to be acknowledged here, and the Scandinavian labour congresses which were established after 1900, with the ambition to foster international peace in an era of hostility between the Scandinavian nations.

By 1914, the nineteenth-century project to unite the three Scandinavian states was long since dead, and with it any residual aspiration to great power influence in Europe. For all three countries the period 1914–39 was thus characterized by their adaptation to their position of vulnerability as small states within an unstable international system. Despite their declared neutrality, the Scandinavian states could not, however, remain isolated from the general problems which beset the continent during the inter-war period, such as economic instability, social tension, and political extremism. The view that was until recently prevalent within the Scandinavian historiography, that threats such as fascism could be seen mainly as foreign imports, is not sustainable. Yet in Europe and beyond there was a growing perception that the Scandinavian countries had been unusually successful in containing these threats and could thus act as models for other countries. The welfare legislation passed during the late 1920s and 1930s was studied with great interest in other countries, for example, as were the policies for the regulation and planning of the economy. The Scandinavian countries had begun to gather a reputation for modernism and innovation in the fields of architecture and design in particular, which was further developed after the war. Although it is not considered here, Finland also became drawn into this stereotype from the 1930s. Pan-Nordic solidarity was to be severely tested by the events of 1939–40, but developments in the inter-war period laid the foundations for closer cooperation after the war.

FURTHER READING

Broberg, Gunnar, and Nils Roll-Hansen (eds.), *Eugenics and the Welfare State: Sterilization Policy in Denmark, Sweden, Norway and Finland* (East Lansing, Mich., 1995).

Esping-Andersen, Gøsta, *Politics Against Markets: The Social Democratic Road to Power* (Princeton, 1988).

Derry, T. K., *A History of Modern Norway, 1814–1972* (Oxford, 1973).

—— *A History of Scandinavia* (Minneapolis, 1979).

Gruber, Helmut, and Pamela Graves (eds.), *Women and Socialism, Socialism and Women: Europe between the Two World Wars* (New York, 1998).

Hadenius, Stig, *Swedish Politics during the Twentieth Century* (Stockholm, 1990).

Johansen, Hans Christian, *The Danish Economy in the Twentieth Century* (London, 1987).

Lewin, Leif, *Ideology and Strategy: A Century of Swedish Politics*, tr. Victor Kayfetz (Cambridge, 1988).

Lindström, Ulf, *Fascism in Scandinavia 1920–1940* (Stockholm, 1985).

Magnusson, Lars, *An Economic History of Sweden* (London, 2000).

Musial, Kazimierz, *Roots of the Scandinavian Model: Images of Progress in the Era of Modernisation* (Baden-Baden, 2000).

Nissen, Henrik S. (ed.), *Scandinavia During the Second World War*, tr. Thomas Munch-Petersen (Oslo, 1983).

Nordstrom, Byron J., *Scandinavia since 1500* (Minneapolis, 2000).

Salmon, Patrick, *Scandinavia and the Great Powers, 1890–1940* (Cambridge, 1997).

Samuelsson, Kurt, *From Great Power to Welfare State: 300 Years of Swedish Social Development* (London, 1968).

Scott, Franklin D., *Sweden, the Nation's History* (Carbondale, Iel., enlarged edn. with an epilogue by Steven Koblik, 1988).

Tilton, Tim, *The Political Theory of Swedish Social Democracy: Through the Welfare State to Socialism* (Oxford, 1990): chapters on the political thought of social democrats Gustav Möller, Per Albin Hansson, Ernst Wigforss, and the Myrdals.

3

Great Britain

Ross McKibbin

INTRODUCTION

Of all the major European powers, Britain's history between 1914 and 1945 is probably the most exceptional. Alone of these powers she fought in both world wars from their beginning to their end. In 1914 she was one of five (six if we include Italy) European states of roughly comparable power. In 1945 she was one of only two; and much weaker militarily than the other, the Soviet Union. But undefeated she remained. She was the first European state to be affected by mass unemployment; but the international depression of the 1930s struck her comparatively lightly. For a substantial part of the population the 1930s meant steadily rising living standards and 'modernity' in social and economic life. Despite real class tension in the early 1920s, the decline of the great Liberal Party, and the rapid growth of a mass working-class party, the Labour Party, Britain's political institutions—unlike those of the other major European states—retained a high degree of legitimacy and supported a remarkably stable political and social structure.

BRITAIN IN 1914

Great Britain, in 1914 the United Kingdom of Great Britain and Ireland, was a constitutional oddity. Of the European states, probably only Austria-Hungary was as odd. It was a unitary state with one parliament, but that parliament governed four nations: the old kingdoms of England, Scotland, and Ireland and the principality of Wales. By treaty Scotland had its own legal and educational systems and also had a consciousness of not being England. Wales was administratively part of the kingdom of England, but over one-third of its people spoke Welsh and its cultural institutions promoted a sense of nationality which governments in London were reluctant to obstruct, and indeed often encouraged, though the Union was dominated by England even more than Prussia dominated Germany. Ireland, as Alvin Jackson points out in the following chapter of this book, was a reluctant member of the Union; but it also comprised two nations: one predominantly Catholic, whose attitude to the United Kingdom was highly ambivalent; another, in the North, predominantly Protestant, possessed of a ferocious British patriotism hardly found anywhere else. Trying to devise a system which would meet Southern Irish demands for some sort of independence while preserving the unity of Ireland and the Union with Great Britain proved to be impossible, but was one of the dominating themes of late Victorian and Edwardian politics.

Sport, as always one of the most sensitive of social and political indicators, gives us some idea of how complicated this hybrid 'nation' was, made even more hybrid by the emergence of Northern Ireland in 1922. In rugby and football an 'international' in 1914 was a match between the constituent parts of the United Kingdom—England versus Scotland, for example. (They are today called 'home internationals'.) It is as though in the German Empire 'international' meant Prussia versus Bavaria. The British Isles were and are represented in the football World Cup by five national sides—something inconceivable anywhere else—but

Figure 3.1. The first FA Cup Final at Wembley Stadium, 28 April 1923.

in the Olympic Games by only two. In rugby there are four national sides. There is, however, also a team, the Lions, which is picked from all four national teams and is made possible because even after the partition of Ireland in 1922, the Irish Rugby Union—almost uniquely—remained an all-Ireland institution. Despite the existence of these self-conscious nations, however, their aspirations, unlike those of Catholic Ireland, could be accommodated within the Union, as we shall see.

In 1914 this constitutional oddity was governed by the Liberal Party, which had been in office since December 1905. As a party it stood for free trade above all; but in defence of free trade it had become an agent of major social reform. In the years immediately before 1914 it had established something like a welfare state, though one by later standards very incomplete. As an electoral force it was heavily dependent upon the Nonconformist churches, on Scotland and Wales, and on elements of the industrial working class. Its geographical bias was towards the north of England and 'Celtic' Britain. It relied for its parliamentary majority, however, on MPs from the south of Ireland and on the Labour Party, which, though small in numbers, with its huge trade union base was potentially very strong. That the Liberals were reliant on these two parties to a considerable extent determined their policies. In particular, it committed them to 'home rule', a form of self-government for Ireland, something strongly supported in the Catholic south of Ireland, but strongly opposed in the Protestant north.

The second great party of the British state, the Conservative Party, was everything the Liberal Party was not: it was weak where the Liberals were strong, and vice versa. It was the party of the Anglican Church, the southern middle classes, metropolitan wealth, the monarchy and most of the aristocracy, much of rural England, and a significant part of the Protestant working class. It was, above all, the party of the Empire and of the Union of Great Britain and Ireland—which is why it was officially called the 'Conservative and Unionist Party'. It had also effectively abandoned free trade and would in government clearly adopt protection if political circumstances allowed.

Britain in 1914 was still the fulcrum of the international financial and trading system. Although its nineteenth-century industrial hegemony was gone, in the face of German and American competition particularly, by specialization in certain sectors it remained the world's largest exporter, and indeed in the Edwardian years there was an export boom. London was the lender of last resort and Britain's huge overseas investments and its willingness to invest and lend abroad stabilized the international economy. The gold value of the pound was the yardstick by which all other currencies were measured. Britain was also the most urbanized and industrialized country in the world. Its commercial and service sectors, its sport and leisure, its theatre and entertainment, its notions of domestic comfort, arguably made it, even more than the United States, the first 'modern' society.

In its external relations Britain looked four ways: to its enormous, amorphous empire—a strange collection of colonies, protectorates, and dependencies with little in common, difficult to defend and a constant drain on British resources;

to the United States, with whom Britain had a close but edgy relationship; to South America, especially Argentina, which was almost part of the empire and integral to Britain's trading system; and, finally, to Europe. There were many in Britain who wished to avoid European entanglements altogether, but no British government had ever believed that was possible. In 1914 Britain found itself allied with France and Russia against Germany—in many ways an unnatural alliance. Britain and France had been imperial rivals until the 1890s and many of the French were still suspicious of Britain. Britain and Russia had also been imperial rivals and had little in common politically or culturally. Britain and Germany, however, had much in common. They were more like each other than any other two European states. Furthermore, the international economic system revolved around them: a fact J. M. Keynes was to remind the world of in *The Economic Consequences of the Peace* (1919). What held this alliance together was a collective fear of German expansionism.

THE EFFECTS OF THE FIRST WORLD WAR

Given Germany's behaviour in 1914, the feeling everywhere that she was in some sense out of control, Britain could probably have done little else than enter the war on the side of France and Russia. Yet the insouciance with which the British political elite did this, the lack of debate, the insistence that it was 'business as usual', is surprising. It has been suggested that the government saw entry into the war as a way out of the crisis over Irish home rule—and war did indeed postpone that crisis (at the price of making it very much worse). This, however, is improbable. It is unlikely that the cabinet thought a war with Germany less dangerous than civil violence in Ireland. The government entered the war because it was not prepared to see Germany impose a punitive peace on France and Belgium (or see the French coast in German hands), and because it underestimated just what the consequences of a war with so formidable an opponent as Germany would be. Although it is possible to exaggerate the degree of enthusiasm for war in Britain, there was little outright opposition to British entry, and this remained true throughout the war itself. Even those thought to be 'hostile' were ambivalent: few believed that Germany should actually be allowed to win. At the outbreak of war all parties agreed to a political and electoral 'truce'. The Irish Home Rule bill was enacted but suspended, and in Ireland both sides supported war.

The country continued to be governed by the Liberals—there was no coalition government, only a 'coalition of opinion'. Yet the Liberal Party was to be the main political victim of the war. In May 1915 it was forced into a coalition with the Conservatives and the Labour Party—though the Prime Minister, H. H. Asquith, deftly ensured that the government continued to be dominated by the Liberals—and in December 1916 its unity was shattered when Asquith resigned and left office altogether, taking much of the Liberal Party with him. Although this new coalition was led by another Liberal, the most dynamic figure in British politics, David Lloyd George, and had the support of the Labour Party, it was primarily a Conservative government, even if wartime circumstances concealed that. After the formation of the first coalition in May 1915 the Liberals were never again to govern in their own right. Indeed, with surprising speed they were overtaken by the Labour Party as the principal party of the British 'left'. There is little agreement among historians as to why this happened and, in particular, what part the First World War played. Nonetheless, whether we think long-term factors were responsible or not, the morale and organization of the Liberal Party undoubtedly began to decay almost as soon as war broke out. This was not because, as some have argued, the Liberals were a *laissez-faire* party and therefore incapable of mobilizing the resources of the state. In 1914 the Liberal Party was not a *laissez-faire* party, if it ever had been, and was perfectly capable of mobilizing the resources of the state. But the war made central those policies, like military conscription, where they were reluctant to mobilize the state. The 'atmosphere' in which the war was fought, the fight-to-the-end anti-Germanism, the militarization of British life, and the increasingly close connections between the government and big business, deeply offended the free trade internationalism which was still fundamental to many Liberals, particularly those in the party's Nonconformist religious networks. Many also disliked the coalition with the Conservatives, who were increasingly assertive and ideologically suited to this kind of war. Furthermore, the electoral truce merely transferred politics from parliament to the press, and the government when led by Asquith was under more or less continuous attack. Asquith himself was an ineffective war leader, whereas Lloyd George was in his element. Had Asquith recognized this, instead of insisting upon his own indispensability, the unity of the Liberal Party might have been preserved. As it was, it got the worst of all worlds. The Asquithian wing of the party was neither a real opposition to the Lloyd George government nor a real ally and paid the price for both, while Lloyd George, though the leader of a victorious government, was a prisoner of the Conservative Party, without whose support he would not have been prime minister. The result was a party whose members felt alienated from an unfamiliar political world and was apparently dependent on its traditional enemies for its survival. In much of the country, therefore, the Liberal Party almost disappeared as its activists simply abandoned political life—or went elsewhere.

Those who gained most from the war politically were the Conservative and Labour Parties—especially the former. The war was not divisive for the Conservative Party. It had a long history of super-patriotic anti-Germanism, and few in it shared the view of one of its former leaders—the Marquess of Lansdowne—that the war was a European catastrophe as likely to breed revolution as anything else. Furthermore, it was better placed—as we shall see—than the Liberals to represent middle-class resentment at the redistribution of wealth for which the war was responsible. It was a more convincing patriotic and anti-socialist party than the Liberal Party. Like the Labour Party, it also gained from the changes to the franchise which were introduced in 1918. Before the war Britain had one of Europe's most restricted electorates: only about 60 per cent of men and no women were enfranchised. All attempts to extend the franchise before the war foundered on the question of women's suffrage. However, the claims of democracy could not be indefinitely denied, especially after the huge sacrifices of the war. The Representation of the People Act (1918) enfranchised all men over the age of 21 and most women over the age of 30. The electorate rose from about eight million to twenty-two million, and the age qualification for women introduced a significant bias in favour of the Conservative Party, as did the enfranchisement of many 'Tory' working men.

The emergence of the Labour Party as the second party of the state was less predictable. The war deeply divided all European socialist parties, the Labour Party not excepted: its leader, Ramsay MacDonald, resigned his post when the Labour Party supported entry into the war. It was divided three ways: into an internationalist wing, of whom MacDonald was a representative, a centre, led by the party's secretary, Arthur Henderson, which supported the war but not unconditionally, and a super-patriotic wing which supported the war more or less without conditions. These divisions, however, were less damaging than they might have been. In practice, the differences between the internationalist wing and the centre were not unbridgeable. MacDonald never believed that Britain could permit itself to be defeated and he even—very ambiguously—supported the recruiting campaign. Henderson thought Germany disproportionately responsible for the war, but also blamed the old diplomacy. The task of peace-making, therefore, was not to punish Germany but to refashion international relations such that war could not break out again. That was a position that nearly all members of the party and the trade unions—Labour's base—were prepared to accept. In 1917 Labour made the final break with the Liberal Party and destroyed the old 'progressive alliance'. Henderson had become convinced that the Russian Revolution demanded the reconstitution of an anti-Bolshevik European social democracy and that a reformed British Labour Party was essential to that reconstitution. During the war, the unions, particularly the miners' unions, largely departed from the Liberal Party and threw their weight behind Henderson's reforms. Labour thereafter followed a double route. Its representatives remained within Lloyd George's coalition until the war's end, while the party simultaneously reorganized itself and devised a new programme for both domestic and international policy which clearly distinguished Labour from the older parties. Unlike the Liberals, therefore, Labour got the best of both worlds: its patriotism was difficult to question, yet as a party of internationalism and social reconstruction it was much more plausible than the Liberal Party—which is why a number of prominent disenchanted Liberals made their way into the Labour Party.

The Labour Party was also favoured by its secular character. It was certainly not anti-religious as such. Many of its early leaders were believing Christians and it was careful not to offend religious sensibilities. But its social networks and appeal were essentially secular. Before 1914, as far as we can tell, religion was the main determinant of voting behaviour. Anglicans were likely to vote Conservative; Nonconformists to vote Liberal. After the First World War that tendency weakened, for which the war itself was partly responsible. By all the indices of conventional religion—church attendance, baptisms, confirmations—Britain was an increasingly secular society. And the causes of 'political nonconformity', like temperance, lost much of their support, as did Nonconformity more generally. The extent of secularism should not, of course, be exaggerated. The Roman Catholic Church continued to grow as Irish migration to Britain had its inevitable demographic effect. Furthermore, a historic Protestantism partly shaped the way many people thought about the world: they derived their ethical systems and their 'morality' (particularly sexual) from this diffuse Protestantism. 'Religion', it was said, 'teaches you good behaviour'. And the formal relationship between the Church of England and the monarchy and the state gave it a presence in the national life its declining congregations probably did not justify. Yet increasingly the driving forces of British life were secular, and the Labour Party was a beneficiary.

The war imposed immense strains upon British society and economy. There was a huge loss of life; Britain spent more on the war per capita than any other combatant—in 1918 Britain had the largest functioning army, navy, and airforce in the world, something she certainly could not afford; she had lent great sums of money to her allies and borrowed heavily from the United States on their behalf; many of her overseas assets had been sold; much of her merchant marine had been sunk. America, formerly Britain's largest debtor, was now its largest creditor, and London had ceded to New York its international financial primacy. Yet Britain emerged from the war much less damaged than any other European combatant. Its standard of living actually rose during the war and, due to state intervention, there was a marked improvement in diet and health. Population continued to increase and London never experienced the demographic disasters that overtook Berlin and Vienna. New industries arose from nowhere to replace German imports—optics, pharmaceuticals (even a substitute for aspirin), chemicals, fine steel, etc.—which were to be the base of much of Britain's inter-war economy. What made this possible was Britain's accumulated wealth, the wealth of its white dominions, its ability to pay for much of its war effort out of taxation rather than inflation, and its credit-worthiness in the United States.

That wealth was augmented by some of its territorial gains from the war: especially, its effective acquisition of oil-rich territories in the Middle East. Yet in a remarkably short time the British began to regret the war and the Treaty of Versailles with Germany which ended it. Britain had acquired responsibilities which she was no longer strong enough to meet and the old international financial and trading system, which Britain felt to be essential for her own prosperity, was still in ruins. Throughout the 1920s, therefore, the main aim of her foreign policy was the reconstruction of as much of that system as was possible. This involved several virtually incompatible policies. Britain had to reassure the French as to their security while making the post-war settlement as acceptable to Germany as she could. She equally had to reassure her imperial dominions that she could defend them against Japanese expansion, should that occur, in the knowledge that she could almost certainly not do so without American support. And coaxing such support from America was almost insuperably difficult. Finally, Britain had to come to terms with the new Russia, the Soviet Union.

While Britain was undoubtedly better off at the end of the war than the major continental powers, her experience differed less from them than is usually believed. The way the war was fought and financed introduced many of the same class hostilities, if less intensely. The war had redistributed wealth both between classes and within classes. It had, first, redistributed wealth downwards. The principal beneficiary was the unskilled working class, though the skilled working class also gained. Many believed that the trade unions were responsible for that. The trade unions had certainly grown spectacularly. In 1919 their membership was eight million—a figure not reached again until after the Second World War. In fact, the unions were not particularly successful in protecting wages, though they did to some degree protect hours worked. The working classes gained because they were indispensable in war and because the labour market was very tight until the beginning of 1920. That the unions were irresistible was, however, widely believed and resented. Those who suffered most from war-finance were the salaried middle class. Although Britain paid for much of the war from taxation, it was also driven to printing money—the result was levels of inflation without precedent in recent British history. Salaries did not keep up with inflation and much of the professional and clerical middle class suffered as a result. The value of certain kinds of middle-class assets also much declined. Owners of houses to rent, holders of shares in railways or shipping or foreign government stocks lost heavily—owners of imperial Russian bonds lost everything—and these were typical portfolios in the rentier middle class. Secondly, wealth moved around within the middle class. While the rentier lost, those in the commercial and service sectors did very well and this explains the popular resentment of the 'profiteer', who was everyone from the local grocer to the great soap magnate Lord Leverhulme. Furthermore, their gains, unlike those of the munitions manufacturers, were permanent. The result of such redistribution was social grievances unequalled in twentieth-century British history.

THE 1920s: ECONOMICS AND POLITICS

In the immediate aftermath of the war much of Britain's heavy industry came close to collapse. Throughout the war itself Britain's industrial 'staples'—shipbuilding, heavy engineering, steel, and textiles—operated at full capacity. In the first year after the war the Lloyd George government, anxious to absorb demobilized soldiers into the workforce, encouraged an economic boom. In industries like textiles, therefore, there was a big increase in capacity. In 1920, however, the government broke that boom (by sharply raising bank interest rates) while international demand for the British staples declined rapidly. This was due partly to the disruption of international trading lines by the war, partly to loss of overseas markets to lower-cost producers like Japan, and partly to changes in the patterns of demand—oil replacing steaming coal, for instance. These industries had always been subject to international trading fluctuations, but before 1914 had always recovered. In the 1920s their recovery was slow and weak. The consequence was a huge rise in unemployment in certain parts of the country—the North of England, South Wales, and the West of Scotland particularly—and high levels of long-term unemployment became characteristic of the British economy throughout the inter-war years. In turn, unemployment became one of the major issues in British politics.

But 'solutions' to the problem of unemployment were usually thought anti-thetical to the interests of the middle classes, and what was as characteristic of the 1920s as unemployment itself was the tendency of governments to put the requirements of the middle classes—which were essentially for deflationary or orthodox economic policies—ahead of those which involved active intervention in the labour market, and a reluctance to believe that such intervention could serve the interests of both the unemployed and the middle classes. This had consequences for British politics. What is striking is how inflexible that system was given the emergence of the Labour Party, the severity of industrial disputes in the early 1920s, the obvious redistribution of wealth that had occurred during and immediately after the war, and the breakdown of the pre-war international trading and financial system. The political and economic logic of Britain's post-war situation pointed to the reconstruction of party politics on the basis of Labour versus a united anti-socialist party, on the one hand, and the abandonment of free trade, on the other. Neither of these happened.

The Lloyd George coalition government could have developed into such an anti-socialist party. It had fought the December 1918 elections as a coalition and had won very easily. Both Lloyd George and the Conservative Party leadership had an interest in perpetuating it. Lloyd George wanted a new party, progressive but non-socialist, untied to traditional vested interests. And since his break with Asquith he had nowhere else to go. The Conservative leadership believed Lloyd George was somehow indispensable and that the Conservative Party by itself was not strong enough to cope either with the Labour Party or post-war social tensions. That view the Conservative leadership held until the end of the coalition government in 1922. It was not, however, held by the national membership of the Conservative Party or by many of its members in parliament. The policies of the coalition government, especially its apparently 'wasteful' expenditure, were unpopular with many Conservatives. Furthermore, members of the Conservative

Party in the country had long memories. Lloyd George might have won the war, but he had also been the scourge of the Conservative Party before it, and many of his cronies were exactly the kind of people Conservatives thought had done too well out of the war. The case for the coalition would have been strengthened had it genuinely held the balance between classes and social forces. This, however, it had not done. As early as 1920 it had largely capitulated to the demands of the Conservative press and various middle-class organizations to adopt deflationary policies whose aim was the restoration of the pre-war ratio of salaries to wages. Having done this it was difficult to argue that his government was better placed to deal with the organized working class than the Conservative Party itself could do. The Lloyd George government had achievements, the most notable perhaps being the settlement of the Irish issue in 1921–2—or at least the extrication of Britain from the violence of Southern Irish politics. But the leadership of the Conservative Party was repudiated by its own members when Conservative MPs voted to leave the coalition and fight an election in 1922 as a purely Conservative government under the former Conservative leader, Andrew Bonar Law. The Conservative Party was convinced that it could establish an anti-socialist party on its own terms.

There were many Liberals, however, who were also unwilling to join such an anti-socialist union. Although it was to become clear that most Liberals, when forced to face the issue, preferred the Conservatives to Labour, there was enough life within the old Liberal networks, particularly where Nonconformity was still strong, to sustain an independent Liberalism. It was a greatly weakened Liberalism with little of its old working-class support, but strong enough to frustrate Conservative attempts in the 1920s at least to appropriate Liberalism within the Conservative Party.

The logic of post-war economics also suggested that Britain should abandon free trade. Britain was in the 1920s the only major 'open' economy in the world. Although free trade had been modified in the First World War by duties on certain kinds of luxury goods, no duties were charged on the great bulk of goods Britain imported. In the circumstances there was little justification for this, and the abandonment of free trade was arguably one way the interests of both the middle class and the industrial working class could have been served. In 1923, the new Conservative Prime Minister, Stanley Baldwin, an old protectionist, surprised many by seeking at a general election a mandate to introduce protection. Baldwin's reasons for doing so have been disputed. Some have argued that he was less interested in protection than in bringing back into the Conservative Party those of its leaders who had remained loyal to Lloyd George. That might have been in his mind, but he actually believed that protection was an effective way of reducing unemployment. Baldwin lost; and as a result the Labour Party formed its first government—a minority government dependent upon the Liberal Party, which had in the election won many middle-class constituencies from the Conservatives. Why did Baldwin lose? In part, because a significant part of the middle class still supported free trade: the election results made that clear. But it was more due to the fact that the Labour Party and its electorate also still adhered to free trade: a remarkable fact, since it was probably the only industrial working class in the world to do so. Like the continued persistence of the Conservative and Liberal Parties, despite the emergence of Labour, the electoral persistence of free trade demonstrated the degree to which people still thought in pre-war terms and assumed that an attempted rehabilitation of that world was justified. The extent to which this was so was further demonstrated by the decision to return the pound to the gold standard in 1925; and not just to make it fully convertible into gold, a risky enough decision, but to restore it to its pre-war exchange rate against the dollar, an even riskier one. There were critics of this step, most notably J. M. Keynes, but it had, on the whole, bipartisan support. It was, however, on any reasonable view, a step difficult to defend: an act of faith which lasted just six years.

The Conservative Party's attempt to turn itself into the sole anti-socialist party came closer to success. Much of the party had been aggressively 'anti-waste' and anti-labour in the early 1920s, digging freely into the seemingly inexhaustible mine of middle-class discontent. In 1924 the Conservatives accepted that protection was temporarily dead and concentrated instead on fairly crude anti-socialism and anti-Bolshevism. The Labour government of 1924 lasted only nine months. It had in domestic policy been very cautious, but it had recognized the Soviet Union and the issue which brought it down concerned the non-prosecution of a prominent Communist for sedition. It was this which provided the Conservatives with their opportunity. In the general election of 1924 the Labour vote remained solid, but the Liberal vote fragmented—most of it going to the Conservatives, who gained a huge majority. It was the closest the Conservatives came in the 1920s to forging an anti-socialist party on their own terms. That victory also permitted the party to settle scores finally with the trade unions. The general strike of May 1926 was the last episode in a struggle that had actually been decided under the coalition government, but which confirmed the effective defeat of the organized labour movement. The general strike, which was a sympathetic strike in support of the miners' unions, was provoked by the government and undertaken reluctantly by the unions. The solidarity of both sides was impressive, but the solidarity of the government and its supporters was the more impressive. The government chose not to regard the issue as an economic matter, miners' wages, but a constitutional one: it portrayed the strike as an illegitimate attempt to force a properly elected government to change policies via unconstitutional means. This was an argument the unions found difficult to deny and that, together with the unity of the non-striking classes, was why the strike collapsed. Both the unions and the Labour Party suffered as a result. By legislation passed in 1927, sympathetic strikes were made illegal and the rules which governed trade unions' political funds were made much less favourable to the Labour Party, even though it was largely a bystander in what was essentially a dispute between the government and the trade unions.

On the whole, foreign policy was less partisan, though there were significant differences between the Conservative and Labour Parties over policy towards the Soviet Union. As noted, the first Labour government recognized the Soviet Union, but relations were broken during the succeeding Conservative government. Conservative attitudes to the Soviet Union were largely determined by the domestic-political uses to which anti-Bolshevism could be put. The Labour Party had no such baggage, and although the Labour Party itself was very anti-Communist, it always took the view that which regime governed Russia was a matter for the Russian people. Otherwise differences were ones of nuance. Fundamentally, the British political elite would have liked to liquidate the Treaty of Versailles, especially war-debts and reparations: this was the international equivalent of its attempts to restore the pre-war world at home. Neither the United States nor France would agree to this, while the Germans were unwilling to accept the permanence of Germany's new eastern borders. The Labour Party was more sensitive to French fears than the Conservatives, though it was under a Conservative government that the Locarno treaties were signed by which Britain (and Italy) agreed to guarantee France's post-1918 borders.

By the end of the 1920s, Britain was in a kind of unstable equilibrium. The position of the middle classes had been restored largely at the expense of the working class, but, despite what many feared and some predicted, outside the coal industry the victory of the government in the general strike did not lead to any sustained attempt to reduce wages and thus labour costs. Much of the economy was operating at way below capacity and much of its workforce, therefore, unemployed. At the same time, however, the unemployed were paid a kind of wage via unemployment benefit for as long as they were unemployed; something no other country did or could afford to do. Britain had attempted to restore the pre-1914 international financial and trading system almost single-handed in inappropriate circumstances, and this mutilated system was clearly imposing long-term burdens on the British economy which were unsustainable. Politically, the two attempts to break with Edwardian politics—a fusion of the Conservative and Liberal Parties and the abandonment of free trade—had failed. The Labour Party had grown rapidly immediately after the war, but its growth had slackened and it was clearly unable to mobilize anything like the whole of the working class. It had disrupted the party system but had not given it a new coherence.

DEPRESSION, RECOVERY, AND THE HEGEMONY
OF THE CONSERVATIVE PARTY

This unstable equilibrium was swept away by two events: the Labour 'victory' in the general election of 1929, and the international depression which began a few months later. In May 1929 the Labour Party for the first time became the largest party in parliament. Although Labour made some real electoral gains, the result was due more to a temporary revival of the Liberal Party and the workings of the electoral system than anything else. Furthermore, Labour was once again a minority dependent on Liberal support. It was a good election for the Conservatives to lose since it left Labour to face the Depression. In Britain the Depression took the form of a major cyclical downturn in demand, which began at the end of 1929, together with (as we have seen) severe 'structural' unemployment in much of traditional heavy industry. Throughout the second Labour government's two years in office (and indeed in the year thereafter) there was a rapid rise in unemployment. How many were unemployed and for how long is difficult to measure, but at its height about one-fifth of the total workforce was out of work.

The Labour Party was ill-equipped to deal with the Depression. Its own history and intellectual tradition, the dogged adherence to free trade and financial orthodoxy of much of the older generation of its leaders, together with the constraints upon a minority government which respected parliamentary rules, increasingly reduced the government to a hand-wringing passivity. Ministers lacked confidence in themselves and in their dealings with civil servants and bankers: they were too easily persuaded by the apparently immutable rules of the game. Furthermore, the Depression was of unprecedented severity; that, and its international character, made it almost impossible for any government anywhere to devise rapid solutions. Labour thus had no active policy; what it had, however, was unemployment benefit. Since benefit was effectively universal and increasingly paid to people who had exhausted their insurance contributions, the ever-rising numbers of the unemployed put relentless pressure on the budget. Conventional opinion demanded cuts in public expenditure, and in particular expenditure on the unemployed. This, however, Labour would not do. While it was not a reflationary party, it was not deflationary, and to most Labour MPs cuts in unemployment benefit would have been an inexcusable betrayal.

It is hard to say how long Labour could have continued in this way. A decision was forced on the government by the European banking crisis of July–August 1931. Britain was not initially part of this crisis, which was essentially one of the central European banking system. It became part via sterling. Under the 'gold exchange standard', which had operated internationally when Britain returned to gold payment in 1925, countries could hold their currency reserves either in gold or in pounds or dollars. But Britain and the United States were obliged to exchange their currencies for gold on demand. It became clear that Britain had insufficient gold reserves to prop up the German and Austrian banks or to defend sterling when an increasingly nervous European financial community began to exchange their sterling holdings for gold. These demands rapidly increased when it appeared that the British budget itself was now dangerously unbalanced. The easiest thing would have been either to have devalued the pound against the dollar or simply left the gold standard altogether and let the pound find its own level. Official opinion was overwhelmingly against such actions and persuaded the Labour government to borrow from American and French banks to provide support for sterling. The bankers demanded, in return, cuts in public expenditure, including cuts in unemployment benefit. The Labour cabinet was deeply divided over this, with one-half of the cabinet, led by the foreign secretary, Arthur Henderson, opposed to any cuts in benefit. On 24 August the government therefore resigned.

Much to everyone's surprise the Labour prime minister, Ramsay MacDonald, formed a 'National' government of all three parties. In fact, it was a government of the Conservative and Liberal Parties with a handful of Labour participants who included not only MacDonald but the unyieldingly conventional chancellor of the exchequer, Philip Snowden: the great bulk of the Labour Party opposed the new government. The National Government (as it was always called) was formed to maintain the gold standard and the parity of the pound against the dollar. To do so it met the demands of the foreign bankers. The budgetary cuts had the reverse effect to that intended. Rather than reassure foreign holders of sterling, the possibility that the cuts might cause civil unrest in Britain—indeed, they caused unrest in the navy—made them even more alarmed. The selling of sterling became an avalanche. Britain in effect ran out of gold. The government was forced to suspend gold payment and allowed the pound to find its own level: it was devalued by about one-third. Those who suffered most were the unemployed, those employed by government, and foreign holders of sterling. The inability of the National Government to preserve the gold exchange standard exposed the fragility of the 1925 settlement and the illusions which underlay it. It also had a liberating effect on British financial policy. The system which emerged was different from that of the 1920s. Exchange control was imposed; it became more difficult for British investors to export capital, while the role of the City of London in the formation of policy was significantly reduced. For the remainder of the decade the pound was a 'managed' currency, with the government rather than the Bank of England largely determining its exchange value. And free trade was finally abandoned. A general duty was imposed on all imports, while a system of so-called 'imperial preference' (by which Britain and its dominions agree to favour each other in trade and financial transactions) accentuated the tendency of Britain to withdraw from the international economy. Many regretted this, but in the circumstances of the early 1930s, when there was a general *sauve qui peut*, and the international economy came close to collapse, Britain had little real alternative. Certainly it was a much more viable and successful policy than that of the 1920s, and the tripartite agreement concluded in 1936 with the Americans and French to manage their currencies in tandem worked much better than the old gold-exchange standard.

The 1931 political crisis was also responsible for a political transformation. From the moment the National Government was formed, and particularly after its fortunate failure to keep Britain on the gold standard, the Conservatives had been rather shamelessly trying to force an election on their Labour and Liberal colleagues, who were in the end forced to agree. The election, in October 1931, resulted in an overwhelming victory for the Conservatives and their allies. And this allowed the Conservatives to do what they had failed to do in the 1920s. They, first, won their mandate to introduce protective duties; and, second, they achieved fusion with the Liberals on their own terms. The Liberal Party did not disappear as an organization, but it was immensely weakened. The bulk of it, the so-called National Liberals, became a wing of the Conservatives and took much of the Liberal vote, particularly in Scotland, with them. The old Liberal Party left the National Government in 1932, in protest at the abandonment of free trade, and went into opposition, but now a rump. The 1931 election established the pattern of the 1930s: complete Conservative hegemony, confirmed at the 1935 election. In much of the country, a two-party system developed—Labour and anti-Labour, with anti-Labour meaning in practice Conservative. In some of the country—especially in rural England—there was *de facto* a one-party system, with everyone, no matter what they called themselves, in the end being Conservative. Stanley Baldwin, who led the party from 1923 to 1937, was the ideal leader in the circumstances, a man who was acceptable to everyone, not least Nonconformist former Liberals.

The 1931 crisis was also important for the Labour Party. Between them the formation of the National Government and the election swept away the generation of Labour leaders who had led the party since its foundation and replaced it with men (but virtually no women) who were less attached to the old party system and less timid in their dealings with businessmen, bankers, and civil servants. Above all, it swept away free trade socialism, hitherto predominant in the Labour Party. After 1931 hardly anyone in the Labour Party advocated a return to free trade. This involved not merely a change in attitude to the fiscal system but to the state as a whole. Although Labour had been notionally interventionist before 1931, in practice it was nervous of state power. This was not true of the post-1931 generation of leaders. However, although the Labour Party recovered from the 1931 disaster—in 1935 its share of the vote returned to its 1929 level—there was little sign that it was gaining new ground before the Second World War; every sign, indeed, that its vote had got 'stuck' at its 1929 level.

By international standards, Britain in the 1930s was a remarkably stable country—more stable than most other major Western societies and more stable than it had been in the 1920s. There was virtually no civil violence, little class tension, and a high degree of stability in all tiers of government. What were the sources of this stability? The most obvious answer is the legitimacy of its parliamentary government. Comparatively few, even those like the unemployed who had every reason to question it, questioned the nature of that government or doubted its ideological fitness. Most believed, on both the political right and left, that the country's problems could be solved within the existing constitutional system, or else that the system only needed modification rather than drastic reconstruction. Those on the left who argued, as some did, that the National Government was Britain's form of fascism never persuaded many. It is nonetheless surprising that a political system that was under real strain in the early 1920s should have been so tough at a time when the political systems of many other countries were either disintegrating or on the edge of disintegration.

There were several reasons for this. The first is the nature of the British economy. The experience of the British economy in the 1930s was unique amongst major countries. Despite the problems of the 'staple' industries throughout the inter-war years, the Depression was milder in Britain than almost any other Western society. In much of the country it was confined to the years 1930–1. Unlike most other countries, where there was a catastrophic collapse in consumption in 1929–30 which lasted several years, rising consumption in Britain merely dipped between 1930 and 1932 and then resumed its steadily upward direction. In the south of England and parts of the Midlands, the Depression was hardly felt at all. As the great industries of the North stagnated, the service and light industries of the South flourished. They were dependent upon middle-class consumption and were closely connected to the private housing boom which was so central to the growth of the British economy in the 1930s. The policies of the National Government played some part in this. Protection channelled demand towards home-produced goods, while the management of the currency allowed the government to keep interest rates very low. Nor was it difficult for people to borrow. Unlike Germany and the United States, for example, Britain's domestic banking system remained intact. There was no threat to savings, while the building societies were awash with cash and willing to lend for house purchase on exceptionally easy terms. Thus the chief characteristic of the British economy was its segmentation. While a town like Jarrow on the River Tyne, the 'town that was murdered', dependent on shipbuilding, had almost universal unemployment, towns like Luton and Coventry, centres of the rapidly growing automobile industry, were 1930s boom towns. Much of the English middle class and a part of the working class began to experience a standard of living which was not to become characteristic of the rest of Europe until after the Second World War.

The segmentation of the economy and the consequent tendency of unemployment to be concentrated in certain areas rendered the unemployed much less threatening to the middle class than they appeared in the United States or Germany. The geographical isolation of the unemployed, together with indefinite payment of unemployment benefit, which to some extent placated them, politically weakened them by concentrating their own 'politics' not on the failures of the economic system as a whole but on levels of unemployment benefit. Unemployment was also socially segmented. Unemployment amongst the middle class, even when the Depression was at its worst, was always very low. Promotion might have been difficult, but finding a job was not. And while most members of the working class were at some point unemployed, only a minority were unemployed long term. Given this, and the almost negligible unemployment amongst the middle class, the pressures to find drastic solutions to unemployment were weak. Paradoxically, therefore, the effect of unemployment in Britain was to stabilize rather than to destabilize politics, and this immensely strengthened the Conservative Party.

In any case, much of the working class supported the Conservative Party. A reason why the settlement of the 1920s—the deflation of the economy after 1920—was so favourable to the middle class was that a large proportion of the working class either supported or acquiesced in it. It is difficult to determine in detail how social classes voted in the inter-war years, but it is self-evident that the Conservatives would not have won as decisively in the 1930s as they did had they not gained about one-half of the working-class vote. In the 1920s that figure was probably lower, but not much lower. It was, certainly, a significantly higher figure than the Conservatives won after 1945. In no other country did such a large proportion of the industrial working class support a right-wing party, and the failure of the Labour Party to mobilize much of its potential vote is perhaps the most important political fact of the period. The result was that all those who felt they had some stake in society never had that fear of the working class, common elsewhere, which might have driven them to extreme politics: which is why the class tension so apparent in the 1920s was largely absent in the 1930s.

Nor was this stability threatened—outside Northern Ireland—by nationalist movements. Given the constitutional make-up of the United Kingdom this is perhaps surprising. The simple reason for the weakness of nationalist movements is that the forces which stood for the Union were always stronger than those which stood against. In industrial Scotland and Wales class politics usually trumped national allegiances; and the Labour Party, already the party of industrial Wales and increasingly so of Scotland, was always opposed to movements which appeared likely to fragment the economy of the United Kingdom. The Unionist Party's *raison d'être* was, of course, the preservation of the Union, and its remarkable success in Scotland after 1931 was a recognition of the fact that to the Scots the Union with England and via England the Empire—the Scots were an imperial master race—offered them more than was available to an independent Scotland. And Scotland did have its own entrenched institutions. In Wales the final disestablishment of the Anglican Church in 1920 removed a major national grievance. Furthermore, much national rivalry was absorbed by sport, which excited national passion but did not disturb the unitary state.

After 1922, Ireland—either North or South—ceased to be an issue which much moved the British. More significant were the consequences of Irish migration to Britain. The majority of Irish immigrants were working class and Catholic. Their inclination—like all immigrants—to cluster meant that British politics, especially in the west of Scotland and in parts of Lancashire, was often as much determined by religion as class. The Irish working-class (and Catholic) vote was overwhelmingly Labour, while the Irish presence drove many other working men and women (often 'Protestant' in some way) into the arms of the Conservative Party and was another factor in its hegemony.

Unlike the 1920s, therefore, British politics in the 1930s was in stable equilibrium. The 1920s had a provisional air, largely because Britain's external economic policies were so obviously provisional. But the politics of the 1930s had nothing provisional about it. A moderate Baldwinite Conservatism was unchallenged, while the Labour Party's growth seemed to have halted. All the electoral evidence suggests that the dominance of the Conservative Party faced no serious challenge before the Second World War. Perhaps war, however, was the one thing which could undermine it: a reason why Conservative governments were so anxious to maintain the peace.

FOREIGN POLICY AND THE OUTBREAK OF THE SECOND WORLD WAR

The policies adopted by or forced upon the National Government pointed to a partial withdrawal from an active intervention in international affairs. The second Labour government had a 'multilateral' view of international relations. Its policies were based upon collective security via the League of Nations, an acceptance that continuing French fears of Germany had at least to be assuaged, an equal acceptance that Germany had legitimate grievances arising from the Treaty of Versailles, and upon a belief that general disarmament was practicable. The policies of the National Government, especially after Hitler came to power in 1933, represented a retreat from multilateralism. Increasingly the aim was to offer a settlement acceptable to Nazi Germany and this was done without much reference to Britain's allies, especially France.

What were the premises which underlay this policy? The first was a moral one: that Germany had been unfairly treated after the First World War, as had those Germans (in Austria or Czechoslovakia, for example) who wished to join the Reich but were forbidden from doing so. This belief was one Hitler constantly exploited. The second was a consciousness that Britain had acquired responsibilities she could no longer meet. The nightmare of British statesmen in the period was the 'three-front war': a simultaneous war against Germany, Japan, and Italy. Britain was not afraid of a war against Italy, for instance, which it had no doubt it could win. It was afraid that such a war would damage Britain sufficiently to make a successful war against Germany impossible. At the same time, as they had in the 1920s, the Asian empire and the Australasian dominions were demanding guarantees of protection against an expansionist Japan. In these circumstances the policy of buying off Germany, which the British always regarded as the greatest danger, via 'appeasement', was attractive. It was also attractive economically. The Treasury feared the costs of rearmament—what it would do to the domestic budget and to taxation; what also it would do to

Britain's external payments, particularly its account with the United States. It was recognized that large-scale rearmament would certainly mean extensive purchases in America, and that could reduce Britain to economic and industrial dependence on the United States. One of the major questions of the period, tacitly asked, was how far could Britain both remain a great power and independent of the United States. The policy of giving Germany all that it could reasonably demand was one answer.

Britain's policy towards Germany, however, was not wholly guided by realpolitik. The extent to which Britain was prepared to appease Germany was limited. There was almost no ideological sympathy for Nazism—although there was some for Franco's Spain—and Britain was never prepared to give Germany a free hand in Eastern Europe, as Hitler wanted. Nor was Britain ready to allow Germany to incorporate non-Germans by force into a greater Reich. The German invasion of Czecho-Slovakia (as it had become after the Munich agreement) in March 1939 cut the ground beneath Neville Chamberlain, prime minister since 1937 and the most determined proponent of 'reasonable' appeasement. It also brought the dominions on side. Hitherto their willingness to support Britain in a war against Germany was doubtful. It was primarily a moral repugnance to Nazism by the British and (on the whole) the dominion populations that forced Chamberlain to give Poland a guarantee of its territorial integrity in the event of German invasion—the guarantee that led Britain to declare war on Germany on 3 September 1939.

But this date does not mark the end of the 1930s or the supremacy of the Conservative Party. There is a sense that amongst those responsible for it the declaration of war lacked conviction, even though the strongest opponent of appeasement, Churchill, was brought into the government, that the so-called 'phoney war', which lasted until May 1940, was appeasement by other means. Nothing was actually done to check Germany or save Poland. There were even some prepared to contemplate war with the Soviet Union (after it had attacked Finland)—which would have been utter folly. The most important date is 10 May 1940, when the Chamberlain government collapsed and Churchill formed a new coalition which included the Labour Party. There were members of Chamberlain's government and of the Conservative Party still prepared to contemplate a peace with Hitler. Neither Churchill nor the Labour Party were prepared to do so. Both were prepared to fight on almost regardless of the consequences. They were thus, even if unconsciously, choosing dependence on the United States rather than subservience to Germany. But the Labour Party demanded a price: that the war should be fought and won 'according to its ideas'. The end of the National Government and the formation of Churchill's coalition was not a result of popular disaffection: even a week before its fall the Gallup Poll suggested that the large majority of the population still supported Chamberlain. It was a result of a crisis within the political elite which rapidly led to major changes in popular political allegiances.

CULTURE: HIGH AND POPULAR

Although Britain was often thought to be culturally rather isolated, arguably it was the most culturally open of the major European states. It was alone in not having a government which did not at some point seriously attempt to exclude outside cultural influences. All a British government could do was prosecute literature for 'obscenity', which is how James Joyce's *Ulysses* was kept out. But this was not aimed at any particular literature and was not very effective anyway. Indeed, the extent of this openness can be seen in literature. Of the two greatest 'British' poets of the period, for example, T. S. Eliot and W. B. Yeats, one was American and the other Irish. British classical ballet, which was to be so brilliant after the Second World War, owed much to Russian *émigrés*. In many disciplines and art forms (and the sciences) the effect of Jewish migration to Britain in the 1930s was almost transformative—paradoxically much strengthening German intellectual influences at the moment Britain was about to go to war with Germany again.

What most distinguished British high culture in the inter-war years from other major European societies was the almost complete absence of state support. Individual authors or composers could receive state pensions, but music, opera, ballet, painting received nothing. High culture was largely commercial. Before 1939 it was not the state but the BBC (of non-private agencies) which did most to support the arts. The BBC had a high degree of independence and large resources. It took over the 'Promenade Concerts' in 1927, turning them into a national institution; it founded its own symphony orchestra; it encouraged interest in French and Eastern European music and composers hitherto outside the canon of classical music; it commissioned plays and provided refuge for a number of European *émigrés* in the 1930s and 1940s. Indeed, the 'Third Programme', established in 1946 and of tremendous cultural rigour, was heavily influenced by such *émigrés* and exposed the British to a European avant-garde which otherwise might never have had an audience.

Although the BBC was never quite certain how far high culture could or should be popularized, it nonetheless thought that culture could be democratic. That belief underlay the attitude of the state to the arts during the Second World War. Assuming that in the circumstances of the war the arts would simply die without state support, it then developed the view that official support for the arts was legitimate and could be legitimated by a democratic theory of society. The most energetic proponent of this view was the economist J. M. Keynes, who had always deplored the cultural withdrawal of the state as an eighteenth-century heresy, and it was he who became first chairman of the Arts Council, established at the end of the war to distribute state support for the arts. Like the BBC, it had considerable independence, but never the resources which the German or French states provided after 1945. It did, however, have a lighter hand.

British popular culture, both what contemporaries called 'middle-brow' and 'low-brow', was intensely commercial. Britain was Europe's only 'mass society'. It was overwhelmingly urban, industrial, and commercial—a mere 7 per cent earned their living from agriculture—and its popular culture reflected that. The British bought more newspapers than anyone else and their newspapers had Himalayan circulations; they read more books than anyone else—best-sellers really were best-sellers, and most of the best-selling authors were also international best-sellers; they went to the cinema more than any other people; they went to dance halls more than anyone else; they watched more sport and gambled more money (usually on sport) than anyone else. Virtually all international sports had their origin in Britain precisely because of its 'urbanness' and advanced class structure. This did not necessarily mean the British were much interested in the international nature of the sports they had invented: here cultural introversion was real. Britain participated in every Olympic Games, but with decreasing success. It did not belong to FIFA and did not play in football's World Cup. Although it played international football matches, they were usually 'friendlies' and not much was thought to hang on them, unlike the 'home internationals'. (The politically sensitive match against Germany in 1938, on which much was thought to hang, was different.) In fact, the most important sporting international for the English (though not the Scottish or the Welsh) was the biennial cricket series, the 'Ashes', against Australia—the oldest sporting international in the world—which left the rest of the world mystified.

Despite the precocity of its own popular culture, Britain nevertheless was subject to constant American influence—particularly via the cinema and popular music. Throughout this period the great bulk of the music played and the films watched were American, and attempts by the state to regulate this by requiring cinemas to show a specified number of British films did something to protect and improve the British film industry but little to control American cultural influence. There were several reasons for this. The first was linguistic. A common language eliminated the most important barrier to American popular culture. The second was the existence of a common Anglo-American popular culture: the vocabulary and conventions of American culture were familiar to the British and easily assimilated. The third was the sheer 'size' of American culture. Even at its most successful the British film industry, for instance, simply could not equal the number of American films. Furthermore, American popular culture had a dynamism which made it very attractive to the British, as to most Europeans. There was a final reason, often overlooked. Britain had a major financial interest in the export of American culture. The two great combines responsible for marketing American popular music throughout America and the world—Decca and EMI—were both British-owned: one reason why so much American popular culture came to Europe via Great Britain. Although the British were sceptical of the claims made by American popular culture and American democracy, their comparative closeness to America certainly contributed to the ambivalence with which Britain looked at Europe after 1945.

THE SECOND WORLD WAR: POLITICS, SOCIETY, AND THE WELFARE STATE

Like the Great War, the Second World War put the British economy and British society under real strain. And for one year (June 1940–June 1941), apart from its dominions, it had no allies. As in the First World War, Britain spent more per capita on the war than any other power. However, unlike 1914, it did not have the accumulated wealth of a century to support it. It emerged from the war heavily indebted not only to the United States, but also to the empire. Most of its dollar assets were liquidated, often on unfavourable terms, and significant aid from the United States only came when Britain's external account—its holdings of gold and dollars—was effectively bankrupt. It also accumulated large debts in the empire, particularly India, and these, the so-called 'sterling balances', were a drain on Britain for many years after the war. The destruction of property was much more extensive than in the First World War. Not only was the merchant marine again destroyed by submarine warfare (though it was largely rebuilt during the war itself), much of the country's industrial and housing stock was destroyed or damaged by bombing. In one area alone was the Second less destructive than the First World War. Although civilian casualties were much higher in the Second (due to bombing) than in the First, Britain had fewer military casualties, and nothing like the number of German or Russian military deaths; and even its civilian casualties were much lower than any of the continental combatants.

As a military power the war had finally confirmed Britain's loss of standing. At the signing of the Treaty of Versailles in 1919, Britain had—as we have seen—the largest military forces in the world. This was true at no point in the Second World War. It was never as strong as Germany and, even with the enormous defensive advantage of the English Channel, it could hardly have defeated Germany by itself. The reason why Britain began the indiscriminate bombing of German cities was that it was the only means she had of attacking Germany militarily. The period between the withdrawal of France from the war (June 1940) and Germany's invasion of the Soviet Union (June 1941) was essentially a holding operation until Britain could acquire a powerful ally—preferably the United States, though Churchill was happy enough to acquire the Soviet Union. Britain's military weakness *vis à vis* both America and Russia was apparent by 1942, and it emerged from the war as one of the 'Big Three' as much for historical reasons as anything else. At the end of the war it had, however, all the burdens of a great power: it found itself with responsibilities much exceeding 1918. Territorially, Britain still occupied all the lands it had held in 1914 or acquired during and after the First World War, and in 1945 in addition found itself in occupation of one-quarter of Germany and Austria, parts of Italy, Greece, the Dutch East Indies, and French Indochina. The military costs of such occupation were high enough, but some of the occupied territories (like Germany) were devastated by the war, and had to be rebuilt. Others were devastated by political and racial divisions which ended in civil war—Greece and Palestine for example. Some of these responsibilities, like the Dutch East Indies or Indochina, were speedily discharged simply by returning them to their former colonial rulers, though with disastrous consequences. Others, like Greece and Palestine, were given up by handing over the obligation to someone else—the United States in the case of Greece and the United Nations in the case of Palestine. Some burdens were abandoned more reluctantly and for many years after 1945 Britain continued to spend more on defence than any other European power.

The Second World War, however, in many ways strengthened British society and indeed its economy. The immense emphasis upon science and techno-logy demanded by defence was to change the pattern of English education and industry. During the war probably only Germany was as technologically

Figure 3.2. Women born in 1919 register at a labour exchange in 1941 following the British government's unprecedented step of conscripting women for war service.

innovative as Britain. Innovation was not just in jet-engines or radar but in genuinely world-historical advances. Perhaps the two most important scientific developments of the war—the synthesis of penicillin and the demonstration that an atom bomb was feasible (with an accurate prediction of its consequences)—were both done in British universities during the war, though it required the resources of the American economy to complete the process. The war also encouraged the expansion of the universities. Before 1939 a smaller proportion of the British population went to university than in any other European country. The big expansion of the university population that occurred after 1945 was a direct result of the experience of the war, as were the brilliant achievements of British science in the next twenty years or so. It was also a result of the view that the problems of British industry in the inter-war years had been due partly to the defects of the education system as well as an unwillingness of British industry to invest in research. The new prestige of science and technology is to be seen in the products of the secondary grammar schools: before 1945 their main function was to train boys and girls to enter the clerical professions; after 1945 more boys from grammar schools went into engineering than any other occupation. The 1944 Education Act was another result of the war. It made secondary education free and compulsory to the age of 15. It was, however, much less successful than the expansion of the universities, largely because the system remained profoundly divided socially: the school system was one area where wartime democracy stopped short.

The war laid the foundations of the post-war welfare state via a major expansion of state intervention. This was to a degree a result of the war itself. The nationalization of the country's hospitals (central to the post-1945 National Health scheme) was due to the very high levels of civilian casualties, something with which the old decentralized voluntary system could not cope. The railways and the mines, both of which were to be nationalized after the war, were taken under state control. The big expansion in maternal and child healthcare was again a result of the needs of war, and the introduction of family allowances in 1945, though the culmination of a long campaign, was also designed to hold down wage settlements. All these changes were to be permanent and extended by the Attlee Labour government. For the fact that Labour was an essential member of the coalition, and that Labour held most of the major domestic and 'social' portfolios, was the other reason for such state intervention, and the reason why the social policies of the Second World War and thereafter were much more successful and extensive than those after 1918—despite the many promises made by the Lloyd George coalition at the 1918 election. Although it is possible to exaggerate the extent of social solidarity in Britain during the war, or rather after May 1940 (there was not much solidarity before then), wartime social welfare policies were an expression of this solidarity, something which remains central to Britain's historical memory of the war.

These social changes were accompanied by a second political transformation (the first being 1931) which was demonstrated by the victory of the Labour Party at the 1945 election. In 1939 the National Government, dominated by the Conservative Party, was politically unchallenged. No one could have predicted that it would be heavily defeated at the next election. Contemporaries were aware of the radicalization of opinion after 1940 which could take the form of an unwillingness to recognize the old social hierarchies, or the widely reported 'rudeness' of ordinary soldiers. The huge sales of books and pamphlets attacking the old National Government and the collapse in the reputation of men like Baldwin and Chamberlain, the success of any 'progressive' candidate at parliamentary by-elections (which, because of a political 'truce', were uncontested by the main parties), or the widespread admiration for the Soviet Union. The *amour-propre* of much of the working class rose as the *amour-propre* of much of the middle class fell, changes due not only to the war—factory workers are much more indispensable than clerical workers—but also to government wartime propaganda which tended to extol certain kinds of people at the expense of others. Such social redistribution also had a material base. As in the First World War, but more so, income was redistributed downwards, with the unskilled working class doing best—a consequence of the end of unemployment (which automatically raised working-class income), wartime wages policies, and much higher taxation on the incomes of the well-to-do.

This radicalization of opinion is generally assumed to be a result of influences felt throughout the course of the war, and we can easily point to these influences. Such evidence as we have suggests that radicalization occurred not as a gradual process but very fast indeed. The crucial fact was the way in which Churchill succeeded Chamberlain. It became clear that in circumstances of possible defeat the country could not be governed without the active participation of the labour movement—which meant the Labour Party in government. This was, in effect, an admission of failure by the National Government. Nor would Labour join a coalition led by Chamberlain, who thus had to go. It was the Conservatives who called in Labour, and this legitimated the Labour Party and its programmes more than anything else. The success of the National Government in the 1930s was based upon the marginalization of the Labour Party; the conviction amongst the electorate that Labour had failed at a crucial moment in the country's history (1931), and would fail again. Before 1939 Labour was conspicuously unable to universalize its political culture. Although it was never to do so, it came much closer in 1945 than ever before. All classes were affected. Labour won significant middle-class support in 1945, but its biggest gains were in those sections of the working class—for example, in Birmingham—who had done moderately well in the 1930s and who had been inclined to be grateful to the Conservative Party for that. Furthermore, most of the political changes which followed the crisis of May 1940 were permanent.

CONCLUSIONS

In 1914 Britain was unquestionably a great power—perhaps the greatest. In 1945 it was a distant third, and soon was to be overtaken economically by Germany, France, and Japan. Yet hers is hardly a story of 'decline'. By most criteria she was in these years the most successful of the major European states. She was militarily undefeated and unoccupied; her democratic political system survived all challenges; and, despite the ravages of long-term unemployment, the standards of life of most of its people rose throughout the period. In 1945 few other states had such a high degree of social solidarity. In most respects, until 1939, she was as 'European' as anyone else. It is a mistake to think there is a model of 'Europeanness' which everyone but Britain fitted. Nonetheless, because Britain's experience of the Second World War was so different from that of most other European states, Britain thought she could encourage forms of European unity without feeling obliged to participate in them. Furthermore, strong cultural and military ties to the USA and the 'white' Commonwealth, which actually strengthened during the Second World War, drew Britain's gaze from the Continent. The result was that Britain was not so much hostile to the idea of 'Europe' as ambivalent about it. Britain was half in and half out.

FURTHER READING

Addison, Paul, *The Road to 1945* (2nd edn., London, 1994).

Broadberry, Stephen, *The British Economy between the Wars* (Oxford, 1986).

Cronin, James, *The Politics of State Expansion: War, State and Society in Twentieth-Century Britain* (London, 1991).

Glynn, Sean, and John Oxborrow, *Interwar Britain: A Social and Economic History* (New York, 1976).

Holt, Richard, *Sport and the British. A Modern History* (Oxford, 1990).

Howell, David, *MacDonald's Party. Labour Identities and Crisis, 1922–1931* (Oxford, 2002).

Hutchison, I. G. C., *Scottish Politics in the Twentieth Century* (London, 2000).

Johnson, Paul (ed.), *Twentieth-Century Britain: Economic, Social and Cultural Change* (London, 1994).

Kennedy, Paul, *The Realities behind Diplomacy. Background Influences on British External Policy 1865–1980* (London, 1980).

McKibbin, Ross, *Classes and Cultures: England 1918–1951* (Oxford, 2000).

Morgan, Kenneth O., *Rebirth of a Nation: Wales 1880–1980* (Oxford: 1980).

Pugh, Martin, *The Making of Modern British Politics: 1867–1939* (2nd edn., Oxford, 1993).

Purvis, June (ed.), *Women's History. Britain 1850–1945: An Introduction* (London, 1997).

Schmidt, Gustav, *The Politics and Economics of Appeasement: British Foreign Policy in the 1930s*, tr. Jackie Bennett-Ruete (New York, 1986).

Seldon, Anthony, and Stuart Ball (eds.), *The Conservative Century: The Conservative Party since 1900* (Oxford, 1994).

4

The Two Irelands

Alvin Jackson

INTRODUCTION

If the years between 1914 and 1945 were a 'dark interlude' for the Irish, then the quality of this occlusion differed from much of the rest of Europe. If the master narrative of European history embodies a story of continental prosperity and expansion, interrupted by the two world wars, then Ireland's 'stories' for the period have been differently shaped. Historicist accounts of Ireland's struggle for liberation from the British (by, for example, Mary Hayden) stretch from the twelfth century to a triumphant denouement with the nation's independence in 1921, in the midst of the European eclipse. For those Irish historians writing in the relatively tranquil and prosperous conditions of the early and mid-1960s (such as J. C. Beckett), the constitutional arrangements of 1920–2 (independence for the majority of the island, devolution within the United Kingdom for the largely Protestant and Unionist North-East) looked like the harbinger, not of a sectarian cataclysm, but rather of one of the most politically settled periods in the island's history. By way of contrast, explanations for the violence of late twentieth-century Northern Ireland (in the work of F. S. L. Lyons, for example) have occasionally highlighted the cultural politics and paramilitarism of the Edwardian era, the supposed apogee of the pre-war European golden age. Yet again, some historians (J. J. Lee, for example), writing against the backdrop of spiralling national debt and public retrenchment in the 1980s, and before the economic 'miracle' of the 1990s, saw the relatively weak performance of independent Ireland as being the dominant motif in its history, including the post-1945 years.

Moreover, Ireland's inter-war years are framed by four, not two, great conflicts: the period has also been defined, to an extent, by two further potential wars which were, in fact, avoided. Nationalist Ireland fought and won its independence in the period between 1916 and 1921, and there is a substantial body of work exploring the vision and the achievements of the revolutionaries. This is, at times, a controversial literature. But, while individual episodes (such as the Kilmichael ambush in County Cork in 1920) and the reputations of individual revolutionary leaders (such as Eamon de Valera) may be fiercely contested, the idealism underlying the conflict, the necessity of the war, and the importance of its results are largely beyond debate.

If there exists a wide consensus linking interpretations of the revolution, and if historians are still broadly fired by the youthful passion and excitement of the insurgents, then assessments of inter-war Ireland tend to labour under the burden of bathos and anti-climax. Fratricidal conflict, economic austerity, unimaginative or repressive government by (mostly) grey men, tend to be the motifs governing general accounts of the 1920s and 1930s. Moreover, certainly until recently, the dominant military struggles of the twentieth century, the First and Second World Wars, have proved harder to integrate into the narrative of modern Irish history than the revolution. The effective disengagement of the dominant Irish separatist tradition from each of these conflicts has meant that, until lately, they have merely provided 'noises off' in the national story. These were Britain's wars, and (as such) were a distraction and an irrelevance.

Recent scholarship has done much to restore the full history of Ireland and the Great War, and this has been linked with a wider popular interest and recognition. It might be argued, however, that much of this literature still concentrates (naturally enough) on the extent of Irish military engagement, on the actions of Irish units and individuals, on issues of sacrifice and commemoration. To some extent the wider social and cultural history of Ireland's Great War—even, arguably, the wider political implications of the struggle for the Irish—remain to be written. In so far as this is the case, then the impact of the Great War on Ireland remains a contested and understated history.

The history of Ireland and the Second World War is a still slighter enterprise, and remains dominated, as with so much else of modern Irish history, by the Anglo-Irish relationship. This, in turn, has provided an emphasis on the question of neutrality and related matters such as intelligence operations and partition. At one time debates within the historiography seemed to represent a continuation by other means of the angry and recriminatory exchanges between Winston Churchill and Eamon de Valera in 1945 over the issue of independent Ireland's wartime conduct. Certainly the critique of neutrality supplied by the prominent historian F. S. L. Lyons, in the early 1970s, has stimulated a series of counter-reactions which have defended the strategy in terms of the consolidation of Irish national sovereignty. Despite pioneering work, independent Ireland's connection with the Second World War is still portrayed in constricted and sometimes defensive terms.

The fourth conflict which has helped to frame the period under consideration is the Irish Civil War (1922–3). The struggle of 'green against green' helped to temporarily overshadow the experience of liberation from British rule in 1922; and, though the numbers of casualties were small (perhaps around 1,200 military combatants fell), the intimate and fratricidal nature of the conflict meant that the impact of these deaths was disproportionately great. To some extent, the history of inter-war Ireland has been dominated by the impact of the civil war, and of the issues arising from this conflagration. To some extent, too, the story of inter-war Ireland is an extension of the narrative of the civil war, rather than an assessment (still less a celebration) of state and nation-building.

Ireland's history in this period was conditioned, not only by the battles which occurred, but also by two smouldering conflicts which might well have erupted into open warfare but which were avoided. It has been suggested (by John Regan) that one of the forgotten determinants of Irish government in the early 1920s was the prospect (however swiftly receding) of renewed conflict with Britain. Related to this threat was the simmering possibility of war between the new Irish state and its northern, Unionist, neighbour. The collective amnesia over the First World War is one 'unseen hand' on the history of Ireland in the inter-war years; but another is represented—for the early 1920s, at any rate—by the threats of war with Belfast and with Britain.

If the role of war in twentieth-century Irish history did not fully correspond with the experience of the rest of Europe, then there are, perhaps, even wider challenges in applying the metanarrative of the continental 'dark interlude'. Though crude arguments for Ireland's exceptionalism are rightly dismissed by scholars, certain aspects of the island's experience in the twentieth century were distinctive. Independent Ireland was, in a sense, a 'successor state' to the old United Kingdom; but, in contrast to the successor states of the old empires of continental Europe, Ireland was fighting and negotiating with an empire which had emerged triumphant from the chaos of the Great War. Ireland, in common with many other new states, fell into civil war in the aftermath of independence; but, while the conflict had some social and economic colouring, it was not fought primarily over class or economic issues, but rather over the precise relationship between the new state and the former 'colonial' power. Independent Ireland, like the new Czechoslovakia (with the Sudeten Germans), or Romania (with its Hungarian minority), or Italy (with the German-speakers of Süd-Tirol), saw itself as having a minority question (the Protestants of Ulster, who generally identified with British rule). But, unlike continental Europe, here the former imperial power, Great Britain, had intervened to impose a settlement (in 1920), namely the partition of the island, together with separate constitutional provision for each of the two new territories: moreover, the British remained in effect the lasting guarantor of these arrangements. In other words, Ireland had its symmetries with the continental European experience; but its political trajectory long after independence continued to be governed by the particular nature of its relationship with Britain.

These, then, are some of the distinctive challenges in writing about the inter-war period in Ireland. The period itself is difficult to define, partly because the social and political impact of the two world wars on the island has not yet itself been fully defined: inter-war Ireland is hard to define, because (in a sense) wartime Ireland is hard to locate. The dominant narrative in twentieth-century Irish political history provides a counterpoint, not so much between pre-war affluence and post-war destitution, as between the achievement and euphoria of the revolution and the bathos and tragedy of partition and civil war. Other parallels with the continental European story and experience may be made, but have inevitable limitations. Indeed, some historians have depicted the independent Ireland of the 1920s not so much in the light of European contemporaries as in that of European history—the pattern of France in the 1790s, of revolution and of counter-revolution. Viewed in this particular way, the government of inter-war Ireland is the Directory without the fear, hope, or challenge of Napoleon.

WARS AND IDENTITIES

The First World War impacted upon political identity throughout Ireland. It reinforced notions of Britishness and Ulsterness among the island's million Unionists, who were concentrated in the North. Members of the pre-war and paramilitary Ulster Volunteer Force were largely recruited after August 1914 into the 36th (Ulster) Division of Kitchener's New Army. The organization and imagery of their army life reinforced the notion of 'Ulster'. The units of the Division were similar to the 'Pals' Battalions' elsewhere in the British Isles, recruiting from local networks of family and friends (and thus ensuring that the experience of life and death in the trenches would be peculiarly intense and resonant). The symbol of Ulster, the Red Hand, was omnipresent for these men: it was on their divisional badge, on the tin hats which they wore, on the New Testaments which they carried, on the divisional gallantry certificates which they occasionally won. This Ulster identity coagulated in the blood of the Somme offensive (July 1916), at Messines and Passchendaele in 1917, and during the German Spring Offensive of March 1918: commemoration of the Somme in particular provided a binding mythology and iconography for successive generations of northern Unionists. The Ulster Division provided military training and a heightened political and cultural identity for those Unionists who helped to forge the Northern Ireland state in 1920–1.

The First World War also served to popularize a more radical form of Irish political identity among the island's three million or so nationalists. There is a superficial paradox here, in so far as the Irish revolution against British authority followed immediately from a war in which Irishmen and -women contributed extensively to the 'British' cause. The question of support for the imperial and Allied war effort certainly divided the dominant Home Rule party and its militant offshoot, the Irish Volunteers, with the overwhelming majority of the latter (around 158,000 out of a total of 170,000) endorsing the party leadership's commitment to the British government. Many of these Volunteers

Figure 4.1. The last hurrah of union: the 1919 Victory Parade in Westmoreland Street, Dublin, to celebrate the end of the Great War—the Union Jack is still flying on top of Trinity College.

and their northern Unionist counterparts (some 30,000) would die as soldiers of the British crown. But Irish service in the British Army in the Great War was by no means consistent with a crude British patriotism: in common with the experience of the Australians (for example), the baleful reality of heroic failure at Gallipoli and other battlefields, the perception of dim-witted British military leadership, and the experience of petty official humiliation all seem to have fed into a consolidation of Irish national identity.

The recruitment of Irish Home Rulers in 1914 to the British Army was also, in a sense, contractual. The (third) Home Rule bill had been enacted on 18 September 1914, but with its operation suspended 'no later than the end of the present war'. Two days later, on 20 September, the Irish leader, John Redmond, spoke at Woodenbridge, County Wicklow, calling on Irishmen to serve 'wherever the firing-line extends, in defence of right, of freedom and of religion in this war'. The two events were, of course intimately linked. Redmond viewed the passage of the Home Rule measure as an historic act of reparation, and wanted to maximize the chances of the speedy realization of legislative independence. In effect, Home Rule and support for the war were interdependent; and, as the chances of the first receded, so, too, did enthusiasm for the other. The relegation of the Home Rule issue in 1915–16, the failure of David Lloyd George's attempted reactivation of Home Rule in May and June 1916, the collapse of the great conference on Irish self-government, the Irish Convention, held at Trinity College Dublin in 1917–18, all tended to discredit Redmond and his constitutional cause, and to provide a fillip for more radical forms of nationalist protest.

If the Great War momentarily raised the possibility of a historic compromise between Irish constitutional nationalism and the British state, then it also created opportunities for those who sought to assert Ireland's legislative rights by force of arms. Traditionally (as with the Irish uprising of 1798 and the Fenian movement of 1858), Irish militant separatists had used the occasion of Britain's foreign entanglements to seek support among Britain's enemies, and to exploit relative British weakness through conspiracy or armed insurgency. In 1916, Irish separatists sought German military aid in planning an insurrection against British rule. With both the 1798 rising and that of 1916, the possibility of foreign support was a factor, though not a decisive factor, in the Irish insurgents' plans.

The war also largely determined the nature and severity of the British response to Irish nationalist insurgency. The Easter Rising occurred at a time of difficulty and of threat for the British, with the failure of Gallipoli (January 1916) still recent and raw, and with the humiliation of Kut-al-Amara in Mesopotamia (29 April) coinciding almost exactly with the rebels' action in Dublin. These defeats, together with the continuing stalemate on the Western Front, were the contexts for the vigorous British suppression of the rising in Easter Week, 1916, for the execution of sixteen rebel leaders, and for the arrest and detention of around 3,500 suspected insurgents or sympathizers. But the British response to Irish insurgency in the past had often included not only armed suppression but also legislative concession; and in 1916, David Lloyd George was commissioned by the prime minister, H. H. Asquith, to explore the possibility of an immediate enactment of Home Rule. The failure of this enterprise, combined with the popular reaction in Ireland against the British counter-insurgency effort, served to promote the rebel cause. The main separatist party, Sinn Féin (founded in 1905, and leading a low-key existence until the war), won a succession of by-elections in 1917–18, successfully reorganized in the summer of 1917, and swiftly (and in 'vampiric' fashion) took over much of the local organization and resources of the old Home Rule party. By the general election of December 1918, Sinn Féin had swept Home Rule aside, gaining around 48 per cent of the total poll in Ireland, and an electoral mandate for the establishment of an Irish republic.

Here again, the context of the war for these developments was central. One of the more intriguing counter-factuals within modern Irish history arises from the question of whether separatism would have prevailed in Ireland in the absence of the war, or in the context of a speedily resolved war. Separatism certainly gained strength from the delays to Home Rule which arose, in part, from the exigencies of the war. Separatism benefited from the diversion of the Home Rule movement into the British war effort. Separatism gained strength, too, from the increased rigour of British counter-insurgency policy, again a development which owed much to the war. The war brought the virtual ending of emigration, widely regarded as an effective safety valve allowing the dissipation of youthful and militant energies. The war brought the more vigorous regulation of Irish industry and (particularly significantly) Irish agriculture, where there was traditionally an antipathy to outside authority, and where tillage regulations pressed hard on the Irish farming class. As in Great Britain, so in Ireland, the war brought collectivist pressures and a recasting of the old social order. As in Great Britain, so in Ireland, the war brought pressure for electoral change, which in turn benefited the Sinn Féin movement.

The Great War also provided a context for the struggles in Ireland in subsequent years (1919–23). It impacted indirectly upon the conflict in the North between Unionist paramilitaries, often veterans of the trenches, and their nationalist opponents. Demobilized veterans of the 36th (Ulster) Division drifted into Unionist vigilante organizations in 1919–20, and into the reconstituted Ulster Volunteer Force in July 1920, which fed (in turn) into the state-sponsored Ulster Special Constabulary, founded in September 1920. While certain acts of violence in the emerging Northern Ireland of this period reflected older traditions of sectarian murderousness, it might be argued that many of the combatants, Unionist and republican, drew upon their experiences and training in the British Army of 1914–18.

The Great War also supplied a critical context for the struggles between militant separatists enrolled in the Irish Volunteers, later the Irish Republican Army, and the forces of the British Crown: this conflict was brewing in 1918, but is traditionally regarded as having begun in January 1919. The shared interconnections between the different combatants in Ireland and the Great War were complex. The Royal Irish Constabulary, who were the chief agents of the British Crown, and the main targets of the IRA, had a strong war record, and were associated in particular with service in the Irish Guards. Other Crown forces were directly recruited from the ranks of British ex-servicemen: the Auxiliary division of the RIC contained many discharged army officers, while the 'Black and Tans' (again an augmentation of the RIC) were recruited from the discharged other ranks of the army and navy. But the volunteers of the IRA were also heavily influenced by the experience of fighting in the British Army in the Great War: and indeed many such men lived to unite the 'Tan' decoration (the Service Medal for 1917–21), awarded in 1941 by the Irish government for action against the Crown during the Anglo-Irish War, with their trio of First World War British campaign medals.

The IRA's war was chiefly fought in three locations, in Dublin, south Munster, and in south Ulster, between 1919 and 1921, and it was characterized by a gradual formalization of organization, and gradual development of scale. In a sense, the war provided a mutual learning experience for the two combatants—at least in so far as there was a perceptible responsiveness to the activities and successes of the other. If the Irish were seeking to regularize and consolidate their activities, then by 1921 the British showed signs of mimicking the fluidity and informality of the IRA's highly successful 'flying columns'. But British politicians and strategists were influenced not just by the successes of their opponents, but by a wide range of other external factors, including domestic liberal opinion and the perspectives of the empire. The international post-war emphasis on self-determination, on partition, and on plebiscites was to some extent reflected in the nature of the evolving Irish settlement of 1920–1. Federalist constitutional notions, highly influential within the British political elite at this time, fed into the Government of Ireland Act (1920), a measure which partitioned the island, and which made provision for Home Rule administrations in a new six-county, and predominantly Unionist, 'Northern Ireland' (with a population of 1.25 million) and in a proposed twenty-six-county, and overwhelmingly Nationalist, 'Southern Ireland' (population 2.97 million). The Government of Ireland Act operated in the North, and provided a constitution of sorts for Northern Ireland in effect between 1921 and its repeal in 1998; but the volunteers of the IRA were not fighting for Home Rule, still less for partition and Home Rule, and consequently the Act was a dead letter outside the Six Counties.

If the Government of Ireland Act bore the influence of imperialist and federalist constitutional thought, then the eventual deal which was brokered between the British government and Sinn Féin also bore some of the imprint of empire. In the midst of the Anglo-Irish War, imperialist ideologues took heart from the British experience in South Africa, which appeared to indicate that a loyal dominion might be created out of the unpromising materials generated by bloody warfare. Imperial leaders, pre-eminently Jan Smuts, were also a moderating influence on the British: Smuts is widely credited as an architect of the ceasefire between the British and the Irish which came into effect in July 1921, and which provided the opportunity for negotiation. But empire was both an emollient and a shibboleth; and this meant that, for the British, there were clear boundaries to what might be conceded in negotiation. In the haggling which took place in London in the autumn of 1921 between Lloyd George and other representatives of the British government and Sinn Féin's plenipotentiaries, led by Arthur Griffith and Michael Collins, the Irish sought to establish a republic by agreement, while the British sought to keep Ireland firmly within the confines of the empire. In effect, the deal that was signed in December 1921 granted the Irish the substance of a republic (embodied within the new Irish Free State) while preserving the vestiges of an imperial connection for the British (particularly through an oath of allegiance to the British king). Northern Ireland, already established through the Government of Ireland Act (1920), was given the right to opt out of the new Irish state, and promptly did so. It was a tribute to the capacity of the imperial imagination for self-delusion (or perhaps to the power of the South African analogy) that the Anglo-Irish Treaty should have been widely hailed by conservative ideologues as a new keystone of empire; equally it was a tribute to the susceptibility of Irish

Figure 4.2. State-builder: W. T. Cosgrove at Michael Collins's graveside, 1922.

separatists to symbolism and to oaths that so many should have been prepared to overlook the substance of what had been achieved in December 1921, and to emphasize instead the distance between the treaty and the republican ideal. This susceptibility would fuel a civil war in Ireland, where the purist opponents of the treaty would seek to defeat those more pragmatic patriots who believed, in the spirit of Henri IV, that Dublin was worth an oath.

STATE-BUILDING

The low-grade warfare fought in Northern Ireland in 1922 between the Crown forces, Protestant Unionist paramilitaries, and the IRA moulded the institutions of the fledgling polity, and left an indelible stain of political and religious bitterness. Much of the security apparatus of Northern Ireland (the police force, special crimes—'special powers'—legislation) was laid down at this time. Nationalists retained bitter memories of anti-Catholic violence perpetrated by Unionists and condoned by the Unionist state: the murder of the Catholic MacMahon family in Belfast in March 1922, probably by the Crown forces, was a particularly bloody and resonant episode. Unionists preserved their own bitter memories of republican violence: the murder of six Protestants at Altnaveigh near Newry in June 1922 by republicans (including, allegedly, Frank Aiken, a future senior minister of the independent Irish state) was one such defining event.

In the South, the Irish Civil War of 1922–3 probably brought little more than 1,500 casualties (as opposed, say, to the 30,000 or more who died in Finland's civil war—a country with population numbers similar to Ireland); but the circumstances of many of these deaths were terrible, and the divisions between former comrades-in-arms and within families ran deep. The youth of many of the combatants together with the ferocity of the conflict meant that the bitterness of the war had a longevity beyond that which might have been expected. This was compounded by the fact that party division within the new Irish Free State largely reflected the disposition of forces during the civil war, with the supporters of the Treaty creating the Cumann na nGaedheal party (1923) as a focus, and with its opponents organizing as Fianna Fáil (1926).

The traditional image of inter-war Ireland is, understandably, dominated by the civil war, and by the prevailing economic austerity of the period. The proponents of the treaty were the immediate victors in the civil war, and their Cumann na nGaedheal was in power between 1923 and 1932. Their track-record tends to be coloured by perceptions of a rigid middle-class Catholic morality, of doctrinaire economic liberalism, and of vigorous policing strategies. Moreover, where once historians tended to emphasize the democratic credibility of the pro-treaty cause (the treaty was endorsed by the Dáil, the Irish parliament, and by its ministers in January 1922, and at a general election in June 1922), on the whole they have become more impressed by the moral ambiguities of the Treatyite stand, which was formulated in the context of British threats, and which was defended with an unremitting ferocity. The corollary of this has been a movement away from overly reductionist assessments of the civil war (characterizing democratic and pragmatic Treatyites and undemocratic and fundamentalist anti-Treatyites) to a more subtle portrayal of Ireland's political culture in the early 1920s—one which lays stress on the shared features and continuities within a superficially riven polity.

Irish republican critics of the new Free State have traditionally emphasized the extent to which it continued, despite independence, to be entangled in the embrace of British imperialism. Ireland, under the terms of the treaty of 1921, was a dominion within the British Commonwealth and Empire, with a British naval presence at various strategically important locations on the Irish coast, and with deputies (TDs) in the Dáil swearing an oath of allegiance to the new constitution and to George V. Ireland remained partitioned, with (from the republican perspective) British occupation continuing in the six counties of the new Northern Ireland. Free State lackeyism expressed itself in (again, from this perspective) a brutal prosecution of republican dissent, both during and after the civil war.

Interpretations of the Irish economy and society in the 1920s have tended to be equally bleak. Both Irish states were launched in a relatively difficult economic context, being burdened by the costs of civil unrest at a time when the immediate post-war boom had ended. Moreover, the first decade of independence also coincided with the global recession associated with the stock exchange crashes of 1929. On the whole, the Irish Free State was underdeveloped industrially, since one of the features of the British regime had been the tendency to define Ireland as a larder for urban England. Only 14 per cent of the working population of the Irish Free State, some 100,000 people, was employed in industry in the mid-1920s, and only 5,000 new industrial jobs were created in the years between 1926 and 1931. Generally high levels of poverty, exacerbated by international economic conditions, were managed by an essentially conservative political elite who were more concerned about demonstrating the new Ireland's financial probity than about evincing social compassion.

Dublin, the capital, was characterized by overcrowded tenements and slums, and by low levels of public housing development (an annual average of just under 500 homes were constructed by Dublin corporation in the decade before 1933): in 1929 it was calculated that almost 44,000 housing units were needed to meet the national need. These conditions were associated with high infant mortality, disease (high rates of tuberculosis), and constrained welfare provision. The Irish countryside was also distinguished by sharp social contrasts, with the substantial farming or grazier class predominating, but with profound poverty and landlessness blighting communities particularly on the western seaboard. Patrick Hogan, the Irish Free State Minister for Agriculture, and author of a celebrated land purchase Act, calculated in 1924 that Ireland was home to a million and a half landless men, who were 'prepared to exercise their claims with gun and torch'.

Depictions of the Irish Free State of the 1920s have often focused on the dominant middle-class, patriarchal Catholic ethos of the country. Modernity, in the form of motor cars and dance halls, tended to be regarded with official suspicion, and a source of threat to the (supposed) traditional virtues and restraint of the country. Sensitive issues such as prostitution or illegitimacy tended to be treated as scandals to be buried rather than as social challenges to be addressed and resolved through reform and improvement. Catholic morality expressed itself in rigorous attitudes towards divorce after 1923 and in the more energetic censorship of films after 1923 and of literature after 1929. Catholic campaigners sought to restrict the accessibility of guidance on birth control; and legislation in 1929 and 1935 dealt with the availability of contraceptives.

But other perspectives are possible. The motifs of the historiography have arisen from a widely shared sense of disappointment that the revolution had ostensibly changed so little, and that political suppression and poverty continued to be features of Irish life. Interpretations of the new Ireland have also been framed within assumptions concerning the socially and culturally repressive ethos of the new administration. Some, though not all, international comparisons, underline this disappointment: economic growth was slower in Ireland than in many other newly established European states of the period, and at least one leading historian of twentieth-century Ireland, J. J. Lee, has strongly and persuasively emphasized the extent to which Ireland was outperformed by comparable and competing European nations.

But economic performance is not the whole story of inter-war Ireland. Ireland emerged after the civil war as a relatively stable and relatively liberal democracy at a time when much of Europe was abandoning liberalism and democracy in favour of more extreme alternatives. Irish women, for example, were fully enfranchised in 1923, whereas their British counterparts had to wait until 1928. The Cumann na nGaedheal government saw off military threats to civilian rule (through the 'Army Mutiny' episode of 1924), dealt with the recurrent threat of political insurgency throughout the 1920s, and tempted its abstentionist and republican rivals, the Fianna Fáil party (founded in 1926), into entering the Irish parliament in 1927. When Cumann na nGaedheal was defeated in the general election of February 1932, there was a peaceful transfer of power, even though the divisions between it and its Fianna Fáil rivals were rooted in the passions of the civil war. Emphases on official repression exaggerate the importance of the state, while obscuring the extent of popular conservatism and acquiescence.

Cumann na nGaedheal sought to bring not only its republican enemies into the operation of the new Irish state, but also its critics from within the former loyalist and unionist community. By way of contrast, Northern Irish Catholics and Nationalists fared worse under the defensive and populist government of James Craig (Viscount Craigavon after 1927). The casualties which this community sustained were disproportionately high in the Northern civil warfare of (in particular) 1922. A combination of Protestant Unionist hostility and Nationalist abstention meant that Catholic interests were largely unrepresented during the formative years of the Northern state. Catholicism was associated in the minds of the Unionist governing classes with political subversion; and very few Catholics were appointed to senior office in the civil service, police, or judiciary. No Catholic served as a minister in the devolved government until the appointment of G. B. Newe in 1971. Some of the limited legal devices which offered protection to minorities were either inoperative (as with the relevant sections of the Government of Ireland Act) or abandoned (such as the use of proportional representation in local elections).

State-building in the Irish Free State was not only a matter of accommodating former enemies; it was also about self-denial, and about the definition of Ireland's new institutions. Legislation passed in 1924 reformed the civil service; but the bulk—some 98 per cent—of the old British administration transferred wholesale into the new Irish service. Some senior supporters of the regime were rewarded, but administrative efficiency and continuity were the desiderata, and there was no thorough-going spoils system. Equally, the new police force of the state, the Civic Guard, or Gárda Síochána, recruited from the pro-treaty members of the IRA, but was not simply a medium for rewarding support: it contained numerous members from the old British police force, the Royal Irish Constabulary; and indeed the British force in Dublin, the Dublin Metropolitan Police, survived the first years of independence, only being stood down in 1925. In general, the government of independent Ireland was characterized by political self-restraint, and by considerable financial probity.

It was also characterized both by a relentless advocacy of Ireland's national interests and by enthusiastic participation in the internationalist initiatives of the era. The government certainly suffered through its failure to secure more territory from Northern Ireland (the treaty of 1921 had made provision for a Boundary Commission, which met in 1924–5, but which did not act as decisively as Dublin would have wished). Though this setback should not be underestimated (it has been argued that it left the Cumann na nGaedheal government 'symbolically bankrupt'), there was some compensation to be had elsewhere in Ireland's international dealings. At the Imperial Conference of 1926 the Irish worked with the Canadians and the South Africans to establish the co-equality of the dominions with Britain. The Irish were also an influence over the Statute of Westminster (of 1931) which effectively abolished the authority of the British parliament over the dominions. They were active, too, in the League of Nations, and were admitted to the Council of the League in 1930.

Nor was Ireland coterminous with its government and ruling elite. Indeed, the independent Irish state was relatively small-scale: the government certainly sought to exercise a centralized control over the lives of its citizens, but it wanted to do so on the cheap (total government expenditure in 1926–7 was a mere £24 million). Formal policing mechanisms existed, but were limited: after the end of the civil war the Irish military establishment was miniscule. The Gárda Síochána was consciously designed not to be paramilitary, and lacked the arms and ammunition which had characterized the Royal Irish Constabulary. Censorship existed, but was founded primarily on religious and cultural principles, rather than upon a desire to eliminate political dissent: the debate in Ireland about birth control, for example, focused on faith and morality rather than (as was the case elsewhere in Europe) on politics, demography, and eugenics. Perhaps the most remarkable feature of Ireland in the 1920s was the extent to which republicans, the ostensible 'losers' in the civil war, and the enemies of the Cumann na nGaedheal regime, were given the space to evangelize and rebuild. Ireland in the inter-war years was policed, not primarily by the Irish state, but by social and cultural consensus.

The Catholic Church more effectively monitored public morals than did the government (though there was a continuum of influence, binding the Church to the administration). The enforcement of a strict morality, particularly evident in sexual issues and with the temperance question, fell to the Church. But here again, as with so much else concerning the history of Ireland in the 1920s, oversimplification is possible. Characterizations of inter-war Catholic Ireland tend to be made from liberal or secularized perspectives, and not in the context (say) of the wider renaissance of European Catholicism in this era. Also, no easy dichotomy can be drawn between the Irish Church and the Irish people, since the two were so closely interrelated. It is certainly true that the Church drew upon, and reflected, certain sections of Irish society, and particularly the prosperous farming classes. It is true, too, that (particularly given the social profile of vocations) the Church hierarchy favoured the Cumann na nGaedheal government and the Free State cause in the 1920s, rather than the republican alternative. But the Church, whatever its unitary aspirations, was not a monolith, and (as was so often the case in its history) priests were divided, often along generational lines, over political questions, and particularly the treaty. Moreover, despite the relative strength of the Irish hierarchy and the proliferation of lay and vigilance organizations, it would be wrong to assume popular subjugation. In the end there was certainly a Catholic moral consensus; but the more extreme aspects of this should not be used to characterize the whole, and the more energetic campaigns of enforcement met with, at best, a highly qualified success. This was a policing regime which could be intolerant, which sometimes demanded obedience, but which was too uneven to effectively extinguish dissent.

In fact dissent expressed itself readily enough in popular refusals to conform, and in the arts, literature, and history. It is true that there was a range of significant artists and historians who were close to the founders of the new Irish state, and who celebrated their achievement: painters such as Sir John Lavery, historians such as John Marcus O'Sullivan or Mary Hayden, and even (for a time) the national poet, W. B. Yeats (the painter William Conor, historians such as Cyril Falls, and writers like St John Ervine performed the same laudatory function for the Unionist state in Northern Ireland). There was a substantial popular literature commemorating the revolution, created by writers such as Piaras Béaslaí or Louis Le Roux (in the North Ronald McNeill celebrated Ulster's stand against Home Rule). But there was a significant tradition of dissent, whether from exiled modernists such as James Joyce or Samuel Beckett, or from those who chose to stay at home in order to rattle bourgeois sensibilities. Mainie Jellett and Evie Hone introduced Cubist art into staid, post-revolutionary Dublin. Seán O'Casey, a veteran of the Irish Citizens' Army and of 1916, came to depict the revolution in highly unromantic (and thus startling) terms through his plays of the mid-1920s. Flann O'Brien vigorously debunked the pieties of the new state in his journalism. The journal *Dublin Opinion* mocked 'national' values in its cartoon art. By the mid-1930s, Irish historians, too, were laying the foundations for a cooler reappraisal of the national story: a new professional manifesto, a new scholarly journal (*Irish Historical Studies*), and new professional organizations paved the way for this evident 'revisionism'.

There is a temptation to equate the Cumann na nGaedheal government with other callous right-wing administrations in inter-war Europe. Such analogies would be mistaken. The rulers of the Irish Free State certainly protected the interests of its middle-class and propertied support, and often took a seemingly heartless approach towards the poor. But, in the end, their state was small, and (after 1923) their capacity to enforce was limited; and they tolerated (perhaps because they could not suppress) a range of political dissent. Ireland's new rulers wanted to consolidate Irish sovereignty, and to create a more centralized administration. But they had little cash, no compelling political vision, and no desire to perpetuate their own command.

NATION-BUILDING

Cumann na nGaedheal also, arguably, taught their republican successors in Fianna Fáil that they did not need to shoot the British in order to secure political rights. The ministers of Fianna Fáil were, for the most part, veterans of the war of independence and of the civil war: some had been suspicious of the truce with the British in July 1921, most remained deeply antagonistic towards the treaty of December 1921, and all were thoroughly distrustful of British diplomacy. In essence, Ireland was now in 1932 ruled by a youthful and hawkish elite who wanted substantial reform in the relationship with Britain.

Yet, despite this potentially explosive chemistry, change within the British–Irish relationship of the 1930s was managed peacefully. The oath taken by Irish deputies to the British king was removed in 1932–3, while the post of king's representative in Ireland (the governor generalship) was quietly downgraded and finally abolished in 1937. Irish citizenship was more tightly defined through legislation in 1935, while Ireland's relationship with the British Crown was loosened through legislation passed in 1936. The culmination of this endeavour was a new constitution, unveiled in 1937, and which defined (in a mixture of liberalism and paternalism) Ireland as a republic-in-all-but-name.

The only conflict that was fought with the British in the 1930s was virtual (though it was intimately connected with sovereignty and independence), and was pursued with tariffs and import bans rather than with artillery. This was the 'Economic War' of 1932 to 1938, and the fact that it was defined in the language and with the vigour of the battlefield possibly helped to acclimatize the retired warriors of Fianna Fáil to the peaceful exercise of state power. But the issues were certainly difficult and sensitive, and might well have generated a more aggressive form of diplomacy than in fact was pursued. A tit-for-tat exchange of recriminatory tariffs and restrictions was pursued by the two nations between 1932 and the signing of an agreement in 1938. This brought some modest financial compensation to the British; but it also, critically, saw the removal of their naval bases from the Irish coast. The 'Economic War' had brought an Irish military victory: the twenty-six counties of independent Ireland had been finally divested of the British military presence through diplomacy, and without the firing of a single shot.

De Valera's genius, and that of his Fianna Fáil party, lay in simultaneously annexing and controlling Irish republican and patriotic sentiment: their particular genius lay in extracting the maximum national benefit, particularly from the British–Irish relationship, at a minimal outlay, and notably without incurring deaths or injury. In part, this was connected as much with British as with Irish diplomacy at this time, influenced (as the former was) by a Gladstonian sense of responsibility and guilt towards Ireland, and diverted by wider economic and strategic considerations. But de Valera's vision, skills, and (his stand in

1922–3 notwithstanding) constitutionalism were also critical factors. His rivals in Cumann na nGaedheal (melded after 1933 into a new party, Fine Gael) had built the independent Irish state, but had continued in the hegemonic traditions of the old Redmondite Home Rule movement, largely heedless of the need to cultivate a popular constituency. De Valera's Fianna Fáil did not make the same mistake, and lavished money and energy in building a national party organization, as well as (when in government) shaping policies which were intended to address patriotic and material needs, and to smother social conflict. At remarkably little cost, de Valera and Fianna Fáil left no political space to dissident republicans within the vestigial Irish Republican Army; equally, their successful harassment of the British throughout the 1930s meant that they undercut possible support for the nascent Irish fascist movement, the Blue Shirts of General Eoin O'Duffy.

Nor could any prospective Irish fascists persuasively appeal to Irish capitalism in the 1930s. Successive Fianna Fáil governments, following in the traditions of Sinn Féin, kept watch over the interests of small businessmen, and were keen in particular to defend them from the ascendancy of British industry. In common with other European governments, the Irish abandoned a de facto free trade regime during the international economic crisis of the early 1930s, so that, by 1937, 288 articles were subject to tariff imposts, with just under 2,000 additional goods being restricted through the application of a quota system. In addition, Control of Manufactures legislation was passed in 1932 and 1934 to prevent non-Irish companies cutting through this protectionist defence by masking their control of Irish businesses. By 1936, the average level of tariff was 35 per cent, as compared with the average level of 9 per cent sustained in 1931 (and the very much slighter range of goods affected). There was an efflorescence of the state, or rather 'semi-state' or 'state-sponsored', sector in the 1930s; but Fianna Fáil was keen to ensure that these semi-nationalized industries were not competing with private business.

The profit/loss account for these endeavours was complex, and it would be quite wrong to characterize the Irish economy of the 1930s as being successful in anything other than some narrow political terms. Local industrial employment and gross industrial output rose sharply, as some native industries flowered in the greenhouse of protectionism; but this was a temporary aberration. Substantial import substitution was attained in some industries; but despite the drive for economic self-sufficiency—indeed, in a sense, *because* of the drive for economic self-sufficiency—reliance on imported raw materials grew. Irish industry developed in a bloated and inefficient manner, protected and uncompetitive.

If Fianna Fáil were able to outbid other, much more dangerous and potentially violent, patriots, and if they were keen to protect the interests of small business, then (equally) they were concerned to address any threat from labour and from socialism. Indeed, Fianna Fáil appeared to have stolen a socially progressive agenda from labour, expanding the application of unemployment assistance through legislation in 1933, legislating for workmen's compensation in 1934 and for widows' and orphans' pensions in 1935, and sponsoring a Conditions of Employment measure in 1936 (an Act which affected working hours and holidays— but which also, controversially, empowered the government to regulate the number of women within industry).

Some qualification is, again, necessary. Industrial unrest certainly remained relatively limited in the 1930s, but was beginning to grow at the end of the decade (with a major strike in the construction industry in 1937): strike action was proscribed during the war, in 1942, but again began to spiral in the later 1940s. The relative peace of the 1930s arose, not wholly because of working-class contentment, but rather because of a weak and divided labour movement, and because of the continuing dearth of employment opportunities (despite some new industrial jobs). If unemployment remained high, then wages (predictably) were relatively low: the gap between British and Irish paypackets was opening up in the late 1930s and during the war, with some inevitable consequences. Migration, traditionally a political and industrial safety valve for the Irish, was comparatively limited through the early 1930s (because of depressed host economies), but grew later in the decade and during the wartime years. Even so, the former Cumann na nGaedheal Minister for Finance, Patrick McGilligan, argued in 1937 that it was only because of emigration to England 'that we still found it possible to limp and hobble along'.

The Unionist government in Northern Ireland presided over a similarly complex piece of political and economic architecture, though with certain critical distinctions and limitations. The Unionist Party, like Fianna Fáil, successfully united strategically important sections of the working classes, the farming interest, and business by offering something to each (welfare provision, continuing land purchase, business credit and investment inducements). But Craig and the Unionists were working with the limited machinery of a devolved administration, and within the confines of a severely divided community; and, unlike de Valera and Fianna Fáil, they were seeking not so much to industrialize, as to defend an existing industrial economic structure. Eastern Ulster had been Ireland's industrial focus—its Ruhr or Catalonia—since the mid-nineteenth century; but this pre-eminence was under threat in the depressed trading conditions of the inter-war years when the demand for Belfast's ships and engineering dried up. Craig's devolved powers did not stretch, as with de Valera and the South, to offering tariff protection to these failing local industries. As with de Valera, however, so with Craig, a heady mixture of intense patriotism and welfarism helped to prevent the conversion of popular economic misery into political activism.

Intense patriotism and welfarism were strategies of state- and nation-building for both leaders and in both polities. But the consolidation of the separatists' vision of the Irish nation and of the Unionists' 'Ulster' involved much more than challenging enemies, British or republican, and subsidizing friends. In each polity there was a low-grade Kulturkampf, fought in the realms of language, nomenclature, ceremonial, and physical environment. This tended to be a more systematic enterprise in the Irish Free State than in Northern Ireland, though the determination of Craig and his supporters to promote a particular vision of 'Ulster' should not be discounted. Both governments were sensitive about the Irish language: in the South language was treated in conventional nineteenth-century ideological terms, as one of the hallmarks of nationality, and great stress, accordingly, was laid upon the propagation of Irish. Just as nineteeth-century Irish nationalists had blamed the British-sponsored National School system for the undermining of Irish, so the leaders of independent Ireland determined to use the schools system for the revival of the language: Irish was to be the sole medium of instruction in the early years of primary school (1926), and was designated as a compulsory subject (in 1934). Knowledge of Irish became a requirement, at least nominally, for a range of positions in the public sector. In Northern Ireland there was no such emphasis on the Gaelic cultural tradition, and the Irish language was wholly excluded from all aspects of official and public life. Here, instead, Craig and the Unionists celebrated the cultural values of the planters (the English and Scots settlers of the seventeenth century), though his enthusiasm did not stretch, as those of his successors would do, to actively propagating the Ulster-Scots language or dialect.

Linked with the issue of language was that of placenames. Each government fretted about the titles of their respective polity. Craig periodically sought to convert the rather anodyne 'Northern Ireland' into the more robust 'Ulster'; in 1937 de Valera abandoned the 'Irish Free State' (a title mired in the politics of the treaty, and with pejorative connotations) for the emphatic 'Ireland'. Placenames, streetnames, buildings, and statuary naturally reflected official cultural emphases: in the South placenames celebrating British royals or heroes were rebranded and gaelicized (King's and Queen's Counties, Kingstown and Queenstown are clear examples). In Northern Ireland, British patriotic, royal, and imperial allusions continued to be used, and there was some use, or attempted use, of the names of Unionist heroes (Craig himself was celebrated in Derry's Craigavon Bridge). Public buildings reflected the power and aspirations of each of the Irish two polities: plans were laid for a grandiloquent reconstruction of central Dublin, while Belfast's law courts (1927) and parliament buildings (1932) projected a triumphal vision of the new 'Ulster'. Public ceremonial, similarly, reinforced the values and authority of the two polities (the Eucharistic Congress in the Irish Free State (1932); royal visits (1921, 1932, 1937); and Edward Carson's funeral (1935) in the North).

In the South, Eamon de Valera blended some of these diverse cultural and political imperatives into a political creed which helped to preserve his state from more extreme alternatives. This complex mixture underlay his new Irish constitution of 1937, a document which (on the whole) preserved liberal values at a time when European constitution-making was abandoning liberalism in favour of authoritarian substitutes: it was also a document shaped by widespread consultation. The new Ireland was indeed to be 'Ireland', and not the 'Free State': it was to be a de facto but not a de jure republic, with a president as head of state, a taoiseach, or prime minister, as head of the executive, and a bicameral parliament, or Oireachtas. It was to be Irish-speaking (Irish was to be 'the first official language'). Liberal and democratic constitutional structures were complemented with Catholic social teaching: the centrality of the family within society was affirmed, divorce was prohibited, and women were located firmly within the environment of 'Kinder, Kirche und Kuche'.

Liberal critics of the constitution have been numerous and vocal, and—from the feminist perspective, in particular—understandably so. Yet (as with so much else in Fianna Fáil's track record), the Constitution was rooted in compromise and in political realities: it was also rooted in de Valera's particular vision and foibles. Ireland was not quite a republic, and retained some vestigial links with the Commonwealth: this, on the whole, reflected de Valera's long-term thought on constitutional relations, and balanced the mainstream separatist imperative with some mild consideration of unionist sensitivities. Republicans were appeased by the assertion that the 'national territory' was the whole island of Ireland, and not simply the twenty-six counties of the South. The special position of the Roman Catholic Church was affirmed; but Catholicism was not established as the state religion of Ireland.

Table 4.1. Religious affiliations in the Six Counties of (after 1920) Northern Ireland

Census	Population	Catholics	Catholic %	Protestants*	Protestant %
1911	1,250,531	430,161	34.4	768,059	61.6
1926	1,256,561	420,428	33.5	781,652	62.2
1937	1,279,745	428,290	33.5	791,540	61.8
1951	1,370,921	471,460	34.4	830,099	60.6

* The main Protestant denominations (Presbyterian, Church of Ireland, Methodist) used for this calculation

Table 4.2. Religious affiliations in the Twenty-Six Counties of (after 1921) the Irish Free State

Census	Population	Catholics	Catholic %	Protestants*	Protestant %
1911	3,139,688	2,812,509	89.58	311,461	9.92
1926	2,971,992	2,751,269	92.57	207,307	6.98
1936	2,968,420	2,773,920	93.45	182,746	6.17
1946	2,955,107	2,786,033	94.28	157,054	5.31

* The main Protestant denominations (Presbyterian, Church of Ireland, Methodist) used for this calculation

The 1937 Constitution defined and reflected the quality of Irish democracy. Ireland was, and was to remain, liberal, patriarchal, and Catholic. Some fundamentals were given direct expression: an all-Ireland republicanism, an assertive Catholicism. Ireland in the 'devil's decade' had thus some ferocious constitutional plumage; but the essential organism was liberal and democratic.

WAR, NATIONALITY, AND WELFARE

Independent Ireland in late 1939 was relatively well equipped to weather the European conflagration. Its defence forces were certainly in a miserable condition: the army was around 7,600 strong, while both the air corps and (more surprisingly) the navy were in a merely nascent state. On the other hand, as a consequence of the 1938 agreement, the twenty-six counties of the South were rid of the British military presence; and the existence of a staunchly pro-Allied government in Northern Ireland mitigated the strategic value of the South, and reduced the threat of British or (after 1942) American occupation. Ireland was thus able to underline its separateness from the looming presence of Great Britain, through a policy of neutrality. The function of this has frequently been explained in terms of the consolidation of national sovereignty; but it is also the case that neutrality was concerned with the internal condition of Ireland. Neutrality, arguably, was the only policy which made sense in terms of national unity, given the cultural hybridity of the island, and the competing traditions of (on the one hand) anti-British hostility and (on the other) participation in the British armed forces.

Neutrality, it was once argued, cut Ireland off from the European mainstream, and corralled its inhabitants into (to use one well-worn analogy) a kind of 'Plato's cave'. In reality, while the Irish state remained largely neutral, Irish people, motivated by personal conviction as well as material need, joined the British armed forces or migrated to work in the British wartime economy: estimates of those in the forces vary between 50,000 and 70,000, with the numbers of casualties being perhaps 10,000. This military and industrial contribution to the British war effort relieved pressure on the faltering Irish economy; but it also tended to elide social barriers and (more generally) to increase Irish susceptibility to British and wider political and intellectual currents. Certainly the work of William Beveridge and J. M. Keynes began to achieve a tentative impact on the Irish political classes at this time, with Seán Lemass (Fianna Fáil Minister for Industry and Commerce after 1941) evincing a particular interest.

Lemass's counterparts in Northern Ireland were being pushed in the same direction, though perhaps for different reasons. In the North the influence and acceptance of the British welfarism were linked to the fear that Protestantism and the Union would be undermined by any divergence in benefits. In the South the reputation of the independent Irish state was to some extent tied up with its ability to deliver on this score; and while the intellectual anchorage was quite different, 'Beveridgeism' did chime in certain respects with the imperatives of Catholic social thought. Welfarism in the Irelands of the 1940s was about community and social justice; but it was also, inevitably, about the national question and partition.

In Britain and elsewhere in Europe, the war was associated with economic dislocation, an expansion of the state, a leftward thrust in electoral politics, and a consolidation of national identity. Despite the supposed isolation wrought by neutrality, Ireland shared much with this broad European pattern (even if there were inevitable local inflections). Pressures grew on the economy of the neutral south, and even on that of the wartime North. For the south, the war (in a sense) compounded the damage done by the protectionism of the 1930s: shortages and restrictions fed into price inflation (74 per cent between 1939 and 1945), with wages failing to keep pace (30 per cent hikes between 1939 and 1945). Rationing, falling living standards, the undermining of some traditionally high-status occupations (such as teaching) fed into mounting social and industrial unrest. In Northern Ireland employment expanded rapidly, but with this growth came the inevitable concomitants of wartime labour—greater restrictions on the workforce, longer hours, industrial tensions. In each of the two Irish jurisdictions the focus of politics moved leftwards: in the South the Fianna Fáil government (which was in power until 1948) continued to develop its social policies, while more socially radical alternatives such as Clann na Poblachta (formed in 1946) began to gather electoral momentum. In the North Unionism survived more or less intact, but only because it took on the colouring of Clement Attlee's reforming post-war administration—and because it benefited from the wider celebration of Britishness that victory engendered for a time after 1945. Indeed, if the twenty years after the end of the war witnessed the last hurrah of old-style unionism throughout the United Kingdom (including England and Scotland), then this was a cry which was also raised in Ulster.

While the Britishness of Ulster Unionism was reinforced by participation in the Allied war effort, Irish national identity was bound and reinforced by neutrality (or perhaps, more accurately, by the ambiguities of wartime policy). Irish republicanism emerged from the war in a relatively strong condition, despite the linkages between some IRA leaders and national socialism. On the whole, Fianna Fáil remained the market leader so far as republican orthodoxy was concerned; but the action taken by de Valera against the challenge of IRA dissent, as well as his failure to deliver on the partition issue, provided others with an electoral opportunity. In particular, the new Clann na Poblachta (given its heady combination of social radicalism, Catholic orthodoxy, and republican conviction) was well placed to exploit this heightened national sentiment. Indeed, it was the first Irish coalition (or 'Inter-Party') government of 1948–51, wherein the Clann was an important partner, that converted Fianna Fáil's aspirational and rhetorical republicanism into action. It was this government, too, which began to convert the quiet intellectual and ideological networks of wartime into a set of formal international connections.

CONCLUSIONS

The grand narrative of twentieth-century European history has some, incomplete, relevance for the Irish. Ireland's inter-war years have, indeed, been characterized as a kind of 'nightmarish parenthesis', though the flanking clauses tend to be different from those relevant to much of the rest of the continent. Nationalist Ireland's early twentieth-century apogee was the revolution, rather the Edwardian decadence of the British *ancien régime*. Independent Ireland's post-Second World War efflorescence only began, arguably, with the economic modernization of the 1960s. If inter-war Ireland was bleak (and this essay has sought to demonstrate some of the complexities of the island's experience in these years), then it was a peculiarly Celtic twilight, with partition and thwarted republicanism, as well as civil war and sustained economic difficulty, casting shadows.

Independent Ireland in 1945 was evidently impoverished, isolated (and in the eyes of the Allies) sullied by its wartime record. It was characterized, apparently, by an assertive Catholicism, and by nationalist chauvinism. The island remained formally divided, but was also torn by cultural and religious allegiance. Northern Ireland (viewed from London and Washington) had had a 'better' war than its southern neighbour; and its economy was in superficially robust condition. But beyond the patriotic bunting of Belfast lay a society riven with sectarianism and guarded intolerance.

It would be wrong to dismiss some of this characterization out of hand. The island clearly remained partitioned throughout the period under examination, and in each of the two Irish jurisdictions there was evidence of ethno-centric politics and cultural triumphalism. Ireland also remained poor. The revolutionaries of 1916–21 had inherited a relatively unindustrialized economy in the South, and had sought—particularly in the 1930s—to develop native industry. But the principal mechanism that they used (as elsewhere in Europe) was protectionism; and this tended to provoke retaliation and to stifle competitiveness. The South was, at least, spared the experience of Northern Ireland, where the undercapitalized, fragmented, and outmoded industrial economy was in freefall in the inter-war years.

The evidence of division and poverty was inescapable; but other aspects of Ireland's inter-war reputation are more susceptible to interrogation. Independent Ireland has often been characterized as both introspective and puritanically Catholic. Yet it was hard to be both wholly isolationist and thoroughly Catholic. Irish artists were influenced by the different expressions of modernism. Irish social activists were influenced by different trends in European Catholic thought. Irish historians were influenced by German and British professional and disciplinary models. Irish diplomats were involved with the internationalist initiatives of the inter-war and post-war years, contributing to the League of Nations and the Council of Europe. Irish economists slowly took on board the ideas of Beveridge and Keynes. Ireland's economy remained protected for most of this period; but there was free trade in the market for ideas.

Ireland's Catholic hierarchy was certainly at the peak of its influence in these years. But the teaching of the Church reflected a broad consensus in Irish society, and indeed was often endorsed across denominational divides. Moreover, the Church provided education and welfare resources at a time when the southern Irish state (though developing in this respect) was relatively impoverished. A few associated with this work were guilty of cruelty and hypocrisy. But this should not wholly mar the wider record of social engagement, compassion, and justice.

Ireland was judged (and found wanting) on the basis of its wartime neutrality. But the fundamentals are clear: Ireland was a small nation, recently liberated from its more powerful neighbour, and anxious to protect this newly acquired freedom. Neutrality was concerned with Irish sovereignty; but it was also about constitutional leadership and national unity. The concept of unity in twentieth-century Irish history tends to be associated with the partition question; but this obscures the fact that the challenge of unification in these years was partly about the integrity of the South. In the aftermath of civil war, Cumann na nGaedheal lured or cajoled both republicans and ex-unionists into the structures of Irish democracy; in the 1930s Fianna Fáil created a support base which united the working classes, small producers, and (increasingly) business. The contribution of each, underpinned by wartime neutrality, meant that parliamentary democracy survived and thrived in Ireland, and that the country was preserved from the spectres of fascism and communism and clericalist dictatorship. But this success was hard won, and was far from being inevitable.

Eamon de Valera ruled Ireland as its prime minister for twenty-one years (on and off between 1932 and 1959), and served as its president for another fourteen years (1959–73). Yet he was no Franco or Salazar, still less a Mussolini. He is said to have cried when he finally relinquished office. But, despite the longevity and the tears, he left in democratic order.

FURTHER READING

Dunphy, Richard, *The Making of Fianna Fáil Power in Ireland, 1923–48* (Oxford, 1995).
English, Richard, *Radicals and the Republic: Socialist Republicanism in the Irish Free State, 1925–1937* (Oxford, 1994).
Ferriter, Diarmaid, *The Transformation of Ireland, 1900–2000* (London, 2004).
Fitzpatrick, David, *The Two Irelands, 1912–1939* (Oxford, 1998).

Follis, Bryan, *A State Under Siege: The Establishment of Northern Ireland, 1920–25* (Oxford, 1995).

Garvin, Tom, *Nationalist Revolutionaries in Ireland, 1858–1928* (Oxford, 1987).

Hennessey, Thomas, *A History of Northern Ireland, 1920–96* (Dublin, 1997).

Hill, J. R. (ed.), *A New History of Ireland: Ireland, 1921–1984*, vii (Oxford, 2003).

Hopkinson, Michael, *The Irish War of Independence* (Dublin, 2002).

Jackson, Alvin, *Home Rule: An Irish History, 1800–2000* (London, 2003).

Kissane, Bill, *The Politics of the Irish Civil War* (Oxford, 2005).

Laffan, Michael, *The Resurrection of Ireland: The Sinn Féin Party, 1916–23* (Cambridge, 1999).

Lee, J. J., *Ireland, 1912–1985: Politics and Society* (Cambridge, 1989).

McGarry, Fearghal, *Eoin O'Duffy: A Self-Made Hero* (Oxford, 2005).

McIntosh, Gillian, *The Force of Culture: Unionist Identities in Twentieth-Century Ireland* (Cork, 1999).

Ó Grada, Cormac, *Ireland: A New Economic History, 1789–1939* (Oxford, 1994).

Paseta, Senia, 'Censorship and its Critics in the Irish Free State, 1922–32', *Past and Present* (Nov. 2003), 193–218.

Regan, John, *The Irish Counter-Revolution, 1921–1936* (Dublin, 1999).

5

Belgium and the Netherlands

Martin Conway and Peter Romijn

INTRODUCTION

Belgium and the Netherlands are the often neglected non-identical twins of inter-war Europe. Over the previous centuries, these prosperous, densely populated, and much contested territories in north-western Europe had been central to the emergence of the commercial economy, social and cultural identities, and state structures that defined modern Europe. Throughout the twentieth century, control of their territory and industrial resources remained crucial to struggles for diplomatic, economic, and military ascendancy in Western Europe, while their respective empires projected their authority as far as East Asia, Central Africa, and South America. And yet Belgium and the Netherlands have been marginal to the ways in which historians write about twentieth-century Europe. This owes something to their relatively small size. Small states, a term that has acquired strangely pejorative connotations during recent decades, lack the evident importance of their larger neighbours: Belgium had a population of approximately eight million, while the Netherlands had almost nine million inhabitants by 1940. Their marginalization also however reflects the way in which neither state fits easily into the conventional narrative of inter-war Europe. The absence of a culture of political violence and the gradual, almost invisible, evolution of structures of socio-economic, religious, and ideological coexistence deprived the Low Countries of the abrupt ruptures of revolution which characterized many other areas of Europe during the first half of the twentieth century.

The purpose of this chapter is therefore to rectify the relative absence of Belgium and the Netherlands (the ordering of which we shall periodically reverse to demonstrate its arbitrariness) from accounts of the years between the First and Second World Wars. In doing so, however, we have been conscious of the need to avoid two errors that it would be all too easy to commit. The first would be to approach the history of the two states in terms of absences or, to put it more crudely, of things which failed to happen. The revolutions which swept across central Europe after the end of the war in 1918, the emergence during the 1920s and early 1930s of Communist and fascist movements in many European states and the descent of almost all of Europe into an interlocking series of military, ideological, and inter-ethnic conflicts from the mid-1930s onwards constitute an obvious agenda for accounts of inter-war Europe. Applied to the Low Countries, they risk however suggesting a rather unsatisfying list of 'dogs which failed to bark'. The relative absence of revolution, of mass movements of the extremes of left and right and of civil war was not the consequence of a failure of collective will or political imagination. It reflected the way that Belgium and the Netherlands developed political systems in which compromise rather than conflict was the defining characteristic. As such, these compromise polities might be regarded as constituting an alternative 'happier' history of the inter-war years from that described in other chapters in this volume. This, however, was true only in the sense that the number of the victims of civil and military conflict was fewer. Violence may not have dominated the history of Belgium and the Netherlands between the end of the First World War in 1918 and the German invasion of both states in May 1940, but the same structures of social inequality, economic oppression, racial discrimination, and political conflict which gave rise to violence elsewhere were present, and indeed omnipresent. The difference lay not therefore in the absence of conflicts but in how these conflicts were mediated.

The second error, and perhaps the most obvious one, would be to approach the history of the two states in terms of a common history. The collective noun 'the Low Countries' encapsulated from at least the fifteenth century until the Revolutionary and Napoleonic wars of the late eighteenth and early nineteenth centuries a shared, if bitterly disputed, socio-economic, political, and cultural heritage. After 1830 this was no longer so. The brief and highly unsuccessful experience of the unitary Kingdom of the Netherlands between 1815 and 1830, which brought together the northern and southern Netherlands under a common northern monarch, demonstrated once and for all the impossibility of political union. The two states were distinguished most visibly by differences of religion and of language: Belgium was largely Catholic in composition while the Netherlands was dominated by a Protestant majority; the Netherlands was almost uniformly Dutch-speaking while Belgium was divided between speakers of French and Dutch. Less visibly, however, the two states were divided by differences of political culture. This became clear in the decades that followed the revolution of 1830 in Brussels and the subsequent secession of the southern territories into what became in 1831 the Kingdom of Belgium. From then on, there were no wars between the two states; but nor did reunion ever seem to be a serious possibility.

Indeed, during the first half of the twentieth century, there were periodic surges in political animosity between the two states. Belgium had been invaded by the German armies during 1914 and suffered a harsh military occupation, while the Netherlands had retained a difficult but in relative terms more comfortable neutrality. These highly divergent war experiences overshadowed bilateral relations in the immediate post-war years. During the negotiation of the post-war treaties at Versailles, Dutch diplomats had to intervene to rebuff Belgian demands and claims for territory at the expense of the Netherlands. Anti-Belgian resentments ran very high in the Netherlands during the 1920s. An agreement between the two states over the centuries-old dispute about the navigation channels to the Belgian port of Antwerp was rejected by the Dutch parliament after a successful protest campaign by conservative and nationalist politicians and further embittered relations between the two states. During the 1930s some intellectual groups on both sides of the frontier, notably Joris Van Severen's Verdinaso movement in Belgium, did try to encourage the dream of a reunified Low Countries. But these ideas never acquired a mass following or elite support. The separation of diplomatic and political convenience initiated in 1830–1 had become a much wider division of political and cultural mentalities, with the consequence that Dutch and Belgians, including the Dutch speakers in Flanders, recognized much more readily what divided them from each other rather than any underlying similarities.

FACTORS OF CONVERGENCE AND OF DIVERGENCE

Belgium and the Netherlands were, throughout the inter-war years, constitutional monarchies which combined the will of the people, as expressed through their elected representatives in parliament, with the executive power of government, which acted symbolically (and sometimes rather more tangibly) in the name of the monarch, and an independent legal system and judiciary. This three-fold division of powers had its origins in the gradual processes of state formation and political modernization that had occurred over the course of the previous century. In Belgium, the founding Constitution of 1831 had imposed on the new country the template of a nineteenth-century liberal state. The initial limited suffrage had been expanded in 1893 by instituting universal manhood suffrage (from the age of 25), while granting additional votes to men overwhelmingly from the middle and upper classes who fulfilled a variety of criteria. The key elements of the 1831 Constitution remained, however, firmly in place. The monarchy, in the person of Albert I who had become king in 1909, occupied a central institutional position, combining the constitutional responsibilities of the King of the Belgians with a wider influence as one of the defining symbols of the new nation.

The centre of gravity of Belgian political culture lay in parliament where the nineteenth-century rivalry between the Catholic and Liberal parties had been supplemented by the emergence from the 1890s onwards of a strong Socialist party, the Belgian Workers Party, which derived its support primarily from the working class employed in Belgium's substantial industrial sector. This tripartite division between Catholics, Liberals, and Socialists proved to be the mould within which Belgian politics continued to operate for much of the twentieth century. While other parties, often dissidence from the three major political families, came and went, the three 'historic' parties monopolized national government as members of the often short-lived coalition governments of the 1920s and 1930s, as well as controlling the influential communal level of local administration. The relative immobility of Belgian electoral politics during the inter-war years was remarkable. In only one election between 1919 and 1939, that of 1936, did support for the three main parties fall below 80 per cent of the votes cast, and support for the Socialists varied over the course of the inter-war years between a high-point of 39.4 per cent in 1925 and 30.2 per cent in 1939, and for the Catholics between 38.6 per cent in 1932 and 27.7 per cent in 1936. The Liberals, by now clearly the smallest of the three political traditions, varied between 17.6 per cent in 1919 and 12.4 per cent in 1936.

In these circumstances, the margin between success and failure for each party lay not primarily in winning over voters from other parties but in maximizing support from voters already sympathetic to its cause. This imposed a conservative logic on the strategies of all of the major parties. They appealed overwhelmingly to slogans and symbols that unified, spurned ideological innovation, and sought to prevent the emergence of dissident groups. This conservatism was reinforced by the social cleavages that had developed over the preceding decades between the Catholic, Socialist, and Liberal communities. In the relatively settled social landscape of early twentieth-century Belgium, family background, education (in Catholic or state schools), membership of socio-economic organizations such as trade unions or insurance leagues and of cultural associations such as youth movements, women's, organizations, or even music groups and football teams served to define most Belgians as belonging to one of these three 'pillars'. This process of 'pillarization' sometimes cut across but also frequently reinforced divisions of social class and linguistic or regional identity, lending to Belgian life its distinct texture of intricate social, linguistic, and ideological divisions.

In the Netherlands, too, the nineteenth century had been characterized by the gradual maturation of a distinctive political culture. This combined a step-by-step evolution towards a liberal constitutional monarchy with the development of movements for emancipation among the lower middle and working classes. The liberal constitution of 1848, drafted by the great constitutional-law reformer J. R. Thorbecke, in many respects laid the basis for the gradual modernization of the fabric of Dutch daily life. This did not, however, occur without difficulty. The monarchs of the House of Orange regarded new notions such as the responsibility of ministers to parliament as an unwelcome development and it was only when the young Queen Wilhelmina (who reigned from 1898 to 1948) came to the throne that the modern idea of a constitutional monarchy took shape. This coincided with a bourgeois cultural offensive, which combined liberal ideas of citizenship with moral discipline as the response to the threats posed by the development of mass society. The process of liberalization during the second half of the nineteenth century brought to the fore a number of closely inter-related developments. The principal Protestant church, the Dutch Reformed Church (Nederlands-Hervormde Kerk), enjoyed a privileged position as the national church in the post-1816 kingdom. The 1848 Liberal constitution formally ended this dominant position, which had already been weakened when more orthodox interpretations of Protestantism had gained a considerable following.

In 1834, an orthodox minority seceded, and later in the century, similar individuals and groups disaffected with the Nederlands-Hervormde Kerk went their own way. In 1892, the political and spiritual leader of the dissenting Calvinists, Abraham Kuyper succeeded in merging a large part of this tendency into the newly founded Gereformeerde Kerk. In the dominant Protestant and liberal culture of the nineteenth century, both the dissenting orthodox Protestants and the long-standing minority Catholic population, located predominantly in the south of the country, were treated as second-class citizens. As a consequence, they organized themselves to demand greater civil and political rights. The Calvinists and Catholics campaigned initially for the right to establish their own schools, without state control, as part of their broader goal of achieving what they termed 'sovereignty in their own sphere'. In contrast to the Liberal concept of an ideologically neutral state school system, the orthodox Protestants of the Gereformeerde Kerk sought to base education on the teachings of the Bible, while the Catholics wanted to do so on the basis of papal doctrine.

The confessional leaders combined the ambition of building space for their own way of life with the goal of their wider emancipation within Dutch society. Calvinists, many of whom belonged to the lower middle class, comprised some 10 per cent of the population. Abraham Kuyper founded the first modern political party in the Netherlands, the so-called Anti-Revolutionary Party (Anti-Revolutionaire Partij). This name indicated fundamental rejection of the revolutionary idea of popular sovereignty in favour of divine authority. Kuyper would serve, between 1901 and 1905, as the prime minister of a coalition government with the Catholic party. The Catholics, who formed roughly 35 to 40 per cent of the population, had long been unable to benefit fully from the division of Church and State which had resulted from the liberal constitution of 1848. Formal equality in no sense brought to an end the long-term informal discrimination against Catholics. Thus, by the end of the nineteenth century, the first modern political parties were established, as a product of these movements for confessional emancipation, and soon thereafter the socialists would follow the same path. This process contributed to the gradual expansion in the suffrage, which culminated in the granting of universal suffrage for men in 1917 and for women in 1919. Thus, a transition to mass politics took shape in the first two decades of the twentieth century.

Their shared quest for emancipation led the different socio-cultural groups to adopt a strategy of separate but concerted campaigning directed towards achieving their common goals. The leaders of these movements for emancipation collaborated with each other but were careful to keep their followers apart. Solidarity within each grouping was reinforced through the creation of networks of newspapers, trade unions, and other social and cultural organizations, whereby in effect each vertical 'pillar' of Dutch society created its own organizational structures. The Socialists too followed this course, and the majority reformist current within the movement in effect abandoned revolutionary goals, hoping that the achievement of universal suffrage would enable them to win over the working-class followers of the confessional movements. In 1917 this gradual process of change found its expression in what came to be termed the 'Pacification' of Dutch political life. This step was made easier by the political truce that had been agreed upon at the start of the Great War. Through mutual agreements between the principal political leaders, the major sources of tension in Dutch politics were resolved. This enabled the introduction of universal suffrage as well as the provision of state subsidies for confessional education. The constituency system was changed by the introduction of the principle of proportional representation, thereby ensuring that the composition of parliament closely mirrored the strength of the different political traditions. It led to stable majorities: in the period 1918–37, the Catholics held between 28 and 32 of the 100 seats in the lower house of parliament, the Calvinists between 12 and 17; the Protestants between 7 and 11; the conservative liberals declined from 15 to 4 while the progressive liberals remained stable between 5 and 7. The Socialists won between 20 and 23 of the seats, while the Communists and other revolutionary socialists held between 2 and 5. The smaller parties never won more than 1 or 2, with the exception of the National Socialists who won 4 in 1937.

In this way, the introduction of modern mass politics in the Netherlands, as well as to a less marked extent in Belgium, led to a system of consensual rule which divided society into ideologically defined compartments. The system of pillarization had derived its origins from the struggle for political emancipation by the lower middle class and the workers and from the campaign for equal recognition by the non-dominant religious groups. But between the two world wars, it grew into an all-embracing system of social ordering, whereby identity was defined less by individual choice than by an affiliation predetermined by birth and upbringing to one or other of the Socialist, Protestant, Liberal, or Catholic communities. At the level of daily life, belonging to a 'pillar' decided which baker and grocer a family would use, which school, trade union, or newspaper they would choose, or which party they would vote for. This social compartmentalization worked well as a means of bridging divisions and mediating conflicts at the top as long as the leaders of the respective pillars were able to maintain firm control over their followers. At the same time, however, pillarization served to forestall the development of clear political alternatives. Consequently, in the 1930s, the system of pillarization came under attack because of its apparent inability to respond effectively to the results of the deep economic crisis of the time, and it came to be seen as synonymous with a certain narrow-mindedness and parochialism. Nevertheless, pillarization favoured the development of a political culture which found the institutional solution to conflicts and problems through the encouragement of negotiation and coalition politics.

Similarities of political culture were reinforced by similarities in state power. In contrast to many areas of Europe discussed in other chapters in this volume where states struggled throughout the inter-war years to assert their supremacy over rival authorities and reluctant populations, the citizens of the Netherlands and Belgium knew who their rulers were. Both were centralized states, where authority was projected downwards through a hierarchy of central and local bureaucracies and parastatal institutions. Both possessed relatively small and subordinate armies and navies, as well as national and local police forces. The frontiers of the two states were long established and, with the exception of the small predominantly German-speaking territories of Eupen and Malmédy annexed by Belgium from Germany by the Treaty of Versailles in 1919, contained no problematic ethnic minorities. Both were therefore nations as well as states. Whereas the Netherlands could claim a long historical continuity stretching back to the United Provinces of the Golden Age of the sixteenth and seventeenth centuries, revitalized by the important political and administrative reforms introduced under the Napoleonic regime, Belgium in its modern form was a creation of the revolution of 1830.

Differences of historical lineage counted, however, for little in the inter-war era. Whatever Belgium might have lacked by way of past history was amply overcome during the harsh German Occupation of the country between 1914 and 1918. The material suffering experienced during those years and the emphatic disregard for the welfare of the population displayed by the German administrators had reinforced the bond that the large majority of the population felt to their Belgian national identity. Discourses of patriotism dominated in both states during the 1920s and 1930s, and were strengthened by the rituals of national commemoration and loyalty to the respective monarchs. There was therefore no crisis either of the state or of the nation in the inter-war Low Countries. The states possessed the material means and the less tangible resources of ideological legitimacy required to confront challenges to their authority, and could count on the mixture of patriotic identification, legal obedience, and occasional self-interested evasion which characterized the behaviour of many West European citizens towards state authority during the twentieth century.

These well-ordered societies were also by the standards of the age broadly democratic. Though the enfranchisement of women in the Netherlands in 1919, boosted by Queen Wilhelmina's accession and the general drive to social modernization would not be followed in Belgium until 1948, the formal power and informal influence of nineteenth-century social elites and institutions had been greatly restricted by the evolution towards parliamentary government. Members of parliament, civil servants, and a broad array of bourgeois professionals, rather than aristocrats or military officers, were the principal rulers of both states during the 1920s and 1930s. Both too had well-entrenched structures of civil and criminal law, staffed by an influential cadre of lawyers and judges. A dominant legal culture therefore constrained the actions of both rulers and ruled, lending a pervasive predictability to daily life. Equality of rights was not, of course, the same as equality of conditions. Both were emphatically capitalist societies, in which the consequent differences of income were merely the most visible element of inequalities of class and gender which dominated all aspects of social experience. Education, employment, housing, and medical and welfare structures were all ingrained with forms of inequality which not so much divided rich from poor as categorized the population into complex and all-encompassing social hierarchies. Both moreover were societies in which the economic elite exercised considerable formal and informal power.

The similarities of mould between Belgium and the Netherlands were, however, mitigated by important factors of divergence. In the Netherlands, the maintenance of its neutrality during the First World War had reinforced a sense of introspection and internal distancing from the conflicts that ravaged other areas of Europe. Politicians and commentators cultivated an image of the Netherlands as a lighthouse of international law and morality in the raging storm of a world at war. In this way, Dutch society came to define itself by its sense of differentness, in which unity was valued more highly than the resolution of conflict or individual initiative. A value structure of social discipline and moral austerity derived at least in part from the long-dominant Protestant churches pervaded many areas of national life and contributed to a slightly self-congratulatory cult of the ruling dynasty of the House of Orange that offset the consciousness of the national decline that had taken place since the Dutch Republic in the sixteenth and seventeenth centuries. The Dutch were, according to this self-image, a historic people, united by a common past but also by shared values that were reflected in a historic orientation towards trade, the sea, and, in more recent times, the substantial imperial possessions in the East Indies (present-day Indonesia) and Dutch Guyana (Surinam).

Few, if any, of these characteristics were evident in Belgium. The brutal shock of the German violation of Belgian neutrality in August 1914, the human sacrifice and the intense material sufferings experienced during the subsequent four years of German Occupation, left many legacies for the subsequent history of the country. Above all, however, it had demonstrated Belgium to be a modern nation-state which through the shared fortitude of its people and their loyalty to King Albert I had proved their worth to the world. The image (and reality) of a martyred nation solidified a tricolour patriotism closely tied to the royal family and the memory of the soldiers who had fought the Germans throughout the First World War from a small area of unoccupied territory in West Flanders. At the same time, the war experience had reinforced the transition to modernity. As the state approached the centenary of its foundation in 1930, it projected a resolutely modern image of a free trade industrial economy, based on the coal and iron and steel industries that had developed since the eighteenth century. Divisions of language or of ideology were secondary to a sense of identification with the dominant values of 'progress' in its various material, social, and cultural manifestations. Empire, in the form of the vast territories of the Congo (nowadays the Democratic Republic of Congo), impinged relatively little on a predominantly industrial society which found its self-image in the confident art nouveau architecture of Victor Horta and the flourishing modernist artistic movements of the principal cities, notably Brussels, Antwerp, and Gent.

These differences of texture and structure were reflected, moreover, in the nature of the internal fault-lines within each society. The Netherlands was a linguistically homogeneous society divided between a fragmented Protestant majority and a homogeneous Catholic minority; Belgium was an overwhelmingly Catholic society (though one in which religious practice was far from universal) divided between speakers of French and the Flemish Dutch language (as well as a German-speaking minority in the territories annexed from Germany in 1919). For much of the previous four hundred years, divisions of religion had appeared more threatening than those of language. But in the Netherlands the tensions produced by confessional division had been gradually blunted during the nineteenth century by the development of pillarization. Each pillar developed separate worlds and, in the words of an expression of the time, pursued strength through isolation. In order to enable the development of the separate communities, a certain tolerance was required, which expressed itself not so much through an interest in other communities as through a focus on introspection and the development of one's own community. The large public demonstrations popular among the different religious communities during the 1920s served above all to promote among their own members a sense of their common purpose and respective power, rather than to win over or to intimidate those from beyond the ranks of their confessional community.

In Belgium, in contrast, the nominal unity provided by Catholicism had given way during the nineteenth century to a bitter rivalry between practising

Table 5.1. Religious affiliations in the Netherlands, 1920–1947

	Roman-Catholic	Nederlands-Hervormd	Gereformeerd	others	not religious
1920	35.6	41.2	9.1	6.3	7.8
1930	36.4	34.5	9.4	5.3	14.4
1947	38.5	31.0	9.7	3.7	17.1

Source: J. Bosmans: 'Het maatschappelijk-politieke leven in Nederland 1918–1940' in: J.C. Boogman *et.al.*, *Geschiedenis van het moderne Nederland. Politieke, economische en sociale ontwikkelingen* (Houten: De Haan, 1988) 404.

Table 5.2. Language divisions in Belgium, 1930

Principal language	%
Flemish Dutch	51.1
French	42.42
German	1.24
Children under 2 and those who spoke other languages	4.13

Source: *Annuaire statistique de la Belgique et du Congo Belge*, lix (Gent: Vanderpoorten, 1937), p. xxii.

Catholics and 'free-thinking' or atheist Liberals and Socialists. Moreover, the linguistic division between French and Dutch speakers gradually became a new source of political tension during the later decades of the nineteenth century. Linguistic identities in Belgium were not simple. The small numerical majority of those who were primarily Dutch speakers, located in the north of the country, was offset by the social and political power of the French speakers in the industrial areas of Wallonia in southern Belgium, and more especially by the tendency of the middle class in all areas of the country to use French as their language of choice. To add to the complexity, the new capital Brussels became during the nineteenth century a largely francophone city located in the predominantly Dutch-speaking area. In the politics of inter-war Belgium, campaigns for equality for the Dutch language therefore went hand in hand with a wider desire for Flemish emancipation. Bitterness felt by some in Flanders at the post-war punishment by the Belgian authorities of the small number of Flemish intellectuals who had participated in the German-sponsored Council of Flanders (Raad van Vlaanderen) during the Occupation of 1914–18 merged with a more diffuse image of the Belgian state as unsympathetic to the interests of the more rural and Catholic north in favour of Brussels and the more secular and industrial south. The image of the Flemish as a disadvantaged majority within a Belgian state controlled by a francophone elite might have been a simplification of history. But, along with the still rather tentative notion of Flanders as a geographical entity, it proved to be a slogan capable of mobilizing a vocal minority of Dutch-speaking Belgians behind its cause. Francophone identities did not possess the same power. A Walloon movement, focused on the cultural and historical specificity of southern Belgium, had developed before 1914 among some intellectuals. It lacked, however, a mass base of support, and excluded the francophone populations of Brussels and Flanders. Throughout the inter-war years, French-speaking interests therefore lacked a clear political goal, beyond the defence of the unitary Belgian state against the supposed 'separatist' ambitions of Flemish nationalists and the defence of the French language against demands of Dutch speakers for full linguistic equality.

Differences of social class, and more especially of the relative weight of the classes, also differentiated the Netherlands and Belgium. In the Netherlands, economic change had added to the already complex social structure. In the provinces of North and South Holland trade and international service industries as well as a number of specialized industries such as metallurgy, shipbuilding, and the diamond industry created an aristocracy of labour alongside the industrial proletariat as well as a long-established and richly differentiated middle class in the major cities. In rural areas, branches of industry had developed, which processed local agricultural produce such as potatoes and sugar beet as well as colonial products, notably textiles. In agriculture, a distinct farming class existed composed either of property owners or tenants, who worked the land independently, and it was in those rural areas where farmers worked as paid labourers on the land that social tensions tended to be greatest. The diversity of social structures ensured, however, that the workers in each industrial sector were obliged to conduct their own struggle. This pervasive social fragmentation moreover was further reinforced by pillarization, which divided the working class by creating separate trade unions for each of the ideological communities. Belgium, in contrast, was a more homogeneous capitalist society, forged under the pressure of an intense and often brutal process of nineteenth-century industrialization. Class frontiers were consequently starker, most notably in the coal and iron industries of southern Belgium, but also in the industrial suburbs of Gent, Antwerp, and Brussels. Here, the living standards of a prosperous upper middle class of bankers, industrialists, and professionals contrasted starkly with the poor living conditions and low wages of a large working class. Between these two poles, there remained, however, a substantial lower middle class of small businessmen and white-collar employees, as well as a significant rural population, most notably in Flanders and the hilly Ardennes region in the south of Belgium.

POST-WAR POLITICS

The political regimes that ruled Belgium and the Netherlands after the First World War were 'old' political entities. This did not, however, mean that they were unchanging ones, and in many respects the dominant theme of political life over the subsequent twenty years would be the attempts in both states to adapt the status quo to the challenge presented by a more modern, more industrialized and more educated society. Radical revolution was ruled out from almost the very beginning. In the Netherlands, food shortages and discontent over the continuing mobilization of the Dutch army led in 1918 to disturbances in several cities and military barracks. The small proto-Communist Party which had split from the Socialists in 1909 saw in these events the opportunity for a revolution on the Leninist model. This would not prove to be the case, even if the collapse of the imperial regime in Germany and the proclamation of the Weimar Republic did have repercussions in the Netherlands. In parliament the Socialist leader P. J. Troelstra declared publicly that the revolution in Germany would certainly not stop at the Dutch border and that he stood ready to take power. He had, however, made no preparations for a seizure of power, and simply presumed that the ruling class was so intimidated by the course of events that they would hand over power to him. Instead, the parties of the right organized a counter-demonstration in The Hague and mobilized former soldiers to create a Home Guard determined to ensure the survival of the established order. Troelstra had no choice but to recognize that he had been mistaken in his assessment of the situation. Moreover, as a consequence of his impulsive action, the Socialists had disqualified themselves in the eyes of the other parties as a potential partner in government. In August 1914, the Socialist leaders had immediately declared a political truce with the non-Socialist parties, but after the war the other parties only proved willing to contemplate the entry of the Socialists into government as a last resort in the case of 'utmost necessity.' That would only finally come about in 1939, in response to the imminent threat of war posed by Hitler's Germany.

In Belgium, social and political tensions ran strong after the harsh suffering of the German Occupation. King Albert I moved rapidly, however, to pre-empt any challenge to the constitutional order. On the day the war ended (11 November 1918), he announced (with somewhat dubious legality) a wide-ranging set of reforms, including the introduction of simple one-man one-vote suffrage for all men aged 21 or over. The leaders of the Catholic Party, who under the former weighted suffrage had enjoyed an absolute majority in parliament since 1884, resented this executive action. The King's decisive action succeeded, however, in rallying the population behind the regime, and most importantly ensured the support of the Socialist Party, which had campaigned vehemently for suffrage reform over the preceding decades. A series of social reforms instituted by Catholic–Socialist–Liberal governments of national unity between 1918 and 1921, including an eight-hour working day and recognition of the legal right to strike, marked a break with the notable parliamentary culture of the pre-war era and the inauguration of a new era of mass politics and social negotiation.

In both Belgium and the Netherlands, the most substantial outcome of the post-war changes was to end rule by one party or social group in favour of a much more complex politics of compromise. This was most marked in Belgium. In the first post-war elections held under the new franchise in November 1919, the Catholic and Socialist parties both gained 36.6 per cent of the vote, while the Liberals won only 17.6 per cent. This pattern of Catholic–Socialist dominance, with the Liberals as a smaller but significant third party, set the pattern for all elections held over the subsequent twenty years. Socialist hopes that they would achieve an overall majority were encouraged by their success in the 1925 elections when they won 39.4 per cent of the vote, but this proved to be their historic high-water mark; and, under the system of proportional representation which Belgium had adopted in 1899, the leaders of the parties were obliged to adapt to the new realities of coalition-building. Unlike in Third Republic France or Weimar Germany as described elsewhere in this volume, the options were relatively limited. The most obvious coalition was an alliance of Socialists and progressive Catholics built on a shared commitment to social reform. This proved, however, consistently difficult to achieve. After a series of Catholic–Liberal governments between 1921 and 1925, a Catholic–Socialist government with the Flemish Christian democrat Prosper Poullet as prime minister, working jointly with the Socialist leader Emile Vandervelde (who became Foreign Minister), finally took office in the wake of the Socialist electoral success of 1925. It lasted only eleven months, and was undermined from the outset by the hostility of more conservative Catholics towards sharing power with the Socialist foe and perhaps more especially towards surrendering the leadership of their own party to a progressive-minded Catholic from Flanders. After the government's resignation in May 1926, the Socialists retreated into opposition, enabling the conservative voices within the Catholic Party to form a new bourgeois coalition with the Liberals. The consequence was to set Belgian politics on a conservative, almost reactionary, course during the later 1920s. Though the reforms of the immediate post-war era remained in place, the prospect of any more wide-ranging democratization of the social and political order had effectively disappeared.

In the Netherlands, the balance of political forces was broadly similar. The Pacification of 1917 found expression in the creation of an almost permanent coalition of the confessional and liberal parties. They formed a stable majority, which in ideological terms was dominated by the Christian parties but which favoured liberal policies in the economic sphere. In this way the continuing modernization of the Netherlands took shape in ways compatible with Christian ethics. This combination of expansion and constraint contributed to a complacency which in times of prosperity was not too irksome but in adversity tended to generate a certain paralysis. With the introduction of universal suffrage, the Catholic party, the Rooms-Katholieke Staats Partij (RKSP), had become the largest grouping in parliament. During the decade after the First World War, they generally provided the prime minister in the person of Charles Ruys de Beerenbrouck, a representative of the South Netherlands rural nobility.

In political terms therefore the post-war era was characterized by a consolidation of the new structures created by the Pacification of 1917, as well as a certain conformism. In other spheres, the 1920s witnessed a rapid modernization of the country. In economic terms, this was evident in the expansion of industry, notably international companies such as Royal Dutch/Shell, Philips, and Unilever. The national infrastructure and urban planning developed through the expansion of the railway and road network, as well as the construction of improved waterways and new dams, which reached its culmination in 1932 with the damming of the Zuiderzee (now renamed as the IJsselmeer). Social mobility increased, and the process of pillarization enabled a more refined civil society to take shape. In some respects, this was undoubtedly restrictive and disciplined but it also offered opportunities for personal development. The colonies provided a new space for Dutch people who sought opportunities in business or public service. In the cultural field, Dutch artists forged links with the international avant-garde. Painters such as Mondriaan and Van Doesburg and architects such as Oud and Rietveld gained an international reputation and national influence. Especially Van Doesburg's connection to Bauhaus linked Dutch designers and artists to the international avant-garde and brought the attention of Mies von der Rohe and Lloyd Wright to their modernist concepts.

ECONOMIC DEPRESSION AND THE POLITICS OF THE 1930s

The economic depression which struck both states during the early 1930s in many respects had the effect of reinforcing the similarities between Belgium and the Netherlands. As industrial and commercial economies, heavily dependent on the lifeblood of international trade, the Low Countries were unsurprisingly strongly affected by the falls in investment, trade, and consumer demand which occurred after 1929. Levels of industrial production and exports fell rapidly and unemployment rose quickly in both countries from 28,000 in 1930 to 234,000 in 1933 in Belgium and 100,000 (3.4 per cent of the registered labour force) to 350,000 (12.8 per cent) in the Netherlands over the same period, reaching a peak of 480,000 (17.4 per cent) in 1936. Misery was, however, distributed more widely than among those who lost their jobs. The price of many agricultural products fell, threatening the viability of small farms; civil servants suffered particularly sharply from the policies of financial retrenchment adopted by the governments; and many small businessmen and members of commercial and ancillary professions were hit hard by the general decline in consumer demand. By the mid-1930s, elements of a tentative recovery had begun to emerge, first in Belgium and with a delay of about two years in the Netherlands. But there was no tangible end to the Depression prior to the war; and in many respects it constituted the defining experience of both societies during the inter-war years, and continued to influence social and political attitudes long after its immediate effects had disappeared.

The decline in living standards embittered social relations and encouraged a radicalization of politics, on both left and right. In both states, the Communist parties became for the first time serious competitors with the Socialist parties; while, on the right, extremist parties emerged, influenced by the style and ideas of fascist movements elsewhere in Europe. These contributed to a tangible increase in political tensions. Large-scale strikes, mass demonstrations, and consequent scuffles with the forces of order did not signify a general descent into violence, but created a pervasive sense of crisis. These parallel processes had, however, rather different outcomes. In the Netherlands, the economic and political difficulties of the 1930s constituted the most serious challenge which the new model of 'pacification politics' established in 1917 had faced. But the principal political and social actors managed to subsume their differences in the pursuit of political stability and continuity. In Belgium, in contrast, the economic depression had a much more corrosive effect. The tentative rapprochement between the Catholic and Socialist parties became more difficult, while the emergence of a vocal Flemish nationalist politics called into question the unity of the nation-state.

In Belgium, the immediate impact of the economic depression was to reinforce the conservative pattern of politics evident since the mid-1920s. The four successive Catholic–Liberal coalition governments between 1931 and 1935 adopted essentially orthodox responses to the economic crisis, seeking to reduce government expenditure to avoid a financial deficit. The sacrifices demanded of the population, and most especially of the working class, created a tense social climate, which reached a climax during the protests and strikes in the winter of 1934–5. The need for a political and social compromise was ineluctable; but the form that it took marked the arrival of a new spirit in Belgian parliamentary politics. The tripartite Catholic–Socialist–Liberal government of national unity headed by the governor of the National Bank, Paul Van Zeeland, that took office in March 1935 was markedly different from those that had preceded it. Van Zeeland was a technocratic figure, and not part of the parliamentary elite. Moreover, his government gave precedence to other relatively new figures, notably Hendrik De Man and Paul-Henri Spaak from the Socialist Party. These latter two figures emerged over the course of the 1930s as the principal advocates of ideological innovation within Socialist ranks. Rejecting the Marxist orthodoxy which had long dominated Belgian socialism, they called for a more activist and nationally oriented socialism which sought to use the mechanisms of the state to achieve economic and social reforms. This new spirit strongly influenced the content of the Plan for Work adopted by the Socialist Party as its campaigning manifesto in 1934, which advocated higher government spending, welfare reform, and industrial modernization.

Within the limits of the parliamentary regime, the Van Zeeland government did mark a new departure. Devaluation of the Belgian franc, long resisted, was carried through in 1935, and a wave of social and economic reforms introduced (notably in response to a further substantial strike wave in the summer of 1936) that marked a substantial departure from the free-market economics that had long been the defining characteristic of Belgium. Van Zeeland was, however, something less than the agent of a renewal of Belgian politics. He re-emerged as the prime minister of a further tripartite government after the elections of May 1936, and won a personal electoral triumph over the young francophone extreme-right leader Léon Degrelle in a by-election in Brussels in April 1937.

Soon, however, Van Zeeland's reputation was tainted by financial scandal, and he resigned in October 1937. Thereafter, the spirit of renewal in Belgian politics dissipated. Though Spaak became the first Socialist prime minister of Belgium from May 1938 to February 1939 his tripartite government achieved little; and, after Catholic and Liberal advances in the subsequent elections in April 1939, the Socialists left government to be replaced by a Catholic–Liberal coalition, led by the very traditional Catholic figure of Hubert Pierlot.

The failure of the Van Zeeland experiment, and more generally of projects of political reform during the 1930s, reflected the way in which the economic crisis made collaboration between the major parties more difficult. None of the three political traditions was immune from the generalized sense of crisis. Within Socialist ranks, the tension ran not so much between left and right as between a predominantly younger generation of Socialist reformers, notably De Man and Spaak, and an old guard of parliamentary and trade union figures gathered around the dominant figure of Vandervelde. The cause of reform might have had some of the best slogans, but De Man's advocacy of ideas of economic and social planning and Spaak's more superficial rhetoric of 'national socialism' was at odds with the more conservative mentalities inherent to a Socialist movement principally concerned with the defence of its established bastions of power in local government and the trade unions. Vandervelde died in 1938, and was replaced in the largely honorific post of party president by De Man. By then, however, the cause of reform had largely disappeared within the Socialist Party and it was his frustration with parliamentary politics which encouraged De Man to declare in a manifesto published in July 1940 that the German Occupation, far from constituting a defeat, was a moment of liberation for the workers of Belgium. Nor could the Socialists claim any longer to be the sole party of the left. The Communist Party, founded in 1921, became a significant rival to the Socialists during the 1930s, winning 6.1 per cent of the vote in the elections of 1936. Though they remained weak within the important trade union movement, the Communists had begun to erode the long-standing Socialist hegemony in the industrial areas of Wallonia, winning, for example, 13.4 per cent of the vote in the province of Liège in 1936.

The crisis within Catholic ranks was more profound. The division between a conservative parliamentary leadership rooted in mentalities forged during the long period of Catholic Party rule before 1914 and younger figures who had emerged from the Catholic social and spiritual organizations of the post-war years was exacerbated by the economic crisis. Catholic trade unionists criticized the party's response to the Depression, while many students and intellectuals denounced the leaders' neglect of Catholic principles in favour of governmental power. This discontent came to the fore in the early 1930s with the establishment of the predominantly francophone Rexist movement led by a charismatic young Catholic journalist Léon Degrelle. Rex, which took its title from Catholic devotion to Christ the King (*Christus Rex* in Latin), was composed initially of students critical of what they perceived as the corruption and indolence of the leaders of the Catholic Party. When, however, Degrelle decided in the spring of 1936 to launch Rex as an independent political party in the forthcoming general elections, it became the rallying point for a much wider constituency of discontented voters. With its populist denunciations of all of the established parties and vague promises of a new Catholic-inspired social and political order, Rex won substantial support among Catholic middle-class and rural electors, notably in francophone Belgium. In the elections in May, the party achieved a remarkable 11.5 per cent of the national vote, and 29.1 per cent of the vote in the southern rural province of Luxembourg, overwhelmingly at the expense of the Catholic Party.

Nor was Rex the only dissidence within Catholic ranks in 1936. The undercurrent of separatist nationalism that had been evident primarily among Flemish Catholics since the First World War acquired a new momentum with the foundation of the Vlaams Nationaal Verbond (Flemish National Union, VNV) in October 1933. The VNV won 13.6 per cent of the votes in Flanders in 1936 (7.1 per cent in Belgium as a whole), again largely at the expense of the Catholic Party, and established itself as the voice of a new generation of Flemish nationalists. Attracted by the models of authoritarian politics prevalent elsewhere in Europe, the VNV's anti-Belgian sentiments merged with a wider hostility

Figure 5.1. Cardinal Van Roey, the primate of Belgium, attends a Catholic rally in Brussels in September 1936.

to francophone values of liberalism and democracy. Its final goal of some form of ethnic homeland for the Flemish people was however less important to its electors than the way in which the VNV expressed a wider alienation, notably among a Catholic intelligentsia and lower middle class, from a Belgian state which appeared unresponsive to Flemish demands. For this vocal minority of the Flemish population, the interminable disputes during the 1920s and 1930s over issues such as Dutch-language rights had led them to the conviction that the Flemish could not be 'at home' within a Belgian state dominated by francophone interests.

The strongly pro-Belgian Rexists and the Flemish nationalists of the VNV were in many respects polar opposites, but their common hostility to the parliamentary system marked a significant departure from the former political consensus. An alliance between the two parties in October 1936 was a short-lived failure, but reinforced the sense of a threat from the extreme right. It also provoked a response from the Catholic Party, the principal loser in the election of 1936, which adopted a new structure composed of largely self-contained Flemish and francophone party organizations. Assisted by the implosion of Rex which, after the failure of Degrelle in his by-election campaign against Van Zeeland in April 1937, rapidly drifted towards an imitation of Italian and German fascist models, this reorganization was sufficient to restabilize the Catholic pillar within Belgian politics. The Catholic Party recovered to win 32.7 per cent of the vote in the elections of 1939, largely at the expense of the Rexists who collapsed to 4.4 per cent. The VNV, with 15.1 per cent of the vote in Flanders, however, also won votes, ensuring that the new Catholic Party was obliged to compete with the VNV as the defender of Flemish cultural and linguistic rights.

The political system in the Netherlands similarly faced the enormous challenge of responding to the disastrous social consequences of the economic crisis. The world economic crisis hit the Netherlands later but harder than most of its neighbouring states. In part, this was the monetary consequence of the success of the economy over the preceding period. Because the Dutch National Bank held considerable reserves of gold and foreign currency it was not initially possible for the Dutch currency to abandon the gold standard. Eventually, the Netherlands did do so in 1936 and began to recover its position in international markets. The problems of the Dutch economy were however exacerbated by the fact that the traditionally important trade with Germany was adversely affected by the monetary, political, and economic situation in that country. The crisis was, in this respect, fundamentally an imported one. It was made worse by the fact that the Dutch government was not able to develop a coherent and effective means of countering the consequences of it. The general policy followed by the consecutive governments headed by the Calvinist prime minister Hendrikus Colijn was the political translation of classic economic theory: in other words, to let the crisis run its course until a new balance could be found at a lower level, and economic growth could again begin.

Figure 5.2. The helmsman: election poster of Hendrikus Colijn, the Dutch prime minister of the 1930s.

This approach was accompanied by an unmistakable moral and moralizing tone. This was particularly evident in the policy of holding to the gold standard for as long as was feasible. To follow other states in letting go of the guarantee provided by gold and devalue would in the eyes of Colijn and his advisers be 'immoral' and an indication of untrustworthiness which could have very harmful consequences for the reputation of the Netherlands. But the effect of this policy was not merely economic stagnation but also a social crisis, to which the dominant political class was only to a limited extent able to provide a response. There was pressure not only from internationally oriented producers to contemplate devaluation, but also from some within the parliament itself. Just as in Belgium, Keynesian economists in the Netherlands developed an alternative to the established economic policy, which they termed (like their Belgian counterparts) the Plan for Work. This was published in 1935, and was seized upon by the Socialists, who used it to develop a new political profile. Despite, or perhaps also because of, energetic propaganda and mass demonstrations in the style of the 1930s the Plan found little political echo in the pre-war years. It was only after the war that its proposers were able to bring their ideas of demand-led economic growth and anti-cyclical economic policy into practical operation.

The most important political consequence of the orthodox liberal approach which the Colijn governments adopted towards the crisis was the way in which it resulted in material hardship and a mood of hopelessness as well as criticism of the established political regime. Behind such emotions lay a sense of despair over the pervasive immobilism: something simply must be done. This criticism was not primarily anti-capitalist in nature, though the membership of the Communist and revolutionary socialist parties did indeed grow. Among young Catholics, Socialists and Liberals there was an activist tendency who felt increasingly discontented with the way in which pillarization had institutionalized ideological divisions. They saw this as a root cause of political stagnation, but also as an expression of the lack of attention paid within Dutch society to the national interest. These denunciations of the structures of pillarization also merged with criticisms of the operation of the only recently achieved democratic regime. In their view, universal suffrage and proportional representation had created a class of professional politicians, who operated under the control of the pillarized elites. In response, they advocated alternative ideas of a more organic corporatist order, which were in part borrowed from Italian or Portuguese examples but which were also rooted in Catholic social teachings.

At the same time, political groupings emerged which in the manner of Mussolini and Hitler presented themselves as an extreme-right alternative to the existing order. Some early and insignificant fascist movements had existed during the 1920s, but it was in 1931 that the most important Dutch representative of this tendency was established, the National Socialist Movement (Nationaal-Socialistische Beweging, NSB). It began as a middle-class and anti-parliamentary grouping which brought together various conservative and nationalist figures. The leader of the party, Anton Mussert, was a qualified engineer employed in the provincial water-board administration but who had discovered in 1925 a taste for politics as one of the leaders of the successful national campaign against the proposed ship-navigation treaty with Belgium. The NSB's programme advocated recovery through faith in national virtues and action against the effects of the economic crisis, but its appeal lay primarily in its forceful advocacy of a strong state, its pervasive martial culture, and its hostility to the class struggle and the workers' movement. Farmers, middle classes, former colonialists, and others who felt their social position to be threatened all saw in the NSB a new hope of recovery.

In 1935, the movement recorded a spectacular victory in the provincial elections, winning almost 9 per cent of the vote. A good part of their votes derived from the electorates of earlier protest parties, but this victory radicalized the movement, in part because Mussert drew from it the conclusion that the Dutch people were waiting for an equivalent of Hitler's Nazi party. When founding the party, Mussert adopted the programme of the NSDAP, while omitting its anti-Semitic paragraphs. Now the movement experienced an influx of radical anti-bourgeois members, who under the leadership of figures such as M. M. Rost van Tonningen came to define the image of the movement. In place of its former solidly reactionary character, the image projected by the movement became increasingly extreme-right and also anti-Semitic. As a consequence, the NSB lost a large part of its following among aggrieved elements of the middle classes. Moreover, Colijn was much more convincing in presenting himself as a 'strong man' than was Mussert, and he issued an administrative decree banning civil servants from being members of the NSB. A broadly based movement developed against the NSB: religious denominations refused the sacraments to party members; a Committee of Vigilance was created by intellectuals; and even a mass movement against fascism was established entitled Eenheid Door Democratie (Unity through Democracy). In these various ways a political cordon sanitaire was established, which forced Mussert back onto the margins of politics. Consequently, in the parliamentary elections of 1937, compared to the elections of 1935, his share of the electorate was halved.

TOWARDS WAR AND GERMAN OCCUPATION

Between 1937 and 1939 most Belgians and Dutch people became newly conscious of the threat of European war. Whether war could be averted was beyond the power of either state; but how any such war might be deflected away from each state's borders was of much more immediate concern. Both Belgium and the Netherlands were neutral states. In the Netherlands, this was a continuation of the long-standing policy of moral aloofness and mercantile necessity. After the First World War, the Dutch Minister for Foreign Affairs Herman van Karnebeek gave priority to the re-establishment of the perception among the victorious Allied powers of the Netherlands as an independent and reliable partner in international affairs. Thus, the Netherlands joined the League of Nations, partly prompted by the need to counter Belgian designs to acquire Dutch territory, but also on the more principled basis that since the time of Grotius the small state of the Netherlands had sought protection in international law. Now, as Patricia Clavin discusses elsewhere in this volume, there appeared to be a realistic possibility of preventing conflicts through international arbitration and fostering world peace and disarmament. Van Karnebeek was at pains to inform the Allies about how a Rhine delta dominated by the Netherlands was essential for a balance of power on the European continent. In addition, the Netherlands campaigned that Germany, which was of inordinate importance for the Dutch economy, should be a full participant in the post-war European order. Thus, the Netherlands held firm to its policy of independence and freedom from any forms of alliance, even if this was based on a rather ambiguous self-image. On the one hand, it was realized in The Hague that the freedom of manœuvre for a small state such as the Netherlands was very limited; on the other hand, the Netherlands saw itself, on the basis of its colonial possessions, as the smallest of the major powers. Dutch diplomats portrayed neutrality as a position of elevated morality and at the same time as an insurance premium against foreign aggression. Thus, it proved impossible to establish effective collaboration with Belgium in the area of defence policy. Yet, with the stagnation of the League of Nations in the 1930s, the Netherlands sought a rapprochement with other small European states through the Oslo Convention of 1932.

In Belgium, in contrast, the return to the pre-1914 policy of neutrality was the consequence of the decision taken in 1936 by the prime minister Van Zeeland and his foreign minister Spaak, strongly encouraged by King Leopold III, to abandon the secret military agreement signed with France in 1920. Henceforth, Belgium adopted what the King declared in a public speech in October 1936 to be a policy of independence from all alliances. Belgium would be an independent state, the territorial integrity of which France, Britain, and Germany all guaranteed to defend against external attack. Neutrality, or independence, could, however, encompass many different nuances. For some, especially those on the left, it was a diplomatic formula which, as the mobilization within Belgium for the Republican cause during the Spanish Civil War well indicated, did not imply a wider neutrality between democracy and fascism. For others, however, including Leopold III, neutrality implied a more wide-ranging withdrawal from any form of partisanship, tinged in some cases with sympathy for aspects of the Nazi regime.

Politics in both states during the late 1930s was increasingly overshadowed by the threat of war. In the Netherlands, the end of an era came with the departure from office of the dominant figure of Prime Minister Colijn. His confessional–liberal coalition fell apart when the Catholics argued for the need for the government to create higher employment and introduce more socially oriented policies. Colijn, with an eye on the rising military expenditure, held firm to a balanced budget and to his policy of cautious adaptation. Thus at last the political opportunity arose for a new parliamentary coalition, in which for the first time the Socialists would be represented. Under the renewed threat of war, the Catholics argued that the conditions of 'utmost necessity' for Socialist participation in government did now prevail. The new government hardly, however, marked a radical new departure, as it still rested on a broad confessional–liberal majority. Moreover, the new prime minister D. J. de Geer was a 69 year old and rather weak-willed representative of the old political class.

He stuck firm to familiar concepts of non-intervention in economic matters and neutrality in foreign affairs. On international and defence matters, a much more active role in preparation for war was played by Queen Wilhelmina. In the First World War, she had sought to demonstrate her solidarity with the soldiers and tried to give an active lead to defence policy. Now, she saw the opportunity to perform a similar role and used her inspection visits to the troops to try to raise their morale. She also played a highly active role in the replacement of the supreme commander of the armed forces in February 1940, because of her differences of attitude with the government in the field of national defence.

In 1914, the Netherlands had used a rapid mobilization of its armed forces to underscore its readiness to defend its neutrality. In 1939, this policy was followed again: when news of the Molotov–Ribbentrop pact broke on 22 August, the first regulations were issued to prepare military mobilization. E. van Kleffens, the Minister of Foreign Affairs, gave his approval to a call for peace which the King of the Belgians issued in the names of the Dutch, Luxembourg, and Scandinavian monarchs. De Geer and a majority of the cabinet were still unconvinced of the need for effective mobilization but, under pressure from Queen Wilhelmina, took the decision on 24 August to allow the armed forces to take up their battle positions. Following a guarantee of Dutch neutrality by von Ribbentrop, Germany attacked Poland on 1 September and declared war on England and France on 3 September. Already on 28 August, the Dutch government had taken a further step and had decided on a general mobilization. From that moment a beginning was made to defence preparations, intended to demonstrate that the Netherlands would defend its neutrality. In the case of a German occupation, the government would abandon the eastern provinces in order to retreat into 'Fortress Holland', behind the traditional water barriers formed by the major rivers and flooded land. If possible, assistance would then be sought from allies willing to help the Dutch to defend themselves. This battle plan took no account of the possible use of paratroopers and other modern methods of war, and under the impact of the surprise attack of May 1940 led to rapid defeat.

In Belgium, too, the outbreak of war in September 1939, led to an expansion of the Catholic–Liberal government of Pierlot to encompass the Socialists, though not significantly the Communists, the Rexists, or the VNV. National unity, therefore, had its limits, and signified more a defensive union of the three major parties and of the state authorities against enemies both internal and external. The underlying problems that had been evident within Belgian politics during the inter-war years remained unresolved. A variety of social, regional, and linguistic grievances had not been effectively addressed, contributing to a widespread sense that the parliamentary regime was unsuited to the needs of the new society that had emerged out of the First World War. Constitutional reforms intended to create a more hierarchical and effective governmental structure were widely discussed during the 1930s. Their enactment on anything more than matters of detail was, however, at odds with a political system which privileged compromise over change. Above all, the two major parties, the Catholics and the Socialists, had not found the means of making common cause. A Socialist–Catholic coalition had been since 1919 the most obvious political coalition in Belgium; but, twenty years later, it remained as far away as ever. The persistence of the division between Catholics and Socialists was in part the result of the ascendancy of conservative interests within the Catholic Party, as well as the reluctance of the Socialists to enter fully into the process of coalition government. At its heart, however, lay the basic fault-line in Belgian society between the Catholic and Socialist 'pillars'. This division between clericals and 'free-thinkers', between the competing ideologies of social Catholicism and a Marxist-influenced socialism and increasingly during the inter-war years between the rival Catholic and Socialist trade union federations, effectively undermined any durable coalition between the two parties until the 1960s. In its absence, however, Belgium was governed either by a centre-right alliance of Catholics and Liberals or by short-lived tripartite coalitions of national unity.

If political change was to come, it would therefore emerge not within parliament but outside. With the collapse of the Rexist challenge, the possibility of any domestic fascism was largely excluded. There remained, however, the monarchy. Leopold III had succeeded his father Albert I after the latter's sudden death in February 1934. The new king, aged 32 when he became monarch, had many advantages, including a marriage to a popular Swedish princess, Astrid, and a young family. In 1935, however, the new queen was killed in a car accident while on holiday in Switzerland. Leopold, who had been driving at the time of the crash, was only slightly injured but the personal tragedy cast a long shadow over the King's reign. Increasingly exasperated by the feuding of the parliamentary elite, Leopold was drawn towards ideas of political reform that would reinforce the power of the royal executive at the expense of the political parties. Such plans never came to fruition. But the King's strained relations with the political elite, and his reliance on a small group of advisers with whom he conducted an increasingly personal foreign policy, created a tension which would turn into bitter conflict after the German invasion in 1940 when Leopold chose to remain in German-occupied Belgium while the government opted for exile in France and eventually London.

CONCLUSIONS

When the long-feared German invasion of the Low Countries finally occurred in the early hours of 10 May 1940, the Netherlands and Belgium were recognizably the same societies and political regimes as those which had existed twenty years earlier. Radical change had been avoided, or suppressed. The political frameworks, but also the societal structures which buttressed them, were largely unchanged. Viewed in the comparative perspective of the emergence of authoritarian and fascist regimes in many other European states during the 1920s and 1930s, the persistence of parliamentary rule in the Low Countries necessarily has something of the character of a victory of democracy. The institutional strength of the parliamentary regimes, and perhaps more profoundly their historical legitimacy, had saved Belgium and the Netherlands from the acute political or social crisis that alone would have provided the opportunity for a surge of extreme-right or extreme-left radicalism from below or a royal or military coup from above which could have displaced the existing political order.

The victory of democracy over Degrelle's Rexists, Mussert's NSB, or the Flemish nationalists of the VNV was, however, something less than heroic. Asked about his experiences during the French Revolution, the French diplomat Talleyrand famously commented, 'I survived' ('J'ai vécu'). Much the same might be said of the Dutch and Belgian political regimes. Their survival was more a product of their resilience than of the construction of a modern form of democracy. It offered, moreover, no guarantee for the future. The violent assault by the German forces on 10 May 1940 and their rapid and apparently definitive victory brought an abrupt end to parliamentary rule in both states. In its place a self-proclaimed 'New Order' was established, operating under Nazi military and civilian aegis, but staffed by many of the same extreme-right groups who had challenged parliamentary rule during the inter-war years. The hopes of the VNV that the arrival of the Germans would bring about an independent Flemish state or of Mussert that it would enable the NSB to create a National Socialist regime in the Netherlands proved to be a cruel illusion. The new German rulers proved unwilling to act as the 'godparents' of local fascist revolutions, preferring in the initial years of occupation to strike pragmatic deals with those civil servants, social institutions, and local elites willing to work with them. Both in Belgium and the Netherlands, the indigenous Nazi parties were employed as reservoirs of reliable personnel for the German cause. As apparent military victory changed during 1942 and 1943 into impending defeat, so the Nazi rulers were forced into dependence on those extreme-right collaborationists willing to commit unconditionally to the Nazi cause. For those Rexists, Flemish nationalists, and Dutch SS who made this choice, the final years of the war brought no tangible political reward. Instead, besieged by the hostility of their compatriots and tied ever more closely to the crumbling Nazi regime, after being severely purged and punished, they followed a course into personal and political oblivion.

Liberation from German Occupation, which came suddenly in Belgium in September 1944 and much more slowly and painfully in the Netherlands during the subsequent winter and spring, brought the restoration of the pre-war regimes. This second victory of democracy over its opponents was perhaps more emphatic and more popular than had been the case before the war. However, as the subsequent evolution of the parliamentary regimes in the two states during the decades after 1945 well demonstrated, democratic government was not a fixed structure but a formula that had to be adapted continually to encompass new social and political demands. The Netherlands and Belgium, together with Luxembourg, became at the end of the 1940s, through the Benelux customs union, core members of the new structures of West European cooperation that dominated the post-1945 decades. It would be misleading to assume, however, that both states were placid epitomes of democratic success. Neither state had been during the 1920s and 1930s democratic in the most direct sense of the term: the majority will of the people did not prevail in any simple or obvious way. Indeed, in many respects the parliamentary regimes as they had developed in the two countries since the end of the nineteenth century were explicitly designed to prevent such majority rule. Proportional representation and the consequent absence of an overall majority for any one party in the Dutch and Belgian parliaments throughout the inter-war years meant that all governments were multi-party coalitions obliged to negotiate compromises between themselves but also with other groups (the trade unions, the churches, the industrial organizations, farmers leagues, and many others) who claimed a share of the decision-making process. These compromise polities were well suited to the complex divisions of class, language, and religion which characterized Dutch and Belgian society. Power was dispersed across a range of political, social, and institutional actors, making it almost impossible to define who was in power and who was not. Thus, for example, the Socialist parliamentary leaders might only have been intermittently members of the government in inter-war Belgium and only became so in 1939 in the Netherlands; but Socialist mayors, trade union leaders, and social insurance officials were in positions of power in both states throughout the inter-war years.

Compromise polities can, however, easily become trapped within a pervasive immobility. In the Netherlands, the evolution of the regime, however hesitant, over the course of the 1920s and 1930s towards a more inclusive character set a political course that would be followed in the post-war era. During and after the German Occupation, reformist elites built strongly on a sense of collective failure in the face of economic crisis and dictatorship. Their alternative assumed the shape of a mixture of moderate socialism and corporatism implemented by 'rooms–rood' (Catholic–Socialist) coalition governments. In Belgium, in contrast, the changes that took place during the inter-war years, and more especially during the 1930s, had created more problems than they had solved. The fissures within the Catholic Party, the authoritarian aspirations of Leopold III and his entourage, and the more marked division between French- and Dutch-speaking Belgians were indications of the strains undermining the constitutional structure. The subsequent war exacerbated these problems, leading eventually to a wide-ranging crisis during the 1960s and 1970s which threatened the very survival of the Belgian state. This divergence between the Netherlands and Belgium had many causes and was not inevitable. It serves, however, to demonstrate that the differences of political regime in inter-war Europe were more complex than is suggested by a simple division between democracy and its enemies.

FURTHER READING

General

Kossmann, E. H., *The Low Countries 1780–1940* (Oxford, 1978).

Blom, J. C. H., and E. Lamberts (eds.), *History of the Low Countries* (New York and Oxford, 1999).

Arblaster, P., *A History of the Low Countries* (London, 2005).

Netherlands

Lijphart, A., *The Politics of Accommodation: Pluralism and Democracy in the Netherlands* (2nd edn., Berkeley, Calif., 1975).

Zanden, J. van, *The Economic History of the Netherlands, 1914–1995: A Small Open Economy in the 'Long' Twentieth Century* (London, 1998).

Leurdijk, J. H. (ed.), *The Foreign Policy of the Netherlands* (Alphen aan den Rijn, 1978).

Bank, J., and M. van Buuren (eds.) *Dutch Culture in a European Perspective, iii. The Age of Bourgeois Culture* (Assen and Basingstoke, 2004).

Wintle, M., *An Economic and Social History of the Netherlands, 1800–1920: Demographic, Economic and Social Transition* (Cambridge, 2000).

Belgium

Stengers, J., 'Belgium', in H. Rogger and E. Weber (eds.), *The European Right: A Historical Profile* (London, 1965), 128–67.

Kieft, D. O., *Belgium's Return to Neutrality: An Essay in the Frustrations of Small-Power Diplomacy* (Oxford, 1972).

Gerard, E., 'Religion, Class and Language: The Catholic Party in Belgium', in W. Kaiser and H. Wohnout (eds.), *Political Catholicism in Europe 1918–1945* (London and New York, 2004), 94–115.

Conway, M., 'Belgium', in T. Buchanan and M. Conway (eds.), *Political Catholicism in Europe* (Oxford, 1996), 187–218.

——— 'The Extreme Right in Inter-War Francophone Belgium: Explanations of a Failure', *European History Quarterly*, 26 (1996), 267–92.

6

France

Joan Tumblety

INTRODUCTION

The French historians who in the middle third of the twentieth century formed what has become known as the Annales school articulated the notion that time for human societies moves at different speeds. First there is the glacial slowness of the *longue durée*, in which human interaction with the physical landscape changes so slowly as to be almost imperceptible; then the structural time in which patterns of human organization and agency can be better perceived; and finally the time of events, or *l'histoire événementielle*, the latter described somewhat dismissively by historian Fernand Braudel as 'surface disturbances'. A survey of the early years of the French twentieth century informed by a longer term perspective may thus not be quite so overwhelmed by the material and human destruction wrought by war. One might see instead the growth of suffrage rights, the establishment of systems of social welfare, the broader benefits of technological innovation, and perhaps even something of a resolution of the great 'social question' that so exercised nineteenth-century reformers. Even taking a short-term view, in fact, one must recognize that—unlike many places elsewhere in Europe—parliamentary democracy in France survived the First World War and the inter-war fascist challenge intact and that the Third Republic, like the Second Empire before it, fell in 1940 only as a result of German invasion.

Nonetheless, it is hardly surprising that historians have come to see the first half of the twentieth century in France through the gloomy lens of war—the anticipation of it, the experience of it, and the quest to avoid it. After all, the body count of French war dead between 1914 and 1918 was exceeded only by that of Serbia, and the memory of the conflict was to have considerable purchase for the next two decades. It is striking, too, how far a narrative of decline dominates much historical writing on the years that followed the armistice. The French are often held to have 'won the war but lost the peace' after 1918, to be a declining world power (albeit one with the second largest empire in the world in the 1930s as in 1914), to have fragmented politically and socially under the centrifugal forces of ideological extremism, and to have slid ineluctably and blindly towards the worst military defeat in their history in 1940. The four years of German occupation that followed, in which the French republic was replaced by the quasi-autonomous authoritarian Vichy regime, have since 1947 been widely characterized as 'the dark years'.

But to focus exclusively on such a narrative of war and decline occludes other ways of seeing the era, not least the significance of longer term political and socio-economic forces. It also renders invisible the extent of alternative preoccupations especially in terms of culture, leisure, and associative life. The first half of the twentieth century was a boom period for such pursuits as sport, tourism, and youth movements and Paris, that iconic modern city, was the home of surrealism, *haute couture*, the cinema, and such extravagant spectacles as the international exhibitions of 1900, 1925, and 1937 and the Olympic games of 1900 and 1924.

This chapter will indeed argue that the experience and legacy of the First World War is crucial in understanding the passage of French history in the period between 1914 and 1945, at political, diplomatic, economic, social, and cultural levels, and will provide evidence of just how and where such memory of the war experience resonated. At the same time, it will seek to correct the 'declinism' of both inter-war contemporaries and later historians, arguing that the collapse of the Third Republic in 1940 was not inevitable even if the defeat of the French armies was overdetermined by earlier tactical and strategic military choices and mistakes. The 'dark' view of France 1914–1945 ought to be tempered by an awareness of the pluralism of the French past and by the recognition that this period witnessed, in addition to war and genocide, the resilience of a social democratic tradition which was reasserted vigorously in 1944–5, a growing consensus among political elites and public opinion on the right of women to citizenship, the expansion of leisure time and activities, and the emergence of mass political and popular culture.

EXPERIENCING AND REMEMBERING THE GREAT WAR

According to the renowned but not universally accepted theory of historian Eugen Weber, peasants had been turned into Frenchmen by 1914 as a result of the introduction of compulsory schooling and the extension of military service in the 1880s. Indeed, illiteracy (if not *patois*) had been almost wiped out by the outbreak of the First World War and children all over the country had grown up seeing maps of France in their classrooms, complete with the territories of Alsace and Lorraine lost to the French after their 1871 defeat in the Franco-Prussian war. It was true to speak of the existence of a deeply entrenched popular patriotic

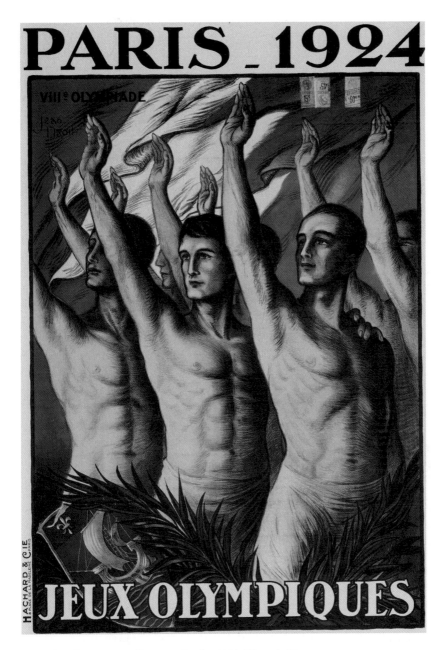

Figure 6.1. 'Paris—1924': poster for the 1924 Olympic Games.

republicanism in both urban and rural France. Yet France went to war in August 1914 not to recover its former national integrity but because of the great European alliance system. Public opinion polls suggest, in fact, that whatever the spirit of *revanche* (desire for revenge against Germany) still meant for those who could personally remember the 1871 defeat or who had come to understand its national importance, the populace met the declaration of war with reserve rather than jubilation.

Still, for a time both high politics and popular culture was marked by a *union sacrée* (sacred union) in support of the war effort, which led to a war cabinet formed of such diverse political personalities as Marxist Jules Guesde and (later) conservative Catholic Denys Cochin. The French socialist party, the Section Française de l'Internationale Ouvrière (SFIO), supported the war despite the traditional pacifism that had determined its opposition to the extension of military service the previous year. Feminists, too, supported the *union sacrée*. The largest suffragist organizations formally abandoned campaigns for women's voting rights and urged women to join the Red Cross instead; some 70,000 women volunteered as nurses during the conflict. There were limits to the *union sacrée,* however, especially in the so-called crisis of morale throughout 1917 and 1918 which similarly afflicted other European nations. Its biggest challenge was an upsurge in worker radicalism fuelled by wage-eroding inflation which in May 1917 led some 300,000 people, many of them female seamstresses, to strike. Throughout spring 1917 tens of thousands of men mutinied in the French army to protest against the insanity of mass slaughter and in 1918 another wave of strikes broke out among metal-workers inspired by the Russian Revolution.

The fact that most of the conflict took place on French soil effectively meant that for at least part of the war three-quarters of French *communes* (townships) in the ten departments behind the lines existed under German occupation, albeit without the armistice or cessation of military hostilities which characterized the occupation of 1940–4. German troops were billeted with French families; mayors in the occupied areas were often kept on by the Germans but dismissed for any sign of 'patriotism'; requisition of food, livestock, and buildings was common (over 80 per cent of the 1914 harvest was seized by the German authorities); and civilians fled the affected areas creating a refugee crisis which anticipated that of the *exode* of May and June 1940. The aftermath of war left a legacy of denuded forestation, over-exploited soil, broken transport infrastructure, and demolished buildings in the industrial heartland of France: only in 1931 was the reconstruction mission deemed complete. By the end of 1914 there were as many soldiers dead as there were men in the 'lost provinces' of Alsace and Lorraine. In total, a full 63 per cent of the active male population had been mobilized by 1918 and of these men 1.325 million (10 per cent of the male workforce) died, with over a million others still receiving a war invalidity pension as late as 1930.

But the transformative nature of the First World War—its significance as a 'watershed' in political, socio-economic, and cultural terms—ought not to be overstated. There were certainly limits to the impact of the war on the organization of French society at a structural level, not least where gender relations were concerned. Although women's participation in the paid workforce during the First World War increased—there were almost three-quarters of a million women munitions workers by 1918—women were conceived by government, industry, and in many cases themselves, as temporary replacements for male workers. Indeed, the French government mobilized women in the war effort reluctantly and, unlike the British, only ever in a civilian capacity. Initially, socialist Prime Minister René Viviani had expected that women's wartime economic role would remain agricultural—he appealed to them as 'soldiers of the harvest' in 1914—and it was only in mid-1916 that Minister of War Albert Thomas ordered industrialists to employ women for the manufacture of munitions. In fact, one must speak not so much of an increase in women's paid employment during the war as a redistribution of it: women left domestic service or were put out of work in the early unemployment (1914–15) in the garment and textile trades and moved into munitions later in the war. Popular attitudes even to female volunteer nurses suggest an engrained and pervasive suspicion of women's autonomy in the public domain of work. In any case, women's participation in the paid workforce decreased in the inter-war period, despite a labour shortage in the 1920s which brought some two million immigrant workers to France, largely from Italy and Poland. Women workers continued to be over-represented among the least well-paid and least skilled segments of the active population, and the sexual division of labour kept them in less highly valued sectors. If women worked in new areas it was mostly as a function of structural changes in the French economy, especially the development of such new industries as electronics and food production and the continued expansion of the commercial sector.

Other European women were being enfranchised in the wake of the First World War (often the result of regime change or the creation of entirely new nation-states that wanted to affirm democratic principles), but this was not the case in France. At the same time, it is important to point out that women's exclusion from the political rights of citizenship until 1944 was not inevitable and, indeed, during the inter-war period, the French Chamber of Deputies voted in favour of women's voting rights on no fewer than five occasions. There was cross-party support for some form of women's suffrage rights by the end of the First World War. René Viviani made an impassioned plea for women's enfranchisement in May 1919 which led the Chamber of Deputies to pass a Bill on the issue by 344 votes to 97; and in 1936 a similar Bill was introduced by arch-conservative Louis Marin and passed virtually unanimously. The persistent bulwark against women's voting rights came not from the Chamber but from the Senate, and in particular from a party at the centre of the political spectrum—the Radicals—whose anti-clericalism, even in this period of reduced church–state tension after 1914, continued to provide a powerful rationale for withholding the rights of citizenship from a female sex deemed devoutly religious and therefore inherently anti-republican. In 1919 Radical senator Alexandre Bérard had urged the Senate not to entertain the novelty of women's vote, warning among many other things that the 'Catholic mentality' of French women 'would lead to clerical reaction'. It was only in the context of transformed political structures in France at the moment of Liberation in 1944 that a debate on women's integral voting rights resulted in their enfranchisement.

Continuities outweigh changes in the economic sphere too. On a fundamental level, France remained a country built on the labours of a landholding peasantry and *petits commerçants* (shopkeepers), despite the existence of economic super-powers such as Renault and Michelin. For the entire inter-war period, a full third of the French workforce was engaged in agricultural labour, although the lines between the agrarian and the industrial could be blurred as much small-scale *industrie* took place in rural areas. Although the urban population overtook the rural by 1931 (compared to 1871 in Britain), it was only in the 1950s that rural France gave way definitively to an urban and industrial economic base. Yet the First World War did alter the face of the French economy at least for a time (it also directly contributed to the demise of the centuries-long French tradition of wet nursing). The organization of the munitions industry during the conflict was both more intensive and more regulated than was the norm for pre-war French industry, and it was not unusual for economic production to follow suit in the reconstructed industries of the former war zones. The production of sugar beet and livestock farming in northern France were rebuilt after 1919 along much more intensive lines, with small firms giving way to larger corporations.

This 'modern' model featuring mechanization and economies of scale was in fact limited in its application until the 1940s and 1950s, but the war nonetheless helped to inspire new visions of economic management. In the 1920s and 1930s, a group of individuals with disparate political affiliations and often graduates of the elite training college, the École Polytechnique, embraced Taylorist models of rationalized production inspired by the United States of America. Ernest Mercier, an engineer and leading businessman in the field of electricity, established a pressure group called Redressement Français in 1926 to further such ideas, and Jean Monnet, later an architect of European economic planning and integration, evangelized about the productive merits of a managed economy. Despite winning the attention of several politicians in this period (Mercier and Monnet both served the government in its organization of the economy during the First World War), these initiatives failed to take root.

The idea that the French economy remained 'backward' in the twentieth century has been widespread, in part thanks to the immensely influential thesis put forward by Stanley Hoffmann in the 1960s that Third Republican France was a 'stalemate society' characterized by a confluence of social, political, and economic inertia in which a disproportionately large smallholding peasantry set a national tone of resistance to change. It has, however, recently come under attack by revisionist historians who point to the relative merits of French economic organization in the modern era. It is true that the economically liberal Third Republic favoured protectionist measures above those that might have stimulated economic growth and was 'Malthusian' in the sense that it showed a reluctance to embrace a model of mass production and mass consumption. Mass-produced goods in France did indeed take hold more slowly than in Britain or the USA, although in the 1930s the low-cost variant of the department store was successful in attracting cash-strapped Depression-era shoppers. Such stores remained politically sensitive, however, and both artisans and small shopkeepers exerted considerable lobbying pressure on the Chamber of Deputies in the mid-1930s to restrict their growth, with some success. At the same time, before 1914 French agricultural growth rates were actually above the European average despite the small scale of production; industrial production in metals and electrics was comparatively respectable; France was the biggest exporter of cars in the world; and French artisan-centred industrial production allowed the economy to remain buoyant where the manufacture and export of luxury goods was concerned. Even during the 1930s Depression French export of its 'quality goods' (for example, in the fields of gastronomy and high fashion) remained buoyant.

The business of managing the economy in the 1930s proved particularly fraught, and it became almost impossible for governments to manoeuvre around the sensitivities of the electorate. Devaluation of the franc in 1926 ushered in a short period of economic growth as investment in French industry increased: some commentators thought as a result that the French might escape the global Depression of the early 1930s. Instead, depression simply hit the French economy later (the high point of unemployment was 1935) and its crisis was arguably deeper and more protracted. French economic production did not surpass 1929 levels until after the Second World War. The Depression affected rural and agricultural areas as well as urban and industrial ones: agricultural prices halved in the first half of the 1930s and agricultural wages fell faster than the wages of industrial workers. A further devaluation of the franc, which may have helped to improve unemployment levels as it did in Belgium in 1935, was associated by the early 1930s with inflation and thus avoided by successive governments until the Popular Front grudgingly accepted it in 1936.

The war may not have transformed the landscape of France at a deep structural level, then, but nonetheless contemporaries in the 1920s and 1930s often came to see political and social challenges through its refractive lens. Socialist deputy Léon Blum opined in 1934 that the post-1918 rupture between generations was 'one of the most important psychological and social phenomena of our times' and communist-turned-fascist Jacques Doriot attempted to rally a whole generation of young men who had experienced the childhood privations—scarce meat and 'lait falsifié' (adulterated milk)—of the First World War. In many ways, this assertion of the significance of the war developed an agency of its own: the figures of the war dead and the war living were subsequently mobilized rhetorically across the entire inter-war period by a range of individuals and groups. Pacifist intellectual and wounded First World War veteran, Jean Giraudoux, was critical of the degree to which inter-war politicians were haunted by the weight of this ghost army. 'If the war dead were asking for sports grounds, I dare say that the Paris municipal councillors would hasten to provide them', he complained in 1928.

Indeed, a veritable cult of the *poilu* (French infantry soldier) was established in the 1920s as part of an extensive and deeply felt memorial culture. One-quarter of French families had a casualty, and 42 per cent of French men after 1918 were war veterans, half of whom belonged to veterans' societies that collectively (although more in rural than urban areas) grouped some 25 per cent of the electorate. Municipalities received state subsidies to oversee the process of constructing monuments to the war dead, which began as soon as the war had ended. By 1930, there were some 34,000 such memorials in France, practically one in every village. From 1919—and cemented in law after 1922—the anniversary of the armistice of 11 November 1918 became a national holiday and the occasion for ceremonies, usually led by veterans' groups, held all over the country. As the work of Antoine Prost has shown, however, this commemoration of the war dead, although patriotic and resolutely republican, tended to mourn rather than to glorify the loss of a generation of men and demonstrates more than anything else how deeply pacifist sentiment was experienced across France in this period.

The scale of human loss in the First World War certainly heightened anxieties about the low French birth rate. From being the most populous country in Europe outside Russia in the late eighteenth century, France's rate of population growth had ever since declined and the population explosion of the nineteenth century experienced in other European countries such as Britain, Germany, and Sweden was simply not felt in France. After defeat in the Franco-Prussian War, military and political elites increasingly drew attention to the imagined consequences of such demographic stagnation for the strength of the nation. It was no comfort to contemporaries that France might be seen as a pioneer for being the first nation to make the so-called demographic transition to a pattern of low births and low mortality. Instead, the low birth rate was universally viewed as a problem and, despite the efforts of a few vocal feminists such as Nelly Roussel, it was practically unheard of to adopt publicly a neo-Malthusian position in favour of birth control. The most tangible early result of this crisis of *dénatalité* was a legislative programme against contraception and abortion. The latter (illegal since 1810) was prosecuted much more forcefully in the 1920s and 1930s than in previous decades and the maximum penalty increased to five years in prison.

Anxieties over *dénatalité* certainly strengthened the political voice of the natalist lobby, whose most prominent member was the Alliance Nationale pour l'accroissement de la population (National Alliance for Increasing the Population), created in 1896 amid reports that death rates had overtaken birth rates. It experienced a rise in membership in the early 1920s of some 700 per cent and became a crucial player in the formulation of government policy on

Allemagne   Italie   France   Angleterre
1.400.000   992.000   616.000   724.000

L'axe Rome-Berlin et l'axe Paris-Londres.
Nombre de naissances en 1937.

Figure 6.2. The battle of births between the Rome–Berlin Axis and the Paris–London Axis: number of births in 1937.

the family. By the mid-1930s, the widely disseminated propaganda material of the Alliance Nationale depicted depopulation as the principal threat facing France—the diminishing size of the cohort of young men eligible for military service in any given year was well publicized—and the organization held both women and men responsible for it. The social vision of the organization was a conservative paean to the traditional family model and prescribed reproductive—rather than productive—work for married women.

In 1932, legislation compelled certain categories of employer (extended in 1938) to pay family allowances to workers with children, with benefits being paid directly to mothers. In fact, this was a formalization of an existing trend that was not entirely motivated by natalist concerns. Before 1932, half of industrial workers and a quarter of commercial workers were already covered by a similar scheme, reflecting the traditional preference of French employers to contribute to the upkeep of their workers' families rather than to provide higher wages across the board. Indeed, the development of family welfare in the first half of the twentieth century as a whole owed much to the campaigns of such socially conservative actors as natalists, industrialists, and Catholic women's groups. The latter, almost all of which refused the label 'feminist', mobilized far more French women than any other sector. Almost without exception, Catholic women's groups emphasized women's duties—specifically as mothers—over their rights. Leading politicians, especially social Catholics such as Jean Lerolle, who introduced the 1931 Bill on family allowances, or Georges Pernot, who presided over the Daladier-appointed committee on the family in 1938, were often members both of Catholic women's groups and the Alliance Nationale, testimony to the political influence of such lobbying organizations. The family code of 1938–9 was the clearest inter-war product of this influence: it extended tax advantages to workers with children, increased family allowances (introducing a bonus for couples producing a child within the first two years of marriage), and raised the maximum penalty for abortion to ten years' imprisonment. Such measures prefigured the more repressive family policy of the Vichy regime, which on the one hand extended family benefits but on the other introduced the death penalty for abortionists.

The Great War also witnessed the dissipation of anti-clericalism among French elites. The 1904 ban on clerical teachers in schools was in effect lifted during the 1914–18 conflict and the state chose not to enforce de-clericalization in the newly reincorporated provinces of Alsace and Lorraine after 1918. Such a weakening of anti-clerical attitudes was felt profoundly at the popular level too: in the circumstances of crisis and loss engendered by the war, attendance at Mass soared temporarily and, as the commemoration of the war dead in the inter-war period shows, French public authorities borrowed the language of mourning (the laying of wreaths, a minute of silence, etc.) from Catholic liturgy and harnessed it to a quite republican schema of commemoration. It was not unusual to find parish priests on the municipal committees established to oversee the erection of local war memorials, and local clergy often played key roles in memorial services in strongly Catholic areas. Such features are hardly surprising in a country where more than 90 per cent of the population were baptized Catholics (fewer than a million were Calvinist or Lutheran Protestants and around 300,000 were Jewish), but were strangely at odds with the secular face of a regime that would not have countenanced such confluence of clerical and secular expressions a mere decade before.

In addition, the 1914–18 conflict helped to forge popular imperialism. By 1914, the French Empire, much of which had been acquired in the previous generation, was second only to the British in terms of its geographical and demographic scope—three million square miles and fifty million people outside the metropole. It was only in the 1890s that colonialism had been able to achieve the kind of political consensus and popular appeal that had been the case in Britain for decades. In the *belle époque,* a combination of the widely publicized falling birth rate and growing concerns about German military rivalry meant that colonial troops came to be seen as a convenient way to bolster French national defences. By all accounts the contribution of 600,000 colonial troops to the war effort was viewed favourably by the French public. The inter-war period witnessed a cultural fascination with the 'exotic'. Images of colonial peoples appeared routinely in this period, often on advertising billboards and consumer products. An increasing number of French films had colonial themes and featured among the most popular of the time, for example, Jacques Feyder's *L'Atlantide*

(1921/1932) and the Jean Gabin star vehicle *Pépé le Moko* (1937). The 1931 Colonial Exposition held in the Bois de Vincennes east of Paris recorded eight million patrons over its duration from May to November and consisted of a series of displays celebrating the territories and colonies in north and west Africa, the Caribbean, south-east Asia, and the Indian and Pacific oceans, acknowledging their importance for the entity known as 'greater France'. The empire was widely viewed as an important trading partner, a military bloc of significance and the chance for France to spread its republican 'civilizing mission' to the rest of the world.

In the late 1930s, the political and popular purchase of empire grew even stronger, not least because its existence meant that France could theoretically counter German military strength with a combined population of around 100,000,000 people. Colonial troops were conspicuously on display during the Bastille Day parade in 1939, which also celebrated the 150th anniversary of the French Revolution, and premier Edouard Daladier, who had visited North Africa earlier in the year, told the assembled crowds that these armies were 'the guardian of your liberties'. Even the French communist party changed its tune in this period. Whereas the Parti Communiste Français (PCF) from its inception had put forward an anti-capitalist critique of imperialism, supporting anti-French colonial rebels in North Africa in the mid-1920s and opposing the 1931 colonial exhibition, the military threat to France posed by Germany at the end of the decade led the party to adopt the SFIO left humanist line that France had a duty to export the values—if not the rights—of the Revolution to the developing nations of its empire.

Indeed, the full legal and political rights of citizenship were withheld from the vast majority of colonized peoples who lived under the French Empire. Instead native populations were subjected to the unequal code of the *indigénat* with its many penalties, including disproportionate taxation and forced labour. Even in Algeria, the North African territory which had been deemed part of metropolitan France since the 1860s, citizenship was reserved for a tiny proportion of the indigenous inhabitants who were in fact obliged to abandon much of their cultural specificity—in particular the Islamic religion—before qualifying as 'assimilated' enough for such rights. That the Blum–Violette Bill of 1936 promised to extend the rights of citizenship in Algeria only to some 50,000 Muslims (from a population of around nine million) is a measure of the entrenchment of imperialist thinking in France even on the left. The benefits of 'Greater France' were thus clearly reserved for those living within the hexagon. Anger generated by the double-think implicit in the French ideology of empire and by the consistent failure of French governments to take seriously the claims of nationalists in the overseas territories, helped to mobilize support for independence across an empire which contributed some 500,000 troops to defend France between 1940 and 1945.

THE 'GERMAN PROBLEM' AND POLITICAL POLARIZATION

The war demonstrated the bite of the 'German problem' and determined the course of French defensive and foreign policy strategies for the next two decades. Hopes that the Versailles conference would create a permanent buffer state in the Rhineland were dashed: permanent demilitarization did not go far enough to appease French political elites that the danger posed by Germany was neutralized. When it became clear that Germany was incapable of paying the agreed reparations to France, the Poincaré government took the ultimately counter-productive measure in January 1923 of occupying the industrial Ruhr to seize payment in kind. In the realm of foreign policy, successive French governments set about securing alliances with Central European states so that France would not be isolated in case of a German attack.

Although this alliance system remained largely in place until the pressures leading up to the Munich crisis of 1938 eroded it, the late 1920s were marked by a more overt quest to seek reconciliation with Germany. After the Locarno Treaty of 1925 formalized German acceptance of the post-1918 borders with France, rapprochement became official policy. Its principal architect was Aristide Briand (foreign minister between 1925 and 1932) who went on to engineer the Kellogg–Briand Pact in 1928 in which over a dozen European nations including France and Germany promised never again to go to war. This was not so much pacifism as war avoidance and it was deemed to make gut sense across the political spectrum. In keeping with this emphasis on defensive measures, the French after 1929 began construction of the frontier fortifications that were designed to protect the north-east from another German invasion—the 'Maginot line', named after the wounded war veteran and defence minister from the Lorraine, André Maginot. In tandem, the length of military service and the number of infantry divisions were reduced. In 1936, when the Belgians declared neutrality, the fortifications were extended to guard the Franco-Belgian frontier with a view to reaching as far as the English Channel. It is not unfair to speak of a 'Maginot mentality' borne of a visceral fear of war that went along with the construction of the material defences along the French border.

Much has been made by historians of the chronic governmental instability of the inter-war period, with its forty-four premierships, as though the quick succession of governments explained the Republic's eventual fall in 1940. In fact, there had been sixty governments in the period between 1870 and 1914 and, as after 1918, such change of government belied a continuity of political elites as the same figures reappeared time and again. The principal political parties, too, survived the war—the socialist SFIO which had been the second largest party in the Chamber of Deputies in 1914; the anti-clerical Radicals, who continued their political domination of inter-war cabinets; the moderate republican centre-right party, the Alliance Démocratique; and the more clerical and conservative Fédération Républicaine. Indeed, it ought to be remembered that democracy in France survived the turmoil of the Great War as well as the political and economic crises that followed it, despite the fact that the inter-war political landscape was marked by the emergence of both communist and fascist challenges to republican democracy.

Communism was formalized in France at the 1920 annual congress of the socialist SFIO when a vote to join the newly formed Third International based in Moscow split the party, a majority opting for a separate organization committed to following orders from Moscow and based on the principles of revolutionary war. The early success of the communist impulse in conjunction with the recent memory of mass strikes and the success of the left at the 1924 elections prompted a response on the right. In the mid-1920s ostensibly 'fascist' movements, modelled in some way on Mussolini's Fascists in Italy, made an impact in the streets and even in the Chamber of Deputies. These groups (such as the 'blue shirts' of Pierre Taittinger's Jeunesses Patriotes and Georges Valois's Faisceau) were not royalist like the Dreyfus-era Action Française and did more to appeal specifically to workers in an attempt to make a mass movement. In general, the stabilization of the franc and economic recovery in the late 1920s temporarily took the steam out of such movements.

In the early 1930s, the onset of Depression, heightened xenophobia connected to a rise in immigration, and the election in 1932 of a left-leaning majority in the Chamber of Deputies supported a new wave of activity on the radical right. On the night of 6 February 1934, around 40,000 rightist demonstrators supported by the 'fascist' and royalist leagues protested alleged corruption in the government. As many as 10,000 individuals clashed with police in the Place de la Concorde opposite the French parliament, calling for the government to resign. Some 1,500 people were injured—fifteen were killed—in the bloodiest civil conflict in France since the Paris Commune of 1871. Yet the night of 6 February 1934 did not constitute a revolutionary moment, and there had been no intention on the part of the demonstrators to bring down the regime. Still, the potential of the rightists to force such a violent display prompted the PCF to call for general strike action and eventually to support an anti-fascist alliance.

The result of this leftist rapprochement was the Popular Front alliance—a coalition of Radicals, socialists, and communists—that won the spring 1936 elections. Its first government in particular, headed by socialist Léon Blum, initiated a raft of redistributive policies to benefit the working classes. In its first twelve weeks in office, the Popular Front enacted some two dozen legislative reforms including general wage increases, the forty-hour week, the introduction of fifteen days of paid leave per year for all employees, the nationalization of the arms industry, a raising of the school-leaving age to 14, and dissolution of the paramilitary 'fascist' leagues.

Despite this success on the left, the threat from the radical right in France actually increased over the next two years. Under war veteran Colonel François de la Rocque, the Parti Social Français (formerly Croix de Feu) had a million members by 1937 and drew cross-class support across urban and rural France. By 1939, it could count 3,000 mayors, 1,000 municipal councillors, and twelve deputies among its followers. The movement desired a spiritual revolution to counter 'flabby' republican democracy, was bitterly anti-Marxist, and, by 1938, espoused anti-Semitism. Historians remain divided as to whether the Croix de Feu/PSF was ever fascist: some like René Rémond and Zeev Sternhell have preferred to see it as an exponent of conservative authoritarianism.

There is, however, general acceptance of the fascist credentials of the Parti Populaire Français (PPF), founded in 1936 by former communist Jacques Doriot one month after the legislative elections that saw the victory of the Popular Front. When Doriot's movement reached its peak (with 100,000 members) in 1938, shortly before the fall of the last Popular Front government deflated its appeal for traditional conservatives, it was overtly anti-Semitic, opposed to immigration, and in favour of stripping French citizenship from the recently naturalized. By 1941, Doriot, the former PCF street fighter, was to play a key role in recruiting for the collaborationist French Anti-Bolshevik Legion and fought in German uniform on the Eastern Front.

More significantly, Doriot's PPF had some success throughout 1937 in forging links with the Fédération Républicaine in an attempt to create a 'liberty front' that could counter the recent electoral success of the left. Doriot elicited the support of Pierre Taittinger as well as the FR's Louis Marin and Philippe Henriot in a show of unity against communism. Hundreds of thousands of French men and women looked seriously to the kind of options provided by the radical right in this period. Yet neither the Croix de Feu nor the PPF ever came close to seizing power by *coup d'état* or by any other means, and such agrarian fascists as Henri Dorgères's 'green shirts' who were ready in 1937 to put down agricultural strikes in the north of France found that the regular police needed no help to restore order. According to Robert Paxton, fascism failed in both urban and rural France because conservatives were not frightened enough to use it to protect their interests. French democracy thus triumphed over the challenges posed by both fascism and communism in this period.

At the same time, the purchase of both anti-fascism and anti-communism helped to shape French responses to the 'German problem'. By the mid-1930s, the traditional humanist pacifism of the socialist left had been eroded by the advent of Nazism. The French communists, keen in the early days to incite revolutionary war, had no real ideological objections to armed conflict in the first place, and the rise of fascism at home and abroad meant that the PCF—and some socialists—wanted to 'fight the good fight' against right-wing extremism, witnessed in their push for French intervention in the Spanish Civil War after 1936 and in their rejection of the Munich accords in September 1938. Concomitantly, the strength of French communism elicited in the conservative and radical right a responding fear of internal subversion. The greater enemy for many conservatives became the PCF and the Third International rather than the traditional German foe, Nazi or otherwise. A minority went as far as to subscribe to the view 'better Hitler than Blum'. At the time of the Munich crisis, the French republican right was almost universally lined up against the so-called 'belliciste' (war-mongering) members of the French parliament who would prefer a war against fascism to the containment of the communist threat at home. Of course, this pro-Munich stance was informed by a number of factors, such as a belief in French military inferiority and the nature of Anglo-French diplomatic relations, but it also shows how an ideological war had overtaken a geo-political one for some sectors of French political opinion. Ironically, in these altered circumstances the humanist Briandism of the 1920s could even provide a rationale for the ideological collaboration with the Nazis that developed after 1940. At the very least, the former helped to provide a language to justify the latter, not least for such inter-war proponents of Franco-German reconciliation as intellectuals Jean Luchaire and Fernand de Brinon, both of whom rose to prominence in fascist-collaborationist circles under the occupation.

ASSOCIATIVE LIFE AND LEISURE

Associative life and leisure activities, too, thrived in France in the first half of the twentieth century despite the fragile political and economic climate. Their development was underpinned by a combination of factors—much improved levels of literacy since the late nineteenth century; increased leisure time due to labour laws introduced after the *fin de siècle* which progressively shortened the working day; and the development of new technologies of transmission (radio and film) and movement (bicycles, motor cars, and then aeroplanes). The number of radios increased from 3.2 million in 1936 to 4.7 million by the end of 1939; cinema receipts rose by 45 per cent from 1934 to 1938. Municipal libraries formed an ingrained site of popular culture by the First World War, and during the conflict itself the library became something of a haven, reflected in its increased use.

A plethora of social, cultural, and sports clubs developed during the inter-war period: societies for swimming, basketball, and ping-pong among a host of others proliferated in number and size. After all, the working day had been reduced to eight hours in 1919, leaving workers with more time to spend on leisure activities. Groups such as the Société sportive des Grands Magasins du 'Printemps' testify to the importance of the workplace itself in supporting sociability among staff. There was already a tradition of employers' organizations for workers, designed with social control as much as philanthropy in mind. A 1930 survey in the metals industry found that around a quarter of employers in that sector already had full-blown worker leisure organizations, almost half of which involved either gardening or sport, with the rest comprising a mixture of musical societies, theatre groups, libraries, cinemas, literary circles, and lecture classes. Employers hoped that such societies would foster discipline and 'respectable' values among the workforce, lure workers away from alcohol and cabaret, and encourage a politically neutral use of leisure time.

On the left it was feared that the involvement of workers in mainstream or employer's sport and leisure organizations would be an instrument of their depoliticization, making workers buy into a consumerist culture that served the interests of bourgeois capitalism. The socialist newspaper *Le Populaire* and the communist organ *L'Humanité* both staged a plethora of sports competitions in the 1930s, from football to swimming, that were designed as an alternative to the undoubtedly more successful mainstream options. To build working-class solidarity and consciousness, both socialist and communist parties established their own sports and cultural associations, which merged after the rapprochement between these two parties in the mid-1930s.

Such overtly politicized attempts to mobilize the masses ultimately paled besides the onslaught of commercialized spectator sport which, despite professing 'political neutrality', in the main of course carried its own values of 'fair play', hegemonic masculinity, and the market. Popular sport took off in the 1920s and 1930s in terms of both mass participation and spectatorship, facilitated by a growing sports press and the advent of radio broadcasting of sports matches. Sports stars, especially in the fields of cycling (Henri Pélissier), boxing (Marcel Cerdan), and tennis (Suzanne Lenglen and Jean Borotra), became media celebrities, fêted by a popular press increasingly attuned to the public's appetite for sporting and cultural spectacles. Aside from the Olympics, the biggest sporting spectacle in France in the first half of the twentieth century was the great cycle race known as the Tour de France, founded in 1903, partly out of the commercial desire to sell newspapers, but which became an event that snaked its way through the heart of both rural and urban France for the rest of the century. After 1930, commercial sponsors followed the column of riders and distributed free samples of their goods to the public. Henri Noguères recalls how the 'publicity caravan' of the Tour galvanized the attention of French men, women, and children in the towns and villages on the race's itinerary. The sports newspaper that invented the Tour de France, *L'Auto*, sold almost as many copies as the biggest national dailies during this annual cycling event.

This was also the era of the—somewhat sectarian—youth movement. From the mid-1920s, the Catholic Church specifically attempted to Christianize the 'red belt' of Paris and the industrial north by recruiting to its male and female youth organization, the Jeunesse Ouvrière Chrétienne (JOC). It faced stiff opposition. The membership of the Jeunesses Communistes soared from 3,500 in 1933 to

288,000 in December 1936, no doubt riding on the crest of popular optimism in the wake of the Popular Front victory. Among the scouts, however, it was the Catholic movement that undoubtedly had the greatest appeal: by 1939 it mobilized 100,000 members, while the secular, Jewish, and Protestant scouts numbered only some 25,000 between them.

Alongside this youth movement developed *colonies de vacances* (holiday camps), which provided holiday accommodation and entertainment for children all over France. At the beginning of the century, such ventures tended to be organized under Catholic auspices (sending a total of 26,000 children away to the countryside every year) but in the inter-war period there was an explosion of secular ones, often flavoured with the political persuasion of the organizers. For example, each summer in the 1930s in the Paris suburb of Ivry-sur-Seine several hundred poor children benefited from free summer vacations to the Atlantic coast provided by the communist municipality. The camps themselves were modelled on a utopian left-wing society, instilling in the children a democratic and anti-bourgeois consciousness. At the other end of the political spectrum, the Croix de Feu staged its own children's holiday camps, and the PPF for its part envisaged the creation of extensive sport and leisure organizations to rival the communist and socialist alternatives, among them youth hostels, scouts, *colonies de vacances*, walking associations, ping-pong, rugby, and theatre groups. In 1938, Doriot claimed that the PPF youth wing had 35,000 members.

The Popular Front governments themselves sought to encourage mass participation in popular sport and physical education for reasons of 'hygiene'—the latter in particular resonated with the era's fixation on the falling birth rate—and to open up previously elite sporting and cultural activities like skiing, aviation, and tourism to a working-class audience. The introduction of these novelties was the responsibility of popular and athletic socialist deputy Léo Lagrange, who was appointed under-secretary for sport and leisure in June 1936. Just in time for the August summer holidays of 1936, Lagrange introduced 40 per cent reductions on train fares for holidaying workers and their families—the so-called 'Lagrange ticket'—and over 600,000 workers benefited from the initiative that summer. The conservative newspaper *Le Figaro* consequently raised fears of the 'encanaillement' of the Côte d'Azur: the measure had in their view let the riff-raff in. Lagrange also introduced an optional sports certificate in primary schools (400,000 children passed it in 1937) and the Ministry of Education set about introducing compulsory physical education in schools and training for physical education teachers. Indeed, the Popular Front is probably remembered as much for its pioneering efforts in the popularization of exercise as it is for the introduction of the forty-hour week and paid holidays.

One relatively overlooked aspect of cultural life in the first half of the twentieth century is tourism. Only from the late 1940s did French participation in tourism—domestic and foreign—assume the proportions of a mass and cross-class phenomenon, although the French have continued to take holidays—and to live—abroad less often than their European neighbours. It is estimated that in the mid-1930s no more than 10 per cent of French people went on holiday. Yet that decade saw the purchase of tourism in France both in terms of the introduction of government legislation that underpinned it and the growth of a consumer culture around travel. Such initiatives helped to attract tens of thousands of foreign visitors to the World's Fair in 1937, including some 20,000 Romanians and about as many Swedes. In fact, tourism flourished in 1937 and 1938, with some 900,000 foreigners travelling to France in each of those years, a figure more than double that for 1936. The increase was experienced in the provinces as well as in Paris and took place, as *L'Œuvre* noted, 'despite international events'.

For the French, battlefield tourism was established as early as summer 1919, when one could take a package day excursion from Paris to Arras and Lens by train. Guidebooks stressed that such visits ought to be approached as pilgrimages, and indeed many early visitors were bereaved relatives of dead soldiers. The French state permitted one free rail trip per year to the site of a soldier's grave for his widow, parents, and children. In 1919, too, the Tour de France passed through the recent war zone and the sports press seized the opportunity to communicate a commemorative reverence to its readers. The Popular Front specifically promoted domestic tourism in France as part of its leisure policies. Camping was promoted as a 'hygienic' form of healthy relaxation and, in addition, as many as 150 youth hostels were created in 1936 alone. The examples in this section have collectively illustrated the common ground among quite opposed political families in addressing issues around sport and leisure. They also demonstrate the awareness in every quarter of the politically mobilizing potential of mass culture.

THE DEBACLE OF 1940 AND VICHY FRANCE

Mythologies of the military defeat in June 1940—when French forces succumbed to the onslaught of a German *blitzkrieg* invasion after a mere six weeks of fighting—grew up almost from the start. It was the view of numerous independent commentators with a range of political loyalties that this spectacular collapse was inevitable, that a fifth column had undermined France from within, that French soldiers had not fought as bravely in 1940 as in 1914, and that French society itself had become fundamentally rotten and 'decadent' in the 1930s amid the politico-economic scandals and crisis of that decade. The Vichy regime's ill-conceived and subsequently abandoned attempt to try Third Republican political leaders such as Léon Blum, Guy La Chambre, Edouard Daladier, and Paul Reynaud for losing the war against Germany—the so-called Riom trials—emphasized this last point in particular. Later historians have been too ready to accept such explanations of the defeat and to see it as a political and moral failure rather than a military one. Even the elegant and largely persuasive account of the debacle, *Strange Defeat*, penned in 1940 by the medieval historian and later resistance martyr Marc Bloch, suffers somewhat from the mistake of reading French unpreparedness for the battle retrospectively from the certainty of the collapse.

Historian Julian Jackson has recently done much to rescue the history of the defeat from the mythology surrounding it. The French airforce was indeed inadequate and the army chaotically organized and under-equipped, splitting up units counter-productively and placing the least well trained troops in the most crucial positions. Yet the French were better prepared than once thought: by the invasion the French had near parity with Germany where tanks and divisional strength were concerned. Contrary to common wisdom, the Popular Front had increased spending on military and defence budgets, and indeed had kickstarted France's industrial rearmament, a programme continued under Daladier. The fighting was fiercer than is often acknowledged and, although at least two divisions panicked when the Germans broke through at Sedan, it should not be forgotten that the French won the first tank battle of the conflict. In addition, as many as 90,000 troops died in the Battle for France and the problem of low morale that characterized much of the phoney war was apparently reversed in May and June 1940. In fact, far from expecting an early French demise, the German military command was itself surprised by the speed of the *blitzkrieg* breakthrough. There is not much evidence either of a fifth column of defeatists operating against the French war effort. A variant of the Briandist desire for reconciliation with Germany did help to underpin both Vichy and the fascist-collaborationist alternatives in Paris that followed the military defeat, but, as Julian Jackson has rightly observed, they did not cause it.

Ironically, the inter-war Republic was probably at its most robust—if not its most democratic—just before its collapse. The government of Radical premier Edouard Daladier that took office in April 1938 set about dismantling Popular Front reforms such as the forty-hour week, arguing that it stood in the way of rearmament. His government put the economy on a war footing, and between 1938 and 1939 the proportion of industrial production based on armaments almost doubled. Daladier, ruling regularly by decree after July 1939, also oversaw the introduction of the conservative family code, the restriction of immigration, the removal of citizenship from some recently naturalized French, and the internment of immigrants, including some 400,000 Spanish republicans. Strikingly, Daladier repressed communism in France even before the outbreak of war, and after September dozens of PCF deputies and thousands of PCF members were arrested. In its authoritarian and anti-communist stance, as well as its appointment of technocrats to cabinet posts, the Daladier administration prefigured the Vichy regime and underlines elements of continuity between republican and Vichy France.

If Daladier engineered an authoritarian republic, however, the Vichy regime was to attempt an antidote to republicanism altogether. Nonetheless, the Vichy regime was legally constituted: once an armistice had been signed, elected French parliamentarians voted on 10 July 1940 by a margin of 569 to 80 to grant Marshall Pétain full powers to rewrite the republican constitution. The Vichy regime nevertheless set about replacing the values associated with the French Revolution—*liberté, égalité, fraternité*— with the conservative and communitarian trinity of *famille, travail, patrie*. No longer were individual liberty and equality before the law to be the driving ideological forces of the French regime. Instead, the patriarchal family replaced the individual as the basic cell of society, and a broadly corporatist rethinking of the economy and social relations served as a counter to the perceived class conflict of the pre-1940 period. It was the tone of Vichy's vision for national 'regeneration' that led the Action Française leader Charles Maurras to record that the humiliation of the 1940 defeat was a 'divine surprise'.

Yet the regime was not strictly speaking fascist. Refusing a single party and mass mobilization (except passively through the popularization of the Pétain cult), the regime was pluralist, staffed at various stages by a combination of technocrats ('experts' such as the classicist Jérôme Carcopino in the Education ministry, the lawyer Joseph Barthélemy in the Justice ministry, and industrialist Pierre Pucheu in Industrial Production); those on the pre-war radical and anti-republican right such as Raphael Alibert and Xavier Vallat who had connections to the Action Française; and social Catholics such as Georges Lamirand and Paul de la Porte du Theil who were dominant in youth matters. Although former PPF members such as Paul Marion enjoyed important positions in the Vichy ruling elite, by and large the dominant pre-war fascist leaders themselves were not represented in the inner circles of power in Vichy France.

The regime was nonetheless built on authoritarian rule and social exclusion. Most remarkably, from the very beginning the Vichy regime overturned the republican tradition of religious tolerance and embarked on a consistent and independent programme of anti-Jewish measures (including internment) that existed in parallel to—and in some ways exceeded—measures taken by the German occupiers. Furthermore, the regime's anti-Semitism led to complicity in the German-imposed 'Final Solution': in a misguided attempt to preserve its own sovereignty, the Vichy regime agreed to the use of French police in the arrest of Jews; administered the 'aryanization' of Jewish assets itself to prevent the Germans from pilfering French property; and offered to fill German-imposed quotas by agreeing to deport foreign Jews, including children, from the Vichy zone before the German authorities had decided to intrude across the demarcation line. As a result, over 75,000 Jews (a third of whom were French citizens) were deported to death camps between 1942 and 1944, the vast majority perishing in Auschwitz. There is widespread evidence of popular anti-Semitism, too, especially in the Vichy zone where such sentiment was heightened by food shortages and the presence of many refugees—including Jews—from the north.

This was indeed a time of widespread privations. The terms of the armistice severely curtailed French sovereignty (and in any case German forces occupied the so-called Vichy 'free zone' in November 1942), around 1.6 million prisoners of war were interned in Germany until spring 1945, some 860,000 billion francs were paid to the Germans in occupation costs, three-quarters of a million French men were drafted to work in German factories, and pervasive and progressive requisitioning of agricultural and industrial produce took place. In addition, real wages fell by 40 per cent, rationing provided most adults with only 1,200 calories a day, and industrial production in 1944 was less than a third of the inter-war high-tide mark of 1929. The nostalgic vision of Vichy's 'National Revolution' must have been unrecognizable in the actual landscape of France under occupation.

Despite or because of such privations and repression, associative life thrived under these circumstances and the football stadium, along with the cinema and the municipal library, became a site of renewed activity. Before the defeat, around a quarter of a million people visited the cinema each year in France: in 1943 the number had risen to over 300,000. Paris municipal libraries, reflecting a national trend, loaned sixty-three books per registered reader in 1938 and ninety-six in 1942. Within three months of the signing of the armistice in 1940, the police claimed that around a third of popular sports clubs in the Paris region, featuring such activities as cycling, athletics, football, and swimming, had successfully regrouped their membership. According to Robert Gildea, a historian who has recently argued that the 'dark years' were not uniformly bleak for all, the small town of Chinon in the Loire valley was 'honeycombed' with numerous clubs and societies, horse-racing associations, and clubs for tennis, cycling, and fishing, even if some had to rebrand themselves (and purge Jewish members) in order to secure permission to continue from the German local authorities. In this way, the German attitude to sports activities in France mirrored their wider 'policy of seduction' of allowing enough liberty of movement in French circles to make the continuation of a vibrant cultural expression possible in a bid to keep the population distracted.

Recent social histories of occupied and Vichy France have reminded us that many French sought what historian Philippe Burrin has called 'accommodation' with the occupiers—an acceptance by both French authorities and the population at large of the German presence and a willingness to engage with it in order to negotiate the best terms possible. Conversely, the German authorities themselves realized the importance of French popular consent in smoothing the course of the occupation. This understanding has come to replace the once dominant binary categories of 'resistance' and 'collaboration' which, not least in their implied moral judgement, were arguably less helpful in understanding the texture of power relations between 1940 and 1944. French mayors often developed close relations with the local *Feldkommandant* in a bid to protect the local community from more extensive German requisitions and brutality: they offered up resources, provided lists of potential hostages usually drawn from 'suspect' locals such as communists, and generally promised to ensure the order necessary for German security. It was not clear either under the occupation or in the post-Liberation courts how far such actions ought to be construed as treasonous and how far they constituted a patriotic civic defence of wider French interests.

Thus collaboration was a broader and deeper phenomenon—and a more ambiguous one—than that evoked by the first generation of post-war historians. Similarly, resistance activities extended far beyond the actions of those who went on to become formal members of combatants' groups (perhaps some 300,000). Especially after the erosion of popular support for the Vichy regime in 1942, resistance became a more thoroughly popular affair. Protests at town halls over diminishing food rations were not uncommon, the largest rallying some 2,000 people. In Montluçon women lay over the railway tracks for hours in an attempt to prevent the deportation of male workers to the German Reich. But resistance was also an affair of high politics, and in summer 1944 General Charles de Gaulle, leader of the Free French and now supported by Eisenhower, assumed the mantle of power when he became the leader of a post-Vichy provisional government based in Paris. Thus France, an ambiguous ally, avoided the indignity of an Allied Occupation to follow on the heels of the German one. By spring 1944, the democratic credentials of Gaullist-led resistance seemed assured: in April the consultative assembly (the resistance forum based in Algiers) had decided to enfranchise women on the same terms as men, and in March the Conseil National de la Résistance (CNR) published a charter which articulated a vision for the post-Liberation period which included the nationalization of key industries, a systematic package of state welfare including pension rights, and a significant element of state control in a planned economy. Indeed, at the level of high politics this Liberation moment was characterized both by the Gaullist impulse for a strong state and a leftist, in fact communist, desire for redistributive social justice.

CONCLUSIONS

Whatever recent historical research may tell us that is new about how the French thought and lived between 1914 and 1945, one can still rightfully emphasize the great weight of the First World War on the brain of the living in the 1920s and 1930s. The resonance of the 1914–18 conflict can be seen everywhere, in worsened *dénatalité* and the resulting debates and measures to raise the birth rate, in a temporarily destroyed economy, as an explanation for a defensive foreign policy and inter-war 'Maginot mentality'. The *poilu* was invoked rhetorically in political debates—often as an appeal for peace—and was ever-present materially in war memorials and ritually in Armistice Day ceremonies across both rural and urban France.

Yet the extent to which the Great War transformed France can be exaggerated, especially in the field of gender relations and economic organization. France remained largely rural and agricultural until at least the 1930s and it was only after 1945 that, amid the '30 glorious years' of sustained high economic growth, full employment, mass consumerism, and a state intervention in the economy fuelled by American post-war loans and economic integration, the French economy was transformed to a 'modern' and technocratic model. The great critic of France's alleged 'stalemate society', Stanley Hoffmann, saw that after the Liberation period both left and right were more prepared to admit a *dirigiste* (interventionist) role for the state in the economy rather than a merely custodial one, and to take the political risks previously associated with any attempt to put economic expansion before the needs of social 'equilibrium'. For whatever reason, it was principally Frenchmen such as Jean Monnet and Robert Schuman who laid the foundations for large-scale, 'rationalized' European economic cooperation after 1945. Monnet, a former adviser to the League of Nations, perhaps attempted to achieve through economic means the European stability that had eluded diplomatic measures after 1918.

Indeed, it was the Second World War rather than the first that provided France with anything approaching a 'watershed' moment, even if the dreams of Liberation embodied in the CNR charter of March 1944 fell some way short of being realized. The Liberation era (1944–6) nonetheless introduced universal suffrage and instigated a comprehensive state social welfare programme (including unemployment benefits) for the first time in French history. And the population decline that had characterized French demographics since the 1789 Revolution was—perhaps inexplicably—reversed in 1943 as the French acquiesced in the wider European 'baby boom'. Despite the association of political Catholics with the Vichy regime and the inaction of the Vatican over the Holocaust of Europe's Jews, Catholicism emerged invigorated from the Occupation period, no doubt due to its ties with resistance activity, and Christian Democracy became a crucial new political force in France in the Fourth Republic in the guise of the Mouvement Républicain Populaire (MRP)—before being overtaken by Gaullism—just as it did more enduringly in Italy and West Germany. Indeed, the anti-clericalism that had fuelled political divisions under the Third Republic seemed a spent force after 1944: several high-profile politicians were subsequently practising Catholics and after 1951 the republic funded private Catholic schools, an act unthinkable in the pre-Vichy period. No wonder the greatest anti-clerical stalwarts of the Third Republic, the Radicals, did not survive in a climate in which state authorities were willing to show such a benign face to Catholic institutions. Still, if this new tolerance led to a more open practising of the Catholic faith among bourgeois republican men (a group previously inclined to leave religion to women), it did nothing to stall the decades-long French decline in attendance at mass.

There were also significant elements of continuity as state assistance to families provided in the 1938–9 family code and extended under Vichy was further built upon after 1944, despite the formal rejection of all Vichy legislation at the Liberation. And despite the noise and fury of the official purges of Vichy-era collaborators between 1944 and 1951, many elites in politics and industry survived to forge careers in public life during the Fourth and Fifth Republics. No doubt continuities were felt more keenly than ruptures, too, in the associative and leisure life of the French population. By all accounts, political and economic crisis, war and occupation, did not do as much as one might expect to interfere with cultural pursuits such as sport, cinema and tourism. The development of such tastes depends on relatively deep currents of social and technological change, however much historical events may punctuate their (free) expression. The history of France in the first half of the twentieth century is indeed marked by the mass slaughter of war, the defeat of an enduringly democratic regime and complicity in a genocide of unprecedented scale, but the darkness of that legacy ought not to eclipse a parallel history in which the lives of millions were affected by the growth of social welfare, an increase in leisure time, and the increasing purchase of both mass politics and mass culture.

FURTHER READING

Burrin, Philippe, *Living with Defeat: France under the German Occupation, 1940–1944* (London, 1996).

Clout, Hugh, *After the Ruins: Restoring the Countryside of Northern France after the Great War* (Exeter, 1996).

Conklin, Alice L., *A Mission to Civilise: The Republican Idea of Empire in France and West Africa, 1895–1930* (Stanford, Calif., 1998).

Gildea, Robert, *Marianne in Chains: In Search of the German Occupation* (London, 2002).

Kedward, R., *France and the French: La Vie en bleu since 1900* (Woodstock and New York, 2005).

Jackson, Julian, *France: The Dark Years, 1940–1944* (Oxford, 2001).

—— *The Fall of France: The Nazi Invasion of 1940* (Oxford, 2003).

Ory, Pascal, *La Belle Illusion: Culture et politique sous le signe du Front populaire, 1935–1938* (Paris, 1994).

Paxton, Robert, *French Peasant Fascism: Henry Dorgères' Greenshirts and the Crises of French Agriculture, 1929–1939* (Oxford, 1997).

Pedersen, Susan, *Family, Dependence, and the Origins of the Welfare State: Britain and France, 1914–1945* (Cambridge, 1993).

Peer, Shanny, *France on Display: Peasants, Provincials, and Folklore in the 1937 Paris World's Fair* (New York, 1998).

Prost, Antoine, *In the Wake of War: 'Les Anciens Combattants' and French Society, 1914–1939* (Oxford, 1992).

Rearick, Charles, *The French in Love and War: Popular Culture in the Era of the World Wars* (London and New Haven, 1997).

Reynolds, Siân, *France between the Wars: Gender and Politics* (London, 1996).

Roberts, M. L., *A Civilisation without Sexes: Reconstructing Gender in Postwar France, 1917–1927* (Chicago, 1994).

Shennan, A., *Rethinking France: Plans for Renewal, 1940–1946* (Oxford, 1989).

Weber, Eugen, *The Hollow Years: France in the 1930s* (London, 1995).

7

Iberia

Frances Lannon

INTRODUCTION

The creation of the Portuguese New State in the early 1930s and the Spanish Civil War of 1936–9 have long dominated writing about the history of the two Iberian countries in the first half of the twentieth century. Uncovering the roots of the New State and the causes of the civil war have absorbed attention in much the same way as tracing the origins of Fascism in Italy and the Nazi movement in Germany. The Portuguese and Spanish Republics have been scrutinized for evidence of failure as closely as the Weimar Republic or the Italian constitutional monarchy. And the miserable teleology of democracy's displacement by dictatorship is all too similar. In the Spanish case it is particularly poignant because of the terrible destruction of life and resources in the civil war that forged Franco's dictatorship. By the time the European war began in September 1939, Spain was already devastated. But it is Spain, too, that provides particularly powerful contrasting narratives of constitutional and social change, extraordinary artistic innovation, political mobilization, and popular resistance. It is not just that they coexisted with the emergence of dictatorship. Their vitality is a large part of the reason why the triumph of counter-revolution in Spain took a more extreme and violent form than it did in Portugal. In both countries the democrats, reformers, and proponents of free speech were defeated. But their convictions and activities nonetheless contributed to the emergence, several decades later, of free, self-governing societies. Their story is not just one of failure and tragedy.

IBERIA AND THE TWO WORLD WARS

Even though the Iberian countries were directly and indirectly affected by the two world wars, they were minor players in these conflicts. Neither Spain nor Portugal formed part of the opposing alliances in 1914. Their geographical position and

Figure 7.1. Poster of the Spanish Republic carrying an olive branch.

lack of great power status placed them rather on the margins, although Portugal's extensive overseas empire and the remaining Spanish territories in North Africa ensured that national and strategic interests were potentially at stake. In both countries elite opinion was divided. But while in Spain the debate was over which side to favour, in Portugal, with its historic relationship with Britain, the question was whether to intervene on the Allied side. Spain remained neutral, whereas Portugal joined the war in 1916 and sent about 55,000 troops to the Western Front and 45,000 to defend its colonies. Heavy casualties in Flanders strengthened internal opposition to the war, and the coup by Bernardino Sidónio Pais in December 1917 opened the way to a scaling down of Portuguese involvement.

In the Second World War neither country was a belligerent, although the famous Spanish Blue Division was sent 'to fight communism' alongside German forces on the Eastern Front. Portugal's dictator Antonio de Oliveira Salazar spent some uncomfortable periods trying to ensure that General Francisco Franco's enthusiasm for the German and Italian axis did not take Spain into the war and thereby threaten Portugal with being drawn in on the other side in support of Britain. He could not afford to alienate Britain, which was in effect the protector of the Portuguese overseas territories. Indeed, Salazar had to agree eventually to allow the allies to use the Azores as a base in 1944, notwithstanding his sympathy for the Axis Powers which had been so obvious during the Spanish Civil War. The Iberian countries were marginal in the international confrontation that eventually resulted in the destruction of the Nazi and Fascist regimes, the defeat of Japan, and the emergence of a bi-polar world order.

Salazar and Franco survived the new and uncongenial post-war context in the democratic West in 1945 and remained in power until 1968 and 1975 respectively. Their opponents' hopes that the victorious allies would complete their destruction of the Fascist and Nazi dictatorships by forcing the Iberian dictators out of power were bitterly disappointed. As the Cold War set in, the impeccable anti-communist credentials of both leaders became more important for the Western powers than the dictatorial nature of their regimes or their stance during the Second World War.

REVOLUTION AND COUNTER-REVOLUTION

Throughout the first half of the twentieth century, the fundamental issue in Portuguese and Spanish politics was domestic. Would power remain in the hands of traditional elites, or would constitutional or social revolutions transfer it elsewhere? Of course the international context was always important. The rise of dictatorships of both left and right in Europe strongly influenced opinion and events in Iberia. Furthermore, Portugal always remained determined to retain its large empire, whatever the regime in Lisbon. And of course Spain became a central focus of international relations during the civil war of 1936–9, as other countries intervened in or sought to control the outcome of the war for their own purposes. But the origins of the civil war lay in Spanish domestic conflicts. Spain stood for a while at the heart of international affairs because its internal struggles mirrored, in a fashion, the ideological oppositions elsewhere between fascism, democracy, and communism.

Political life in both Spain and Portugal was marked in the first decades of the century by constitutional crisis and breakdown. Monarchy failed. It ended definitively in Portugal in 1910 (notwithstanding attempts for some years to revive it), and collapsed in Spain in 1931 until a much later restoration after Franco's death in 1975. Republican replacements in both Iberian countries proved divisive and unstable. But the establishment of Franco's dictatorship in Spain and Salazar's in Portugal in the course of the 1930s did not resolve the problem of legitimacy. Franco's power was based on military victory over fellow Spaniards in the dreadful civil war. And although both regimes enjoyed significant domestic support, they also used authoritarian methods, including violence, to control and suppress dissent. They institutionalized counter-revolution in what had been politically divided societies.

This triumph of counter-revolution was much more bloody in Spain than in Portugal. Indeed, a comparison between the two Iberian countries helps illuminate the strength of revolutionary movements in Spain. The Portuguese comparison also throws into sharp relief the scale of social change and political mobilization in Spain. If civilian politicians failed to establish any stable regime in Spain, this was largely because rapid economic and social development had created a society of sharply opposed interests. It proved easier to mobilize these than to reconcile them. The ambitious agendas of both revolutionaries and reformers challenged conservative traditionalism but were unable to supplant it.

PORTUGAL

Portugal at the beginning of the twentieth century had a population of about six million—less than one-third the size of Spain's. About 58 per cent of the working population was engaged in agriculture. The country had virtually no heavy industries, with tiny numbers employed mainly in small units. The approximately 25 per cent of the working population employed in secondary industries based on agricultural produce in 1900 rose only marginally in the decades that followed. In 1900, not more than 10.5 per cent of the population lived in towns of over 20,000 inhabitants, and this proportion increased modestly to still under 14 per cent by 1930. Lisbon had no near rival as a major urban centre. Portugal was predominantly rural and agricultural. Illiteracy rates were well over 60 per cent, and improving very slowly. The Portuguese economy and Portuguese society were, then, much less differentiated than the Spanish.

It is equally striking that, as every history of Portugal rightly emphasizes, the country exhibited some kinds of continuity and homogeneity that made it not just unlike Spain, but unlike many other Western societies. Its frontiers were unchanged since the thirteenth century (apart from the partial and anomalous exception of the period 1580–1640 when Portugal was added on to Spain through inheritance by Philip II). It had no internal linguistic or national minorities. Less unusually, it had no religious minorities of any significance. From the point of view of anyone interested in exercising political power, the difficulties associated with the lack of economic resources must have been mitigated by the unifying force of a common history, language, and culture. These strengths were reinforced by the historic continuity and pretension to great power status afforded by the empire.

The Portuguese constitution of August 1911 created a secular, liberal, parliamentary Republic. It was secular in the same mode as the French Third Republic on which it was modelled; that is, it was anti-clerical. The revolution of the previous year had resulted in the breakdown of relations with the Vatican, and the proclamation of the Republic on 5 October 1910 was swiftly followed by the banning of Catholic teaching in schools, the establishment of divorce and civil marriage, and then the separation of Church and State. The Spanish Second Republic of 1931 would follow the same model, with the same flurry of secularizing legislation. It is notable, however, that urban intellectual opposition to Catholicism in Portugal was not accompanied by the violent popular anti-clericalism that was so prominent a feature of Spain in the first decades of the twentieth century. Although there was a good deal of worker agitation in the first years of the Portuguese Republic, and again in the 'red' years of 1919–22, these had a limited demographic base. Moreover, the cultural agenda of middle-class anti-clericals remained distant from the economic preoccupations of the workers' movements, in which wage levels and the eight-hour day (formally attained in 1919) were paramount.

Catholic reactions to anti-clerical republicanism in Portugal were varied and potent. The Academic Centre of Christian Democracy in Coimbra University laid the foundations for the Catholic Centre Party. It brought together laity and clergy who were to lead the defence of Catholic interests in the 1930s, most notably Salazar himself and Manuel Gonçalves Cerejeira, who would be cardinal patriarch of Lisbon for the whole long period of Salazar's supremacy. But Catholic interests were also furthered by initiatives from beyond the frontiers of civilian politics. The 1917 military coup by Major Sidónio Pais overthrew the regime of Alfonso Costa, leader of anti-clerical republicanism, and restored relations with the Vatican. This dictatorship was short-lived because Pais was assassinated in late 1918, and the 1911 constitution was reinstated. But the 1917 coup nonetheless set the precedent for another in 1926 by General Carmona which had the backing of conservative republicans and social Catholics. Salazar himself was not involved, but it was this coup, and the resulting regime in which Carmona remained president until 1951, that was the foundation of Salazar's extraordinary political career. He left his post as an economics professor at Coimbra University to become finance minister in 1928 on terms of his own choosing, most notably financial control of the other ministries. Army support was always vital, but the regime Salazar fashioned was not a military dictatorship.

The other exceptional aid to Catholic defence was the series of Marian apparitions to three young cousins at Fátima, near Leiria, in central Portugal, between May and October 1917. To the sceptical observer it seemed no accident that these occurred in the year of revolutionary crisis in Russia, and under an anti-clerical regime in Portugal. To the devout, they represented succour from on high at a time of siege. Fátima became a Marian shrine surpassed only by Lourdes in Western Europe in its attraction for national and international pilgrims. The famous secrets entrusted by the Virgin to the children in the apparition led many Portuguese Catholics to believe that their country was the site of special divine favour in a troubled world. For the Church, it was a heaven-sent opportunity to rally the faithful and strengthen popular devotion. It is interesting that similar Marian apparitions also occurred in Spain some years later when the new Second Republic began to introduce anti-clerical measures. The visions at Ezkioga in the Basque country in 1931 attracted huge numbers of pilgrims. But the local bishop, Mateo Múgica, declared in September 1933 that the visions did not have a supernatural character. The next year, the Vatican reached the same conclusion. Ezkioga did not become a Spanish Fátima.

After the coup of 1926, Catholic defence in Portugal was shaped even more decisively by civilian politicians than by the army or the Church's own devotional culture. It was led by Salazar. His success as a counter-revolutionary lay in his ruthless determination to establish tight political control while also compromising when necessary. Between 1928 and 1933, Salazar consolidated his power. After his appointment as finance minister in 1928, he balanced the budget largely by reducing public expenditure. In July 1930, the National Union was created, following the model set by General Miguel Primo de Rivera's Patriotic Union in Spain a few years before. It gathered together several conservative strands in support of the government. Two years later, Salazar was appointed prime minister and devised a new constitution. By means of the 1933 constitution and the legislation that followed it, Salazar's New State was created. Although the constitutional order was anti-democratic, it carefully retained a façade of representation and consultation, with a weak National Assembly. Salazar himself became leader of the National Union in November 1932 and other parties—including the Catholic Centre Party—were disbanded in 1934. The army was respected but tamed. In 1936 Salazar added the Ministry of War to his range of responsibilities, and cut the number of officers and the size of the army. Meanwhile workers' organizations were replaced by toothless corporatist ones. Dissent was suppressed with carefully targeted violence. It is notable that

Figure 7.2. The three 'Fátima visionaries': Jacinta, Francisco, and Lucia.

Salazar understood the limits of possible action. There was no attempt to restore the monarchy. The separation of Church and State was not reversed.

Scholarly debate about the nature of Salazar's regime continues. There has long been interest in its stability, with discussion often concentrating on how far this relied on suppression of dissent and how far on maintaining in balance several major interests, including the army, the Church, and rural and business elites. Salazar's aim of establishing 'government without politics' suited well those who prized order, even if some would have preferred a monarchy or military rule. His Catholic conservatism reassured many religious traditionalists who would have preferred to see the separation of Church and State reversed. Recent analyses of the regime emphasize that Salazar's room for manœuvre was always limited by the need to keep different interest groups satisfied or at least pacified. One historian even refers to the New State as 'a precarious enterprise'. This is a useful reminder of the skill Salazar deployed. It may well have saved Portugal from a more extremist challenge from either left or right.

Of course, for many the costs were intolerably high. Liberty was curtailed and democracy set aside. Economic development was very slow. Literacy rates remained low. The triumph of counter-revolution was, however, relatively moderate when set beside contemporary equivalents. It was certainly less repressive than the Franco regime. But Portugal was not Spain. Salazar had numerically small elites to deal with, none of which was powerful enough to impose its own agenda unilaterally. These elites were largely content with Salazar's top-down government by administrative methods of a mainly uneducated, rural, and politically apathetic society which he was determined to keep that way. Spain between 1914 and 1945 was a different matter altogether.

SPAIN

The 1914–18 war had a destabilizing effect on the Spanish economy, society, and politics. Industries that gained new export markets during the war became hugely profitable. These included iron and steel, shipping, and textiles. The production of iron and steel doubled between 1913 and 1917. Some sectors, however, such as orange growers, lost export markets and suffered as a consequence. Others, including wheat growers and coal mining, benefited from the collapse of foreign competition within Spain. Rapid growth in heavy and manufacturing industry created inflationary pressures, but wages moved up more slowly than consumer prices. It has been estimated that prices rose on average by about 62 per cent during the war, but wages only about 25 per cent. Moreover, the labour market changed rapidly. Between 1910 and 1920, the percentage of the labour force employed in agriculture decreased by 15 per cent, while the size of the industrial labour force shot up by 40 per cent in the same period. The combination of inflation and rapidly changing circumstances created enormous discontent. It is not surprising that in the war years the two major trade union organizations, the socialist UGT and the anarchist CNT, expanded significantly. In the summer of 1917, they combined for the first time in a general strike and openly stated that its aim was to change the political regime. Even though the August strike was poorly coordinated and fizzled out swiftly in Madrid and Barcelona, it had greater strength in coal and iron mining areas in Asturias and Vizcaya respectively. The government's response was to send in troops to restore order by force.

If the constitutional monarchy established by the constitution of 1876 had been robust, this economic crisis would not have been so threatening. But the regime was already under pressure. Catalan regionalists wanted devolution, and went as far in July 1917 as convening a Catalan Assembly in Barcelona to demand a new federal constitution. Meanwhile, army officers pursued their own aims of higher wages and a revised promotions system through the organization in 1916 of military *juntas* that acted very like military trade unions. Government attempts to dissolve the *juntas* failed. Instead, in June 1917 many of their demands were met, to the detriment of government authority. With recalcitrant army officers, and trade unions and Catalan regionalists calling for a new constitution, the monarchy was in crisis. A first attempt at a national, cross-party government under the Liberal Manuel García Prieto in November 1917 failed. On the insistence of King Alfonso XIII, a second one was assembled in March 1918 under the Conservative Antonio Maura and lasted longer, but still for less than nine months. The old system in which Liberal and Conservative elites rotated in government had collapsed, unable to take the strain of anti-dynastic political movements including republicanism, socialism, and regionalism, and social unrest. Coalitions were no more successful. Government followed government at bewildering speed. Employment levels fell as industries that had temporarily expanded and flourished in war conditions contracted again. A new wave of worker protest swept over the rural south, especially Andalusia and Barcelona, as the 'Bolshevik' post-war years began, threatening to make Spain ungovernable. The fundamental agenda in Spain from then on, throughout the 1920s and 1930s, was social revolution and how to avoid it.

Southern Spain erupted in confrontation and violence in 1918 as unions, especially anarchist unions, mobilized agricultural workers to seek better pay, better working conditions, and the new world pioneered by the Bolsheviks in which landed elites would tumble and power would be exercised directly by workers. The extent and intensity of social confrontation were unprecedented. The owners of the great estates in the south despaired of government. Eventually, in the summer of 1919, as the rural strikes began to lose cohesion, the government dispatched 20,000 soldiers to restore order through the use of force, arrests, and the closing down of union offices. But in Barcelona the unrest continued, taking the form of strikes, street violence, and assassinations. As in Andalusia, the mobilization was led by the anarchist union federation, the CNT. Employers responded with lock-outs and attempts to sabotage the unions. From just before the beginning of the 1917 general strike through to the military coup of September 1923, at least 300 people were killed in Barcelona province. It was not difficult in Barcelona in these post-war years to believe—with either enthusiasm or terror—that this was the revolution in action. The country reeled from the assassination of Prime Minister Edward Dato in March 1921, and Cardinal Soldevila, archbishop of Zaragoza. The government was discredited.

PRIMO DE RIVERA'S DICTATORSHIP

When General Miguel Primo de Rivera launched his coup in September 1923, it was greeted with relief by a very broad spectrum of Spaniards. Not many lamented the suspension of the constitution and the demise of ineffective parliamentary politics. Primo took power under the King and opened his famous 'parenthesis' in Spain's political history. Order was restored. It was the first time since 1874 that the military had wrested control of central government from civilian politicians.

Counter-revolution remained the underlying priority of many social sectors, institutions, and organizations in Spain. These included the army, the Church, propertied elites, and many rather frightened members of the middle classes. A further breakdown of order was a more immediate issue for many than whether Spain had parliamentary government, or was a functioning democracy. The dominant preoccupation of British and American historians writing about Spain has often been why democracy, as represented by the Second Spanish Republic of 1931–6, did not survive, and whether it could have done so. But it is easy to exaggerate the extent to which parliamentary democracy was the salient issue, even for many of the Republic's supporters and leaders. If one begins with 1917 rather than 1931, it becomes clearer why so many Spanish politicians and citizens gave parliamentary democracy only qualified support. Overturning the existing social order or preserving it were often more immediate priorities.

The Spanish population at the end of the First World War numbered about twenty million. Approximately 60 per cent of the workforce was employed in agriculture, as in Portugal. But Spain had significant industrial developments on the periphery, the greatest concentrations being textiles and other manufacturing industries in Catalonia, coal mining in Asturias, and iron ore mining, metallurgy, and shipbuilding in the Basque province of Vizcaya. Such industries employed 18.5 per cent of the workforce. Economic historians have often described Spain in this period as having a dual economy, with an agricultural heartland flanked to the north and east by modern industry. While in Portugal barely 10 per cent of the population lived in towns of over 20,000 inhabitants, in Spain more than 10 per cent lived in large towns of over 100,000 inhabitants, with more again than that in towns of 20,000 to 100,000. There were strong patterns of internal migration, from the south and centre to the north and east, and from country to town.

This differentiation was superimposed on older cultural differences. The north was more observantly Catholic, and generally speaking formal religious practice dropped as one went south. The Catalan and Basque regions had a profound sense of historic cultural identity that was heightened as they became the powerhouses of the Spanish economy. Indeed, economic growth and inward migration from other parts of Spain stimulated the rise of regional nationalism and calls for autonomy by the end of the nineteenth century. Social and cultural identities were therefore sharply debated. Issues concerning class, religion, and region were all capable of mobilizing sectors of the population, as trade unions, regionalist parties, anti-clerical movements, and organizations for the defence of Church or property rallied their supporters. These issues often criss-crossed one another in highly complex ways. Governments in Spain faced an extremely difficult task navigating the cross-currents. It was not made any easier by the persistence of republicanism in many Spanish towns, or by the wider context of the loss of empire in the nineteenth century, culminating in the traumatic withdrawal from Cuba after defeat by the United States in 1898. Indeed, a new imperial crisis was unfolding in Spain's remaining territories in North Africa, and the catastrophic defeat in Morocco in 1921 at Annual was part of the background to Primo's coup in 1923, which saved the King from a parliamentary inquiry into responsibilities for the defeat.

When Primo dismissed the politicians and took control, he assumed responsibility for a country immersed in imperial and post-imperial uncertainties, with an unpopular monarchy, disagreement about the role of the state, a disillusioned army, conflict between anti-clericals and defenders of the Church, and virtual class war raging in parts of the country. The contrast with the situation in Portugal when Salazar became finance minister in 1928 is stark. Portugal still retained much of its empire, the monarchy had already been abolished, there were no regional nationalist movements, and the demographic and organizational bases of worker protest were quite limited. Portuguese national identity was clear. Spain's was contested.

Miguel Primo de Rivera made no pretence of political sophistication. He aimed to sort out the country's problems by authoritarian action, and then guide it into a new—as yet unspecified—constitutional normality. His most spectacular achievement was the eventual defeat of Abd-el-Krim's forces in Morocco in 1925 and 1926, made possible by cooperation with the French, who were equally concerned to assert control over their own more extensive Moroccan colony. This ended twenty years of struggle by Spain.

In Spain itself, the suppression of dissent was often accompanied by reformist, modernizing policies. There had never been any doubt that Primo de Rivera would repress the anarchist movement. Its newspapers and offices were closed down, and its trade unions survived only clandestinely. But his policy towards their socialist rivals was unexpected. The socialist party was not dissolved, and its trade union wing, the UGT, was allowed a major role in the new arbitration committees created by minister of labour Eduardo Aunós in 1926 to deal with labour disputes. At every level, these committees had an equal number of representatives from employers and workers, with a state-appointed chair. Members of the small Catholic unions gained some elected places as worker representatives, but the UGT was the dominant group. The arbitration committees decided matters such as wage levels and working conditions. The inspiration for them was drawn from social Catholicism and its corporatist view of social and employment organization. Aunós was also influenced by Mussolini, and indeed the Labour Code issued in 1926 was obviously based on the Italian Labour Charter. But the *comités paritarios* were not the corrupt corporatism that developed in fascist Italy or later under Franco, which was essentially a façade for employer control. They were a genuine effort to facilitate inter-class negotiation under independent chairmen, and employers' associations frequently did not like the results. Unfortunately for Primo, owners of the great agricultural estates in southern and central Spain refused to cooperate when the dictatorship extended the arbitration committees from industry into agriculture in 1928. The dictatorship lacked both the resources and the will to impose them. A few years later, the Second Republic reinvigorated the *comités paritarios*, recognizing their reformist potential. But it also inherited the problem of recalcitrant agricultural employers and decided to tackle it head on. Where Primo de Rivera had left rural property untouched, the Republic embarked on an ambitious programme of land reform. But the Republic, like the dictatorship, was hindered by the inherent weakness of the Spanish state when seeking to implement reforms that propertied elites found unacceptable. This was something that neither Salazar nor Franco ever attempted.

On other social issues, too, Primo introduced useful if limited reforms. A Royal Decree of 21 June 1926 granted subsidies to workers and state employees with large families. The pro-natalist inspiration behind this is revealed by the fact that workers of either sex were eligible, and illegitimate as well as legitimate children counted. A Royal Decree of 22 March 1929 established an obligatory maternity insurance scheme for women workers, which was eventually put into force by the Republic in 1931. Primo appointed thirteen women to the National Assembly he convened in 1927, and several others as municipal councillors. Government expenditure on education went up by 58 per cent in the 1920s and on health and social services by even greater rates.

Primo was determined to modernize the economy, and used state intervention without any hesitation. A public works programme created a network of good highways and additional employment, and stimulated production. There was state investment in the railways and irrigation schemes. The chain of outstanding state-owned hotels in historic buildings, the *paradores*, was begun. State monopolies proliferated. The most audacious was the petrol monopoly, CAMPSA, set up to divert some petrol profits to the state. Regulatory committees sought, with mixed success, to control a whole series of different industries. Mining and industrial output rose substantially. The growth of industry attracted migration from a countryside in crisis to urban centres. By 1930, over 40 per cent of the Spanish population lived in towns of over 10,000 inhabitants.

Primo's brave attempt through finance minister José Calvo Sotelo in 1926 to introduce a single direct tax on all sources of income was shot down by the financial sector and the press. Spain had to wait many decades for an effective income tax. In the meantime, state expenditure including public works was financed by loans serviced from ordinary revenues. Not surprisingly, bankers considered some of Primo's financial and economic measures unorthodox and inflationary, while many businessmen resented state interference. The drop in value of the peseta from 1928 onwards gave extra force to their criticisms.

Primo also attempted to modernize the army. He was right to see that the officer corps was too large, and that promotions based only on seniority led to inefficiency. But his solutions were ineffective. He reduced the size of the officer corps enough to create fear, but not enough to modernize and professionalize the army. And his head-on collision with the artillery corps over its closed system of promotions in 1926 was disastrous. He suspended the entire corps. It had little choice but to give in. The price, however, was widespread criticism in the army of the dictator's methods. There was some military backing for a botched coup attempt by conservative politicians in July 1929 in Valencia. Finally, when Primo asked the captains general of the Spanish military regions in January 1930 whether he had the full backing of the army, their unsatisfactory response led immediately to his resignation.

He left behind a constitutional and power vacuum. When he first seized power, his governmental changes had seemed effective. He appointed military colleagues to work under him in a governing directorate. At local level, this was replicated by military delegates replacing town councillors and provincial governors. The next and more difficult stage was the reintroduction of civilian participation. In April 1924, Primo created the Patriotic Union (model for Portugal's later National Union) as the official state party. Its members were favoured for government jobs, and it was meant to provide an administrative phalanx of reliable supporters. In December 1925, he appointed a largely civilian government. But the future remained unclear. The consultative National Assembly he convened in September 1927 to make proposals for a new constitution was not successful. Many of those invited to participate declined. The eventual draft constitution published in July 1929 was never taken any further. No consensus emerged. On the contrary, political and intellectual opposition to the dictatorship and its plans gathered pace across a wide political spectrum.

Regionalism had remained a problem. Like most, if not all, Spanish generals, Primo was a centralist, intent on maintaining national unity. His coup was launched from his position as captain general of Catalonia, with at least tacit support from some Catalan elites who were relieved to see the restoration of order on the streets and in the workplace. But he was deeply suspicious of Catalanist political ambitions. He insisted on the use of Castilian Spanish, not

Catalan or Basque, in schools and public administration and in religious services. The Law of the Provinces of 1925 made clear his determination not to allow the development of regional-level government. Catalan and Basque nationalists were alienated as surely by this as liberals, democrats, and republicans were by the failure to restore constitutional government. Primo neither undermined nor conciliated any of these groups. Rather, he merely silenced them for a while, only for them to re-emerge more determined.

In the end, Primo ran out of ideas and support. In January 1930, he tendered his resignation to Alfonso XIII and took off for Paris. He had seized power in 1923 to restore order. But he tried to do much more than that. Primo's ambition to bring social and economic improvements to the people of Spain differentiates him from both Salazar and Franco. While Salazar was content with social stagnation and Franco with social control, Primo de Rivera attempted to use the state to promote economic growth and modernization. It is impossible to know whether a more politically skilled leader could have secured greater agreement. But the rapidity with which institutions, organizations, and interest groups turned against him when his policies did not favour them shows clearly the limits of his room for manœuvre.

No constructive way was found to close the parenthesis opened in 1923. Alfonso appointed General Berenguer, and then Admiral Aznar, to do the impossible. While they tried to ease the way back to the constitution abandoned in 1923, a revolutionary committee of several parties was formed to overthrow the discredited monarchy. A premature and uncoordinated military rising failed. But in the end violence was not necessary. In April 1931 municipal elections were held as a preliminary to general elections. The Republican-Socialist bloc triumphed in Spain's major cities, and although pro-monarchist candidates gained more votes overall, it was immediately recognized that the public opinion that mattered had rejected the monarchy. On 14 April, Alfonso left Spain. The Republic was proclaimed, with the revolutionary committee as its provisional government.

THE SECOND REPUBLIC

The Second Republic was hailed with popular delirium. This was the regime that would right historic wrongs, and promote the interests of the masses that had never before been directly represented in government. It never, however, established a clear legitimacy. From the beginning there were unreconciled Alfonsist and Carlist monarchists and anti-democrats on the right and a sceptical and dissatisfied revolutionary left. Even for many politicians operating within the Republic and its democratic structures, loyalty depended on whether it would forward their vital interests.

Elections for a constituent parliament were held in the summer of 1931, when the political right was in disarray after the monarchy's disappearance.

The Socialists emerged as much the biggest party, followed by the Radicals and Radical-Socialists. They, together with the Left Republicans led by Manuel Azaña, set the constitutional agenda. They decided on a unicameral legislature, autonomy for Catalonia and other regions that chose it, equal legal status for women (including, after some controversy, female suffrage), the separation of Church and State, compulsory secular schooling, the introduction of divorce, and the right of the state to confiscate property in some circumstances. The cultural revolution against the Catholic Church was, for Azaña and many others, the essential breakthrough into secular modernity. This included banning the religious congregations from teaching, and restricting religious practice to the home and the inside of churches. Zealous local councils in some parts of Spain forbade priests to lead funeral processions with a crucifix, and the ringing of church bells. To Catholics, of course, all of this was an authoritarian exercise of state power to curtail their liberty. The constitution of the Republic was never the broadly accepted framework it needed to be if the Republic was to establish its legitimacy. Other legislation sought to bring about radical improvement for workers and landless peasants. The eight-hour day, a minimum wage, the reinstatement of Primo's arbitration committees, and the extension of state education all promised a better future for the masses. Moreover, the Republic ventured where Primo had not dared to tread, with ambitious agrarian reform. The question was whether these reformist measures would be enough to undercut demands for a social revolution, especially on the great estates and in the big cities. The Socialist party maintained its reformist line, arguing that cooperation with 'bourgeois' democratic parties was the appropriate way forward. But it was hard to convince its supporters that this was good enough.

By the time the constituent parliament was dissolved, and the first general elections under the new constitution called for November 1933, the political situation was very different from what it had been in April 1931. First of all, former monarchists who were willing to use parliamentary means to defend property, religion, and the family had created a modern mass Catholic party, the CEDA, under the leadership of José María Gil Robles. It used modern methods of propaganda and organization, including sections for women and youth, to mobilize support. It was particularly successful among the Catholic middle classes and peasant smallholders, both of whom disagreed with the attack on religious schools and feared the undermining of private property rights and the traditional family. The Radicals, meanwhile, moved right as their anti-monarchist and secularizing agenda was fulfilled. The Radicals and CEDA constituted what had not existed in the summer of 1931, a broadly conservative coalition capable of winning a majority of seats.

The Socialists had achieved a great deal. In particular, they had introduced significant labour reforms that were of real benefit to their supporters. But legislation on wages and working conditions did not suffice in the rural south and centre. Great numbers of landless labourers continued to suffer seasonal unemployment with no social welfare provision. Conditions were harsh. To many labourers it seemed obvious that what they needed was their own land. The Agrarian Reform Law of September 1932 was an attempt to redistribute land, but the state lacked the resources to implement it. There was very little money to pay compensation for expropriated land, and there were endless legal challenges about which land qualified for expropriation. Only tiny numbers of peasant families were actually resettled. Rural frustration flamed up in a series of violent incidents that met a predictable response from the Civil Guard. The names of Casas Viejas and Castilblanco became infamous for murderous repression. Battered by criticism that in power they had kept order in the countryside by the same bloody methods as the monarchy, and feeling compromised by their experience of coalition, the Socialists went into the 1933 elections alone.

The small pro-Republican Catholic movement under Niceto Alcalá Zamora and Miguel Maura was left stranded between the successful CEDA and the Republic's anti-clericalism. Its fate symbolized the flight from the centre taking place on both sides in the Republic. If there had been mass support behind Azaña and Alcalá-Zamora the history of the Republic might have been different. But they were outflanked by the Socialists and the CEDA respectively, and these in turn were always aware of openly anti-parliamentary forces further out beyond them.

In the November 1933 elections the coalition of Radicals and the CEDA triumphed. Although the Socialists obtained far more votes than the Radicals, because the electoral system favoured coalitions their representation in parliament was halved. The new Radical government, with full support from the CEDA, set about repealing or simply not implementing much of the reforming legislation of the previous parliament. It was not surprising that in the European context of 1933 and 1934 many on the left feared that they were witnessing the first stages of an authoritarian takeover by parliamentary means. This was exacerbated by the entry of three CEDA ministers into government in October 1934. In a fatal move, a revolutionary rising broke out in Barcelona and elsewhere which was readily suppressed except in the Asturian coal mining areas. There a workers' revolution seized control and held it for two weeks, until it was put down by General Francisco Franco and his army of Morocco. The repression was brutal. The Spanish left was in disarray, divided between those like Indalecio Prieto who concluded that the conquest of power must be by democratic and not revolutionary means, and others who had little faith in the Republic's ability ever to bring about by legislation the transformation of property and class that they desired. On the right there was a similar division between those like Gil Robles who hoped that the next election would give Catholic conservatives a parliamentary majority, and those like Franco who decided that the left was irrevocably committed to social revolution and was illegitimate. While Prieto worried about how to harness the revolution, and find a reformist way forward, a great swathe of Spanish conservatives decided that an electoral victory of the left would be intolerable.

The general elections of February 1936 brought victory for a Popular Front alliance with much the same programme as had been enacted in the 1931 constitution. Manuel Azaña succeeded Alcalá-Zamora as president. The alliance created a weak government, run by minority Republicans without direct participation by the Socialists or the small Communist party. This was poorly placed to deal with the alarming tendency of several different forces to take matters into their own hands. Large-scale strikes and land occupations signalled the impatience of many workers and peasants with parliamentary processes. The small but growing Spanish fascist party, the Falange, under its leader José Primo de Rivera (son of Miguel) adopted another form of direct action, gunning down its enemies on the streets. A group of generals decided that the political experiment had failed, and conspired to effect a military coup. But when the rising began on 17 July 1936, it was only partly successful. Crucially, it failed in both Madrid and Barcelona, as well as in several other cities. A combination of popular resistance, and specialist forces such as the Assault Guards sometimes staying loyal to the government, defeated the rising in the capital and in Barcelona. Spain experienced not a military takeover like that effected by Primo de Rivera in 1923, but three years of devastating civil war.

The Republic had represented an attempt to modernize Spain's cultural life as well as its constitution and society. Most of the country's famous leading philosophers, creative writers, and artists looked to the Republic in 1931 to curtail the influence of the Church in education and censorship, and to usher in a new era of artistic freedom and creativity. They included the philosophers Miguel de Unamuno and José Ortega y Gasset, and the poets Antonio Machado and Federico García Lorca. They, like many of the leading Republican politicians of the left and centre-left, including Manuel Azaña, were associated with the Free Education Institute, an extraordinarily influential secular school that had long nurtured Spain's intellectual elite. No less a figure than Federico García Lorca headed one of the Republic's most famous cultural initiatives, 'La Barraca' (The Shack), touring a theatre company through Spain in the early years of the Republic, especially in rural areas, giving performances of Spanish classical drama. The experience of rural Spain helped inspire his sombre, brooding plays of this period, *Bodas de sangre* (Blood Wedding, 1932), *Yerma* (Barren, 1934), and *La casa de Bernarda Alba* (The House of Bernarda Alba, 1936). La Barraca was part of a drive by the Ministry of Education to take culture to the masses with travelling libraries, film shows, and art exhibitions as well as theatre. The approved culture was humanist and secular (the Catholic monarchs were cut out of Lope de Vega's 1619 play, *Fuenteovejuna*). Not surprisingly, Catholic traditionalists were suspicious of the whole enterprise.

The 1920s and 1930s were a golden age for Spanish letters, art, and film. Luis Buñuel's surrealist film *Un chien andalou* (An Andalusian Dog) was made in France in 1929, with the surrealist artist Salvador Dalí helping create the script. Buñuel's searing documentary *Tierra sin pan* (Land without Bread) followed in 1932, set in the remote Las Hurdes area of Extremadura, and depicting utter destitution. The poets Juan Ramón Jiménez and Vicente Aleixandre were both later awarded the Nobel Prize for Literature, while others, including Jorge Guillén and Rafael Alberti, also gained international recognition. In Catalonia, the extraordinary modernist exuberance of the turn of the century generated continuing experimentation in architecture and painting. Antoní Gaudí continued to work on his great church, the Sagrada Familia (Holy Family) in Barcelona, up to his death in 1926. In painting, Joan Miró and Pablo Picasso chose to work in Paris, but their artistic roots were in Catalonia.

Gaudí was a devout Catholic. In this, he was the exception that proves the rule. The other writers and artists mentioned here belonged to a very different, humanist cultural world, with which the Republic became identified, and to which it gave hope. When Manuel Azaña famously said in the Spanish parliament in October 1931 that Spain was no longer Catholic, he meant that its high culture was not Catholic. He was right. When Franco took up arms against the Republic, he was also taking up arms against an intellectual and artistic golden age which he abhorred, and which he repudiated as alien to Spanish tradition and identity. The civil war would inevitably be a war about culture, as well as about politics and resources. One of its early victims was Federico García Lorca, shot as both an intellectual and sexual deviant (he was homosexual) by the insurgents in his home city of Granada on 19 August 1936. Pablo Picasso created one of the most famous icons of the twentieth century when he painted *Guernica* for the Republic's stand at the International Exhibition in Paris in 1937, in protest at the horrors of the war in Spain, and especially the air bombardment of civilians. At the end of the war, when the Republic was defeated, a whole long generation of creative artists, writers, and philosophers joined the hundreds of thousands going into exile, most of them never to return to Spain again.

THE CIVIL WAR

The military rising of July 1936 destroyed the authority of the Republican government. Power ebbed away, as many regular soldiers deserted and crowds in the streets demanded arms. The social revolution that had been hoped for by some and dreaded by others since the end of the First World War now occurred as government control collapsed. Peasants collectivized land and killed landlords. Workers seized factories and turned on employers. Over 6,000 priests and some nuns were killed in an anti-clerical rampage. Churches were desecrated and destroyed. Franco and his fellow conspirators unleashed this storm when they took up arms against the government. Meanwhile, in areas where the rising succeeded, the army and Carlist and fascist militias also turned on their opponents, including unarmed workers and other civilians, with terrifying ferocity. In the first weeks of the war, just being in the wrong place, caught on the wrong side, swiftly turned into a death sentence.

In the days after the attempted coup, the division of territory and resources in Spain seemed to favour the Republic. It held Madrid, Barcelona, Valencia, more than half of the total population and territory, the industrial concentrations of Catalonia and the Basque country, the resources of the Bank of Spain, and most of the navy and tiny airforce. The insurgents held great swathes of rural Spain in the centre and north, Seville, Granada, implausibly—and by trickery—the erstwhile revolutionary centre of Oviedo in Asturias, and quite crucially, Spanish North Africa. Both sides faced the problem of disconnected territories. The Republican north coast was cut off from the rest of the areas that remained loyal, while the insurgent territories in the south-west around Seville were cut off from those further north. It seems quite likely that if Franco had not been able to get the army of Africa over to the mainland, the armed rising would eventually have failed. The very early, but independent, decisions by both Hitler and Mussolini to extend aid to Franco were therefore of central importance to the outcome of the war. On 29 July 1936, German military transport planes began ferrying Spanish and colonial troops from North Africa to Seville.

While General Mola's forces advanced on Madrid from the north-east, north, and north-west, Franco moved at great speed north from Seville towards the capital. Mola reached the outskirts of Madrid, but was unable to get any further, stopped by a combination of loyal Republican forces and hastily organized militias. Franco swept north as far as Mérida, pausing only to mop up Badajoz near the Portuguese frontier with one of the most ruthless actions of the entire war. In Badajoz, and throughout this march to Madrid, the policy was to leave no enemies in the rear, and to move fast. It was easier to kill than to take prisoners. Opponents, often unarmed, were gunned down in pitiless massacres. From Mérida the army of Africa turned north-east towards the capital. It slowed down only for a diversion to Toledo, to relieve insurgent forces surrounded by a Republican siege. By the beginning of November, Franco was at the approaches to Madrid. But here he ran into the first international mobilization in support of the Republic, as Soviet planes repulsed German bombers, Soviet tanks went into action, and the International Brigades of volunteers organized through the Communist International reinforced Spanish defenders of the city. A truly desperate, building by building, hand-to-hand battle resulted in the western outskirts of Madrid. But the city held, and the front remained pretty well where it was until the very last stages of the war. New attempts on Madrid from the north-west at the end of 1936, from the south across the Jarama valley in February 1937, and by Italian forces from the north-east to Guadalajara in March 1937 all made some progress but then failed. Madrid became identified with the Communist leader and orator Dolores Ibarruri's slogan 'They shall not pass'.

Between November 1936 and April 1939, the main military course of the war was essentially a steady capture of the rest of Spain by the insurgents, now calling themselves the nationals or nationalists, with almost the last conquest being Madrid itself. On the Mediterranean coast, Málaga and the surrounding area was taken, with Italian help, in February 1937. The Basque province of Vizcaya with its iron ore mines and heavy industry fell in the campaign of March to June 1937. It was in this campaign that German bombers destroyed the town of Durango on 31 March and Guernica on 26 April, providing a new model of modern warfare, the aerial bombing of civilian populations with no means of defence. A Republican offensive heading west out of Madrid in July 1937 took Brunete but was then repulsed. Similarly, a Republican advance at Teruel in Aragón at the end of 1937 brought victory at first but was short-lived.

In April 1938, the nationalists cut right through Republican territory to the Mediteranean at Vinaroz, between Barcelona and Valencia. With its territory depleted and divided, the Republic tried one final, immense onslaught in the second half of 1938, determined to drive the nationalists back west across the river Ebro. The Ebro campaign enabled the Republicans to advance impressively, but they could not hold their positions. Months of counter-attacks slowly forced them to relinquish what they had won, until by mid-November 1938 they retreated back across the Ebro. There was little now to stop the nationalist advance into Catalonia. Barcelona fell on 26 January 1939. As hundreds of thousands of refugees trailed over the frontier into France, the nationalists turned south and west. They eventually entered Madrid on 28 March 1939, and remaining Republican centres immediately afterwards. On 1 April 1939, Franco declared that the war was over.

The nationalists owed a good deal of their success to Hitler and Mussolini, whose personal decisions to intervene had tipped the balance towards them in the very first days of the war, and who continued to supply military equipment, specialist personnel, and in Italy's case thousands of troops. They also owed a lot indirectly to Britain. In August 1936, in an attempt to prevent the war from escalating, Britain developed a policy of non-intervention and by the end of that month all the major powers, including Germany and Italy, signed a non-intervention agreement in which they pledged to prohibit the export of arms to Spain. When the non-intervention committee met for the first time on 9 September in London, it was therefore already obvious that the agreement was being broken. It did, however, make it extremely difficult and costly for the Republic to secure arms. Only Mexico was willing openly to defy the embargo. When the Soviet Union decided in October to provide arms to the Republic in exchange for Spain's gold reserves, this offer could not be refused. Soviet intervention kept the Republic fighting, and at times its military equipment was superior to that supplied by Germany. But it came with a cost beyond the inflated prices charged. Along with it came Soviet military and political advisers, and increasing Soviet pressure on the beleaguered Republican government.

The Republic faced a double challenge from the beginning—how to defeat the rebel generals in a largely hostile international context and how to hold together the diverse Republican parties and movements. By the end of the summer of 1936, it seemed obvious to many that the first of these could not be achieved while revolutionary groups sought to create a collectivist utopia behind the lines, and militias organized by trade union or political affiliation resisted military discipline. The Socialist trade union leader Francisco Largo Caballero was appointed prime minister on 4 September in an attempt to bring the revolution within government. In October the militias were incorporated into the new Popular Army. On 4 November the anarchists took the quite extraordinary step of entering the government, thereby also giving Spain its first ever woman cabinet minister, Federica Montseny, who became minister of health. But tensions remained, and Largo Caballero became increasingly frustrated by the pressure put on him by the Soviet Union through its ambassador Marcel Rosenberg, and by the growing Spanish Communist party, to restrain the anarchists and revolutionary socialists. In early May 1937, in the midst of what was for the Republic the disastrous campaign in the Basque country, a civil war within the civil war broke out in Barcelona, where revolutionaries and their opponents fought out their dispute on the streets. The anarchists were defeated and the small dissident group of anti-Stalinist communists, the POUM, were destroyed. Largo Caballero was replaced by the more pro-Soviet socialist Juan Negrín, who remained prime minister until the end of the war. Negrín shared the view of the Prieto wing of the Socialist party, the Communists, and the Soviet Union that a disciplined and all-out war effort was the essential priority.

What did the Republic stand for by late 1937? It maintained, of course, that it was the continuation of the democratic Republic established in 1931. The government traced its legitimate origins to the Popular Front victory in the general elections of February 1936, and civilian politicians remained in control. Every effort was made to keep a broad coalition. But many erstwhile Republicans were disillusioned. The early revolutionary and anti-clerical violence had totally alienated some Catalan nationalists, Catholics, and moderates. The increasing dominance of the Communists did not bode well for any restoration of parliamentary democracy. On the other hand, the dismantling of the revolution left many anarchists and left-wing Socialists wondering if this regime of order, property, and imposed discipline was really worth fighting for. Their aim of an egalitarian, collectivist, atheist society had seemed within reach in August 1936, but was now very far away.

On the nationalist side, politics were brutally straightforward. Martial law was declared wherever nationalist forces penetrated. As early as the end of September 1936 Franco was named by his fellow generals as both supreme military commander and head of government. He immediately arrogated to himself also the role of head of state. Power was militarized, unified, and personalized. The CEDA disbanded. The Alfonsist monarchists could only hope—fruitlessly as it turned out—for a restoration when the war was won. In April 1937, Franco merged all political associations into one mass party of which he became the head. To the dismay especially of the Carlists and the fascists, their separate organizations were fused into a great conglomerate called the Spanish Traditionalist Falange (FET) whose very name—Traditionalist for the Carlists, Falange for the fascists—declared it to be a kind of depoliticization. There were parallels between the defeat of the revolutionaries in May on the Republican side and the emasculation of the Carlists and fascists on the Nationalist side in April. Some fascist and Carlist leaders felt betrayed. Where was the monarchical restoration, or the fascist revolution, for which they had been fighting? Franco's emerging military and personal dictatorship was far from their ideal. However, it was obviously far preferable to the triumph of the revolutionary, anti-clerical mob which they feared above all else.

In July 1937, the vast majority of the Catholic bishops made their support of the military rising plain in a joint pastoral letter addressed to Catholic bishops throughout the world. For them, too, the issues were stark—Franco's order or persecution. The only sizeable group of Catholics to take a different view were the Basque Nationalists. They hated the idea of a centralized military dictatorship, and for a while, from October 1936 to the fall of the Basque city of Bilbao in June 1937, experienced—albeit in dire circumstances—the autonomous Basque government within the Republic that they had long desired. Apart from them, only a few Catholic democrats stayed loyal to the Republic at war.

FRANCO'S DICTATORSHIP

On 1 September 1939, Germany invaded Poland. Two days later Britain and France declared war on Germany. The greater European confrontation that Negrín had hoped might force Britain and France at last to the defence of the Spanish Republic had begun, but too late. Franco's sympathies were clearly with Germany. These were greatly reinforced when Hitler invaded the Soviet Union in 1941. But apart from the Blue Division sent to fight on the Eastern Front, Spain kept out of the war. It was hardly in a position militarily and economically to participate. About half a million Spaniards had died. Economic production had collapsed. Living conditions for millions were appalling.

Franco's victory was not followed by any attempt at reconciliation. Knowing that would be the case, hundreds of thousand of Spaniards chose exile in France or Latin America if they were able to get out before frontiers and ports were closed. A whole generation of liberal intellectuals and professionals left the country. The dictatorship turned usual notions of justice on their head by retrospectively defining bearing arms in defence of the Republic as 'military rebellion'. About

50,000 people were executed under military justice after the war was over, and huge numbers imprisoned. In another piece of retrospective legislation, the Law of Political Responsibilities of February 1939 made anyone who had supported the Republic or failed to support the 'national movement' from the time of the revolution in October 1934 liable to prosecution and having their assets seized. As though that were not enough, there was a political purge of teachers and many other professionals, who were dismissed, fined, moved away from their home town, or at the very least denied promotion if they were found to be ideologically unsatisfactory.

Franco's dictatorship abolished democracy and devolution. It restored property rights (except for the defeated), religion, and patriarchal authority. Trade unions were banned. The Church was given extensive powers over education and censorship. Women's rights and opportunities were severely curtailed. Nor did Franco have Primo de Rivera's appetite for using the state to promote economic modernization. Indeed, his autarkic policies had the opposite effect. The Spanish economy took many years to return to pre-war levels of production.

Counter-revolution had triumphed, not just over the social revolutionaries of 1918 and 1936 with their vision of a collectivist egalitarian society, but also over the reformist initiatives of liberals and Socialists between 1931 and 1933, and over the intellectual and artistic achievements of Spanish humanist culture. It had triumphed in a more extreme and ruthless form than the regime of either Primo de Rivera or Salazar. Franco's power and legitimacy were based on conquest. The great institutions, the army and the Church, were beholden to him, as were the industrial and agrarian elites. There was no king above him, and he had no intention of relinquishing power. The onset of the Cold War removed any possibility of the Western democracies making life difficult for him. Franco famously found running the country quite simple. To a much greater extent than either Primo or Salazar he had destroyed his enemies. The 1940s were known in Spain as the years of hunger. Much later, in the 1960s, more liberal economic policies facilitated growth, gradually improved living standards, and indirectly created aspirations towards self-government. By the time Franco's successor King Juan Carlos had to respond to new calls for democracy, freedom, and devolution in the second half of the 1970s, the country's economy and society had changed so radically that there were almost no revolutionaries of either right or left to be found.

CONCLUSIONS

Historical perspective constantly changes. It has been argued in this chapter that the fear of revolution that proved so potent in Spain and Portugal in the 1930s is best understood by looking not just at the immediate sources of Salazar's New State and Franco's dictatorship in that decade, but at the underlying struggle for political control in both countries from the beginning of the twentieth century.

Similarly, if one considers the situation in both Iberian countries in 1945, the end of the period studied in this book, the two Iberian dictatorships were internally secure and free from external intervention. Their fate was sealed for decades to come. Whereas Hitler and Mussolini died defeated, Salazar and Franco remained in office. But neither internal dynamics nor external developments can be fully controlled even by successful dictators. The Salazar regime, it is true, survived the incapacitating illness of Salazar in 1968 and his death in 1970. Marcello Caetano succeeded him as prime minister. The regime continued. The dramatic army coup of 25 April 1974 that swept it away, however, did not appear out of nowhere. Probably most important of all was the anti-colonization movement sweeping through all the Western European empires in the 1950s and 1960s. Goa was lost in 1961. Sections of the Portuguese army became convinced that Angola and other colonies could only be held by unacceptable methods and the commitment of vast resources. The rhetoric of defending Christian and Western civilization in Africa rang ever more hollow. At the same time, the political and economic success of democratic Western Europe, and especially the European Economic Community, exerted an almost irresistible attraction. The Portuguese population looked at the experience of the EEC countries and wanted to share it. Salazarism was too old-fashioned, defensive, and insular.

The dismantling of the Franco regime was done differently, not by the army but by civilian politicians from within the system, aided and encouraged by King Juan Carlos. When Franco died in November 1975, the restoration of the monarchy which he had planned seemed a reversion to the past. But Juan Carlos, like so many Spaniards, had decided that a transition to democracy was essential for the country. Without it, it was impossible to join the EEC, which Spain had first applied to do in 1962. Moreover, more dramatically in Spain than in Portugal, society had changed almost beyond recognition since the early 1940s. A new wave of industrialization transformed the economy in the 1960s. Rising levels of education and purchasing power led to widespread aspirations for a different and more modern kind of life. The dictatorship seemed a hindrance to a society it had once controlled. At the same time, the Church had changed. In the later stages of the Franco regime many priests and bishops became advocates of civil rights and social justice, especially in relation to Spanish workers and regional movements. As early as June 1977, democratic elections were held, and in 1978 parliament approved a democratic, secular, and devolutionary constitution.

It would be foolish, of course, to argue that Franco's and Salazar's dictatorships were what Primo de Rivera's claimed to be—a parenthesis in the political life of the country. They determined the fate of millions. Their repressive measures blighted and destroyed lives, with particular ferocity in Spain. As counter-revolution, both were successful. By the time they were destroyed, many of their enemies had also been destroyed. But it is right to recognize that the reformist, democratizing movements of the first decades of the twentieth century re-emerged with greater, indeed unstoppable, support in the 1970s, in an international context that was incomparably more conducive to their success than had been the case in the inter-war years. In the long, long historical retrospect from the early twenty-first century, it seems clear that the democrats whose day had not come, the unsuccessful campaigners for human rights, and the artists and writers who paid a great price for claiming freedom of expression, all contributed much more than they could know at the time to the eventual emergence of self-government.

FURTHER READING

Portugal

Costa Pinto, Antonio (ed.), *Modern Portugal* (Palo Alto, Calif. 1998).
—— *Salazar's Dictatorship and European Fascism: Problems of Interpretation* (New York, 1995).
De Meneses, Felipe Ribeiro, 'The Origins and Nature of Authoritarian Rule in Portugal 1919–1945', *Contemporary European History*, 2 (2002), 153–63.
Gallagher, Tom, *Portugal: A Twentieth Century Interpretation* (Manchester, 1983).

Spain

Beevor, Anthony, *Battle for Spain: The Spanish Civil War 1936–1939* (London, 2006).
Ben Ami, Shlomo, *Fascism from Above: The Dictatorship of Primo de Rivera in Spain 1923–1930* (Oxford, 1985).
Blinkhorn, Martin, *Spain in Conflict 1931–1939* (London, 1986).
Esenwein, George, and Adrian Shubert, *Spain at War: The Spanish Civil War in Context 1931–1939* (London, 1995).
Gibson, Ian, *Federico García Lorca: A Life* (London, 1989).
Graham, Helen, and Jo Labanyi (eds.), *Spanish Cultural Studies: An Introduction* (Oxford, 1995).
Holguín, Sandie, *Creating Spaniards. Culture and National Identity in Republican Spain* (Madison, 2002).
Lannon, Frances, *The Spanish Civil War 1936–1939* (Oxford, 2002).
Meaker, Gerald, *The Revolutionary Left in Spain, 1914–1923* (Stanford, Calif., 1974).
Nash, Mary, *Defying Male Civilization: Women in the Spanish Civil War* (Denver, Colo., 1995).
Preston, Paul, *Franco: A Biography* (London, 1993).
Seidman, Michael, *Republic of Egos: A Social History of the Spanish Civil War* (Madison, 2002).

8

Italy

R. J. B. Bosworth

INTRODUCTION

It so happened that I saw a market day in Bolzano [a natively German-speaking city in the Süd Tirol or Alto Adige, annexed to Italy after 1918], to which hundreds of peasants had come from one of the remote fastnesses, the Val Sarentino. The men looked like people visiting this world for the first time. They were tall, awkward, but deliberate in movement, silent among themselves, and painfully shy in the town streets. They had matted flaxen hair which bunched out in straggles, like a wig, round the lean weather-creased napes of their necks. Pale blue eyes. Tiny cone-shaped felt hats rested on rather than fitted their heads; trousers made of a fustian-looking felt, which only reached down as far as their shins; small Tyrolese jackets with very short sleeves; and, instead of a waistcoat, a most extraordinary leather contraption consisting of, not a breastplate, but a bellyplate of thick leather, on which is lettered their name, village and their birthday! More leather gear—enough for a horse—over their chests and shoulders. Grey stockings and mountain boots. And, as if to give a last touch to this singular attire, every man wears a green apron, which conveys to the initiated a whole who's who and what's what concerning the wearer, according to the various ways in which it may be hung from the waist, folded over or rolled up.

So, in a book published in 1934, Ion Munro, a Scottish journalist, sympathetic to the Fascist dictatorship then controlling Italy, portrayed a moment of everyday life in that country. For a decade, Fascist authorities had proclaimed their intention to forge a totalitarian state and society. The image of the *fascio* (a bundle of rods bound about with rope and reinforced by an axe threatening punishment to any who did not comply) promised national unity. Fascism and the rule of the dictator, Benito Mussolini (1883–1945) were, it seemed, directed first and foremost at uniting and nationalizing the Italian masses. The dictatorship was needed to drive Italians, whether willing or not, to national modernization (and readiness for mass war). Yet here in Bolzano, not in the economically backward South of the country but on its relatively prosperous northern borders, were peasants, men (no women were present) who used a host of markers to express a local and a seemingly timeless or premodern identity rather than a national, ideological, or modern one.

To some extent, Munro may have been expressing that combination of romance and anxiety which has often characterized the response of citizens of an industrialized world towards the rural. Munro may have seen 'Italy' with British eyes. Nonetheless, his vignette raises deep questions about inter-war Italian history and its place in the story of Europe at large. Why was it that Italy was the country that first abandoned its officially liberal institutions and fell to some form of fascist dictatorship? What sort of dictatorship was it, whether in its theory or in its practice? Was its tyranny idiosyncratic or a model for those other dictatorships destined to spread across inter-war Europe from Portugal to Poland? When the Fascists pioneered 'totalitarianism' (the word passed from 1920s Italy into other countries), what was the effect on the everyday lives of its subjects? To what extent, at various moments after 1918 in Italy, were religion, the family, patron–client relations, the evident gap between city and countryside, class and gender difference, and a slew of other topics, matters to be understood as nationalized and/or fascistized? Or should each topic be allowed to stand on its own and be accorded its own historical comprehension and analysis?

Given the arrival of Fascism to power in October 1922, after the so-called 'March on Rome', half paramilitary coup, half cabinet crisis, it might seem that Italy was the prime locus of that interpretation which views the inter-war decades as 'locust years' and defines Europe bleakly as a 'dark continent'. Yet, maybe such phrases depend on the focus chosen. Mussolini's dictatorship was scarcely benign. Yet histories beyond the political continued to thread their way through Italian lives. They thus to some extent countered and diverted Fascist tyranny. Despite the encouragement given by Mussolinian totalitarianism to brutality and cynicism, Italians continued to negotiate their identities and behaviour across competing currents—national, international, and local. Simultaneously the victims of Fascism and its practitioners, they also never ceased to be Italians, *paesani* (villagers), and a part of humankind.

WAR AND DIPLOMACY

Italy had joined in the First World War in May 1915 and thereafter fought what was essentially its own conflict against mainly Austro-Hungarian armies. All but routed in the aftermath of the Battle of Caporetto in October 1917, Italian forces rallied and, on 4 November 1918, drove their Habsburg enemy to defeat and its empire to collapse. Thereafter patriotic commentators loved to remember that the victory of Vittorio Veneto had occurred a week before the German surrender on the Western Front.

Despite this seeming success of the Liberal system, Italy was soon cast into crisis, both at home and abroad. Self-publicizing poet Gabriele D'Annunzio took to talking about a 'mutilated victory' and the phrase stuck in political discourse as a summary of the discontents of 1919. Territorially the peace-making rewarded Italy with Trieste, Istria, parts of Dalmatia, and the Trentino-Alto Adige up to the Brenner watershed, plus some minor imperial gains. By 1945, all but Trieste and Trento had been lost by Fascism and, furthermore, France had made adjustments in its favour on its Alpine border with Italy, while all of the pre-1914 Liberal empire was now taken from Italian rule. During the peace-making in 1918–19 and, in many senses, also during the Fascist years, Italy continued to play the part of the 'least of the great powers', that role which it had occupied in international diplomacy since the Risorgimento. As Bismarck had put it abruptly, Italy had 'a large appetite and very poor teeth'. It was thus, frequently enough, a restless power but was rarely able to command the international scene. At Versailles, the 'sacred egoism' proclaimed as its war policy by conservative Foreign Minister, Sidney Sonnino, squared badly with Wilsonian rhetoric about the 'new diplomacy' and, in May–June 1919, Italy became something of the butt of proceedings, while the Liberal leadership remained anxiously unable to fuse their liberalism and their nationalism. In that last regard, since its formation in 1910, the Associazione Nazionalista Italiana (ANI, Italian Nationalist Association), although numerically small, had achieved a dominance over the thoughts about Italy's proper grandeur among many of the best and the brightest of the new generation, and its ambition and aggrieved sense that foreigners were unfair and disrespectful to Italy flowed easily into Fascism.

In the 1920s, the dictatorship mostly pursued policies not out of kilter with Italian traditions and, even in the next decade, its line did not dramatically break with the past. In his international dealings, Mussolini painted himself as an arch-realist, sardonic about the Kellogg–Briand peace pact (1928), for example, and the League of Nations, but nonetheless a signatory of the one and an active participant in the committees of the other. The invasion of Ethiopia in October 1935 was accompanied with violent Fascist fanfare, but Italy had attempted to seize the African empire also in the 1890s, and thereafter patriots had never ceased to dream of revenge. By the end of the 1930s, Italy was the Axis ally of Nazi Germany and, in June 1940, nine months late, it would join it in the Second World War. The explanation of this alliance was partly ideological and partly structural. In the special circumstances of a war which Germany in the summer of 1940 seemed to have won, it was natural for Italy to try to place itself on the winning side, hope for booty, and look to a continuation of schemes that might raise it some way up the hierarchy of great powers.

POPULATION AND POLICY

Any review of Italy's international posture between the wars needs to be set into the background of national history as a whole. There some facts should be established. When, in 1914, all the great powers except Italy entered the First World War, it was reckoned that there were thirty-five million Italians. Thirty years later, at the end of a Second World War which, since July 1943, had been partially fought out over Italian territory and which resulted in the overthrow of the Fascist regime, the total had grown to some forty-five million. This growth had occurred despite 650,000 deaths in combat in the First World War (in addition, 100,000 perished as POWs of the Germans and, especially, the Austrians) and the disabling (*mutilati* was the graphic Italian term) of a further 700,000. Unlike many other European states, Italy in losing 450,000 soldiers and civilians, killed in the Second World War, suffered less than in the First, although more than half of the deaths occurred in 1943–5, while the front passed across Italy and while Italians themselves engaged in a sort of civil war. The losses did not cease in April 1945 with the collapse of Fascist forces. Rather, over the next months, a further 12,000 died in revenge killings with ideological or personal impulse. Social murder of a different kind was never wholly eliminated from the South, despite Fascism's tough-sounding campaigns against the Mafia. After liberation in 1943, the murder rate in such regions rapidly resumed the high level that had led the criminologist, Cesare Lombroso, before 1914 one of the few Italian intellectuals with a global reputation, to aver that Northern and Southern Italians sprang from a different racial mix.

The earlier Fascist wars and colonial campaigns had been bloody, especially for Italy's enemies. Some 1,500 white soldiers died invading Ethiopia in 1935–6 (according to Ethiopian historians, Fascist forces in combat and when governing from 1936 to 1941 caused up to half a million Ethiopian deaths). Italy's colonial armies killed 100,000 Arabs as they pacified Libya in brutal campaigns at the end of the 1920s and the beginning of the 1930s. In all, after Italy seized the territory in 1911–12, the native population of Libya fell from an estimated 1.4 million to 850,000 in 1933. When Italian generals talked about imposing a 'Roman peace' on what they labelled the barbarous native inhabitants of Libya, they were not joking. Then and thereafter, some ambiguity was provoked in the racial purpose of Italian imperialism from the national tradition of utilizing natives from established colonies in the armed forces. In 1936, Giorgio De Vecchi, the son of Cesare Maria De Vecchi, a First World War hero and one of the chiefs of the March on Rome, hailed these soldiers as 'black *arditi*' (crack forces celebrated for their alleged heroism 1915–18). Although some of his phrases were predictably patronizing, Giorgio De Vecchi was nonetheless expressing 'Africanist' sentiments of a sort that squared uneasily with the more 'scientific' and fundamentalist racism of Nazi Germany, by then emerging as Italy's grand, frightening, and menacing ally.

In 1941, with the swift collapse of the new Fascist empire, only fifty-six Italian colonists were murdered by the victorious Ethiopians, testimony to the Africans' humanity and to the rapidity of their rout of Fascist forces but also proof that Italian imperialism shared more with that of Western European countries than it did with the exterminationist and ideologically driven imperialism of Nazism. To be sure, Fascism did not merely thrust into Africa. Some 4,000 Fascist so-called volunteers (where the volunteering had often been notional) died fighting in the Spanish Civil War and 12,000 were wounded (according to official figures), while hundreds of Anti-Fascists perished on the Republican side of the conflict. Mussolini had typically ordered that any Italian Anti-Fascists taken prisoner should be shot out of hand (although, equally typically, he did not follow the matter up and expressed shock at the bloodiness of Spain when it was described to him by a rumbustious Fascist boss, Roberto Farinacci, who had travelled there).

To this lamentable tally of the effect of Fascist rule, there should be added the 3,000 killed in the political and social disturbances occasioned by the rise of Fascism from 1920 to 1924. The initial coalition government, formed under Mussolini's leadership in October 1922, had not seen the end of political killing. Rather, the Fascist murder of moderate socialist, Giacomo Matteotti, on 10 June 1924, proved that violence was an inescapable element of the Fascist mix. When, prompted by party radicals, on 3 January 1925, Mussolini opted for open dictatorship, he symbolically took responsibility for, and so endorsed, all the mayhem his movement had fostered since its foundation in March 1919. Then and thereafter, through its various aggressive wars and as a result of its other retrograde social policies, the dictatorship bears responsibility for at least a million premature deaths.

No doubt quite a few of the casualties of Fascism might be as well understood as victims of the Italian version of European imperialism. Yet the empire, confined as it was to Libya, East Africa, and the occupied Greek Dodecanese islands, scarcely attracted Italians as settlers. By 1941, only 3,200 Italian farming colonists survived in Ethiopia, while, in Libya, the trumpeted immigrations of '*Ventimila*' in 1938 and 1939 (in practice, more like 10,000) had scarcely been settled with any permanence when war broke out in 1940, soon turning the territory into a battlefield. Most commentators have dismissed the impact on metropolitan Italian lives of this *imperialismo straccione* (empire of rags and patches). As an unforeseen result, after 1945 decolonization was a less significant problem for Italy than it was for the other major European states, although the current re-emergence of racism, vented mostly against 'Third World' immigrants, is a reminder that Italy's imperial story is another chapter of national history which could do with a more critical telling to the national populace.

Although the modern empire scarcely replicated that of classical Rome, to the overall tally of Italians might be added tens of millions living in an informal imperium created by a massive emigration to France, Belgium, and other Northern European states, to the Americas and to the rest of the world. The only question in this regard is whether the peoples who migrated there should be counted as belonging to Italy or to 'the Italies'. The emigrants were, in other words, often men and women whose identities sprang from local and familial loyalties more surely than they did from national ones. Confronted by a divided great world in the Second World War, Italian-Americans, for all their flirtation with Mussolini's charisma before 1940, in overwhelming majority backed their new country and its armies, rejecting any idea that they should take up the Fascist cause of their original homeland.

HEALTH AND TECHNOLOGY

The physical well-being of Italians remained precarious throughout the inter-war period. Despite Fascist chatter about launching a welfare state, Italy retained a lowly rank on international indices about health. In 1914, 138 children per 1,000 perished before their first birthdays and, although the establishment of the Fascist Opera Nazionale per la Protezione della Maternità e dell'Infanzia (ONMI), in 1927, allowed some improvement to trickle down to the poorest classes, infant mortality remained high relative to the surrounding countries and was especially bad in such poverty-stricken provinces as Calabria, the Basilicata, and Abruzzi. Even in 1939, overall infant mortality was still above 100 per thousand births. Contrary to myth, Italians were not an especially prolific people, with a birth rate in 1913 of 21.7 per thousand. Despite noisy Fascist pronouncements that the dictatorship was engaged in a 'battle of the births', the number of live births fell steadily, although the population rose given the spread of some modern health practices (especially in regard to childbirth and infant illness). The death rate declined from 17.2 per thousand in 1926 to 13.6 in 1940. The median age of death of all Italians rose from an appalling 5.56 in the decade after 1861 (when almost half the deceased did not reach the age of 5) to 28.44 in 1911–20; 43.81 (1921–30) and 56.36 (1931–40). If children below 5 are eliminated from this statistic, the improvement went from 49.19 in 1861–70 to 67.14 in 1931–40, and then fell to 64.84 (1941–50).

In its favouring of improved health for the nation or 'race', the dictatorship gave much media space to the military and patriotic virtues of sport, arguing that athletic endeavour would hone Italians into trimly healthy soldiers. Football and Fascism went well together. Italy won the World Cups of 1934 (in Rome) and 1938 (in Paris) and, from the 1920s, ambitious *ras* spared no expense in erecting new stadia in such provincial capitals as Bologna and Florence. The various party scouting organizations (Balilla, Piccole italiane, and the rest) similarly fostered sport at a more popular level, certainly for boys and, with doubts and hesitations lest their reproductive potential be curtailed, also for girls. Yet, in many ways, the majority of Italians in 1945 were not yet wedded to the sporting life and indeed had never contemplated play on a sports field or beach. Achille Starace, the Fascist Party Secretary 1931–9, may have taken pains to display his rippling musculature while dressed in shorts and jumping through a fiery hoop, and Mussolini may have enjoyed entertaining admiring pressmen while engaged in a (carefully programmed) tennis match with the national champions, but quite a few of their compatriots could not imagine owning sporting gear. Most Italians exhausted their physical strength in work not play.

In very many ways, in 1914 Italy was, and in 1945 remained, a poor country. Every year malaria, pellagra, and simple starvation sent Italians early to their graves. Abortion, the favoured birth control of the poor, was a common solution to the dilemma of an extra mouth to feed and, although the regime condemned the practice, Fascist repression remained uneasy, worried by popular hostility towards the removal of a needed demographic safeguard. Peasant and working-class Italians regularly spoke as though they were unsure where the next meal was coming from and, for example, in the late 1930s a lingering discontent with the prospect of battle against Britain and France owed much to the popular assumption that the states beyond the Alps were wealthy countries by comparison with their own. With the war after 1940 and the drastic failure of the regime's feeble attempts to institute a socially fair rationing system, poor Italians had to subsist on a calorie intake similar to that offered by the Nazis to their subjects in occupied Poland. Mod cons of any type did not reach most Italian homes until the 1950s and 1960s, decades of the so-called 'economic miracle'. In 1919, there was one telephone for every 392 Italians, as against one for every 12 Americans and 45 Germans. Twenty years later, phones were still a luxury item—127,333 subscribers in 1925 rose hesitantly to 566,768 in 1940. The Fascist secret police happily took over from Liberal Italy the habit of tapping the phones of political opponents, loosely defined, given that many Fascists and even Mussolini had their calls recorded (among those thus given historical record were the dictator's dismally banal conversations with his young last mistress, Claretta Petacci).

Despite the regime's fondness for the spoken word, even radios penetrated Italy slowly and partially. In 1926, a meagre 27,000 receivers could be found in Italian households and the number was still only one million in 1939. Put another way, 0.43 per cent of the population took out subscriptions to the national radio service in 1930, 1.28 per cent in 1935, and 4.10 per cent in 1942. It was true that some radio listening was collective: 2,685 elementary schools were said to have receivers in 1934 and 18,780 in 1939. But, often, listening in such places must have resembled the scene in a Southern *paese* memorably recounted by the Anti-Fascist political prisoner, Carlo Levi, where forcibly assembled peasants only heard from the crackling loudspeaker on the village square an incomprehensible chant of *CEDUCEDUCEDU* (actually *Duce! Duce! Duce!*). Since many peasants clung stubbornly to dialects that could be largely incomprehensible from one agro-town to the next, rich and poor, urban and rural Italians frequently spoke different languages when they sought to portray the world and themselves.

EDUCATION AND CULTURE

In further reflection of its disunity and its technological backwardness, Italy remained a partially literate society, with a telling example of the weakness of Fascist totalitarianism compared, for example, with the communist kind being displayed in the Soviets rapidly teaching their populace to read whereas, in Italy in 1930, 30 per cent of the population were still registered as illiterate. This figure rose to 60 per cent and above in the South, while women were always less likely to have been instructed about reading and writing than were men. Quite a bit of Italy's feeble military performance after 1940 can be explained by the inadequate education of the troops. If for different reasons, neither officers nor men were primed for the demands of mobile and technologized warfare.

Schooling beyond the elementary level remained territory largely confined to middle-class boys and girls, with the latter composing about a fifth of a typical *liceo* (high school class). At university, in 1931 it was estimated that only 3 per cent of students sprang from the working class (down from 5 per cent in 1911). Fascist chiefs, led by Giuseppe Bottai, regularly minister of this or that, editor of such key party journals as *Critica Fascista* and *Il Primato*, and always an aspirant intellectual, talked glibly about a cultural revolution and were generous in subsidizing approved publications, art exhibitions, museum displays, and theatrical events. Primed by the patronage of Bottai and other party chiefs, many young men and women after 1945 destined for major intellectual careers, whether out of ideology or self-interest happily called themselves Fascists. In 1935, cultured Italy was in great part Fascist, although just what the conversion to this ideology really entailed must remain a matter of debate. Then the young and talented were anxious to join the dictator in 'going to the people' and so rendering their culture more 'real' or populist (and increasing their sales and status). The

Figure 8.1. A school for Jewish children in Italian Libya (1937).

actual penetration of the poor by the touted ideas of the moment remained problematical, however. Fascism boasted that allegiance to the nation had swept aside class distinction but, in fact, the cultural gap between the bourgeoisie and the working class and peasantry (as well as that between men and women) was huge, obvious, and acknowledged by all. The comment by a clear-eyed townsman of Messina in 1908 that, here 'we automatically address any member of the bourgeoisie as "Professor"' had not lost its meaning and relevance in 1945.

Of the various cultural forms, film was the arena where Italians won most acclaim, at least in Europe, and certainly men and women flocked to the cinemas. In 1938, 343 million cinema tickets were sold in Italy; 469 million in 1942. A national cinema, if one with a raffish aristocratic and international cast, had begun to flourish before 1914. With the 1920s came some financial difficulties; 220 films were produced in 1920, nine in 1930. But the Fascist regime was generous in its sponsorship of an art form which Mussolini had labelled quintessentially modern and which Bottai had advised should be allowed its independence. Too much overt propaganda, he counselled, would drive audiences out of cinemas. Even Pope Pius XI acknowledged that film was a crucial educative device, although the Church advocated censorship, especially of any hint of lubricity, more eagerly than did the dictatorship. In the 1930s cinema revived. By the end of the decade, the industry could rely on the patronage of Mussolini's eldest son, the laddish Vittorio (born 1916). Cinecittà, a modern production centre on the outskirts of Rome, opened in 1937 with rich government subsidy. Quite a number of avant-garde Fascist films were made there and elsewhere. *Squadrone Bianca*, directed by Augusto Genina (1936), and set in Italian Libya, for example, contains some marvellous visual effects in its portrayal of heroic desert war and its moral tone owes at least as much to orthodox European imperialism as it does to a cultural revolution. Continuities were evident. Roberto Rossellini, a young Roman man about town, made a trilogy for the Fascist (and Catholic) war in 1941–3 (*La nave bianca, Il pilota ritorna,* and *L'uomo della croce*) before producing the Anti-Fascist and 'neo-realist' classics, *Roma: Città aperta, Paisà,* and *Germania: Anno zero* (1944–8).

Other ambiguities can be noticed. The most popular films were less those with themes of battle than 'white telephone' romances, such as *Una romantica avventura* and *Rose scarlette* (both 1940) in which a blonde draped herself alluringly over that luxury item, the phone. Moreover, in the years leading up to war in 1940, the Italian industry was under severe commercial (and, more implicitly, ideological) challenge from Hollywood. In 1938 almost three-quarters of tickets were sold for American films. Such dismal failure to compete encouraged protective measures, ones fitting the general economic line of 'autarchia' or self-reliance adopted by late Fascism. Nonetheless, adolescents continued to dream of the US as the paradise of sex and modernity, and their hopes were only partially channelled back towards Fascism by the common claim of regime propagandists, at least until the outbreak of the war, that F. D. Roosevelt was some sort of Fascist and that his 'New Deal' owed a great debt to Italian economics.

MONARCHY

Constitutionally, Italy had entered the First World War as a liberal monarchy. The King was Victor Emmanuel III. He had come to the throne in disturbed circumstances in 1900 after his father, Umberto I, was assassinated at Monza by an anarchist returned from a stint as an emigrant at Patterson, New Jersey. Victor Emmanuel remained king until 1946, when a belated abdication installed his sleek but vacuous son, Umberto II, briefly on the throne. Shortly afterwards, on 2 June, a closely contested referendum turned post-Fascist Italy into a Republic. Victor Emmanuel was not a natural celebrity and, for the most part, did not directly interfere in politics in the way that Alfonso XIII of Spain, Edward VIII in England (especially when Prince of Wales), or King Carol of Romania did. Mostly Victor Emmanuel confined himself to misanthropic and anti-clerical aphorisms. Women, he thought, should concentrate on knitting socks and being taken to bed; priests, he warned, 'in their long gowns have long arms'. Victor Emmanuel's hobbies were such private ones as photography and coin-collecting. He let it be known that he never left his palace without his Kodak. By 1942, he possessed more than 100,000 coins and had an international reputation as a numismatician. He did, however, remain true to his class in not forgoing hunting. During the 1930s, it was a sign of a new austerity when his expected daily bag fell from 350 to 200.

Victor Emmanuel may have been more moderate than some royals but he was scarcely a democrat. Not for nothing did the army officer corps between the wars remain more loyal to the monarchy than to the regime. Although his diminutive size made some aspects of military life troubling, Victor Emmanuel always strove to embody a *re soldato* (soldier king). The civilian sphere was of lesser significance in his eyes than that connected to the barracks. Before 1922 Victor Emmanuel viewed parliament as an unseemly battleground between 'wolves and rabbits' and he cohabited cheerfully with the dictatorship once it was installed. It was to be expected that, from time to time, his natural malice would cast doubt on some flight of Mussolinian grandiloquence, just as the dictator regularly mused sullenly about abolishing the monarchy. There were few signs of action in that regard until July 1943 when Victor Emmanuel sacked the *Duce*. Once the Fascist chief was reinstalled by German arms in northern Italy in September, Mussolini finally ousted the monarchy, calling his puppet regime a 'Social Republic' (the Repubblica Sociale Italiana, or RSI).

Before that testing time, Victor Emmanuel retained a sort of reserve charisma, secondary to the dictator, but always there and frequently hailed in the regime's publicity. To quite a degree, Fascist Italy was a dyarchy where children and crowds on public occasions successively sang a national anthem (the Royal March) and a Fascist party one invoking Mussolini (*Giovinezza*) and where, in offices and school-buildings, the wall was adorned with photos of both the King and the dictator. Victor Emmanuel as soldier king always gave the military salute (even to greet Adolf Hitler) and ostentatiously avoided the stretched arm 'Roman salute' of Fascism. No wonder, when the *Führer,* on an official visit to Rome in 1938, had to stay at the Quirinale, or royal palace, he remembered the event as constituting the unhappiest days of his life.

CHURCH

Sometimes a third man joined the King and the dictator in official glorification. Italy was, after all, the home of the Catholic Church and of the three Popes of the inter-war period, Benedict XV (1914–22), Pius XI (1922–39), and Pius XII (1939–58). No history of Italy can omit an account of the charisma, ideas, and policy of the Vatican and of the less 'disciplinized' religiosity of ordinary Italians. Benedict XV had a difficult papacy coinciding with a First World War in which Catholics fought on both sides. It was natural for him to seek compromise peace—in 1917 he sorrowfully defined the endless battles as 'useless slaughter'. The Church, however, scarcely carried sufficient political weight to stem the conflict and Benedict XV was left with a reputation in Nationalist circles as a traitor to the nation. Mussolini, ardent advocate of war, damned him as 'Pope Pilate XV'. Benedict's Church was also troubled financially, and it was little surprise that his successor did not style himself Benedict XVI.

The tough—Fascist journals hailed the 'sublimity' of his sporting prowess as a mountain-climber and fencer—authoritarian and ambitious Pius XI was luckier in his historic moment. It was under his rule that, on 11 February 1929, he and the *Duce* signed the celebrated Lateran Pacts. This agreement resolved the 'Roman question' that had dogged Church–State relations since the Risorgimento. Now the Vatican city-state came into existence and the Church earned generous monetary compensation for the territory it had lost in 1870. Pius XI was soon spending the cash in massive building works, notably in Rome, aiming to express an 'imperial papacy' that yielded little in its public profile to the Fascist dictatorship. Pius even stated in early 1932 that his Church was as happy to be as 'totalitarian' in its sphere as the Fascist regime was in the lay world. More informally, the Lateran deal restored Church authority in the fields of early childhood education and adult social behaviour. The Church, as much as the Fascists, favoured a patriarchal view of gender relations and opposed abortion, divorce, and any modernizing talk about female equality. It was the Church, in its preparation of its priests, which demanded that trainee clerics be rigorously separated from their families. Fascism, by contrast, was much more hesitant about intruding into the realm of the hearth and home, and almost all its cadres, including the dictator, retained familial identities to which any more modern and 'political' ideology had to adapt. In general, rather than Fascism ruthlessly hammering its totalitarian ideas into the Catholic sections of national life, the two forces worked together with aplomb. John Pollard, a historian of Vatican finances, has concluded that, from 1929 to 1943, 'Italy was . . . under a kind of joint Catholic–Fascist hegemony in all spheres, political, cultural, social and economic'.

As the 1930s wore on, however, cracks began to appear in the relationship between the political and religious arenas, especially given that Pius XI had never yielded in his view that 'the education of the child belongs to the Church and not to the State'. The fissure deepened when Mussolini began to move into a closer Axis with Nazi Germany. Despite persistent suggestions among some commentators that Eugenio Pacelli, from 1939 Pius XII, was a 'Nazi Pope', in fact both this pontiff and his predecessor deeply mistrusted Nazism as an atheist enemy of Catholicism (if, doubtless, a lesser evil than was the Bolshevik regime in the Soviet Union). Reflecting these doubts about the Italian regime's drift in international relations, from 1935–6 the Church began to adjust its investments away from Fascist Italy. Pacelli, while still Papal Secretary of State, visited the USA in October 1936, and the Church readied itself to cope with a post-Fascist Italy. Cannily, Alcide De Gasperi, an Anti-Fascist Catholic politician who had served both in the Austrian parliament before 1914 and the Italian one leading up to the imposition of dictatorship, had been kept primed for political resuscitation, while employed in the Vatican library. De Gasperi lived in a flat across the river in central Rome and walked to work each day, invulnerable to the Fascist police given his priestly protection. During the 1930s the Church continued to train a new generation of Catholic leadership, including later prime ministers, Amintore Fanfani and Aldo Moro, with a clerical Fascism that could drop the Fascism if need be and transmute into Christian Democracy. Alcide De Gasperi was to be prime minister eight times between 1946 and 1953.

Although the Church of Pius XI and Pius XII (the latter's enthusiasm for an imperial image was, if anything, even greater than his predecessor's) was committed to 'Romanization', that is, an ever tighter centralization of religious administration, and demanded that non-Italians accept the fact, within Italy one episcopal see and one parish could still differ from the next. The scholarship sorely needs a thorough modern social history of Italian Catholicism but it is known that members of the hierarchy varied in the extent of their Fascist enthusiasm. At one extreme, the cardinal archbishop of Bologna greeted war entry in 1940 as divine proof of Italy's providential mission, while other prelates were less ready to place the nation's cause above their dedication to humankind. The papal newspaper, *L'Osservatore Romano*, throughout the war offered its readers news about the conflict not identical with that purveyed in the Fascist party press.

Out in society, the meaning of religion was complex. Some intellectuals talked of being purist integralists and crusaders for the Catholic cause—in the Spanish

Civil War (1936–9), for example. However, especially in the South, more ordinary Italians preserved a religiosity of the kind that anthropologists codify as based on 'saints and fireworks'. In the Gargano, Padre Pio was beginning a career in saintliness and publicity that would give him a huge following after 1945 and encourage the arch-populist John Paul II (1978–2005) to sanctify him. In a more humdrum sense, ordinary Italian men and women continued to regard the Church in general and their local priest in particular as a potential fount of generosity and an ultimate safeguard and sanctuary in times of trouble. Accounts of the Salò Republic, for example, regularly indicate that villagers then looked to the Church for protection and hope. Throughout the dictatorship, perhaps the best index of the survival of popular religion in Italy is provided in the role given to the *festa* of each village saint. Although the regime had Fascist festivals, the State had monarchical and military ones, and the Church cultivated its ceremonies at Christmas, Easter, and on the special days of the Virgin or leading saints, nonetheless, for many Italians the most sincere expression of their collectivity occurred when the local saint had his or her one day of the year. Similarly, Italians who lived outside Italy were much more likely to rally spontaneously in memory of their village saint than in the commanded but tinsel celebrations of the Italian nation-state or of the ideology of its dictatorship.

LIBERAL INSTITUTIONS, BELIEFS, AND PRACTICE

In 1914 Italy was a realm where power seemed centred in the parliament, itself a two-house body composed of a Chamber of Deputies and a Senate. Among careless writers, it is still possible to find this regime called democratic. Liberal (of a certain kind) it may have been; democratic, if the term is meant to embrace any sort of social equality, it certainly was not. It was only in 1912 that Italy had moved towards something approaching universal manhood suffrage (Italian women were denied the vote until 1945). Although there were hesitant signs of the organizing of modern political parties, with the Socialists being the plainest example, the great majority of parliamentarians, when the First World War approached, were still elected through local deals and dealing. Belief was subordinated to the practical. Patron–client networks mattered more than did ideological commitment. Sociological analysis has demonstrated that, whatever their formal allegiance, the majority of deputies were lawyers (52 per cent in 1913) or were otherwise sprung from the humanist middle classes. Businessmen and workers rarely took up seats and, both in 1913 and 1919, the elections failed to return a single peasant, then still the most numerous group of Italians. Senators were older and even more likely to belong to the Risorgimento establishment, frequently being retired military men, ex-diplomats or officials, and politicians whose careers had taken a turn for the worse. Change in this regard was not rapid under Fascism. Very many leading Fascists, despite their automatic condoning of Fascist murder, were lawyers, the most notorious and best rewarded of whom was Roberto Farinacci, the *ras* or boss of Cremona. This rough and tough party radical had shamelessly plagiarized the thesis which won him his law degree and the rich remuneration that followed. Mussolini, knowing something about the ancient technique of divide and rule among his immediate juniors, carefully preserved a copy of Farinacci's thesis and the copied original in his office desk, with an attached bureaucratic note that plagiarism of that kind was ordinarily punished with six months in gaol.

It is true that, by 1939, when the lower house had been renamed the Chamber of Fasces and Corporations, its members were not as likely as they had been a generation earlier to be practising lawyers. They were instead often employed as technocrats of some kind, risen in the luxuriant bureaucracy of the Partito Nazionale Fascista (PNF, National Fascist Party) and its numerous linked 'para-state' bodies. Yet very many still held degrees in jurisprudence. Moreover, even in its courses in engineering and medicine, a lot of Italian training gave greater place to the verbal than was the norm in Northern European societies. Such educational practice and vocabulary left Fascism perennially coloured by humanist words and ideals in a fashion that differed from the Nazi German equivalent, even though such seeming values, perhaps always freighted with self-interest, could readily be twisted into an authoritarian and murderous 'humanism'.

After all, until 1922 the most characteristic expression of the Italian version of liberalism was not a zealous devotion to Adam Smith, free trade, industrialization, banking, and the business life but rather membership of the Freemasons, a qualification that was all but essential for members of the pre-Fascist parliament of whatever stripe. However arcane were some of its ceremonies, Masonry was scarcely a sinister conspiracy as its clerical and later Fascist enemies were to claim. Rather, its adherents pledged to accept a rational understanding of life, a hope in science and progress, and a practical willingness to work fruitfully with each other as patrons and clients long had been accustomed to do. For Masonic parliamentarians and the doctors, accountants, teachers, and public officials who could be found in the best cafés and restaurants of each beautiful but somewhat old-fashioned provincial capital across the peninsula, their good sense and civilization were what made Italy liberal and modern. Simultaneously, this 'culture' and its forms were what separated town-dwellers from the uncultivated and even dangerous world outside the city's ancient walls. There resided the imponderable peasantry. The late nineteenth-century nationalist prime minister, Francesco Crispi, himself a Sicilian lawyer by origin, expressed the all but automatic view that such people were, for the present and foreseeable future, barbarous. Even in the gentler and kinder days of the *belle époque*, most of the ruling elite believed that now was the time for all good men to come to the aid of the humanist bourgeoisie. Simultaneously, a deep pessimism about the masses limited the liberalism of most of those involved in politics and provided a key unspoken assumption in explaining the rise of Fascism.

The prime ministers in the Liberal system varied in their power, given that governments rose and fell with an average life of under a year. Nonetheless, Giovanni Giolitti, five times holder of that office at periods in 1892–3, 1903–14, and 1920–1, like Agostino Depretis and Crispi in the 1880s and 1890s, was charged by some with being a parliamentary dictator. All three used their authority freely, while always being aware of the requirement to hold a coalition together. When Italy invaded Libya and annexed the ex-Ottoman territory in 1911–12, Giolitti found few impediments to his decision-making and acted with clarity, efficiency, and ruthlessness. To the wider public, Giolitti and the other political chiefs were nonetheless distant figures. Little spin sold their charisma to the masses. Although Italy had a flourishing press before 1914, its paper with the greatest prestige, Milan's *Il Corriere della Sera*, sold only 350,000 copies, a significant tally but far fewer than the populist sheets already commanding the market in Britain, the USA, and France. Moreover, with the partial exception of the Socialists' *Avanti!*, Italy lacked a national paper and Italians in the know reinforced their world view with local papers and local news. Fascism, by contrast, awarded a major propaganda role to Mussolini's own *Il Popolo d'Italia*, founded with the help of Italian and French secret service money in November 1914 to advocate war entry. This daily was edited after 1922 from Milan by the younger Mussolini brother, Arnaldo, until his death in 1931, as a national paper, the organ of a regime which was anxiously exercising a steadily more obsessive control over the press. Yet, even under the dictatorship, most literate Italians for preference still first scanned the local newssheet and used its information to dream of local and not national, let alone global and ideological, advantage.

FASCIST AND MUSSOLINIAN DICTATORSHIP

Was there much difference between Mussolini and his Liberal predecessors as executives? Technically the answer to this question is yes. What, it might be thought, is the point of being dictator unless you dictate? Moreover, the ideology of Fascism at its base endorsed the idea of the Great Individual dominating his fellows, while party propaganda imposed onto Italians an image of their *Duce* (by the 1930s almost always their *DUCE*) as a living God. Fascism understood human society to be arranged hierarchically, with movement up the ranks being possible if a man was sufficiently tough and dedicated but where, ordinarily, the social order held and where all was pinned together by the immanent, infallible, omniscient, and ubiquitous dictator (he even penetrated Italian dreams).

One of the pervasive and, in retrospect, most absurd slogans of the regime (except that the Pope, since the Vatican's defeat in the Risorgimento, had already claimed infallibility) was *Mussolini ha sempre ragione* (Mussolini is always right). The florid personality cult around the dictator has left most historians assuming that Mussolini did indeed exercise total power. Certainly the queries prompted

Figure 8.2. An Arab admirer of Mussolini.

by the suggestion that Hitler, and even Stalin, may have been a 'weak dictator' have rarely been raised about Mussolini. Yet a careful examination of his character and habits does suggest that the *Duce* was, on most occasions, as ready to follow 'opinion' (somehow defined) as to lead it. The key may have lain in Mussolini's practice as an executive. Some of his time was expended in tours around Italy, during which he typically made propaganda speeches in numerous small centres as well as more wide-ranging pronouncements in Rome, Milan, Genoa, and the other major cities. Here he was dictator as speechifier, an activity which, to some extent, foreshadowed that of our contemporary politicians looking for 'grabs' for TV, more travelling salespeople than thinkers.

When he sat at his office desk (and he never ceased to be an assiduous reader of files), Mussolini occupied his mornings and sometimes his afternoons, too, in a stream of interviews. On these occasions, pioneering the role today occupied by the radio talkshow host, the *Duce* was thus required to display a seeming mastery of a huge variety of subjects while also possessing the verbal dexterity to leave most of his interlocutors content with their meeting and convinced that the dictator had placed himself on their side. The atmosphere of each meeting was given a 'modern' and Fascist purpose by a clock which stood ominously ticking on the leader's desk, ideally signalling that time was running out for this plan and conversation as was appropriate and necessary in the febrile modern world. It is thus no surprise to find Mussolini swiftly acquiring a reputation among his more knowing colleagues as a chief who, on many occasions, adroitly said what his listeners wanted to hear. Whether, through such interchanges, a decision was being made was a matter to be resolved by subsequent events, by the functioning of party and state bureaucracy and by the stamina and contacts, beyond the dictator's office, of the person fortunate enough to have talked with Mussolini. Ian Kershaw has argued that many Germans, after 1933, worked towards their *Führer*. In Fascist Italy, the more common situation was that Mussolini worked towards those Italians who counted. The Lateran Pacts, for example, saw the *Duce* directly involved in the detail of negotiation, wheeling and dealing to the early hours of the morning. Nonetheless, the move towards an agreement had begun in 1919 and the actual terms were more a triumph for the Church than for the dictator, let alone for the idea that he was revolutionizing his country through a cultural turn that would render Catholicism obsolete.

No doubt there were occasions when Mussolini did enforce his will on the nation. The decision to opt for a high value to the lira, the national currency, in 1926–7 and the determination to invade and conquer Ethiopia in 1935–6 were examples. Yet, frequently, Mussolini was more the politician as tactician than the grand strategist or fanatical ideologue. Much about his dictatorship is exemplified by an examination of its police force, headed from 1926 to his death in 1940 by Arturo Bocchini, a career official who used, with jovial sexism, to say that he was only a Fascist from the waist up. Bocchini saw Mussolini almost every day—for all his apparent power and celestial charisma, the *Duce* was perpetually and even neurotically alert to the possibility that Anti-Fascism might lurk still in Italian minds. Although the secret police were not numerous, Bocchini's men were efficient and patrolled the after all not huge number of Italians with modern political ideas ruthlessly and effectively, being especially adroit in utilizing such ancient weapons of discipline as corruption, blackmail, and exploitation of the (yawning) divisions among its opponents. By the mid-1930s, there were few glimmerings of public or organized Anti-Fascism within Italy. Outside the country and notably in Paris or in Moscow, where Stalin watched ruthlessly over the fate of Italian communists, a handful of, often squabbling, opponents of the regime survived and the Spanish Civil War provided occasion for them to rally. But their influence on Mussolini's subjects remained thin to non-existent.

The irrelevance of Anti-Fascism does not necessarily prove that Fascism had fully occupied the hearts and minds of all Italians. The contrast between Bocchini's policing and that of Himmler, presiding over the cancer-like 'SS-state' in Nazi Germany, is striking. Himmler aimed at a Third Reich that was still more surely ideologized, fanatical, and 'fundamentalist' than that presently controlled by the *Führer*. Bocchini, a Scarpia come to life, aimed instead at an Italy that was tranquil and depoliticized. His authoritarianism, which owed quite a bit to the principles that had been pursued in this regard in the Liberal regime where he had been trained, happily watched over Fascists as well as communists. Himmler wanted the Germans to think in only one way; the Fascist secret police preferred that Italians did not think at all.

Equally emblematic of the regime was its key political punishment system of *confino* or relegation to a mountain or island commune, usually in the South. The implication of such penalty was that, contrary to noisy rhetoric about a seamlessly united modern nation mustered to serve its *Duce*, Italy was in fact a country where levels of 'civilization' and comfort varied starkly from one place to another. Prisoners themselves regularly expressed this view, one fallen Fascist eloquently complaining that his place of confinement in the South lacked any human being with whom a man of his cultural level could converse, while a communist woman was appalled by the sight in her *paese* of confinement of a teenage girl gunning down her seducer in the streets as though such an act was still the natural form of justice.

Some 14,000 Italians fell victim to internal exile, among them such celebrated political and intellectual chiefs as communist Antonio Gramsci, socialist Sandro Pertini, the liberal democrats, Fausto Nitti and Emilio Lussu, and a number of dissident priests. Nitti and Lussu dramatically escaped but Gramsci and Pertini had their five-year terms automatically rolled over until they were released, the first by death and the second by the fall of Fascism. The typical *confinato*, however, was a more everyday figure who had been picked up for whingeing about national foreign policy, berating Mussolini, or singing the *Red Flag*. Some women were arrested after exasperatedly wishing cancer on their leaders, while at least one dreamt publicly of emasculating her *Duce*. These 'Anti-Fascists', loosely defined, were rarely forced to serve out their full terms since the regime continued to have many excuses (an imperial triumph, a royal birth, a religious festival) to offer amnesty to those of its prisoners ready to apologize and able to engage friends and patrons to plead their cause. Italy was studded with prison-sites of one kind or another but they did not really function in the same way as the camp system of Nazi Germany or even the *gulag* (if Soviet gaols were also characterized by many unspoken assumptions).

RESISTANCE AND ANTI-FASCISM

Despite Fascist repression, the other great ideologies of the twentieth century eddied somewhere beneath the surface of Fascist totalitarianism. Most persistent in a disciplined opposition to the dictatorship were followers of the Italian Communist Party, founded in January 1921. Despite occasional moments of flirtation with the idea of rapprochement with the regime, the communists never ceased to watch for their own scientifically determined victory (there were also Fascists who, in the mid-1930s, wondered whether Stalin was leading the Soviet Union to a Russian form of fascism). Certainly in retrospect, the key member of the PCd'I was Antonio Gramsci, the party leader, historian, and philosopher, who spent the last ten years before his death in 1937 in Fascist gaols. There Gramsci, despite great suffering from the harshness of his imprisonment and from the debilitating effects of Pott's disease, was able to pen his *Prison Notebooks*, which, carefully marketed by Palmiro Togliatti, Gramsci's successor as head of the party, offered worthy proof that Italian Communism had avoided the worst crudities of Stalinism and retained a loyalty to humanist traditions. Gramsci, it was said after his death, had mapped an 'Italian road to communism' and it was true that local communism rejoiced in a history of its own, forged in its opposition to dictatorship. The experience of being the prime target of Fascist policing and, especially in the latter stages of the war from 1943 to 1945, the active participation in a fighting resistance while allied with liberals, Catholics, and other anti-Fascists did give what was reorganized as the PCI a distinctive face and a cherished memory of its own history.

Fascism had certainly done its best to eliminate communist ideas from Italian society but it never quite achieved its purpose, partly because its own line on equality and the possession of property was vague and contradictory. It talked often of being revolution of the masses and, in 1943–5, under the RSI refurbished the slogans of its first years about a commitment to the 'socialization' of the economy. Similarly, regime foreign policy, even if it did debouch into Operation Barbarossa in 1941, was not fanatically anti-communist and it is scarcely surprising to find Mussolini, already in 1942 and on a number of occasions after that, baffled by Hitler's lack of responsiveness to the idea of a compromise peace in the east (the better to fight the present 'plutocratic' and liberal enemies of Italy in the Mediterranean).

At home, Fascist economic policy was similarly mutable. Mussolini sometimes talked as though he wanted to privilege rural life but he was equally ready to celebrate industrialization and to appease his nation's bankers and businesspersons. Whether by planning or accident, the official policy of the 1930s of 'autarky', however much on occasion troubling Italian business with its renunciation of the sacred laws of Adam Smith, had led vast sums of government money to flow to industry and banking, especially through the umbrella Institute for Industrial Recovery (IRI), while national capitalism sought with difficulty to recover from the world Depression. In 1939 Italy was the country outside the Soviet Union with the highest proportion of its economy being 'state-owned', even if the 'para-state' style of ownership owed much to earlier traditions of patron–client deals. It was typical that, when the two para-state bodies coping with tourism, always the most lucrative national industry, quarrelled irredeemably, the regime simply created a third body to supervise the other two. This fondness for what would come to be called *lottizzazione* (a word describing what happens when real estate is chopped into blocks) long survived after 1945 as a Catholic or Christian Democrat version of 'state capitalism', more crudely damned as corruption by some puritan Anglo-Saxon commentators. In this, as in so many other zones of Italian life, Fascism, despite its programme to nationalize the masses, had never been able to liquidate universalist and localist ideas, contradicting or compromising that project.

During the 1930s, the most active opposition to the dictatorship apart from the communists was marshalled from exile in Paris by the Justice and Liberty (Giustizia e Libertà) movement, headed by the liberal socialist patriot, Carlo Rosselli (he and his brother were murdered in France at Fascist behest in 1937). The Rossellis and their followers kept alive Western European ideals about democratic social organization and, in 1945–6, Italy's first post-war government was led by Ferruccio Parri, another patriotic and liberal-democrat ex-soldier from the First World War who had endured a period of *confino* before he was amnestied. Also significant is the fact that the Rossellis were Jewish; they belonged to an elite with an intimate and long-standing connection to that radical democrat and nationalist sector of the Risorgimento best incarnated in Giuseppe Mazzini. Their families had celebrated the unification of Italy as the time when they were for ever freed from the ghetto and, for example, from the automatic anti-Semitism of Pope Pius IX (1846–78).

RACE, THE GERMAN ALLIANCE, AND WAR

A year after the Rossellis were assassinated, Fascist Italy began introducing its own anti-Semitic legislation in a process that culminated at Verona in November 1943, when the outline constitution of the RSI listed Jews as the 'enemies of the nation', with the somewhat curious qualification 'for the duration of the war'. Such policy has sometimes been seen as the result of the Axis with Nazi Germany and so a matter of self-interested and cynical mimicry rather than a profound or scientific racism. Historical analysis, however, shows that Italians between the wars did not escape the curse of racism. Rather, racial prejudice was possessed of an Italian history differentiating it from the German story. If a body count is attempted, the Fascist regime committed its most numerous crimes against Arabs, blacks and Slavs, this last especially during its wartime occupation of much of ex-Yugoslavia, where, in 1942, party secretary, Aldo Vidussoni, at least talked about the liquidation of all Slovenes. Nonetheless, after September 1943, officials of the RSI did assist the collection and the dispatch of more than 7,000 Italian Jews to the death camps to the east, while 173 were murdered on national soil during those years.

This participation in the horror of the Final Solution went against that history which had made not just the Rossellis but all Italian Jews natural fans of the Risorgimento as the victory of a nation that was by definition the modernizing enemy of traditional clerical anti-Semitic thought and practice. This natural alliance with Italian nationalism had ensured that Jewish Italians to 1938 generally thought of themselves as Italians with a somewhat different religious or cultural inheritance rather than as members of a diverse 'race'. Despite the endorsement on occasion of anti-Semitic stereotypes, few gentile Italians demurred. Although Mussolini, as ever, said one thing one day and another the next, mostly he averred that anti-Semitic policy had no place in Italy. Rather, ironically, he like many other Italians was probably quicker to detect 'primordial difference' between Italians from different regions than to expatiate about other forms of racism. The Neapolitans, the *Duce* maintained in a typically cavalier and drastic manner, were naturally feckless and unmodern and could only be cured by a ruthless purge of their city. In his heart Mussolini, like many of his subjects, feared that 'Africa' began somewhere south of his own birthplace in the Romagna and contended that this fact helped to explain why 'civilization' still did not reliably command all Italian lives.

Only a very few Fascists blindly took up German ideas about racial science, with the regime's preference being instead to emphasize 'will'. The first site of Fascist racial legislation was actually the empire, after the conquest of Ethiopia swiftly raised the issue whether Italians were fit to be imperial administrators and stern but just overlords of native peoples. In a fashion that could be paralleled with developments in British South Africa or the Belgian Congo, from 1937 a sort of Apartheid system began to be adopted in Ethiopia, designed to prove that Italians were worthy to shoulder the White Man's Burden. Favoured by such young party intellectuals as Indro Montanelli, after 1945 an enduring Italian radical conservative, discourse began to flourish stating that the long-delayed Fascist revolution could at last be made genuine through the mobilizing effects of racism. Their backs straightened by a sense of their 'blood', Fascist new men and new women could stand tall both abroad and at home.

It is not completely clear how enthusiastically most Italians took up this new line. The Catholic Church was unconvinced if, to a degree, it was willing to go along with racial separation, and so in large part were the rest of the elite, be they fervent Fascists or fellow-travellers, nearer to the monarchy, the army, and the lingering liberal world. Very many Italians, not excluding Mussolini and Farinacci, were ready to find special cases in which their Jewish friends might be saved from the general persecution. Similarly, Oscar Sinigaglia, a Jewish businessman who had been prominent in nationalist causes, did not altogether escape a racism of his own. In July 1938, he wrote to his *Duce,* disgusted that his lifetime dedication to Italy was to be thrown away. 'Is it really possible', Sinigaglia lamented, 'that I must feel separated from my *patria* and made to belong . . . among Mongols and the Negroid?'

Where the Italian version of racism might have led is obscured by the Fascist regime's dismal performance as a warrior society in the Second World War, once that conflict was entered on 10 June 1940. The disastrous attack on Greece, begun on 28 October, eighteenth anniversary of the March on Rome, rapidly reduced wartime Italy into being Nazi Germany's ignoble second. This failure Nazis like Joseph Goebbels were quick to ascribe to what all German nationalists, except Hitler, believed was the inevitable racial inferiority of the 'Mediterranean race'. Italy, it was soon apparent, was to experience a Second World War which, even more than in France or Poland, cast doubt on whether there was, or should be, any such thing as an Italian nation. On 8 September 1943, proof of the inadequacy of the ruling elite and of its willingness to abandon the people to their fate was given when King Victor Emmanuel and his soldier prime minister, Pietro Badoglio, cravenly and precipitously fled Rome to escape the invading and vengeful Germans. Under what was widely called the test of war, they were unable or unwilling to defend Italians within Italy or to give any clear orders to those Italian soldiers still stationed abroad. The elite of the elite patently rejected the view that it was sweet and fitting to die for the nation.

CONCLUSIONS

What was it about Italian society, culture, politics, and economy that produced this wartime disaster? What can explain the abject inability of the national economy to produce war material and of the political culture to rally Italians in the fashion expected of a modern state? After all, Italy, alone of the combatants, failed to increase the percentage of its product directed to the war effort after it entered the conflict and its men remained poorly equipped and of low morale in almost every battle.

To a major degree the answer lies in the inadequacies and failings of Fascism and of the dictator since, by most indices, Liberal Italy was better at mustering its populace in the First World War, however unpopular among the peasants and the working class, than it was in the Second. Yet Liberal Italy, too, had laboured with the business of war and the structures of being the least of the great powers did much to condition Italy's international behaviour and limit its military and political achievement.

Nonetheless, the 'disaster of 8 September' and the calamity of the rest of the war should not be exaggerated in their significance. The year 1945 did not signal a final terminus for Italian history. Even Fascism did not altogether disappear since the Italians were soon voting in appreciable number for a neo-fascist party, the Movimento Sociale Italiano (MSI, Italian Social Movement). More importantly, the theory and practice of religion, the character and imprint of the family, the functioning of 'corruption' and patron–client networks, the interplay between national, regional, and local identities, the relativities of gender and class, each continued to condition Italian lives into the post-war era. For all Fascism's pretensions to constitute a 'revolution', the change that did indeed massively alter Italians and the face of Italy would come from the 1950s with the 'economic miracle' and national membership of a uniting Europe. The inter-war years were important ones for Italy. But they were not decisive.

In sum, among the ideologies of the twentieth century Fascism was an Italian invention. Its resultant regime is well called the 'Italian dictatorship'. There can be no doubt that Mussolini's rule repressed the populace for a generation and bequeathed a negative legacy to many sectors of national history. On the other hand, just as Italian liberalism had varied from that familiar in Western Europe, so Fascist totalitarianism needs to be understood in its specific context. To be sure, Hitler long admired Mussolini, drew comfort from his rise and, to 1933, self-consciously followed the Italian model. To the disgust of his party comrades who believed automatically that Italians were racially inferior to the peoples of the north and unjustly occupied Germanic lands from the South Tyrol to the Adriatic, the 'artistic' *Führer*, dreaming of his own eventual retirement to Florence, set aside his German nationalism and racism to embrace an alliance with Italy which he repeatedly advocated before his rise to power and sought and achieved after himself becoming dictator. Nazi Germany, to a significant degree, bore the imprint of what happened before and after the March on Rome. But the practice of Fascist Italy needs to be understood on its own terms and not as some half-baked imitation of Nazism. Italy's First and Second World Wars, and the tyranny that misgoverned Italy in between, were Italy's own. The generation of Fascists from 1915 to 1945 were also Italians.

FURTHER READING

Absalom, Roger, *A Strange Alliance: Aspects of Escape and Survival in Italy 1943–45* (Florence, 1991).

Ben-Ghiat, Ruth, *Fascist Modernities: Italy 1922–1945* (Berkeley, Calif., 2001).

Bosworth, Richard, *The Italian Dictatorship: Problems and Perspectives in the Interpretation of Mussolini and Fascism* (London, 1998).

—— *Mussolini* (London, 2002).

—— *Mussolini's Italy: Life under the Dictatorship* (London, 2005).

Clark, Martin, *Mussolini* (Harlow, 2005).

De Grazia, Victoria, *How Fascism Ruled Women: Italy 1922–1945* (Berkeley, Calif., 1992).

Dunnage, Jonathan, *Twentieth Century Italy: A Social History* (Cambridge, 2002).

Gentile, Emilio, *The Sacralization of Politics in Fascist Italy* (Cambridge, Mass, 1996).

Knox, Macgregor, *Common Destiny: Dictatorship, Foreign Policy, and War in Fascist Italy and Nazi Germany* (New York, 2000).

Mallett, Robert, *Mussolini and the Origins of the Second World War, 1933–1940* (Houndmills, 2003).

Morgan, Philip, *Italian Fascism 1919–1945* (New York, 1995).

Pollard, John, *Money and the Rise of the Modern Papacy: Financing the Vatican, 1850–1950* (Cambridge, 2005).

Quine, Maria, *Italy's Social Revolution: Charity and Welfare from Liberalism to Fascism* (Houndmills, 2002).

Zamagni, Vera, *The Economic History of Italy 1860–1990* (Oxford, 1993).

9

Germany

Stefan Berger

INTRODUCTION

The period between the outbreak of the First World War and the end of the Second World War is a period of dramatic changes in German history: the negative balance sheet is marked by responsibility for two world wars, political violence, economic crises on a scale unprecedented in the twentieth century, National Socialism, and, above all, the Holocaust. But even in Germany, where the first half of the twentieth century were indeed dark years, the period also has a positive balance sheet including the revolutionary breakthrough to parliamentary democracy and republicanism, a vibrant cultural scene (at least until 1933), the extension of the welfare state, and remarkable economic recovery. Overall these are roller coaster years of German history—a roller-coaster which did, in the end, crash badly, leaving the country as well as much of Europe in ruins. But do we have to judge the entire ride from the vantage point of the crash in 1945? The story of Germany in the first half of the twentieth century has often been told as a linear story of catastrophes leading straight from the Versailles Treaty to the victory of National Socialism, the horrors of total war, and genocide. This essay will attempt to take a more kaleidoscopic view which allows for the plural realities of Germany at several different moments of time and for the hetero-temporality of events. Without trying to belittle or counter the horrors of the world wars and the Third Reich, it will be suggested that even this darkest period of German history had its brighter moments. In some respects the foundations for the happier second half of the century were laid during those years.

In August 1914 few people in Germany greeted the outbreak of war with the kind of resignation captured in Sir Edward Grey's famous statement that the lamps had gone out all over Europe not to reappear during his lifetime. The reasons for the outbreak of war have been hotly contested ever since, but, whichever way one looks at it, the imperial German elites have to shoulder a large part of the blame for deliberately risking war or, at the very least, doing nothing to prevent it. But war was popular in Germany in the summer of 1914. Apart from a powerful wave of straightforward jingoism flooding the country, there was also, among intellectuals and the ruling elite, the notion that war would point a way out of a deep cultural and political crisis. It would stop the decadence and the disunity and lead to a renewal and rebirth of a stronger and more unified Germany.

More recently, however, historians have stressed that one should not overestimate German enthusiasm for the war. Especially among the rural population and the working classes there was often little support and widespread fear. When the full horrors of modern trench warfare became apparent, opposition to the war increased. On the home front the increasing shortages of food, clothing, and other items important to everyday life and the growing militarization of workplaces also contributed to the first stirrings of unrest. Mass strike waves radicalized sections of the working classes, many of whom declared their solidarity with the Kiel sailors who, on 30 October 1918, mutinied against the decision of the chiefs of the navy to seek one decisive battle against the British fleet. Workers' and soldiers' councils were set up in many cities and towns. They took control of municipal affairs and toppled the monarchies and governments across the German states. The Kaiser went into exile in the Netherlands. For a while it was wide open where the German revolution of 1918 would lead. But the moderate Social Democrats were eventually successful in steering the revolution in the direction of a republic and parliamentary democracy. Questions concerning a different social and economic order were postponed.

The birth date of the Weimar Republic was 19 January 1919, when elections for a constitutional assembly produced an overwhelming majority for those parties in favour of republicanism and parliamentary democracy. It looked as though the German people had at long last freed themselves from the fetters of an authoritarian political regime and were tumbling into a brighter, freer, and more democratic future. Yet the key event which cast its long shadow over the entire period was the First World War. It had led to the near total mobilization of German society. Thirteen million men, a fifth of the German population, served in the army, while the home front suffered under the impact of the Allied blockade. The war impoverished Germany and many of the economic and political crises in this period were directly related to wartime decisions and events. The soldiers at the front were traumatized by the experience of mechanized mass slaughter. It paved the way towards the legitimization of violence in the post-war world on a hitherto unprecedented scale. Former soldiers active in the paramilitary *Freikorps* and the paramilitary street-fighting formations, such as the National Socialist Stormtroopers (SA), the Communist Red Front, and even the Republican Iron Front, often consisted of men brutalized by four years of organized mass killing. Political violence, uniforms, marching, and political terrorism marked the inter-war years to a degree that was unthinkable in the period before 1914.

Right-wing anti-republican veterans' organizations, which counted their numbers in the millions, glorified the soldierly wartime experience as a school for manhood and upheld the military ethos of war in peacetime. The Veterans' Association Kyffhäuser (42,000 branches with more than four million members) and the Stahlhelm were among the most vicious opponents of the Republic and the Versailles Peace Treaty which ended the war on such unfavourable terms for Germany. Republican veterans' organizations, especially the Reichsbanner Schwarz-Rot-Gold, fought an uphill battle to draw different lessons from the war. They stressed the horrors of war and preached international reconciliation and the prevention of armed international conflict. The war undoubtedly produced strong pacifist sentiments, which were expressed powerfully by Erich Maria Remarque's *All Quiet at the Western Front*. And yet the negative perception of the war in Germany was far less popular and widespread than was the case in Britain or France.

The idea, however, that the German people were united behind the German war effort and supportive of the imperial German army and state was a myth produced immediately after the war by the anti-republican right, which was keen to lay the blame for the loss of the war and the Versailles Peace Treaty at the feet of republican politicians. In fact, the war produced considerable resentment and rejection of imperial Germany, as people suffered from food and other shortages and struggled to make ends meet while their loved ones died like flies in the trenches of Northern France. In particular workers were deeply dissatisfied and began mobilizing behind those who demanded an end to war and the democratization of the political system. The revolution of 1918 has engendered a good deal of debate focusing on the question of its success or failure: was not enough achieved in 1918? Were the old elites largely left in place to bounce back and destroy the republic? Was too much achieved, that is, would less have been more? After all, was Germany really ready for parliamentary democracy and one of the most liberal constitutions of the world? Might not some sort of constitutional monarchy with more authoritarian features have stood better chances of survival? Was the revolution aborted, even betrayed by those who put themselves at its helm, especially the Social Democrats? Undoubtedly the democratic revolutionaries made mistakes. They did not trust the revolutionary masses and instead relied too much on a dubious alliance with the old imperial elites. They failed to be open about the responsibility of those elites for the outbreak of war in 1914. But at the end of the day, they managed to establish a republic and a parliamentary democracy in extraordinarily difficult circumstances. Seen in the context of those East-Central European constitutions created after 1918, the Weimar constitution was arguably the most successful and long-lived—despite all the problems that Germany was facing after the war. Weimar democrats also reshaped industrial relations, for the first time removing all legal restrictions to the existence of trade unions as independent representatives of workers' interests. And culturally, the 'roaring twenties' were at their loudest in Berlin—making it a European Chicago, attracting close to two million tourists every year by the mid-1920s.

The republic folded in the midst of economic depression, when Hitler seemed to many (albeit never a majority of) German voters the only solution out of a deep economic and political crisis. It was replaced with the National Socialist dictatorship which ruthlessly persecuted political opponents of the regime and those deemed not part of the 'people's community', above all the Jews. Total war and the Holocaust marked the horrendous endpoint of Germany's march into the abyss. The National Socialist regime was a genuinely popular regime among many German *Volksgenossen* who were all too happy to share in an economic upturn and social policies deemed to benefit the Aryan part of the population. Sebastian Haffner once said that, had Hitler died in 1937, he would have died as one of the most popular German politicians ever. This chapter would like to trace the development of Germany from 1914 to the end of the Third Reich in 1945, focusing, first, on the development of politics, secondly, the economic, social, and cultural sphere, and, finally, on Germany's international relations during this period. Throughout, it will be suggested that the catastrophic events which cast their long shadow over the entire period were never offset by but were accompanied by events and developments which planted the seeds for a happier second half of the twentieth century.

POLITICAL DEVELOPMENTS

The Weimar Republic has often been described as a republic without republicans or a democracy without democrats. Undeniably those parties most committed to democratic change in 1918/19, that is, the Social Democratic Party (SPD), the left-liberal German Democratic Party (DDP), and the Catholic Centre Party, took a beating in the first national elections of June 1920. The SPD's share of the vote went from 37.9 per cent in 1919 to 21.7 per cent in 1920, while the DDP plummeted from 18.5 to 8.3 per cent, and the Centre Party went from 19.7 per cent to 13.6 per cent. Disappointment about the course of the German revolution and the outcry over the Versailles Treaty were among the most important reasons for this collapse of the democratic vote. Yet various coalition governments broadly supportive of the republic saw off challenges from both the left and the right during the turbulent early years of Weimar. The newly founded Communist Party (KPD) followed an insurrectionist policy line until 1923, when the pathetic Hamburg rising ended all hopes of taking power in Berlin along similar lines to the Bolsheviks in Russia. The political right, often supported by the military and the old elites of imperial Germany, also attempted to get rid of parliamentary democracy and to return Germany to more authoritarian forms of government, most notably through the Kapp–Lüttwitz putsch in 1920. Eventually, and despite the law courts' lenient treatment of right-wing terrorists, which stood in marked contrast to the judges' feverish persecution of the political left, the republic managed to pull through and, against the odds, establish a liberal parliamentary democracy ruled by a constitution committed to individual rights and social justice. In the circumstances this was a huge success for the democratic parties in Germany.

Party politics in the Weimar Republic has often been perceived as messy and unsatisfactory. For a start, each and every party, even the most pro-republican, contained elements which were critical of the republic. Furthermore, the parties often seemed unable to forge compromises and agree on anything, which made coalition governments very difficult and led to the frequent collapse of governments and new elections. For sure, political parties had little experience playing the parliamentary game, as there was no parliamentary government in Germany before 1919. The imperial governments were responsible to the Emperor, not to parliament. Hence the Reichstag was a stage where politicians of various parties enacted their party programmes and beliefs. Cooperation between different parties existed pre-1918, but it was not paramount for parliamentary parties to reach compromise in order to maintain coalition governments. It is hence not surprising that coalition politics was difficult after 1919. Nevertheless, up until the economic depression of the late 1920s the republican parties managed reasonably well. In fact, two parties which started off impeccably opposed to the Weimar Republic, the German People's Party (DVP) and the German National People's Party (DNVP), came to support coalition governments, albeit, in the latter case, somewhat reluctantly. Under Gustav Stresemann the DVP turned into a staunch supporter of the republic. Under Count Kuno Westarp the DNVP was at least willing to play the parliamentary game. Only under the chairmanship of Alfred Hugenberg after May 1928 did the DNVP turn sharply to the right again, seeking to distance itself from the republic as much as possible.

Rather than emphasize the failure of party politics in the Weimar Republic, one could equally stress what an impressive and steep learning curve party politics underwent in the 1920s. Some extremely talented republican politicians emerged, and it was a tragedy that so many of them were either murdered by terrorists (Walter Rathenau, Matthias Erzberger, Karl Gareis, and Kurt Eisner) or died prematurely, hounded to death by their political opponents (Friedrich Ebert, Gustav Stresemann). Given the lack of a strong parliamentary and republican tradition in Germany, the overall dearth of committed republicans is perhaps not surprising. But the republic managed to produce a reasonable amount of people who accepted and, in time, supported it as the only viable alternative following the collapse of the constitutional monarchies in 1918. During the middle years of the republic, parliamentary politics began to work better, although compromise and coalition politics were still hindered by the pillarization of German society into tight social milieux which corresponded to voting blocks for particular parties. Each party felt that it had to speak for and represent the interests of its particular social milieu: the SPD and the KPD those of the working class; the

DDP and DVP those of the Protestant middle classes; the DNVP those of the agricultural interests; and the Centre Party those of the Catholics.

The relative success of the Centre Party, but also of the SPD and the KPD, in retaining voters when challenged by the Nazi Party (NSDAP) in the final years of the republic, had much to do with the tight milieux in which these parties operated. They were part of a vast network of social and leisure-time organizations, which ranged from kindergartens to burial associations, from sports clubs to organizations for particular occupations, and from choirs to educational associations. Women's and youth organizations, were prominent both in the Catholic and the working-class milieux. For Catholics, Socialists, and Communists it was possible to spend their lives from cradle to grave with relatively little contact with other pillars of society.

It was the Protestant middle-class milieu and the farming interests which were least capable of resisting the National Socialist onslaught in the final crisis years of the republic. Farming was in perpetual crisis throughout the 1920s. The hyper-inflation of 1923 impoverished wide sections of the middle classes and the Great Depression after 1929 did nothing to inspire confidence in democratic politics. The status of many professional groups in society was in free fall, and the republic had been unable to protect civil servants and white-collar professionals from economic misery and social decline. The National Socialist share of the vote rose from a mere 2.6 per cent in 1928 to 18.3 per cent in 1930. Within two years it had almost doubled, and the elections of July 1932 saw the National Socialists emerge as biggest party in the Reichstag with 37.3 per cent of the vote and 230 members of parliament. Although, with hindsight, the threat from the political right to the Weimar Republic was always far more real than the threat from the political left, one should not forget that Weimar Germany boasted the strongest Communist Party in the world outside the Soviet Union. The KPD's vote also rose during the years of the Great Depression, peaking in November 1932 when the party got 16.9 per cent—a mere 3.5 per cent behind its Social Democratic rival for the working-class vote. An alleged Bolshevik threat drove the conservative middle classes even more into the arms of the National Socialists.

The National Socialists were the first genuine catch-all party in German history. They were successful in presenting a slightly different face to different constituencies and drawing support from all milieux in Germany. However, those who had not been part of the Socialist, Communist, and Catholic milieux were most prone to fall for the Nazi Party. But ultimately the National Socialists did not come to power through the ballot box. Parliamentary democracy ceased to function in 1930, when the democratic parties in the Reichstag were unable to produce workable coalition governments. In line with the letter (if not with the spirit) of the constitution, the president appointed so-called presidential cabinets. The Weimar constitution had set up the president as the closest substitute for the emperor, reflecting the desire of the makers of the constitution to create a strong executive as counterbalance to parliamentary rule. Elected directly by the people only every seven years, his powers included the appointment and dismissal of cabinets, the command over the army, the dissolution of the Reichstag, and the right to call new elections. He appointed the chancellor and he held vast emergency powers which included the temporary suspension of civil liberties.

In the hands of a staunchly pro-republican president, like Ebert, these powers were used to save the republic and strengthen it. But in the hands of an anti-republican president, like Ebert's successor, Paul von Hindenburg, they were turned against the republic. Under the chancellorship of the Centre Party politician Heinrich Brüning between 1930 and 1932, presidential cabinets tried to weather the economic storm and the political crisis which threatened to engulf the republic. The beginnings of the presidential cabinets spelt the end of the parliamentary democracy of Weimar. Hindenburg and his entourage had plans to use the cabinets to bring to an end parliamentary government. Brüning himself knew of those plans, although it is unclear to what degree he shared their ambition. But the presidential cabinets marked the slippery slope towards more authoritarian forms of government. As parliament grew weaker, interest group representatives, the army, and the civil service acquired more influence on how the country was run.

It was an army man, General Kurt von Schleicher, who suggested building a 'cross-front' (*Querfront*) including both the trade unions on the left and the National Socialists on the right. During von Schleicher's short time at the helm of a presidential cabinet between November 1932 and January 1933, he failed to bring about any such 'cross-front'. Neither in 1930 nor in 1932/3 was it a foregone conclusion, however, that Hitler would take power. Hindenburg resisted his appointment as chancellor for a long time. It was his entourage, and in particular Franz von Papen, who convinced Hindenburg in the end to agree to the appointment of a cabinet in which the National Socialists were supposed to be ruled in by a range of other national-conservative forces. But when this new cabinet with Hitler at the helm was sworn in on 30 January 1933 the Nazis quickly dubbed it their 'seizure of power' (*Machtergreifung*), turning what was in effect the appointment of Hitler by Hindenburg into a revolutionary act of sweeping away the republic.

Over the next weeks and months, the National Socialists established their dictatorship. Presidential decrees limited the freedom of the press and the freedom of assembly and gave Hitler special emergency powers. Meanwhile the Stormtroopers (SA) terrorized political opponents. The Enabling Law, passed in the Reichstag in March 1933, brought to an end parliamentary democracy, as it allowed the government to pass laws without the legislative's consent. The opposition of the Social Democrats and the Centre Party together would still have left the National Socialists without the two-thirds majority required for the passing of the law. Yet in the end, only the Social Democrats were courageous enough to oppose the Nazis and stand up for parliamentary democracy. In a deeply moving speech Otto Wels defended the republican spirit: 'we stand firm by the principles of the rule of law, and the equal and social rights enshrined in it. In this historic hour we Social Democrats solemnly profess our belief in the principles of humanity and justice, freedom and socialism. No Enabling Law gives you the right to obliterate ideas which are eternal and indestructible . . .' In July 1933 the Social Democrats along with all other remaining political parties were abolished and a one-party state came into being.

After Hindenburg died in 1935, Hitler's position was unassailable. The whole National Socialist state was 'working towards the Führer' (Ian Kershaw) — several competing institutions, ranging from the military, to civil administrations to party institutions, were all vying for influence and the ear of the dictator. An 'institutional Darwinism' (David Schoenbaum) was implemented which produced administrative chaos as well as restless dynamism and activism. Federal structures were abolished and replaced by a system where Reichsstatthalter and Gauleiter ruled over administrative units and were directly responsible to Hitler. Self-confident and power-hungry regional satraps emerged which often attempted to protect their authority against that of the Reich bureaucracy and increased further the degree of administrative chaos. But all of that did not make Hitler a 'weak dictator' (Hans Mommsen); he mattered in the National Socialist system, as no decision could be taken without his consent. As the leadership principle was adopted throughout society, the ultimate leader, Hitler, made the key decisions. His 'blessing' was necessary to give his satraps the security that they were acting with the consent of their *Führer*. That was true for the Holocaust as much as for decisions of domestic and foreign policy and the conduct of the war. Without Hitler the Third Reich would have looked very different.

At the same time National Socialism was not Hitlerism. It has often been described as either a variant of fascism or totalitarianism. Although generic concepts such as fascism and totalitarianism are important in comparing aspects of National Socialist Germany with aspects of other dictatorial regimes, National Socialism's unique features are not captured by these concepts. Its radical propagation of a racial state, ruled by belonging to a racial community, set it apart from other fascist or totalitarian regimes. Race became the new religion, and National Socialism had indeed many elements of a political religion. Prayers were dedicated to Hitler in the Third Reich and the *Führer* was depicted as the new Messiah, leading his people into the promised land of Aryan supermen. Germany had been reborn under the Nazis. Sections of the National Socialist movement, in particular the SS under Heinrich Himmler, were hostile to Christianity and practised Teutonic paganism, but other National Socialists were far more willing to come to an arrangement with the Protestant and Catholic Churches, provided the latter accepted the National Socialist state.

The Protestant Churches in particular had been largely hostile to the Weimar Republic. When the Versailles Treaty was signed they had declared a day of national mourning. Both the Catholic and Protestant Churches were highly critical of the more libertarian aspects of Weimar culture and frequently called for a return to traditional moral values. In 1917 the Protestants had celebrated the 400th anniversary of Luther's posting of the famous ninety-five theses. Luther had long been a major national hero for the Protestant community, and the festivities in 1917 were again steeped in nationalism. Protestant supporters of Hitler often compared him to a second Luther. They assembled in an organization entitled 'German Christians'. It was founded in 1932 and led by Pastor Ludwig Müller. Entirely in line with the National Socialist idea of the racial state and virulently anti-Semitic, it attracted 3,000 of the 17,000 Protestant pastors in Germany, a far greater number than those who joined the oppositional Confessional Church. The Catholic Church had traditionally a much greater distance from the German state and the authorities than the Protestant Churches. But the Catholic Church also tried to come to some form of agreement with the Nazi state which would ensure the survival of the strong Catholic associationalism in Germany. Hence a concordat was signed in 1933 between the Pope in Rome and the Nazi government which seemed to guarantee the autonomy of the Church in exchange for guarantees that the Church and its clergy would stop playing a part in political affairs. Individual Catholic bishops, such as Clemens August Graf von Galen, protested against specific Nazi crimes, such as the murder of the mentally handicapped in 1941. But overall there was, for example, little protest over the anti-Semitic measures taken by the Nazi regime. For the majority, both the Catholic and Protestant Churches seemed content to come to an arrangement with the new Nazi regime.

The National Socialists had important allies among other traditional elites, above all, in the army, in the civil service, and in industry. These elites were steeped in the values of the authoritarian imperial German state. But the National Socialists were always the dominant party in any power cartel, as they penetrated the state bureaucracy with great efficiency. They could rely on the popular support of large sections of the wider population willing to collude with Hitler and the National Socialist regime to produce one of the most barbaric dictatorships in history. The Gestapo, the SS, and the SA were the terroristic face of the regime. It is, however, easy to overemphasize the degree to which German society under Nazism was a totalitarian octopus governing every aspect of individual lives.

Gleichschaltung, the process of bringing into the National Socialist orbit all organizations of civil society, was for real. Thousands of organizations and groups were forcibly dissolved or decreed their own disappearance or merger with National Socialist organizations. The terror apparatus of the regime was efficient enough to deal ruthlessly with acts of political opposition, but it could not control all aspects of society. It had to rely on the willingness of the wider population to conform with National Socialist values and ideals. And many among the German *Volksgenossen* were all too willing to follow suit. Thus, for example, the Gestapo was inundated with calls from ordinary Germans keen to denounce alleged enemies of the National Socialist state—among them neighbours, colleagues, friends, and family. The solidarity and fascination of wide sections of the German population with Hitler was real. Yet popular support for the Third Reich was not constant. Thus, for example, levels of support for the regime fell dramatically the year before the outbreak of the Second World War. Nevertheless, the 'Hitler myth' (Ian Kershaw) created a special bond between many Germans and the dictator which did not even falter during the final phase of the Second World War. Criticisms of his paladins and the National Socialist regime mounted, but Hitler remained exempt, retaining frightening levels of popularity even in the early years of the Federal Republic.

The *Volksgemeinschaft* was a central ingredient in the ideology underpinning the National Socialist racial state (Michael Burleigh and Wolfgang Wippermann). The idea of a people unified by racial characteristics produced policies of the National Socialist state aimed at undermining social inequality. It also helped to erode the social milieux which had been such a characteristic of German society before 1933, but it needed the war to obliterate the traditional milieux and pave the way for catch-all parties after 1949.

Although the notion of *Volksgemeinschaft* appealed to many Germans, not everyone wanted to be part of it. Active resistance to National Socialism inside Germany was restricted to small clandestine groups which remained relatively ineffective. Foremost among them were Communists, Social Democrats, Christians, and members of those groups deemed not to belong to the racial community, above all Germans of Jewish faith. By 1935/6 almost all resistance groups within Germany had been infiltrated by the Gestapo and its members were either dead or in concentration camps. By 1939 about 150,000 Communists and Social Democrats had been interned in concentration camps. Tens of thousands of Germans had fled the country and were living an often precarious existence as political refugees in Europe and elsewhere. 12,000 Germans had been convicted of high treason and 40,000 were imprisoned for lesser political offences. During the war, civilian courts handed out 15,000 death sentences for opposing the National Socialist state. Communists suffered the greatest loss of life in the fight against Nazism, but they did not pose the biggest threat to National Socialism. It was resistance from within national conservative circles and in particular from within the military which was dangerous to the regime. But the military coup against Hitler in July 1944 came very late in the day. Even if it had been successful, it would not have marked a return of Germany to republicanism and parliamentary democracy, as most of the plotters were deeply anti-democratic. Most had initially supported Hitler and the German war effort and turned against the dictator only after things had started to go wrong.

Yet opposition went beyond active resistance. Many Germans partially rejected specific aspects of the National Socialist regime and in their everyday life tried to bring into line their personal ideas and beliefs with the demands made on them by the National Socialist state. This did not produce active resistance, but it did lead to acts of defiance or complaints about particular practices and policies. Arguably the majority of Germans were neither fervent National Socialists content with every aspect of the regime nor active opponents of National Socialism determined to topple the dictator.

ECONOMY, SOCIETY, AND CULTURE

The new republican Germany dealt successfully with the legacy of the lost war after 1918. Six million soldiers needed to be demobilized and integrated back into civilian life. Above all, they needed jobs. Hence women, who had been recruited into the factories and offices during wartime, were either directly thrown out of a job or enticed back to domesticity by a strong discourse about maternalism and the duties of married women around the home and in social welfare. Yet the republic also gave nineteen million women the right to vote for the first time. Extremely diverse images of women stood next to each other: the voter, the consumer, the proletarian worker, the emancipated employee, and the mother and carer. But Weimar Germany was perhaps most frequently identified with the phenomenon of the 'New Woman', who stereotypically was wearing fashionable clothes, had short hair, held a job, smoked, and could be found regularly in the cinemas and dance halls of the cities. It was, of course, very much a male projection of a modern-day femme fatale. But the promise of greater emancipation of women was there in the republic, which witnessed major debates surrounding the female body. While many saw motherhood as a national duty, some were keen to introduce more voluntary concepts of motherhood. Sexual knowledge became more readily available to women than ever before. Diverse methods of contraception were used more widely, and women set about to reclaim their bodies and demand more rights. The economic crises of the 1920s were far more important than images of the 'New Woman' in threatening traditional gender roles. Among the now impoverished middle classes, wives, mothers, and daughters found it difficult to retain their home-bound status, as they were forced by sheer economic necessity to think about gainful employment. Overall, the feminization of the workforce gathered pace throughout the 1920s. Positions such as stenographers, typists, and telephonists were now routinely filled by women. All of this met with a ferocious backlash, as misogynist representations of women were directly proportional to the rising promises of emancipation. Anti-republican organizations were particularly outspoken on identifying the republic with women's emancipation and denouncing both.

The discursive processes concerning gender issues reached out and overlapped with welfare issues. Caring for the many war disabled and war widows became a prime political issue after 1918 and led to a massive extension of welfare services, in which women often played a prominent role. In 1913 Germany spent one billion Reichsmark on welfare. In 1929 that sum had increased ninefold to nine billion Reichsmark. Even considering that the value of the Reichsmark had decreased between 1913 and 1929 this was a massive increase in state expenditure for welfare. The 1922 Youth Welfare Law, the 1924 National Welfare Decree, and the 1927 Unemployment Benefit Law were milestones on the road to guaranteeing social security to the vast majority of citizens. Progressive labour laws, new pension schemes, and massive housing programmes added to the ambition of the republic to turn Germany into a comprehensive welfare state. The principle of the welfare state was enshrined in Article 151 of the Constitution, but time and again the ambition came into conflict with economic reality. Too often the republic could not deliver on the promises it had made to diverse groups of people whose expectations of better welfare had been raised by republican politicians. In other countries, such as Britain, caring for the victims of war was left far more to private charities and welfare organizations. In Germany the state took prime responsibility, arguing that social rights had to be expanded to honour the people's sacrifices for the nation in wartime. But the expectations could not be fulfilled by a republican welfare state which was always overburdened. Hence the state was blamed for failing the veterans and the war dead. As disappointment frequently turned to despair, many veterans blamed the republic for their fate and moved to the anti-republican right.

Taking care of the veterans' needs was widely perceived as the least the republic could do in exchange for their sacrifice to the nation. With so many dead, crippled, and injured, the memorialization of the war became a major issue. Almost every town and community across Germany built its own memorial to their dead, as commemorating the war became a means of reasserting militaristic values that had been so prominent in the empire. The military establishment was still the backbone of such militarist sentiment. It felt humiliated by the stipulations of Versailles reducing the German army to a token force. Many officers were steeped in Prussianism and resentful of everything that smacked of republicanism and democracy. Officially, they declared that they wanted to keep the army out of politics, but in reality they were building a force which was infused with anti-republicanism. Popular among the generals in the 1920s was the idea of a 'military state' (*Wehrstaat*), where all resources would be geared towards the militarization of social life.

If the military elite was unhappy with the republic, the same can be said for the industrial elite. In the early years of the republic the state subsidized many industries in order to secure jobs. Republican politicians virtually guaranteed full employment to head off further social discontent. The republic also fundamentally reshaped industrial relations. During the war, in the Auxiliary Services Law of 1916, trade unions were recognized as legal representatives of the workers for the first time. Following the revolution in 1918 unions were in a powerful position to demand economic changes. There was a groundswell of working-class support for demands for the widespread socialization and nationalization of industries. But trade union leaders settled in the end for the introduction of the eight-hour day and the notion of social partnership between unions and employers, which found institutional expression in the Central Working Community (Zentrale Arbeitsgemeinschaft, ZAG).

Many employers, however, and in particular the influential leaders of heavy industry, found it deeply unpalatable having to negotiate with union leaders. They wanted to return to the 'master-in-their-own-house' attitude that had governed industrial relations in imperial Germany. Denouncing the Weimar Republic as a 'trade union state', they did everything to scupper the success of the ZAG, increase working hours, reduce wages, and undermine notions of social partnership. Undoubtedly sections of the German economy suffered from high wage costs, high social welfare costs, and high taxation. In a climate in which world economic growth was weak, all of these factors further hindered the dynamic growth of the economy and turned the industrial elites against the republic. Their anti-republicanism did not, however, make them into early supporters of the National Socialists. In fact, few prominent industrialists backed Adolf Hitler before 1932. Yet they certainly did not mind when the National Socialists demolished the last remnants of parliamentarism and implemented a dictatorship in which many industrialists were happy to gain from the economic advantages that the regime offered them. The troublesome union movement was destroyed by the National Socialists. As the leadership principle was introduced into the factories, the managers and employers once again became 'masters-in-their-own-house', although they now had to reckon with the National Socialists. Undoubtedly economic interest groups declined in importance in the Third Reich and the relationship between industrialists and the state varied enormously in different branches of industry. The National Socialist state intervened heavily in economic decision-making. Industry had to comply with the aims and ambitions of the National Socialists, not vice versa. But much money was still to be made, important leaders of industry were appointed to leading positions in the direction of German industry and, by and large, the industrial elite in Germany was happy enough to play alongside the National Socialist regime.

If many representatives of the traditional German elites were unhappy with republicanism and parliamentary democracy, the revolution and the subsequent republic unleashed an explosion of cultural creativity. Many of those working in the culture industry welcomed the crumbling of the edifice of an imperial German state widely perceived as philistine. Artists and writers were enthused by the energy and dynamism of the revolution, which brought greater freedom for cultural producers. The richness and diversity of Weimar culture is an expression of this release of energy after 1918. The modernist movement, which had its origins well before 1914, came fully into its own in the Weimar Republic. German expressionist film was the only cinema in inter-war Europe to hold its own against Hollywood. In the realm of architecture the Bauhaus set new international standards in modernism. Its style became closely associated with the democratic style of the republic. It was all about clarity, usefulness, and

Figure 9.1. The Bauhaus in Dessau.

honesty of lines and materials. There was no pretence. The beautiful merged with the practical. It also had a social vision which found expression in some of the most famous new housing estates of the republic, such as the *Hufeisensiedlung* in Berlin. The leading modernist architects of the 1920s, such as Walter Gropius and Bruno Taut, were keen to contribute to the making of a new Germany through a style of 'new sobriety', a style that consciously tried to disassociate itself from the architectural pomp of imperial Germany.

Berlin itself became the very symbol of urban modernity, even if small-town Germany always remained more typical of German everyday life than the much-hated and much-maligned metropolis. Berlin had the museums, theatres, concert halls, cabarets, restaurants, nightclubs, music halls, jazz cellars, cinemas, and bordellos. It had a world-class university and one of the foremost institutes for psychoanalysis. Magnus Hirschfeld's famous Institute for Sexology was at home in a city which seemed to encourage and tolerate all sorts of sexual experimentation. Radical artists, be they Dadaist, Futurist, or Cubist, challenged the contemporary understanding of art. Christopher Isherwood's *Farewell to Berlin* is a lasting tribute to the magneticism of Berlin for many European intellectuals of the inter-war period. But in small-town Germany Berlin was denounced as 'Babel of sin' and a symbol of 'sexual Bolshevism'. Here half-timbered houses (*Fachwerk*) dominated the skyline, people liked to listen to traditional folk music, they cherished realistic genre paintings, Christmas was celebrated as the ultimate symbol of German 'Innerlichkeit', and mountain and *Heimat* films were popular. Not for nothing did National Socialist propaganda identify small-town Germany with the health of the nation, whereas the metropolis stood for illness and decay.

The flowering of culture under Weimar did not mean that Weimar culture was, on the whole, pro-republican. Art, architecture, and culture more generally were often difficult to pin down politically. Several Bauhaus architects, for example, continued to work in Germany under National Socialism. The National Socialists denounced expressionism as un-German, but there were expressionists, such as Emil Nolde, who were violent anti-Semites and would have been all too glad to serve the master race. In fact the cultural sphere just as much as the political sphere was characterized by processes of radicalization and polarization. Many well-known cultural producers in the Weimar Republic veered either towards the Communist or towards the *völkisch* camp. On the left the atrocious social injustices about which the republic apparently could do little drove artists and writers into the camp of Communism. Bertold Brecht and Hanns Eisler were directly involved in some of the Agitprop activities of the KPD. Käthe Kollwitz and Heinrich Mann veered from support of left liberalism and democracy to sympathy for the Communist position.

Germany was a highly developed civil society which had a vibrant mass media, but much of it was anti-pluralist, intolerant, and xenophobic. The *Frankfurter Zeitung* was the flagship of the democratic and liberal Germany and republican media magnates, such as Mosse and Ullstein, published many of the republic's finest authors. But the anti-republican right could rely on the support of the media empire of Alfred Hugenberg. A great number of authors wrote literature which praised the virtues of the Volk or produced war novels which spread the mythologies of the community of the trenches and glorified wartime experiences. National-conservative intellectuals such as Ernst von Salomon, Ernst Jünger, and Arthur Moeller van den Bruck, representatives of the so-called 'conservative revolution', saw themselves on a quest to reproduce the mythical wartime collectivity and promote *Volksgemeinschaft* ideals. Among the young, there was a widespread desire for wholeness which turned to anti-rationalism and found expression in the *Wandervogel* movement. The young, more generally, but specifically university students, turned to the right in the early 1930s. To them the republic seemed elderly, unexciting, and plodding. Struggling with dim job prospects and the feeling of having missed out on the experience of the trenches, they came to identify the Weimar state with musty paternalism and encrusted structures. The *völkisch* right enticed them with a more intoxicating brew of youthful dynamism and activism.

If the young were disappointed with the republic, the latter had been trying its best to make things work. After the war republican governments subsidized industries and distributed welfare in an attempt to head off further social unrest. Under such circumstances the republic found it impossible to pursue deflationary policies which would have put the country's finances on a sounder footing. Germany had financed the war by printing more money rather than by raising taxation levels. Financial policies after the war should have been more stringent, but this would arguably have dug a hole for the republic at a time when it was desperately trying to survive. One cannot blame republicans for trying to prevent the premature collapse of the republic, even if, with hindsight, post-war financial development pointed in the direction of hyper-inflation which finally caught up with Germany in the wake of the passive resistance to the French Occupation of the Ruhr in 1923. Hyper-inflation produced immense social hardship for the working classes and impoverished wide sections of the German middle classes. It alienated wide sections of the population from the Weimar republic which was blamed for this financial disaster.

If politicians at the beginning of the republic were caught between the Scylla of inflation and the Charybdis of risking further social unrest which might have ended the republican experiment prematurely, did they not have more options in combating the even deeper economic crisis associated with the Great Depression after 1929? The economic historian Knut Borchardt caused a long-running debate with his powerful argument that the republic was equally without a feasible alternative after 1929. Already before the onset of the economic depression, according to Borchardt, the Weimar economy was fatally weakened by rapid rises in real wages which exceeded productivity and wage rises abroad. High taxes on industry were used to fund the welfare programmes of the republic. Uncompetitive and without the money to make necessary investments, German industry was hit particularly hard by the economic slump. As Borchardt sees it, no economic policy could have made a difference in the context of the distributional conflicts of Weimar democracy, fixed exchange rates, and the gold standard.

Many historians have disagreed, arguing that it was largely lack of imagination and the fear of reproducing inflationary tendencies, which prevented Weimar governments from adopting Keynesian economic policies. John Maynard Keynes, an influential economist, argued that governments could spend their way out of economic crisis by increasing government debt short-term, in order to promote industrial growth and employment. His ideas of counter-cyclical economic policies were implemented to different degrees, but in both cases successfully, in Sweden and the United States to combat the Great Depression in the 1930s. Yet republican politicians from the left and the right clung to financial orthodoxy. Although they were undoubtedly restricted in their actions by the Bank of International Settlements and the Young Plan, they could have tried to gain greater room for manoeuvre. Instead, they pursued deflationary policies in an attempt to balance budgets, thereby exacerbating the crisis and missing an opportunity to cushion the politically disastrous effects of this worst economic crisis to engulf the industrial world in the twentieth century. By 1932, Germany counted seven million unemployed. The depression caused unprecedented social misery with which the welfare system could not cope. It was this economic failure which provided the backdrop to Hitler's rise to power.

Hyper-inflation and the Great Depression battered industrial life in Weimar Germany. Many working in agriculture were also hit hard by economic crisis. Cheap imports of grain from North America threatened their very existence. On the vast East Elbian estates the Prussian Junkers still dominated the political interest groups and the social life of the population. Elsewhere in Germany, small farmers dominated the scene, but they too participated in a wide range of often radical and violent agricultural protest. Whereas Junkerdom was still influential enough to make right-wing governments subsidize their large estates east of the river Elbe, smaller farmers were often left to fend for themselves. As hundreds of farmers were forced into bankruptcy, the agricultural vote became easy prey of the anti-republican right.

National Socialism had some of its earliest and most stable pockets of support in rural areas. Its 'blood and soil' ideology appealed to many people living on and from the land. It promised redemption from a modern agricultural capitalism which seemed to push them towards extinction and held out the vision of a protected niche where their traditional ways of life would be preserved. A healthy *Volksgemeinschaft*, the National Socialist propaganda implied, was rooted in the land. The racial stock of those who worked the land would be crucial in moulding the image of the new Aryan man propagated by Hitler's rural ideologues, such as Richard Walther Darré. Although the National Socialists could not stem the long-term trend towards further de-agrarianization, they raised the social status of farmers. Rural ways of life were equated with true Germanness. Once in power, the National Socialists did protect the Aryan German farmer and his property. They could not be expropriated any more, but at the same time they were also de facto tied to the land. With the government in full control of markets and prices for agricultural products, the agricultural community could do nothing but follow the National Socialists' ambitious plans for achieving autarky in the provision of food for the German people.

But the ideal of the *Volksgemeinschaft* meant more than a happy community of stocky German farmers. As the central ingredient in the National Socialist world view it appealed to many different elements of the German population and rallied diverse social groups to the banner of National Socialism. The National Socialist *Volksgemeinschaft* had a medieval and a modern face. It incorporated *Thingspiele,* where people dressed up in medieval garments, performed Teutonic rituals, and celebrated ancient Germanic values. But it also included the vision of a high-tech, mobile industrial nation at the forefront of science and technology. The *Autobahnen* were supposed to revolutionize the German transport system. The 1936 Berlin automobile show was geared towards presenting Germany at the hub of the new age of the automobile. The Berlin Olympic Games in the same year were meant to showcase the National Socialist *Volksgemeinschaft.*

Workers were wooed by the National Socialists through promises of social and economic advancement. The National Socialists did not produce an economic miracle but they benefited from and built on policies implemented under the chancellors von Papen and von Schleicher in 1932. Yet millions Germans experienced the period from 1933 to 1936 as improvement: workplaces were secure again and living standards were rising. The National Socialist propaganda included an array of positive proletarian images. The National Socialists made International Labour Day (1 May) a national holiday, praised the German workers' 'quality work' and emphasized the 'honour of manual labour'. Organizations such as Beauty of Labour and Strength through Joy were meant to improve working conditions, give more social status, and promote better lifestyles for millions of Aryan workers. Family loans, tax breaks, a consumer revolution (symbolized, above all, by the radio, dubbed *Volksempfänger*, and the car, called Volkswagen) and an authoritarian welfare state were among the promises made by the National Socialists. They remained, by and large, promises. The *Volksgemeinschaft* of the 1930s was more propaganda than social reality. But the National Socialists missed no opportunity to claim that social distinctions between working classes and other social classes were broken down systematically.

Of course, the promises of National Socialism were available only within the parameters of the racial state. Access to services, goods, and benefits were regulated by belonging to a racial community. Rigorous exclusion of those not belonging to this racial community, above all the Jews, was an integral part of the system. The forging of the 'people's community' depended vitally on the construction of internal and external enemies as the 'other' which threatened that community: Jews, Bolsheviks, Slavs, feminists, pacifists, homosexuals, Roma, Jehovah's witnesses, and republicans. Their maltreatment, harassment, imprisonment, and, ultimately, elimination was a central ingredient in the National Socialist vision of *Volksgemeinschaft*. In the racial state the 'healthy' had to be separated from the 'degenerate'. As the body of the Volk took priority over the body of the individual, the state had a responsibility for providing welfare and services for Aryans and weed out those who were allegedly weakening the 'people's body'. Welfare and elimination were two sides of the same coin. The national discourse became medicalized and biologized to an extent unknown before. *Völkisch* ideas were centred around notions of healing the 'people's body', which had been threatened with disease and decay by sectional interests, party politics, alien Western ideas, Bolshevism, sexual promiscuity, and other evils. All aspects of society were racialized. Racism penetrated state policy at every level. The cult of physical health, the emphasis on 'racial purity', the rise of eugenics as a scientific discipline in the Third Reich and the practice of euthanasia testify to the overriding importance attributed by the Nazis to issues of 'racial health and hygiene'. Skulls were now measured to prove racial purity; those deemed genetically deficient were forcibly sterilized and the mentally ill were murdered; at the same time, war, struggle, and violence were celebrated as true expression of German warriordom. 'Jewish music' was banned from the concert halls, 'Jewish art' removed from the museums, and books by 'Jewish authors' were burnt. National Socialist architecture aestheticized power and celebrated a cult

Figure 9.2. *The Eternal Jew*, anti-Semitic film poster, 1940.

of the Germanic hero which also found expression in the arts in the powerful, belligerent, and self-confident male nudes produced by Arno Breker.

The National Socialist pantheon was, by and large, male. Women's national vocation was motherhood. Mother's Day was made a national holiday, and mothers were awarded crosses of honour in bronze, silver, and gold, depending on how many offspring they reared. Aryan women benefited from exemplary population and family policies, while those excluded from the racial community were forcibly sterilized and murdered. National Socialist anti-feminism led to a wave of dismissals of women from positions in the higher echelons of the civil service and the professions, but overall the National Socialists could not reverse the trend towards greater employment of women which had been such a notable feature of the Weimar Republic. Many women undoubtedly supported the racialized *Volksgemeinschaft*. National Socialist organizations such as the Association for German Girls, the Reich Labour Service, and the National Socialist Women's League offered millions of women a range of opportunities outside the sphere of the home. Women also participated actively in the race war on the Eastern Front and in the Holocaust.

The racial state found its most horrific apogee in the systematic murder of European Jewry. Anti-Semitism in Germany had been no worse than in many other European countries before 1933. Violent anti-Semitism and calls to cleanse the 'people's body' of Jewish 'parasites' were restricted to *völkisch* groups on the far right. The National Socialist Party was openly anti-Semitic, although it did not emphasize that aspect of its programme much before 1933. After 1933, however, pogroms against Jews started almost immediately, and their rights as German citizens were curbed and reduced more and more during the 1930s. The infamous Nuremberg laws of 1935 made any sexual contact between Germans and Jews a criminal offence, and the Law for the Protection of German Blood and Honour stipulated that only those of 'German or German-related blood' could be citizens of the Reich. In 1938 the Night of Broken Glass saw most synagogues throughout Germany go up in flames and thousands of Jews maltreated. The systematic Aryanization of Jewish property benefited thousands of German businessmen. During the war German victims of Allied bombing were often given furniture of Jewish families who had been sent to the gas chambers. The Wannsee conference of 1942 had laid the foundations for the systematic murder of European Jewry in annihilation camps in Poland and Eastern Europe. Mass shootings and mass murder of Eastern European Jewry had predated the Wannsee conference and were part and parcel of National Socialist warfare in the East almost from the beginning.

The widespread support of the German people for the National Socialist regime continued, even when the war began to bite. The ordinary man in the street had never been asked to bear the full brunt of the costs for war. No direct taxes for the mass of the population were ever introduced to finance the war. The National Socialists did attempt to curb consumption and siphon off any spare capital into the war economy, but they also ruthlessly exploited the occupied territories and robbed European Jewry of its property. Ethnic cleansing in Eastern Europe was meant to make way for German colonizers who would repopulate the region. Heinrich Himmler's 'socialism of the good blood' enticed many Germans to undergo 'race tests' in the hope for better homes and careers in Eastern Europe. Millions of slave labourers from across Europe (finely graded according to the categories of race) helped the German war economy and made it largely unnecessary for the National Socialists to draft women into the factories. German men often experienced occupational advancement and upward social mobility, as they were put in charge of the slave labourers. The harsh treatment of them at the hands of the *Volksgenossen* testifies to the degree to which ideas of the racial community had penetrated everyday life in National Socialist Germany. The very barbarity of the racial war on the Eastern Front was further testimony of the impact of racialism on wider sections of the German population. Even during the final months of the war, when everyone knew that the war had been lost, millions of Germans continued to fight until the bitter end, although increasing numbers of *Volksgenossen* also began to opt out of the National Socialist vision—just waiting for the inevitable and hoping to survive. Carpet bombing had reduced German cities to heaps of rubble, and millions of ethnic Germans were fleeing the advancing Red Army in the East. The war had come home to the Germans with a vengeance.

INTERNATIONAL RELATIONS

After 1918 the lost war and the Versailles Treaty left the overwhelming majority of Germans with the desire to revise the stipulations of a peace treaty which they regarded as deeply unjust and humiliating. Under the treaty Germany lost almost 15 per cent of its arable land, three-quarters of its iron ore, and one-quarter of its coal. The Saar basin was separated from Germany for fifteen years to be administered by the League of Nations, while its coal output was to benefit France. The Rhineland was demilitarized and occupied by Allied soldiers. The Allies prohibited Austria from joining Germany. All of Germany's overseas investments and properties were confiscated. It lost its colonies. It lost its merchant shipping. Severe restrictions were put on Germany's military. And on top of all this, the country was to pay massive war reparations and declared the sole guilty party in the outbreak of war in 1914.

Although, at first sight, these seem indeed harsh peace terms, none of them prevented Germany from quickly re-establishing its position as one of the most important economic powerhouses in Europe and a great nation among the other great nations of Europe. It was by no means as harsh a peace as was depicted in the contemporary German press. Much of the reparations were never paid. And although no German was willing to admit it in the inter-war period, the

First World War was a bid for German hegemony in Europe which directly aimed at extending its borders and penetrating vast areas of East-Central and Eastern Europe. Some territories were going to be directly incorporated into a much bigger German Reich, whilst a range of vassal states would do Germany's bidding in Eastern Europe. The treaty of Brest-Litovsk between Germany and a defeated Russia in the spring of 1918 gave the world a feel for things to come had Germany won the war against the Western Allies. The high-pitched hopes for German dominance, re-enforced at Brest-Litovsk, were confronted with the widespread loss of territories determined at Versailles. The nation was about to be rudely awakened to the realities of a lost war. While republican politicians were willing to consider the territorial losses in the West and the North, the much more substantial losses in the East were never accepted.

The extensive loss of territories meant that the issue of borders and bordering became hugely important. German foreign policy tried to strengthen that part of Germandom in Eastern Europe that found itself outside the borders of the German Reich after 1918. German politicians argued that for centuries Germans in Eastern Europe had fulfilled a colonizing and civilizing mission. It was territory deeply imbued with German culture. The Tannenberg memorial in East Prussia, which was officially opened in 1927, became an important symbol for German cultural superiority over the Slav East. State-funded German Ostforschung provided 'scientific' expertise to legitimate the territorial ambitions of Germany in East-Central and Eastern Europe. The traditional anti-Slav impetus of German nationalism strengthened the desire to bring the lost territories in the East back under German control. Republican Germany was quite successful in effectively penetrating East-Central European markets, which were perceived by many German economic experts as 'natural markets' for German industry. German economic muscle was an important element in strategies for the revision of the Versailles Treaty.

When, in 1922, Germany and the Soviet Union signed the Rapallo Treaty, alarm bells were ringing in the West European capitals. Were the two outcasts of post-1918 Europe about to join forces to bring about a revision of borders in Eastern Europe? Given the prevalence of anti-Slav sentiments in Germany, the country was far more likely to seek reconciliation with the West. Many representatives of Weimar democracy argued that Germany should demonstrate its goodwill by trying to fulfil the payment schedule for war reparations laid down in the aftermath of the Versailles Treaty. The Allies would see that these payments had a crippling effect on Germany and would in turn be willing to reconsider their demands. German politicians could indeed count on a fairly sympathetic hearing from Britain in the 1920s. Jingoism and anti-German sentiments peaked immediately after the war, but soon those who, like Keynes, had warned about the dire consequences of keeping Germany impoverished won the upper hand. British foreign policy became an important ally in attempts to revise Versailles.

The Dawes plan of 1924 opened the path to a peaceful revision of the Versailles Treaty. It recommended evacuation of the Ruhr by the French, the setting up of a special bank to receive reparations payments from Germany, and the granting of a generous international loan to Germany. If hyper-nationalists in Germany denounced the Dawes plan as a devious plot to enslave Germans for generations to come, there could be no mistaking the fact that the tone of the Allies had become more conciliatory. And indeed two years later Germany was admitted to the League of Nations. Franco-German relations were set on the road to a genuine reconciliation under the Locarno Treaty of 1925. Its architects, Gustav Stresemann and Aristide Briand, made the first steps to overcome the alleged 'hereditary enmity' between the two nations. They shared the Nobel Peace Prize in 1926 for their endeavours and went on to become early champions of the idea of a European Federal Union. The Young Plan and The Hague conference were also important in furthering Franco-German détente. The Kellogg-Briand pact of August 1928 was essentially a pact to outlaw war, but it provided an important opportunity for Stresemann to push his case for a peaceful revision of the Versailles Treaty and an early return of the Rhineland under German control.

If representatives of Weimar democracy sought to bring about an end to the perceived injustices of Versailles by furthering genuine reconciliation—at least with the former enemies among the Western countries of Europe—the anti-republican right remained impeccable and immovable in their opposition to all reconciliation. Already under Brüning Germany's foreign policy moved from Stresemann's idea of a peaceful integration of Germany into a new European order to the notion of a strong 'central Europe', in which Germany had a hegemonic position. On a superficial level, National Socialist foreign policies were a continuation of Weimar foreign policies, as both National Socialists and Weimar politicians put the revision of the Versailles Treaty at the top of their agenda. But ultimately Hitler quickly abandoned the peaceful search for a revision of the stipulations of Versailles. In October 1933 Germany left the disarmament conference and the League of Nations. Hitler's confrontationist tactics wanted to push the Allies to the limit while, at the same time, actively preparing for a new war, which was perceived as the only possibility of achieving the old aim of hegemony in Europe and ultimately in the world. It also had an intensely ideological component in that it was directed against Jewish Bolshevism. Preparation for war and racialist anti-Semitism had not been part of Weimar's foreign policy.

The National Socialists showed themselves flexible enough to forge short-term alliances with the Soviet Union in 1939, but the short-term gain did not mean that the National Socialists lost sight of their ultimate goal: an ideological and aggressively expansionist war in Eastern Europe fought on behalf of a *Volk ohne Raum* (people without space). For this purpose the Anti-Comintern Pact was signed by Germany and Japan in November 1936. In May 1939 Italy joined to make it the 'Pact of Steel' between these three deeply anti-Communist and expansionist nations. When war broke out in September 1939, it looked as though the totalitarian dictatorships were ready to take over what remained of liberal parliamentary democracy in Western Europe. But when Britain could not be defeated quickly, National Socialist Germany made the mistake of attacking the Soviet Union. After initial successes, the German armies got stuck in the Russian winter. When Japan attacked Pearl Harbor, it brought the United States into the war on the side of Britain. In 1942–3 the battles of Stalingrad and El Alamein marked the turning point of the war. By 1945 the Communist Soviet Union and the Western democracies had jointly defeated fascism.

CONCLUSIONS

Any balance sheet of the years 1919 to 1945 in German history has to start with the Holocaust and the National Socialist dictatorship. How did a project of such primeval barbarity succeed in a highly civilized and modern society? Ideas of a negative German *Sonderweg*, paving the way for Hitler and the National Socialists and reaching back far into the nineteenth century and beyond, gained widespread support in the 1960s and 1970s. The loss of the First World War and the Versailles Peace Treaty, others argued, contributed much to the failure of the first German republic, as it was unjustly but effectively blamed for the lost war and the 'treaty of shame'. The onslaught of the political right against the republic coincided with the rise of *völkisch* nationalism after 1918 which contributed to the victory of National Socialism in 1933 and the setting up of their racial state thereafter.

And yet, one should not forget that, despite its eventual collapse, parliamentary democracy had its own glorious moments between 1919 and 1933. The revolution of 1918 marked the promise of a more democratic, more liberal, and more emancipated future. Social rights were enshrined in the Weimar constitution for the first time in German history, and the experimentation with welfare state policies was extraordinarily progressive in the 1920s. The concept of social partnership between trade unions and employers, established for the first time with the ZAG of 1918, was pointing towards future developments in the second half of the twentieth century. There were also some real openings for Franco-German cooperation and European economic integration, which in the end came to nothing, but which also pointed in the direction of developments post-1945. Furthermore, the Weimar Republic paved the way for greater women's emancipation. In the arts, the period between 1919 and 1933 produced some of the great classics of twentieth-century culture. Republicans successfully defended democracy against left-wing and right-wing extremism in the early years of Weimar. Monarchist and anti-republican right-wing parties became integrated more closely in the middle years of the republic. The pillarization of society held back the progress of parliamentary politics. Ironically, the National

Socialists unwittingly began to dismantle this by stressing the egalitarianism of the *Volksgemeinschaft*, but it needed the devastation of total war to shatter Germany's social structures for good and allow for the emergence of catch-all parties in the Federal Republic. Courageous acts of resistance against the National Socialist barbarity came from all walks of life—many Communists, Socialists, Democrats, Christians, and conservative nationalists made clear their hostility to National Socialism. Many paid for their courage with their lives, but post-war Germany could build on their examples of civil courage and their vision of a 'different Germany'.

This chapter has attempted to stress throughout that the 'dark years' approach to the period 1914 to 1945 is somewhat problematic even in German history, where these were dark years indeed. But there were also many events and developments which pointed to the potential for a brighter future. Without wanting in the least to convey the impression that National Socialism was just an unfortunate break in an otherwise smooth development towards more democracy and freedom in Germany, what needs to be emphasized as well is the hetero-temporality of events and developments. While National Socialism could build on a range of historical precedents, other stories and lines of development pointed in different directions. Between 1919 and 1945 Germany was not lacking in modernity. Already by the beginning of the twentieth century it was one of the most modern industrial nations in Europe. But after 1918 Germany suffered from a severe crisis of modernity (Detlev Peukert), which buried the Weimar Republic and paved the way towards the pathological modernity of the National Socialists. All too many Germans perceived the post-1918 period as a time of crisis in which the traditional social order was being eroded. Urbanization, atomization, insecurity, and the consequences of 'mass society' all seemed threatening phenomena. Hence radical ideas of re-establishing order were popular in the 1920s and 1930s. Modernity itself is, of course, a Janus-faced phenomenon. German history in the twentieth century revealed some of its worst and some of its best aspects. Bringing modernity in line with the values of parliamentarism, democracy, and the rule of law was the central achievement of German politics of the second half of the twentieth century.

National Socialism cast a long shadow over Europe. Yet the majority of Germans chose to forget questions of their own guilt for the first one and a half decades after the end of the war and instead concentrated on constructing themselves as victims—victims of war, of Hitler, and of the Allies. At the same time they focused on rebuilding their country with amazing speed. Only from the 1960s onwards did more self-critical views of National Socialism come to the fore. Yet views of Weimar remained almost entirely negative. The Weimar system was blamed for the failure of the first German democracy, which was also a means for politicians and the German elites more generally to avoid awkward questions about their own responsibility for the failure of the first German republic. 'Bonn is not Weimar' became the rallying cry of all post-war

West German governments, indicating how much distance the second German democracy was putting between itself and its predecessor. However, as this article has shown, Weimar was by no means a one-sided failure. Its successes foreshadowed developments in West Germany during a happier second half of the twentieth century, when economic and political developments were far more conducive to building a successful democratic state. Today's Germans remember in their majority the democratic traditions and the dark sides of their modern history together. The Holocaust in particular has become a major part of public national remembrance. All this does not amount to 'normality' which remains elusive, as there is no norm in matters of national identity, but it contributes to a stable democracy—even in times of social, economic, and political crisis, as in the middle part of the first decade of the twenty-first century.

FURTHER READING

Bridenthal, Renate, Atina Grossmann, and Marion Kaplan (eds.), *When Biology Became Destiny: Women in Weimar and Nazi Germany* (New York, 1984).

Burleigh, Michael, and Wolfgang Wippermann, *The Racial State: Germany 1933–1945* (Cambridge, 1991).

Crew, David (ed.), *Nazism and German Society 1933–1945* (London, 1994).

Evans, Richard J., *The Coming of the Third Reich* (Harmondsworth, 2004).

——, *The Third Reich in Power* (Harmondsworth, 2005).

Fritzsche, Peter, *Germans into Nazis* (Cambridge, Mass., 1998).

Robert Gellately, *Backing Hitler: Consent and Coercion in Nazi Germany* (Oxford, 2002).

Gerwarth, Robert, *The Bismarck Myth: Weimar Germany and the Legacy of the Iron Chancellor* (Oxford, 2005, paperback 2007).

Herf, Jeffrey, *Reactionary Modernism: Technology, Culture and Politics in Weimar and the Third Reich* (Cambridge, 1984).

Hiden, John, *Germany and Europe 1919–1939* (2nd edn., London, 1993).

Kershaw, Ian, *The Hitler Myth* (Oxford, 1987).

——, *The Nazi Dictatorship: Problems and Perspectives of Interpretation* (4th edn., London, 2000).

Kolb, Eberhard, *The Weimar Republic* (2nd edn., London, 2005).

Mommsen, Hans, *The Rise and Fall of Weimar Democracy* (Chapel Hill, NC, 1996).

Peukert, Detlev, *The Weimar Republic* (London, 1993).

Usborne, Cornelie, *The Politics of the Body in Weimar Germany: Women's Reproductive Rights and Duties* (Ann Arbor, 1992).

Wright, Jonathan, *Gustav Stresemann: Weimar's Greatest Statesman* (Oxford, 2002).

10

The Successor States

R. J. W. Evans

INTRODUCTION

In East-Central Europe, empires went to war in 1914; nation-states emerged after it. Few there in 1914 had doubted the future of their existing empires (except the Ottoman one, by now marginal to the region anyway). During the war, *émigrés* in the West were first to urge a radical restructuring, especially of Austria-Hungary, to facilitate the defeat of the Central Powers. But the possibility of a separate peace with the Habsburgs, and fears of revolution following the collapse of Tsarist Russia, blunted their campaign. By 1918, dismemberment became an Allied war aim, but the main determinant of that outcome was a domestic upsurge against the imperial regimes, channelled by existing political groupings at home.

The chief casualty was the Habsburg monarchy, which lacked any clear nation of state to fall back on, since all its dozen peoples were minorities of the population as a whole. Austria-Hungary had been a complex polity: advanced in some respects, with sophisticated parliamentary and part-federalized structures, a rule of law, economic dynamism, and cultural florescence; but undermined by political crises, oligarchies, backward peripheries, social and national unrest; and with traditional dynastic, aristocratic, military, and religious bonds that proved wasting assets over time. None of its 'successors' was comfortable with its legacy; but all were stamped by it.

These successor (or succession) states, as the new or reconstituted countries of the area came to be collectively known, formed an integral part of the post-war liberal-constitutional order across the continent and of the international system guaranteed by the League of Nations. Indeed, they were a touchstone for the politics and diplomacy of the 'New Europe', with universal suffrage and personal freedoms proclaimed across the region, and the whole panoply of contemporary political and social causes brought into public debate there. Yet individually, the states were all weak and attempts at collaboration could not conceal the huge native differences between them, or their very divergent and often mutually antagonistic foreign agendas. Let us first briefly survey the various kinds of purportedly novel and transformed polity, dividing them for convenience into three pairs.

THE NEW STATES

Austria and Hungary were the two rump states from the heart of the old empire, small and top-heavy, with friction between a now overblown capital and a largely rural hinterland. They contained few ethnic minorities. Jews formed some 5 per cent of the population in each case, with a disproportionate economic, professional, and intellectual role, though whether they actually constituted a minority was a moot (and important) point. Besides them there were fifth columns within the ruling nation and grave social tensions exacerbated by economic prostration post-1918. Both countries were reckoned guilty for the war, and for the sins (now much exaggerated) of the Habsburg system. They were correspondingly harshly treated at Paris (by the treaties of St Germain and Trianon respectively)—that is how they were left so ethnically homogeneous—and still viewed with much suspicion thereafter. In both, the instability and resentments from 1918–20, above all the brief Bolshevik regime of Béla Kun in Budapest, turned out to be decisive for the whole inter-war evolution.

Did Austria and Hungary really perpetuate pre-1914 arrangements? In some ways clearly so, especially Hungary, albeit on a pettier level. But there was little continuity of personalities: it is striking how, by contrast with the rest of the area, none of their main political figures had been important before the war; and they distanced themselves from the dynasty, though Hungary remained nominally a kingdom. They faced some similar problems; but also carried over deep differences from Habsburg days, notably the open confrontation in Austrian politics, with fully fledged party conflict ending in parliamentary breakdown and spilling over onto the streets, versus a solidarity front of the main vested political interests in Hungary, restraining mass movements from the early 1920s onwards, with parliament operative till the bitter end, railing now against the peace settlement rather than the Austrian link. And no cross-border cooperation emerged, except between sectarian groupings on right and left (the territorial issue of the 'Burgenland', transferred from Hungary to Austria, fomented discord). Thus a Habsburg restoration was possible in each, but never in both together. As we shall see later, Austria would be the first of our states to collapse, and Hungary the last.

Czechoslovakia and Poland grouped together closely related peoples, now in two republics, both created anew but claiming continuity with monarchies of an earlier era. Each was formed for one ethnic group; but their frontiers, part ancient, part novel, embraced large minorities, particularly the Germans of

Table 10.1. Ethnic composition of the Successor States
c. 1920 *(approximate figures)*

Country	Total	Chief ethnic population groups	%
Austria	7 million	Germans	90
		Jews	5
Czechoslovakia	13 million	Czechs	50
		Germans	23
		Slovaks	15
		Hungarians	6
Hungary	8 million	Hungarians	85
		Germans	7
		Jews	5
Poland	27 million	Poles	69
		Ukrainians	14
		Jews	8
		Germans	4
Romania	18 million	Romanians	72
		Hungarians	8
		Jews	4
		Germans	4
Yugoslavia	12 million	Serbs	43
		Croats	23
		Slovenes	8
		Bosniaks	6
		Macedonians	5
		Germans	4
		Hungarians	4
		Albanians	4

Bohemia, who came henceforth to be known as 'Sudetens'. Besides, their 'state-nations' were split: in Poland the inheritance of the former tripartite division proved not insuperable, but left all kinds of frictions; whereas the 'Czechoslovak' concept of Czech–Slovak homogeneity grew weaker with time, until it broke down altogether.

Both Czechoslovakia and Poland profited from much Western goodwill: they counted as important members of the post-Versailles system of alliances. They sought to stress links with the West and full membership of the democratic camp. That was truer of Czechoslovakia, with coalition governments throughout the period legitimized by regular free elections, than in Poland, where a coup by the wartime leader Józef Piłsudski in 1926 soon eliminated most of the parliamentary process. In any event, their claims soon generated a gap between appearance and reality, and placed supreme strains on the institutions of both states by the 1930s. Yet worse, they found no common ground: in a classic instance of the failure of Slav brotherhood, the whole ethos of their public life was, or was perceived to be, divergent. Thus the two most powerful successor states (with a joint population greater than that of France) failed to perceive their mutual interest, as will appear below in connection with the territorial clash over Teschen.

Romania and Yugoslavia were both vastly expanded kingdoms, with backward landed economies. Hence, they had, on the one hand, an overstretch in administration and communications; and on the other, the added dimension of dynastic politics, an unsteady and sometimes unsavoury world of German princelings and Serbian pig-breeders recast as rulers. Like Czechoslovakia and Poland, they had minorities proper: especially Romania, with its many Magyars and Jews. More crucially, they too had rifts in the 'nation of state': in Romania (like Poland) the bridgeable but fraught gap between Regateni, citizens of the old state, and the rest; in Yugoslavia (like Czechoslovakia) the artificial and in time abortive attempt to create a single Serbo-Croat (and also Slovene etc.) identity. Meanwhile, dissident politicians from the Regat and Serbia were always ready to ally with 'outsiders'.

Both Romania and Yugoslavia passed through a decade or so of more or less parliamentary government, faction-ridden and barren. False hopes of improvement emerged in the late 1920s; then authoritarian solutions took over—not just because of the Depression—under royal control. But the basic domestic contest was different: in Romania an effete central establishment versus right-radicals; in Yugoslavia, Serb–Croat antagonism with other groups as bargaining counters. And two of Europe's most virulent fascist movements played opposed political roles: in Romania preaching integral nationalism; in Yugoslavia (as in Austria) feeding on its frailty. In both cases (as in Austria and Hungary), fascists actually attained some fruits of power in the end, fleetingly, with German help. Romania and Yugoslavia pursued a somewhat more kindred line of foreign policy than Czechoslovakia and Poland; but again external power ambitions were abetted by their absence of common purpose.

THE NEW ESTABLISHMENTS

Tomáš Masaryk, the exile philosopher and politician catapulted to presidency of Czechoslovakia, called his memoirs of the period 'The World Revolution'. But how revolutionary were the events of 1918–20? In their territorial effects, indeed so; but in social-political terms, far less. There was chaos on the ground, especially in Hungary and Austria, in the immediate aftermath of the war, including a short-lived Communist coup and military campaigns across the new frontiers. But we must look deeper, at continuities with the pre-war world which explain much that was orderly on the surface of its successor, but which would perpetuate, even aggravate, the underlying weaknesses of the region, both in individual states and collectively.

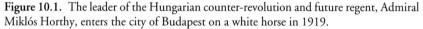

Figure 10.1. The leader of the Hungarian counter-revolution and future regent, Admiral Miklós Horthy, enters the city of Budapest on a white horse in 1919.

The new establishments were mostly formed from existing national interest groups, and their hold on authority became correspondingly tenuous as they faced complex and interlocking challenges from rivals old and new. All suffered, albeit in varying degrees, both from ethnic exclusiveness, and from a narrow social and institutional base. In Austria the Christian Social allegiance dominated; in Hungary the governmental bloc around the Regent, or acting head of state, Miklós Horthy, and his prime minister of the 1920s, István Bethlen. In Czechoslovakia the preponderantly Czech parties of the so-called Pětka, or quintuple coalition, held the reins of power; in the complex Polish situation the National Democrats, or Endecja, came nearest to that at first, until replaced by Piłsudski's purgative (*Sanacja*) regime. Control in Romania fell mainly to the Liberals from the Regat; whereas the strongest force in Yugoslavia, which explicitly announced itself as encompassing the South ('Yugo') Slavs as a whole, was the 'market-place' (*čaršija*) of old-Serb elites based in Belgrade. At the same time certain embattled anti-governments, like the Socialist-run Viennese municipality and the Croatian party organization in Zagreb, acted as a kind of mirror-image to their hegemonic rivals.

These successor establishments sought to consolidate their position in the 1920s, sensing peril from further change. By the 1930s, they increasingly felt the need to buttress themselves with various kinds of authoritarian structure, abandoning party-political rule where necessary. This was an upper middle class, defined by economic, functional, and educational-intellectual features, fending off mass involvement at the price of some concessions to the old order. Let us briefly consider those several elements in turn.

The inter-war elites could build on earlier prosperity, especially in Bohemia and parts of Austria, Poland, and Hungary. One of their components was an entrepreneurial class with political clout, such as the group around Prague's Živnostenská bank, the Endecja with its Prussian roots, and the Romanian Liberals. They faced three problems, however. Even Czech and Austrian industrial output stood at only 70 per cent of the West European average; elsewhere the ratios ranged from about 50 per cent to less than 20 per cent. Then came post-armistice prostration, inflation, and war debts, all exacerbated by protective tariffs and expensive loans, mainly abroad, and by the collapse of agrarian prices after 1929. Few new railways were built, though communication needs had changed; motor vehicles hardly made a difference. Moreover, the established bourgeoisies might be alien to the changed purposes of state, as with Sudeten Germans in Czechoslovakia, Transylvanian Magyars in Romania, and above all Jews, who now experienced an altered atmosphere, particularly ominous in the early shift towards anti-Semitism in Hungary, where they had hitherto felt most welcome.

The establishments were also bureaucracies: a Habsburg legacy, which now often endured in its vices of arrogance and peculation rather than its virtues of diligence and integrity. Austria and Hungary henceforth had a distended administration; the other countries had more to rule, with rewards to bestow on loyal cadres. In both cases the implications were Parkinsonian. Higher taxation was needed, but it could not yield enough, hence widespread corruption. This officialdom, like the loyal economic elites, promoted, and was legitimated by, the mentality of nationalism, entrenched through education. National ideology could conveniently be turned against enemies at home and abroad, and used to mobilize groups otherwise held at arm's length. It ensured respect for schooling, and generated important cultural movements; but chauvinistic assumptions regularly diminished its broader appeal and brought clashes with Jews in the professions.

The new elites proved largely capable of containing the region's traditionally privileged groups, aristocratic, ecclesiastical, and military, though in some cases significant accommodations had to be made. Nobles lost wealth and sway in proportion to the implementation of land reform, which proceeded furthest in Czechoslovakia and Romania (alongside Yugoslavia, where Serbia's large estates had been eliminated in Turkish times). Elsewhere the nobility retained a role: a circumscribed one in Austria and Poland; a more conspicuous one in Hungary. These last countries had substantial numbers of déclassé and ex-gentry elements in their bureaucracies. They were also the places where the Catholic Church remained most powerful, though in Hungary it stood in an uneasy relation with East-Central Europe's only major Protestant minority. As an oppositional force,

Catholicism could count on support among many Slovaks, Croats, and Slovenes. But there were few actual confessional parties, and Orthodox influence in Serbia, Romania, and eastern Poland played itself out in largely non-political ways. The army was significant especially in Poland, after the Piłsudski take-over, and in Yugoslavia, where it could build on its wartime exploits—and these two states alone would in due course resist Hitlerite aggression. Elsewhere soldiers wielded less prestige, even in Czechoslovakia, which boasted the best-equipped and staffed troops—who would see no action.

For all their distance from earlier equivalents, ruling groups between the wars acquired many aspects of a backward-looking mentality, broadly conservative, exclusive, and immobile. What had begun as flexible groupings, growing out of genuinely progressive initiatives, were frozen on the crest of a wave in 1918, under the overwhelming emotional experience of national 'liberation' or humiliation, deceiving and self-deceived about the permanence and authenticity of the solutions vouchsafed to the region by the peace conference. As those proved incomplete, unstable, and unworthy, ideals of national regeneration turned into idols, democracy into intolerance, confidence into disillusion. By the same token, ethnic minorities were the most elemental antagonists for regimes which claimed to rest on the rights of self-determination and to have merged state and nation; and the situation was especially dangerous where counter-establishments could mobilize dissatisfied groups, either inside the now dominant ethnicities, as with Slovaks in Czechoslovakia and Croats in Yugoslavia, or linked to powerful co-nationals abroad, as with the Sudeten and other German interests.

CHALLENGES 1: PEASANTS

Competing political and socio-economic ideologies constituted hardly less of a menace to the mainly bourgeois-national leaderships of the successor states. The real confrontation came with three kinds of mass movement. It is logical to examine first the peasant issue, since peasants were far the largest social constituency over most of the region. They made up a third of the population at the beginning of the period even in Austria and Bohemia: 40 per cent in Czechoslovakia as a whole, since more numerous in Slovakia (60 per cent). The figures for Hungary and Poland were higher (56 and 65 per cent respectively), in Romania (75 per cent) and Yugoslavia (79 per cent) far higher still. Where these proportions fell slightly thereafter, the absolute numbers did not, given high birth rates and the brake on emigration abroad.

Peasants benefited from land reform, where it took place. By 1930, only 10 per cent of the land in Yugoslavia belonged to estates over 50 hectares in extent, 20 per cent in Czechoslovakia and Poland, 32 per cent in Romania. In Hungary, with its minimal transfer, the figure was still 46 per cent. But dwarf holdings now predominated even more than before: two-thirds of the total in Poland and

Figure 10.2. The Czech composer Leoš Janáček (centre) on a visit to London in 1926. Jan Masazk, the Czechoslovak minister to the United Kingdom, is on the right.

Yugoslavia, three-quarters in Romania, higher still in Hungary. There was a desperate need for credit, for innovation, for cooperative forms of husbandry and marketing. Yet the state cushioned industry, raised indirect taxes, and chased prestige goals. Then came desperate overproduction as the Depression took hold from 1930, with a calamitous widening of the price-scissors in favour of manufactures.

Why did peasantries find no escape from their poverty trap? Partly because rural populations were so disparate, ranging from the better-off peasants proper (increasingly described by this time as 'agriculturalists', 'smallholders', or the like), down gradations of 'cottagers', those who typically possessed a dwelling but no land, to the many rural proletarians in varying degrees of destitution. That endangered the cohesiveness of peasant parties, and contributed to the wider problem of their frequent failure to develop effective political programmes. Austria's solid *Bauern* voted in the Christian Social interest, and their Czech equivalents were likewise represented by bourgeois leaders, who took a major role in government through the Pětka—the most impressive of them, Hodža, was actually a Slovak, who proved unable to satisfy the larger demands of his countrymen. Hungary's peasant groups, dislocated and chastened by the post-war troubles, largely withdrew from the fight, leaving their followers, the most marginal and deprived of all, seemingly also the least enfranchised. Poland had two (and sometimes three) rival parties, the most notable of them a platform for their doughty leader Wincenty Witos; but by the time these managed to unite, the parliamentary system had been destroyed. In Romania a coalition of peasants and nationalists broke through dramatically in the late 1920s, but failed to sustain its momentum. In Yugoslavia Serb peasants formed the backbone of the Radical camp, but exerted little influence thereby; whereas Croatia nurtured a dynamic rural party which embodied grievances of the whole nation, especially under its leader Stjepan Radić until his assassination in 1928.

The efforts of peasant politicians were not a complete failure. They belonged among the more honourable public figures of the inter-war era, and the extent of common ground between them is revealed by serious attempts at cross-frontier organization: an Agrarian Bureau, pursuing technical and managerial matters under the direction of the Czechs, which then mutated into a so-called Green International; and its more militant and startling rival, the Moscow-inspired Krestintern. Yet both these initiatives ran into the sand; and their course mirrored a loss of direction and diluted or deflected programmes at home. The contest in the successor states between urban and rural visions was an uneven one. The theorists of the latter were at the best of times inclined to be romantic and impractical; their extremer demands terrified the establishment, besides being divisive and economically faulty. However, compromise brought disorientation. Peasant leaders found themselves out of their depth, easily persuaded by appeals to a factitious 'national' interest, alienated from the electorate. They either abandoned rustic dress or held to it merely as a self-conscious fashion. While the elite swallowed up careerist churls, it held its idealized countrymen at a safe distance. The village stimulated some genuine and creative literature and art (I shall return to that point later); yet the folksy idiom of the day cocooned villagers in a largely ersatz confection of patriotic historicism

CHALLENGES II: SOCIALISTS

Peasant movements were outflanked to left and right by socialists and fascists, both of whom—but especially the latter—succeeded in manœuvring with other interested parties to gain a share of power at crucial junctures. The Socialists were the oldest of the mass political groupings in the area, and the only one with a significantly international stance. They had drawn inspiration from the disciplined German movement, the most formidable in pre-war Europe, and from the turbulent politics on the left in Russia, especially during 1905–7. But their main precursors were the Monarchy's Social Democrats, the largest party in the Austrian parliament from 1907 and a powerful extra-parliamentary pressure group in Hungary, as well as a seed-bed for the major theorists of the Austro-Marxist school. These Social Democrats had not been immune to ethnic rivalries; but they had held them more or less in check, with parallel union and party structures. Almost all had approved the war in its earlier stages; but from 1917 they were poised to exploit elemental revulsion against its continuation and against the social system which seemed to have brought it about.

A wave of Socialist popularity in 1919–20 across the region sufficed to frighten the establishments, but not seriously to threaten them, even in Hungary and Austria, where leftish regimes briefly enjoyed at least the appearance of power. Soon the Socialist–Communist split provoked by the Bolsheviks became manifest everywhere; and the subsequent fortunes of the two branches illustrated the frailty of Marxist assumptions about working-class solidarity and the industrial proletariat as a revolutionary class. What occurred was a clash between patriotic reformers and international Marxist-Leninists: between the solid trade-unionism of Austria and Bohemia at one end of the spectrum and the inchoate radicalism of Yugoslavia at the other, with Hungary in a middle position. In this scenario, Romania and Poland corresponded more or less to Yugoslavia and Hungary respectively, but with the modifying factor in their case of elemental anti-Russian attitudes. Everywhere those nearer the new centres of power were apt to be Socialist; while neglected provinces, disregarded communities, and disadvantaged minorities became Communist.

A decline of the left during the 1920s was accelerated in various proportions by these squabbles, which reached their nadir by 1929 with the Comintern's new confrontational line; by repression on the part of the authorities; and by comparative prosperity and stability. Support fell away particularly in Romania, less than 10 per cent of whose labour force was in manufacturing industry as late

Figure 10.3. The architectural flagship of 'Red Vienna': Karl-Marx-Hof, 1930.

as 1930, and Yugoslavia. Communists were proscribed there and in Hungary, where the Socialist movement fell into the hands of rightish, indecisive trade unionists cowed into a pact with the government which minimized their scope for activity. In Poland revulsion against the Soviet Union, which had invaded the country in 1919, left the Socialist party (PPS) as the only force on the left, and placed it in a false position from 1926, when its ex-leader Piłsudski re-emerged as a dictator with his programme of national regeneration. Its Austrian equivalents faced a tense stand-off with the ruling Christian Socials, their radical municipal projects in 'Red Vienna' aggravating relations with the rest of the country. Even in orderly Czechoslovakia a plethora of left-of-centre parties attenuated their overall share in government. Besides mainstream Socialists, with a parallel grouping among the German minority, the Czechs also had National Socialists, who preached patriotism, even a chauvinist egalitarianism; while the fully legal Communist party was genuinely cross-ethnic.

In the 1930s, Socialism enjoyed a revival, but this remained surprisingly limited. In Austria it was broken by the notorious shoot-out with the authorities in 1934. Elsewhere the more legalistic Social Democrats were held down across much of the region by police surveillance, as well by their own lack of remedies for the economic crisis. The bravura resistance of Communists was trumped by fascists, then debilitated by purges of their exiled leadership in the Soviet Union. The call for a Popular Front arrived too late and lacked sincerity, except in Czechoslovakia, where it lent the domestic Communists new national credentials, and Yugoslavia, where it revived tarnished ideals of South Slav unity in the clandestine circles around Tito and his like. Elsewhere it yielded curious alliances, sometimes with the right, as in Hungary and Romania. Then came the acrobatics of the Hitler–Stalin pact, which killed any such cooperation and deprived militants of whatever fruits had been gained by their individual bravery against fascism over the previous years.

By that point, in the autumn of 1939, things had reached a low ebb. The Social Democrats stood outmanœuvred and forlorn, if not openly persecuted. The Communists were led from the wings by mostly obscure new men. The whole left was forced underground, like the representatives of the peasantry. Yet both lay poised, thanks to the very circumstances of their exclusion from power, to bounce back as soon as the new wartime order faced its nemesis.

CHALLENGES III: FASCISTS

The strong Socialist boost from 1917–18 onwards helped lend local proto-fascists an anti-Bolshevik momentum; but they had native roots too. Their activities were not at all homogeneous: they generated little international contact, beyond a loose debt to Italian and German models and some help from these later; they demonstrated widely different levels of appeal and forms of evolution. They are best understood as a series of self-contained movements, isolated from each other by their ultra-national motive force, where foreign influence served to lend some shape and direction to a spontaneous, incoherent, and highly fractious upsurge.

Yet certain common features are apparent. The upheaval of 1918 introduced a first stage of small inchoate groups, with wild theorists and violent methods. They fed on expectations of change, on a sense of uprootedness and a (para-)military ethic, especially in the defeated states, Austria and Hungary, with many *déraciné* soldiers and officers. The doctrine of hyper-nationalism functioned as an emotional focus for those caught up in a disruption of traditional communities who found few secure economic opportunities elsewhere and no effective help from above. In all this there was a clear debt to the semi-authoritarian habits and the lack of civic responsibility widespread in the old empires. Altogether the upsurge looked much more like an attack on the new establishments (and on their predecessors) than a defence of them, though they faced no immediate threat from it.

The Depression ushered in a second stage, as signs of spiritual as well as material turmoil spread. Disillusion with the rational-cum-liberal-parliamentary nostrums of the Versailles era grew apace, though the fascism of the successor states was no more a product of anti-democracy alone than of anti-socialism (these countries had had too little experience of either). By now serious movements were afoot, with a broader social base and aspirations to political power. The real contest came to be revealed as one between this new right and more traditional conservative forces. Repressive and themselves quasi-fascist regimes defended establishments unwilling to seek popular backing. In that they proved successful for the most part: the third stage, that of fascist government, tended not to be reached, except as an imposition from abroad. Everywhere in the region (by contrast with contemporary Italy), anti-Semitism operated as a touchstone for fascist sympathizers: it was intricately linked to xenophobic and defensive ideologies. At the same time (by contrast with Germany), such sympathizers still usually made appeal to Christian principles, whether Catholic or Orthodox. We can distinguish three varieties of local fascist organization from the late 1920s.

First, the trappings of fascism were regularly assumed by authoritarian governments. They moved towards political dictatorship, the elimination of parties, maybe of all representative bodies, and perhaps of the constitution altogether, with a rigid centralizing drive and a tamed judiciary. Corporatist slogans might be brought in, and probably some institutional forms too from the same stable. There was use of plebiscites (where they could be guaranteed to work), and of the 'leadership principle' up to a point, with some attempt at 'national' forms of organization to underpin it. Paramilitary guards became *de rigueur*, or else a prominent place was accorded to professional soldiers, with associated youth movements, uniforms, coloured shirts (typically green ones), salutes, and so on. And normally some anti-Semitic measures were introduced by the end.

Right across the area, except in Czechoslovakia, we encounter such a development: from the Austria of Dollfuss and his 'above-party' Vaterländische Front; and Hungary, with its *numerus clausus* as early as 1920 to restrict higher education for Jews, then the regimes of Gömbös and Imrédy; through the Poland of Piłsudski. and the colonels, with their camp followers in the government support organization OZN (Obóz Zjednoczenia Narodowego); to the royal variants in Romania, where King Carol gained approval by a plebiscite of 99.872 per cent for his Front of National Renaissance, and Yugoslavia, where King Alexander ruled as a strong man from 1929 till he was assassinated in 1934, then premier Stojadinović established his solidarity bloc in the Jugoslavenska Radikalna Zajednica. All these remained distinctly weak versions of an Italian model. They were not seriously totalitarian, and they invaded more the public than the private sphere. Besides, they were still politically vulnerable, especially in Hungary and in Yugoslavia after 1934, where they depended on a non-fascist head of state. They exhibited little real ideological or social dynamic (imagine Dollfuss's drab successor Schuschnigg as a charismatic figure!); and even with liberal utilization of police methods they struggled to steal enough clothes from their radical rivals.

Nazism, our second category, was distinct. As an openly German creed, it was largely restricted to ethnic Germans in the region and to a few proselytes (with a corresponding tendency to alienate non-Germanophiles). That meant mainly Austria and the Sudetenland, where 'National Socialism' had already emerged well before the war as a political movement among workers protecting their jobs and national culture from Czech inroads, under the influence of the fanatical pan-German, Georg von Schönerer. In Austria things were more complex than the eventual *Anschluss* and attendant flag-waving might suggest. Austria's Great-German camp behaved in a rather staid and conservative manner from 1918, while the anti-Communist and anti-democratic, Catholic-tinged patriots of the paramilitary defence leagues (*Heimwehren*) looked to Mussolini as their protector.

Even in the 1930s, native Nazis in Austria operated in underground, provincial, and ambivalent ways, while the Sudetens fed on the crisis of state in Czechoslovakia only late in the day. Elsewhere Nazism spread through fifth columns. The free city of Danzig comprised one of these: a sore on the Polish body politic. Two million Danube Swabians and Saxons, spread out across Hungary, Romania, and Yugoslavia as self-contained and not particularly oppressed minorities, were swept along after 1933 by ideas of the *Herrenvolk*. They pressed the authorities for, and eventually gained, autonomy statutes, even nominal control over the territory of the Yugoslav Banat by 1941.

Thirdly, indigenous mass right-radical movements made headway among the non-German populations. They had a following in Poland, with young Endecja cadres, Bolesław Piasecki's Falange, Rutkowski's youth association Związek Młodzieży Polskiej (ZMP—the 1930s abounded in acronyms), and others. They mobilized national and Catholic *ressentiments* among the Slovak and Croat oppositions in Czechoslovakia and Yugoslavia respectively, assuming a markedly anti-Semitic character among Slovak Nástupists and the Hlinka guard, whereas the vicious extremists of the Croatian Ustaša would turn their full force on the local Orthodox Serbs. The main cases in East-Central Europe, however, are those of Hungary and Romania.

The Hungarian white terror, unleashed by the Kun episode and by the severest laceration inflicted upon any national community as a result of the First World War, had already revealed much of the later chauvinist and racist mood in the country, notably through its sudden and sanguinary animus against the highly integrated but still 'alien' and now scapegoated Jews. It revived with added fury in the 1930s, exacerbated by the frustration of many workers, peasants, and redundant, underpaid officials and intellectuals at what they perceived as the Semitic-aristocratic-latifundial miasma in public life. Running fights ensued between a subversive but gentlemanly fascism located within the establishment and a petty-bourgeois crusade for social-moral rebirth. By 1939 the deranged megalomaniac Ferenc Szálasi and his band of Arrow-Cross thugs (the Nyilaskeresztesek) became the leading gang snapping at the heels of government.

In Romania right-radical ideology worked at a yet more primitive, mythopoeic level, and produced a yet more charismatic folk-hero in Corneliu Zelea Codreanu. Some extreme hatred of Jews and other kinds of 'foreign' domination had taken root in the Regat earlier, and it was acted upon by populist censure of exploitation and modernity in the name of rural anti-capitalism. Codreanu established his Legion of the Archangel Michael in 1927, with the Iron Guard (Garda de Fier) as its paramilitary arm: both fiercely anti-democratic and ritualized organizations which declared war upon what they saw as the corrupt, cynical, materialist, secular, and degenerate royal regime. The same trial of strength took place in Romania too, with regimes alternately temporizing and persecuting; the same genteel semi-fascist politicians, led there by Alexandru Cuza and Octavian Goga, sought to exploit their position as mediators. But in Romania the showdown came sooner, with a campaign of terrorism, the assassination of Codreanu, and a final struggle between Carol and the Guard which brought nemesis to both sides by the beginning of 1941.

INTERNATIONAL RELATIONS

Thus the successor states were progressively debilitated by domestic discord, which was exacerbated from the end of the 1920s by the Depression. They were terminally threatened, however, only by the wider crisis of Europe's post-war settlement, as Italy, Germany, and the Soviet Union fished in the murky waters of the 'lands between'. The diplomatic and then military solutions imposed by *force majeure* demonstrated how little common purpose had been engendered among the beneficiaries of the new order in East-Central Europe. Certainly the diplomatic dimension was crucial to their survival. We must follow this back to the Parisian treaties, which placed the settlement for the area on an explicitly international plane.

The treaties had two prime kinds of failing. The first were territorial. The peace-makers probably encouraged Poland and Czechoslovakia to swallow too much; Hungary they treated vindictively, and Austria as well to some extent. But much of this was either a *fait accompli*—thus, for instance, the Allies played a minimal role, despite the myth, in the Russo-Polish war of 1919–21—or else it reflected problems insoluble at the time. What could have been done about rump Austria? Where should the Sudeten Germans go? Or the Szeklers, a Magyar people now stranded in the middle of the new Romania? More plebiscites might have helped, according to some. But the evidence from those that were held was unclear. Southern Carinthia, parts of Upper Silesia, small portions of the Prussian–Polish borderland, the Sopron/Ödenburg salient in western Hungary: all raised at least as many difficulties as they solved. It was hard to pose or answer simple 'yes'/'no' questions in such a situation of flux; harder still to design satisfactory 'constituencies' for the vote.

Secondly, the settlement proclaimed principles and created expectations. The 'New Europe' would depend on a massive infusion of political and economic models from the West; but these could not be made to stick. In this respect Paris offered the worst of both worlds. It laid a false veneer over underlying East-Central European problems and methods, without the wherewithal to keep it polished. For example, those clauses introduced into the treaties to protect minorities: they would be unnecessary if democracy were really implemented, and constituted an offence to the *soi-disant* 'democratic' states on which they were imposed; but they proved wholly ineffectual anyway, and thus only compounded the grievances they were supposed to allay.

Altogether the victors soon began to lose interest. Political and humane concern to restore order and prosperity quickly evaporated. Official loans had to be supplemented by private investment during the 1920s; then both were mostly extinguished by the Depression. Western governments were unwilling to underwrite their commitments through positive trade policies or other inducements over any length of time. More insidiously—though also to some extent more honourably—doubts soon surfaced about the legitimacy and defensibility of the settlement itself. These led first to the Locarno Treaty, with its implications by default (by *not* guaranteeing frontiers there) for the east of the continent, then in the 1930s to France's lack of offensive military preparedness and the start of British appeasement. Yet this disengagement could only be rhetorical: note the irony, and inanity, of Chamberlain's famous comment after Munich about a 'far-away country of which we know nothing', whereas Czechoslovakia was avowedly the pride of post-First World War interventionism, and he had just sent a high-level fact-finding mission there.

The Western response was further fuelled by disappointment at the lack of collective action within the region. Why was such self-help so neglected? The 1920s furnished the only chance for communal, not to say confederal initiatives. But they lay too close to the real or supposed rancours of the past. We have already seen how few contacts existed between political groups in the separate countries. And their numerous paper treaties often had no more content. Minorities, of course, usually bedevilled relations between neighbouring states, just the ones which needed mutual security (and practically *every* border was fraught, once 'self-determination' had been enunciated as a goal). There was need for independent-minded and free-standing diplomats; but the foreign services depended heavily on the given ethnic establishments, with little vision or flexibility. It was easier too for regimes to insist on economic autarky, and buy off noisy domestic critics with privileges and tariffs. Trading policy became largely an arm of politics, and even honest officials had little scope. When France eventually floated the Tardieu plan for economic rapprochement in the Danubian area in 1932, it arrived just in time to be sunk by a resurgent Germany and Italy. Home-grown proposals by Hodža and others came far too late—or just a little too early, given the exiles' discussions during the Second World War and developments thereafter.

Paris left three classes of successor state: favoured and quite strong allies (Czechoslovakia and Poland); approved, but feebler and more distant allies (Romania and Yugoslavia); and former enemies, to be at best patronized (Austria and Hungary). This brief conspectus must concentrate on Czechoslovakia and Poland, as the key foreign-political operators within the region; and with a word on Hungary, as its only internal peace-breaker. Czechoslovakia was personified (the word is not too strong) by Dr Beneš, most conspicuous and celebrated of all inter-war statesmen from the east of the continent. Decent, thoughtful, rather aloof, reasonably honest but sinuous, a tenacious figure with uninterrupted responsibility, direct or indirect, for his country's diplomacy between 1918 and 1938, Edvard Beneš was a man of the League of Nations (six times chairman of its Council) and viewed collective security as crucial to his country. But he recognized its limits; therefore he added bilateral arrangements from 1924 on. Francophile in many things from military hardware to cultural influence—that doctorate he so valued was a French one, in political science—he also esteemed the Anglo-Saxon world, although that was cultivated more by Masaryk and then especially by the latter's son Jan. Whereas both Masaryk and Beneš always mistrusted Germany and felt cool towards Russia and Italy, Beneš was ever ready to manoeuvre.

The one fixation of Beneš (less so of Masaryk) was the *bête noire* of the old Habsburg world and his consequential fears of a restoration in Austria and especially Hungary. Hence his largest diplomatic achievement: the 'Little Entente' (so named by the Hungarians), through which Czechoslovakia joined with Romania and Yugoslavia for action against common enemies. The alliance foiled ex-King Charles's Hungarian adventures in 1921, then showed its mettle intermittently through to its condemnation of the Austro-German customs union ten years later. But was not Beneš here chasing a phantom? Hungary remained weak militarily, economically, and politically. And the alliance was no use against anyone else. It could not even do much to promote good inter-Entente relations. Despite the commitment of the Romanian Nicolae Titulescu and of certain Serb politicians, the awkward partnership was never much beloved of the Bucharest or Belgrade establishments.

Worse followed the breach with Poland over Teschen, a small but valuable piece of the old Bohemian lands in Upper Silesia, the subject of complicated historical and ethnic claims. Czechoslovakia held on to most of it while Poland was distracted in 1919–20. There were deeper reasons why Těšín/Cieszyn (the Czech and Polish variant spellings, with near-identical pronunciation) could sow such mischief, and why even some cooling of that issue could not yield amity. The two states projected very different styles of government and public ideology: the one 'Masarykian' humanist, bourgeois, and anticlerical; the other 'Piłsudskian' romantic, chivalrous, and Catholic. Each was rather jealous of the other's international status and sceptical of its viability (especially *vis-à-vis* Germany, in the 1920s as in the 1930s). They nursed very discrepant estimations of Russia, which grew out of a nineteenth-century heritage; and of Hungary, likewise a tradition not to be exorcised by any mentality of a 'New Europe'.

Poland had a French alliance from 1921, as a similar cornerstone of her defence diplomacy. But otherwise she stood in a partly self-imposed isolation, which went with great confidence in her superficially redoubtable army, fresh from its triumph over the Soviets, and the sense of a commanding political role in the region. Was not Poland grander than the petty Danubian realms? Her internal weakness had debilitating results: a profound clash from the first between civil and military authorities, and *within* the army; then army morale was restored by Piłsudski and his acolytes at the expense of representative institutions. The largest threat would clearly be her alienation of Germany and Russia at the same time. Poland was too confused and proud to play off one against the other, and she placed exaggerated reliance on her two neighbours' inability to cooperate, though the Rapallo agreement in 1922 already sowed the seed for 1939.

None the less, the problems of the area still appeared manageable during the 1920s. The only immediate threats to its international stability were the local revanchism of Hungary and the wider ambitions of her sole foreign backer at this stage, Mussolini's Italy. What of Mussolini? On the one hand, he sought gains along the Adriatic as part of his revived 'Roman Empire': a clear danger to Yugoslavia despite the 'other' Rapallo treaty, negotiated in 1920, only ratified in 1924 because of the two countries' dispute over the status of the port of Fiume/Rijeka, but then renewed as late as 1937. An associated ploy was for Italy to hold the Croats in a cleft stick, for deployment against the Serbs if required. On the other hand, Mussolini desired a larger protectorate over the Danubian basin as part of an arbiter role in Europe. Between the mid-1920s and the mid-1930s, Italy indeed looked to have a large stake in the region, thanks to her treaty with Hungary in 1927, her patronage of Austrian fascists, and the Rome protocols by which she reaffirmed her backing for Austria and Hungary in March 1934.

But this, like so much else, increasingly proved to be a façade, as Hitler developed a far greater foreign-political dynamic from 1933. Here is no place to consider his plan for East-Central Europe, but there were evidently two prongs to it, the *Mitteleuropa* dimension being exploited first, perhaps in case the German army and public should be satisfied with acquisitions further north which might be thought to lie merely in the Prussian tradition. What matter here are the responses on the ground to his continuously forward, adventurist policies, with their support for autochthonous Nazis and fascists, at least if governments would not play ball. Now the situation of 1914–18 repeated itself, in peacetime, and with no Habsburg Monarchy to moderate the German bid for hegemony.

The only immediate political taker, naturally enough, was the Hungarian premier Gömbös, the first foreign leader to pay an official visit to Hitler, who favoured a German–Italian 'axis' (the word was apparently his own coinage) to help his country's revisionist programme. Despite all the hesitations of the Budapest establishment, this policy proved irreversible and—in the short term—successful. The 'Versailles' reaction was orchestrated by Czechoslovakia. Beneš now tried belatedly to give real teeth to the Little Entente. Backed by Titulescu, he set up a permanent secretariat for it. Their efforts culminated in the 1934 diplomatic campaign of the French foreign minister, Barthou, for a system of eastern alliances. Then Barthou died (murdered with King Alexander of Yugoslavia on the quayside at Marseilles); but there were other reasons too for the collapse of the project. Poland was already out of step, having signed a non-aggression pact with Germany in January 1934. Great Britain stood on the sidelines, contemplating a similar *démarche*. Overtures to Austria foundered on her ambivalent attitude to Germany and on the Social Democratic stumbling-block. The Little Entente itself was emasculated, with the advent of Stojadinović in Belgrade, then the toppling of Titulescu in Bucharest in 1936; Yugoslav and Romanian priorities were anyway different.

Worse soon came with the Abyssinian fiasco, which threw Mussolini into Hitler's arms. Thus Austria was rendered defenceless (her Anschluss with Germany imminent), and the other countries lost any real room for manœuvre *between* Italy and Germany; while the Western powers' half-measures dismayed their remaining friends across the region. Moreover, the sanctions imposed on Italy tightened the economic strings in the German bow. Prostrated peasant exporters looked more and more to the Reich, where Schacht and the Reichsbank directed a system of barter, guaranteeing high prices for agrarian commodities in return for purchases on the German market. Now the beggar-my-neighbour policies of the new states, accentuated by the Depression, really came home to roost, above all playing members of the Little Entente off against one another. Romania and Yugoslavia were economic rivals in any case, whereas Czechoslovakia's Agrarians desperately held on to their own home customers. All three delivered more and more to Germany, spending from tied bank accounts to stimulate German industry and further depress their own, giving German investment and know-how ever greater scope in the East.

What of the only other possible guarantor of peace, the Soviet Union? The burning anti-Communism of most regimes, alongside obvious fears of the Comintern, had kept contacts to a minimum and prevented any genuine rapprochement. Poland and Romania did reach non-aggression pacts with the Soviets in 1932 and 1933 respectively, but only because of the latter's temporary preoccupation in east Asia. Hungary was hardly less antipathetic, for different reasons; Yugoslavia seriously feared Bolshevism at home. Only Czechoslovakia always sounded out the possibilities of a link, from the economic agreement signed as early as 1922. Even there, public opinion did not allow a treaty until 1935. It strengthened domestic solidarity among the Czechs, but yielded a doubtful ally; and it exposed Czechoslovakia to increasing international isolation, as the Nazi regime orchestrated propaganda against this 'Bolshevik bridgehead' (which moreover was also a haven for German and Austrian Socialist exiles).

It is no accident that Communists' identification with the Czechoslovak state accompanied a rising tide of Sudeten disaffection from it, while Poland and Hungary rekindled all their latent animosity. Czechoslovakia by 1938 was badly out of step in its whole public stance; and that, as much as anything, concentrated Germany's campaign on the Sudeten issue, Poland's on the (ultimately trivial)

Teschen, Hungary's on Slovakia (less heartfelt than the country's claims against Romania in respect of Transylvania), even the indigenous complaints of the Slovak clerical-fascists. And of course the coincidence of all these factors fortified each individually.

The outcome was Munich. The great powers came together again—at last—to dismember Czechoslovakia; and the successor states—whether lambs or hyenas—were excluded from the process. Maybe there had been no saving the Czechs after the Austrian Anschluss; maybe they should have fought; maybe they did something to deserve their fate. But the real tragedy of the 'betrayal' at Munich was that poor 'democratic', 'Western' Czechoslovakia found herself saddled as a lone scapegoat with the miscalculations of the post-First World War settlement. In that sense the Allies betrayed themselves.

As we know, Poland—that less conscientious steward of the trust of 'Versailles'—would soon follow. The Piłsudski–Hitler treaty of 1934 looks like the beginning of the end, but was it? It meant a breach with the West, and abandonment of a possible pre-emptive strike against Germany; it confirmed the anti-Soviet line, to which little alternative existed anyhow. Hitler was not necessarily picking an early quarrel with Poland, assuming some concessions—after all, he thenceforth effectively cut off pan-German propaganda about the Corridor for five years. In any event, the Poles used the respite to go off the diplomatic rails by 1938; then the Anglo-French guarantee of their frontiers in March 1939 confirmed their *folies de grandeur*: in the aftermath of Germany's invasion of Bohemia-Moravia, appeasement was replaced by light-headedness. Britain even gave a simultaneous guarantee to Carol's Romania, less than a month after Bucharest's comprehensive trade agreement with Berlin.

Western reliance on these feeble relics of the post-war system in East-Central Europe hastened the logical move which neither Britain and France nor the successor states themselves had foreseen: the Hitler–Stalin (or Molotov–Ribbentrop) pact of 23 August 1939. We now look back in a blasé way at this last nail in the coffin of independent Eastern Europe. But we should recall the astonishment of contemporaries, from died-in-the-wool, philo-fascist conservatives to Communist activists. The stage was set for the immediate destruction of Poland and the reimposition of empire, direct or indirect, throughout the region.

THE SECOND WORLD WAR

War began for the successor states with German and Russian invasion in September 1939. But their frontiers had already been sharply modified: through the Anschluss of Austria to Germany in March 1938; the transfer of Czechoslovakia's Sudeten districts to the Reich and of some Magyar-inhabited ones to Hungary later that year; then the Nazi occupation of rump Bohemia-Moravia and the foundation of a separate Slovak state in March 1939. This initial phase of

destruction of the inter-war international order we have been examining was
completed with the speedy new partition of Poland, the whole country being
overrun in six weeks while the West looked on. Then followed a respite in the
open combat in our area till the launch of the Balkan front, as by early 1941
Italian ineptitude forced German intervention to sustain the Axis hold there and
precipitated the equally speedy break-up of Yugoslavia when the Serbs resisted.
That led straight on to the decisive and fateful stroke: Hitler's attack on the
USSR in late June 1941, which unleashed four years of non-stop hostilities over
most of East-Central Europe.

By that time, the Soviet Union had overrun large tracts of Poland, roughly as
far as the 'Curzon' line, that is, the provisional demarcation of the boundary with
Bolshevik Russia in 1919, as well as parts of Romania (primarily Bessarabia).
Yet the bulk of the region lay in degrees of thrall to Germany. Austria had been
wholly integrated into the Third Reich (losing even the name); her territory was
ruled mostly by outsiders, but plenty of Austrians occupied important positions
elsewhere. The same applied to the Sudeten areas; whereas the rest of Bohemia-
Moravia subsisted as a protectorate, with a stooge government (an Agrarian
party-dominated conservative front). This was destroyed when it showed flickers
of life, giving way to the brutal regime of Reinhard Heydrich and Karl Hermann
Frank, which became even more merciless after Heydrich's assassination in 1942.
Meanwhile Slovakia, nominally an independent ally, was in fact a puppet, with
a Catholic priest as premier, who tried without much success to limit the extent
of sell-out. The rest of former Poland lay prostrated, parts of it incorporated in
the Reich, the remainder constituted as the General-Gouvernement, a slave land,
with hardly any vestige of Polish authority at any level. Even the revival of First
World War Pilsudski-ite loyal subordination was ruled out by the Germans' own
barbarity, which progressively undermined also any option further east, among
Ukrainians, of seeing the Nazis as a lesser evil.

In the southern theatre, the Serbian residue of former Yugoslavia kow-
towed to Hitler, trying, at least initially, to conserve its resources. Meanwhile,
Croatia, another titularly independent state (like Slovakia), indeed on paper a
kingdom—ruled by an Italian princeling, who never arrived—fell under the
domination of Ustaša gangs. The rest of old Yugoslavia was parcelled out: the
coastlands to Italy, slivers to Hungary, Bulgaria, and the local Germans, with
part of Slovenia even attached to the Reich. Hungary, having with German and
Italian backing realized substantial claims against the Trianon settlement—with
four bouts of frontier revision in as many years, the largest recapturing half of
Transylvania from Romania—needed in return to join the Nazi war on Russia.
At best she proved a grudging ally, locked in her own domestic strife between
real fascists and Nazis, on the one hand, and an increasingly anti-German establishment, alongside modest liberal oppositional groups, on the other. Romania,
balanced against Hungary by that Transylvanian award in 1940, saw the need to
recover German favour, and plunged into energetic cooperation against Russia

to recapture her territory lost to the Soviets in the same year. But under the self-reliant dictatorship of Ion Antonescu, Romania too was ready to look elsewhere if any alternative emerged to the stiff German terms. Meanwhile, millions of Jews throughout the region faced the most monstrous fate of all: the final solution, employed first in the General-Gouvernement and the new Reich territories, then elsewhere, reaching much of Romania and finally Hungary in 1944.

This was never a stable situation anyway; less and less so when the pact of 1939 gave way to another Russian campaign in the manner of 1812. As in 1914–18, so in 1939–45, new circumstances were born during the wartime dislocation of the old; but now an extra interpenetration of old and new, and the lack of synchronicity, made the picture still more confused. We can distinguish three trajectories whereby the area was restructured. I shall outline them in three subgroups, pairs of states with roughly similar experiences.

Longest to survive in unmodified form were Romania and Hungary. The former was the only country not invaded by the enemy. Her active military partnership with the Nazis encountered no significant resistance until the extent of impending defeat on the Eastern Front became clear. Then a clique of old moderates and new Communists organized a coup led by the young King Michael, which on 23 August 1944 flipped Romania straight onto the other side, fighting together with Russia. Bessarabia was lost (again) to the Soviet Union, now as the 'Moldavian SSR'; yet Transylvania could be regained under Russian auspices. It was unclear who would come to dominate when the war ended: the reviving peasant interest or a more motley crew of Communists (they still only numbered a thousand or so in 1944). And what about the regenerated monarchy? Nevertheless, in the short term Romania's transition was uniquely smooth for the region.

Hungary's inter-war establishment likewise stayed in the saddle almost till the end. But growing German vexation (precisely because she was a *less* reliable ally than Romania) issued in a partial military take-over in March 1944. Now the inner circle around Horthy desperately sought to jump ship as Russia approached, especially once they had been upstaged by their Romanian rivals. A bungled coup on 15 October only left Horthy as a German prisoner and brought in Szálasi. Now Hungary fell victim to both enemies at once. Six months of chaos and mayhem ensued, especially in besieged Budapest. The old world of landowning aristocrats, gentry officials, Jewish businessmen, and Catholic conservative culture disintegrated. That would provide a huge boost to the left, especially the Communists returning from exile, though the main immediate beneficiaries were the 'Smallholders', that is, the recrudescent peasant (and partly bourgeois) interest, poised to win nearly 60 per cent of the vote in free elections.

Yugoslavia and Poland formed a pair of resisters where, despite fragmentation and devastation, capitulation was never quite complete. The Yugoslav idea actually recovered ground from 1941. The post-coup government fled into exile and was reconstituted in London with Allied support under King Peter. Mainly Serb-conservative in attitude, it encouraged like-minded resistance back home from bands of Chetniks. But more dynamic opposition emerged on the left, from the Partisans organized under Tito with an explicitly Yugoslav range and agenda. They had the advantages of youth, and of a vigorous and broader leadership, which offered a radical escape from the inter-war quagmire. Moreover, they operated in the centre and west of the country, which afforded more scope for guerrilla tactics and a feebler Italian enemy (while leaving Russia at a safe distance). By late 1943, the West came to see Tito as a better bet and switched its backing to him. So when the Germans' pressure relaxed, and the regimes of their Serb and Croat satellites began to implode, the Partisans were placed to take their chance and achieve 'liberation' from within. Utterly ruthless towards other parties or groups, and feeling no obligation towards any of the Allies, they could consolidate their still multi-ethnic appeal.

Poland was likewise pulverized at home and had an exile government in London. Similar attempts to sustain insurgency were fractured between official pro-Western and Communist pro-Eastern resisters, which became unbridgeable after the Russian massacre of Polish officers at Katyn came to light. Here the authorities in the West, under the experienced and charismatic Władysław Sikorski until his death in a plane crash in 1943, retained more legitimacy: many Polish troops fought under their aegis, and those in the Home Army (Armija Krajowa) were significant on the ground too. However, major clashes over the future restoration of frontiers could not be avoided, especially once Russia entered the war. By late 1944, the Soviet Union—having ignored the Warsaw rising—was ready to invade the rest of the country, placing the exile regime in a dilemma. The revived Polish Communist party, still small and with little-known leaders, could demand a strong, even a leading, role in the provisional government. Whereas in Poland—as in Hungary and Romania—the right was eliminated from practical politics, peasant interests could not be ignored for the moment. Yet Russian patronage would be decisive, especially with the occupation of former German lands (in place of those now lost in the East) and the expulsion of the German minority.

Finally the two re-creations. The lands of Czechoslovakia remained much quieter than Yugoslavia or Poland during their longer subjection. Early discontent was pitilessly suppressed; then only the murder of Heydrich and the resultant vengeance were exceptions to prove the rule. The pre-Munich government was reconstituted in London under Beneš. This managed to overcome most squabbles with the Slovaks, and the 'independent' Slovak state was thus isolated (though a revolt there in 1944 proved ill-fated as its Polish equivalent). Meanwhile *émigré* anti-Nazi Sudeten representatives were kept at a distance. From 1941, Beneš showed himself much more prepared than were his Yugoslav or Polish opposite numbers (and than Romanians or Hungarians till later on) to seek an arrangement with the Soviet Union. He actually traded off his pre-war eastern outpost of Ruthenia in the expectation of post-war 'democratic' solidarity. But the government of national unity, set up when Russian armies reached the border of

Slovakia, already had a built-in Communist dominance. That became confirmed when the rest of the country was liberated and its Germans expelled. Parties of the right were discredited in both halves of the country; and a centre-left coalition—which revived inter-war political practice—soon came under threat from the Communists, who would take almost 40 per cent in the free elections of 1946.

Austria was last as well as first in the whole wartime chronology. She offered no resistance to speak of, and looked like other parts of the Reich till the very end, in April 1945. Then came a four-power occupation, but on a separate basis from Germany's. The same arguments applied as in 1918 for setting her up again as a distinct state. They were helped by a belated and convenient Austrian revulsion against the German link. The possible development of a real Soviet zone here (like that further north) lost its viability as early as the end of 1945 with a woeful electoral performance by the Communists—part of the legacy of the inter-war Austrian left. Replacement of earlier antagonism with cooperation between Social Democrats and the Catholic People's Party did the rest to ensure the country's future.

CONCLUSIONS

From the autumn of 1944, then, our successor states were restored as quickly as they had emerged in 1918–19, and more quickly than their large-scale abolition in the immediately preceding years had taken. Moreover, they reappeared mostly within their 1919–20 boundaries, with Poland as an only partial exception. Thus they regained legitimacy—and perhaps a stronger version of it this time, for being reasserted in such different circumstances. However, the rest of their inter-war order was largely swept away, more completely than had been the case in 1914–18. That was in part due to the unspeakable cruelty and savagery of the conflict on the Eastern Front and its far greater damage overall, including much total destruction; in part also because certain problems were resolved by the belligerence itself and its immediate aftermath, especially the eradication of some minorities in the Holocaust and through ethnic cleansing, along with the—temporary—renewal of solidarity among the 'nations of state' in Czechoslovakia and Yugoslavia. But mainly there took place a basic mental and ideological shift. Now genuine hopes sprang up for a new start on the left—and many with suspect pasts also needed to climb on that bandwagon. By the same token, it was a 'revolution' very different from that witnessed just under thirty years previously.

Yet the states regained only a simulacrum of sovereignty, less than they had enjoyed within the constraints of the inter-war system. Not really because of any injection of (con)federal ideas, though some talks to this end had taken place during the war, particularly between Poland and Czechoslovakia; nor because of the impact of German economic coordination (*Grossraumwirtschaft*) and the recognized need for more collaboration in that sphere. The largest factor was the power of Stalin, the physical presence of the Russian army, and the foreign-political need to defend the Soviet zones in Germany and Austria in the first phase of the cold war. Along with this went a willingness in the West to concede the region as a sphere of influence, a tendency evident already during the war in the hesitancy about even existing commitments to Poles, Czechs, and Serbs.

That was one crucial inheritance from the perceived failure of earlier arrangements. Otherwise the Eastern hegemony for the next forty years over almost the whole area (all but Austria and in some respects Yugoslavia) sought to efface the traces of inter-war politics and society. After 1989 many of the attitudes, structures, and problems we have encountered in this chapter returned to haunt the—once again—newly emancipated states of the region. By then, however, they were 'successors' in more senses than the one treated here, and the years from 1918 to 1945 can now take their place in a more coherent understanding of the longer term evolution of that part of Europe, as well as providing much comparative material for students of the continent as a whole.

One of the themes of the present book is to strike a new balance in our understanding of Europe between 1914 and 1945, whereby the successes and achievements of the period come more to the fore. It may well seem that the East-Central European evidence, as outlined in this chapter, does little to sustain such a view. Indeed, it was a record of rising intolerance, disorder, brutality, and misrule, introduced and terminated by wars of unprecedented ferocity and devastation. No audit of material factors could yield more than limited and temporary benefits: some gains in political participation, mainly in the first years; isolated cases of economic innovation, like the Baťa shoe works at Zlín; the land reform programmes, above all in Czechoslovakia and Romania; certain kinds of communal provision, notably in Vienna; a measure of social inclusion, at least on paper. Cultural developments, however, afford some degree of final recompense.

Of course, much culture in the successor states was determined by the new establishments and took on hyper-national forms. The universities overproduced humanities graduates inculcated with highly patriotic sentiments; and governments funded much propaganda, for domestic and foreign consumption. Yet modernist currents, already incubated in the pre-1914 years, could be accommodated, at least by more progressive regimes. Thus Karel Čapek was an intimate friend of President Masaryk, and Ivo Andrić a long-serving diplomat in Yugoslavia; the radically innovative architect Jože Plečnik won a series of commissions in Austria, Czechoslovakia, and his native Slovenia. Moreover, the comparative openness of public life over much of the region until the late 1930s afforded scope to outré talents like Stanisław Witkiewicz in Poland. Other artists might be more closely associated with marginalized or oppositional forces, as a string of composers—Janáček or Kodály, Szymanowski or Enescu—evoked peasant themes in music. Some writers consorted with fascism: for example, Mircea Eliade and Emil Cioran in Romania. A larger number stood somewhere on the left, such as Miroslav Krleža, a Communist party member and ally of Tito, and Hungary's 'proletarian' poet, Attila József.

With time this East-Central European culture made an increasing impact in Western countries. That process was fuelled by exiles. Some moved voluntarily, as did the anthropologist Bronisław Malinowski or the philosopher Ludwig Wittgenstein to Britain. Others found themselves forced by political circumstances, beginning with refugees from the chaos of post-First World War Hungary: Moholy-Nagy, Lukács, Balázs, Mannheim, and other creators of 'Weimar' culture. Then followed the emigration of the 1930s, led by Austrians, many of Jewish background, under threat from Nazism: the logical positivists of the Vienna Circle or writers like Robert Musil, Franz Werfel, Joseph Roth, Stefan Zweig, and Ödön von Horváth. They would be joined by many more as crisis deepened and the war ensued: from masters of the surreal, Eugen Ionescu and Witold Gombrowicz, to those apostates from Romanian chauvinism, Eliade and Cioran. The great Croatian sculptor Ivan Meštrović joined his Romanian colleague Brancusi in emigration, and the whole movement was much strengthened by its most immediately adaptable export component: music and musicians, headed by Arnold Schoenberg and then Béla Bartók. It is a fine irony with which to conclude that so much of the intellectual and artistic legacy of the inter-war successor states lived on after 1945 outside the region, in places which had displayed so little appreciation of them at the time.

FURTHER READING

General

Berend, Ivan T., *Decades of Crisis: Central and Eastern Europe before World War II* (Berkeley, Calif., 1998).

Rothschild, Joseph, *East-Central Europe between the Two World Wars* (Seattle, 1974).

Mendelsohn, E., *The Jews of East-Central Europe between the World Wars* (Bloomington, Ind., 1983).

Seton-Watson, Hugh, *Eastern Europe between the Wars* (Cambridge, 1945; repr. 1986).

Sugar, P. F. (ed.), *Native Fascism in the Successor States, 1918–45* (Santa Barbara, Calif., 1971).

Austria

Barker, Elizabeth, *Austria, 1918–72* (London, 1973).

Carsten, Francis L., *The First Austrian Republic, 1918–38* (Aldershot, 1986).

——, *Fascist Movements in Austria* (London, 1976).

Gehl, Jürgen, *Austria, Germany, and the Anschluss* (Oxford, 1963; repr. 1979).

Czechoslovakia

Bruegel, J. W., *Czechoslovakia before Munich* (Cambridge, 1973).

Mamatey, V. S., and R. Luža (eds.), *A History of the Czechoslovak Republic* (Princeton, 1973).

Wiskemann, Elizabeth, *Czechs and Germans* (Oxford, 1938; repr. 1967).

Hungary

Macartney, C. A., *Hungary and her Successors* (Oxford, 1937; repr. 1968).

——, *October 15: A History of Hungary, 1929–45* (2 vols., Edinburgh, 1956–7; repr. 1961).

Poland

Cienciala, Anna M., *Poland and the Western Powers, 1938–9* (London, 1968).

Davies, Norman, *White Eagle, Red Star: The Polish-Soviet War, 1919–20* (London, 1972; repr. 2003).

Jedrzejewicz, W., *Piłsudski: A Life for Poland* (New York, 1982).

Polonsky, Antony, *Politics in Independent Poland, 1921–39* (Oxford, 1972).

Romania

Hitchins, Keith, *Rumania, 1866–1947* (Oxford, 1994).

Yugoslavia

Pavlowitch, Stevan K., *Yugoslavia* (New York, 1971).

Banac, Ivo, *The National Question in Yugoslavia* (Ithaca, NY, 1984; repr. 1988).

Hoptner, J. B., *Yugoslavia in Crisis, 1934–41* (New York, 1962).

11

The Balkans

R. J. Crampton

INTRODUCTION

The Balkan peninsula takes its name from the Balkan mountains, the Haemus range of the Ancients, which run east–west through the centre of present-day Bulgaria. The word, which is derived from a Turkic term meaning a wooded upland, was first applied to the peninsula by a German geographer in the early nineteenth century and for much of the remainder of that century it had little more than topographic significance, the political term used for the region being, generally, European Turkey or Turkey in Europe. It was not until the late nineteenth and early twentieth centuries that 'the Balkans' began to be used regularly as a political definition, and increasingly with pejorative implications. The Balkans, it was believed, were synonymous with struggle, inter-ethnic rivalry, disorder, and danger. Thus the wars of 1912–13 were not the wars of Ottoman succession but 'the Balkan wars'. The Balkan wars were held to epitomize the rapacity of the small Balkan nation-states.

Those states had emerged during the nineteenth century as successors to the Ottoman Empire in Europe. Local chieftains in Serbia had revolted in 1804 against the failure of the Ottoman central government to control local warlords and from this uprising eventually emerged a distinct Serbian political entity. The Hellenic kingdom was a result of the Greek revolt of 1821 in Wallachia and the Peloponnese and the subsequent war of Greek independence. The Serbian and Greek states were consolidated in the 1830s, and thereafter Montenegro, which had remained an independent bishopric since the Ottoman conquests of the four-teenth century, also began to assume the form of a modern or modernizing state. Romania's two constituent principalities, Wallachia and Moldavia, had enjoyed considerable autonomy in the eighteenth century and were virtually autonomous after the Russo-Turkish war of 1828–9; they fused in 1859 to form the Romanian state. Bulgaria was a creation of the Russo-Turkish war of 1877–8 which followed upon the ill-fated Bulgarian national uprising of April 1876. The last successor state of the Ottoman Empire to appear was Albania. Albanian nationalists declared independence in November 1912, during the first Balkan war, and this was endorsed by the great powers. All states, however, were saddled with national grievances. All had territorial claims upon one or more of their neighbours, large or small, and almost all such claims were based solely or primarily on the existence, or alleged existence, of communities of fellow nationals in other states. Looked at another way, all states had national minorities within their own borders.

The Balkans were condemned as hotbeds of ethnic and religious rivalry and hatred. But was this confined to the Balkans? The policies pursued by the Berlin government in Prussian Poland or by British administrations in Ireland or Wales were hardly based on notions of equality and minority rights, whilst the Russian record in this regard is simply appalling. Nor should the plains of North America or the hills of Tasmania be left out of the moral equation; when a Romanian deputy from Transylvania complained in the Hungarian Diet of discrimination against Romanians, a Magyarized German, Paul Hunfalvy, advised him, 'Don't provoke us to employ towards the other nations the methods of total extermination employed by the Anglo-Saxons towards the Red Indians of North America.'

The association of 'the Balkans' with disorder and danger has continued into the early twenty-first century, with an increasing tendency to use the term for the areas of the former Yugoslavia which are still far from settled: Bosnia and Hercegovina, Kosovo, and Macedonia. It has also now become a seemingly unshakable article of faith that 'the Balkans caused the First World War'. This is cultural chauvinism. There were numerous 'Balkan' crises which did not cause a European war—1885, 1897, 1903, and 1908, to name but four. The First World War broke out because of decisions by the 'statesmen' of the great powers not by the leaders of the Balkan states.

THE FIRST WORLD WAR

The First World War offered each state the chance to redeem its national claims. The assassination of Franz Ferdinand in Sarajevo had itself been a gesture by Serbian nationalists in Bosnia. The Serbian government in Belgrade was held accountable for this by Austria-Hungary, and thus a Balkan conflict was transformed into a world war. The decisive factors in the war were the forces of the great powers, not those of the Balkan states. The main fighting occurred in the southern Balkans in 1915 and 1918, and in the north of the area in 1916 and 1918.

Serbia, amazingly, repelled the Habsburg forces launched against it in 1914, but in September 1915 it could not withstand a combined assault from Austria-Hungary, Germany, and Bulgaria. The latter had bided its time. Its objective was to secure its national _terrae irredentae_ in the Dobrudja, Thrace, and Macedonia.

But the greatest of these was Macedonia. By the late summer of 1915 the Central Powers seemed to offer the best bet. The Entente Powers were bound to Serbia, which refused to cede one inch of its claims in Macedonia. More importantly, the Western Allies seemed not to be in good military shape: the Russians were fleeing post haste from Poland; Italy's intervention seemed to have little effect other than to complicate the territorial claims in the eastern Adriatic and therefore to entrench Serbian determination not to relinquish any of Macedonia; and the gamble at Gallipoli had failed.

The Albanian state had been created in 1913 but by the summer of 1914 it was scarcely functioning and the country fell into the hands of local chieftains. They were soon replaced. Greek forces moved into southern Albania, which Greece had claimed in 1912, and the Italians occupied the central area. In 1915 the Serbs and Montenegrins also took part of the country, only to be driven out by the Bulgarians and the Austrians. For the remainder of the war the zones of occupation in Albania fluctuated but at no point was there a functioning Albanian government. Montenegro fell under Austro-Hungarian occupation.

The position in Greece was complicated by the rivalry between the German-leaning king and the pro-Western prime minister, Venizelos. When Allied troops retreated from Gallipoli to Salonika Venizelos seized his chance. He had been forced to resign as prime minister so in the summer of 1916 he joined the Allied forces in northern Greece. The Allies eventually recognized him as the legitimate leader of Greece but only after their troops had occupied Athens, suffering heavy losses in the process.

After the Central Powers' offensive of September 1915 there was relatively little action in the southern Balkans until 1918. The theatre of war shifted to the north. Romania, like Bulgaria, had played a waiting game. Romania, unlike Bulgaria, was theoretically committed to the Central Powers thanks to a secret alliance dating back to the 1880s. When Romania did commit itself, however, it was against the Entente Powers but, in contrast to Bulgaria, it was the Allies who were most likely to deliver the desired lost territories, in this case Transylvania, the Banat of Temesvar, and the Bukovina, both of which were Habsburg lands, though Romanian claims on Russian-held Bessarabia complicated matters at least until Russia's exit from the war. As with Bulgaria, it was the fortunes of war that determined the timing of Romania's entry into the contest. The Western Allies pressed hard for a Romanian commitment before they launched the offensive on the Somme, and when Russia's General Brusilov began his successful thrust against the Austrians the Bucharest government decided to join the war. But the Romanian army was not ready for action until the end of August 1916, by which time Brusilov's advance had ground to a halt and the Somme had degenerated into hideous and pointless slaughter. The Romanians began their campaign by taking some of Transylvania but in September a combined German and Bulgarian army attacked from the south. A few weeks later, German and Austrian forces attacked from the north-west; by December Bucharest had fallen and the Romanian army had withdrawn across the River Seret. Here, in August 1917, it held a renewed German offensive at Mărăşeşti, but it was a Pyrrhic victory which exhausted the Romanian troops and commissariat. With Russia declining into impotence and chaos the Romanians sued for peace. The Germans were now given control of Romania's oil industry and, even more critically, access to the wheat reserves stored in Constanţa. This was not quite the end of Romania's war. In a move of sublime opportunism Romania rejoined the Allied side on 10 November 1918.

By then Bulgaria, the last state to join the Central Powers, had become the first to desert them. After the Allies had advanced into Bulgarian-held Macedonia and then into Bulgaria itself, the government in Sofia signed an armistice in Salonika on 28 September 1918.

Bulgaria's fighting capacity had been much reduced by the food shortages which by the summer of 1918 were affecting the army and the home front alike. The other Balkan states had similar experiences and in both Bulgaria and Romania there were outbreaks of unrest amongst both the military and the civilian population.

Despite this, there was no Balkan equivalent of the Russian Revolution. Most Balkan populations responded to the slogan of 'Bread, Peace, and Land' but when they had been given peace their revolutionary ardour abated, the more so because their political masters had promised that they would receive land after the war. This being so, the political elites who had ruled the Balkan states before the First World War were not immediately destroyed, though coping with the social dislocation occasioned by the war was to be a major task for them. And, with the exception of Bulgaria, it was the old elite who were required to implement the peace terms which the victorious Allies had devised.

THE PEACE SETTLEMENT

The factors which guided the Allies in deciding the terms of the peace settlement in the Balkans were: the need to punish the vanquished and the guilty; the desire to reward the victorious and the virtuous; and the determination to create a new state system which would produce stability and order in the region.

According to these precepts Bulgaria, the only state in the region, apart from the Ottoman Empire, to have fought on the side of the Central Powers, lost territory on the Aegean coast together with small enclaves on its western borders which were ceded to Yugoslavia. Bulgaria was also burdened with arms limitation clauses and with hefty reparations. As a compensation it was promised economic access to the Aegean, though no one had any idea how this might be achieved. It never was in peacetime. The Ottoman Empire lost control of Constantinople and the Straits as well as virtually all its imperial holdings beyond the Anatolian heartland. Romania, thanks to its last-minute opportunism, received huge areas of new land, and Serbia was made the core of the new kingdom of the Serbs, Croats, and Slovenes (Yugoslavia). Albania was restored to its pre-war borders. Greece, thanks to Venizelos's efforts, was rewarded with much of Thrace, and was encouraged to stake its claim to chunks of Asia Minor with large Greek populations.

The need to secure stability was the most important of the determining factors at Versailles. It was widely believed that the cause of the First World War had been the struggle of subject peoples to liberate themselves from imperial domination and establish nation-states. The empires had self-destructed during the second half of the war but the creation of pure nation-states in the Balkans remained a chimera. The victorious powers, as will be seen below, attempted to circumvent the dangers with mechanisms born of the liberal ideology of the new Europe, but at the same time the peace-makers could not ignore hard-headed strategic considerations. The new system had to be capable of containing Habsburg revanchism, and, more immediately, the militant communism emanating from Béla Kun's Hungary and from Lenin and Trotsky in Russia; Italy's grandiose pretensions in the Adriatic were also a factor to be considered.

The most prominent features of the 1919–21 peace settlement in the Balkans were the creation of Yugoslavia and the expansion of Romania. The new Yugoslavia was seen as the home for all South Slavs; it was also intended to prevent Habsburg or Hungarian encroachment into Slovenia and Croatia. Romania's acquisition of Transylvania was justified on the ground that it had an ethnic Romanian majority, but its transfer to Romania would also serve to limit Hungarian strength, just as the same state's possession of Bessarabia would help keep the dreaded Bolsheviks at bay. With a strong Yugoslavia established in Slovenia and along the Dalmatian coast Italy's eastward expansion would also be made more difficult.

To draw up a territorial settlement conditioned by strategic rationality was relatively easy; to devise one grounded on ethnic justice was impossible. The states which emerged at the end of the First World War were therefore far from ethnically homogeneous, as the tables in the following text illustrate. This was not just because the region contained so many nationalities, it was also because those nationalities were frequently intermixed or living in close proximity. Macedonian towns and villages, for example, could host Slavs, Greeks, Turks, Tatars, Vlachs, Roma, Jews, Armenians, and others; Transylvanian towns had mixed populations of Germans, Magyars, Jews, and Romanians; Bessarabia had a very mixed population which included Ukrainians, Jews, Bulgarians, Gagauze, and Tatars, whilst the Banat, also acquired by Romania, was more ethnically diverse than anywhere in the region, and even included some French-speaking settlements. The peace-makers were fully aware of these difficulties. They knew they were creating not nation-states but states dominated by one ethnic group and that in such states the minorities would be vulnerable and discontented. Their solution was to require all states to sign minority protection treaties, and to trust in goodwill and the League of Nations to ensure that these problems would be overcome.

This ethnic mixture meant that most of the post-First World War Balkan states faced huge problems of integration and assimilation. But the problems of integration and assimilation were not only ethnic. The settlement involved bringing together into single states areas with enormously varied historic backgrounds. Yugoslavia's core and most influential element was the pre-war kingdom of Serbia, including central Macedonia which it had acquired from the Ottoman Empire in 1913; the former independent statelet of Montenegro was also part of new state, to which were added Slovenia, formerly part of the Austrian half of the Habsburg Empire, Bosnia and Hercegovina which had been administered by a minor part of the Habsburg bureaucratic machine, and Croatia, most of which had been part of the Kingdom of Hungary but whose coastal strip, Dalmatia, had been within the Austrian section of the Monarchy. Romania acquired Transylvania which had been part of the Habsburg's Hungarian kingdom, Bessarabia which had been part of Tsarist Russia, the Bukovina which had been within the Austrian section of the Dual Monarchy, and southern Dobrudja, which Romania had acquired from Bulgaria in 1913 and retained in 1918. Territories with different historical origins had differing legal systems, different social structures, and different political cultures. Knitting these areas into one system was never easy and in some cases impossible. In some instances it was made even more difficult because the population being absorbed, or part of it, regarded itself as culturally more advanced and politically more sophisticated than the absorbers; Transylvanians, Hungarian, Romanian, and German, regarded their political establishment as more developed and less corrupt than those in the 'Regat', or the pre-war Romanian kingdom. Similarly, Croats regarded some Serbian customs which were adopted in the new Yugoslavia as backward.

Rates of social and economic development were as varied as ethnic groups and historical backgrounds. Slovenia and Croatia had some areas of economic sophistication far beyond that which could be dreamt of in Kosovo or Macedonia. In Romania, too, there were vast disparities, Transylvania's economy being far more advanced than that of Bessarabia or of much of the Regat itself. Tenurial systems, a critical consideration in the vital process of land reform, also varied enormously. Most of Macedonia had until 1913 been part of the Ottoman Empire and some of its idiosyncratic landlord–tenant relationships still existed and these bore little resemblance to the systems operating in Slovenia or Croatia. In Bessarabia landholding patterns were very different from those in Transylvania or the Regat; and this was a particularly sensitive issue in Romania whose pre-war kingdom had been rocked by a violent peasant uprising in 1907.

In addition to these problems came those of standardizing legal systems, tariffs, customs and excise, trade regulations, tax systems, currencies, and weights and measures. Furthermore, the existing infrastructure in the new and expanded states had been built to serve other purposes than those now required of them.

In Bessarabia the railways operated with the Russian rather than the standard European gauge, whilst the entire rail network of the former Hungarian kingdom had been predicated primarily on the need to supply Budapest and the other major cities with food and fuel. This did not meet the needs of a Transylvania or Banat attached to Romania, or of a Croatia which was part of Yugoslavia. Greece was to face different problems of absorption in the 1920s. Here, as will be seen, it was a question of absorbing people without any increase in territory.

The problems of absorption and integration underlay many of the issues which came to the fore in the inter-war years in the Balkans, and it is seldom recognized how much progress was made, especially in areas such as legal codification, the unification of currencies and weights and measures, and in the imposition of new tariffs and tax systems.

POLITICAL EVOLUTION IN THE INTER-WAR YEARS: GENERAL BACKGROUND

For all Balkan states the first post-war years were dominated by social tensions. The war had occasioned enormous dislocation and after it came the problems of returning economic production to a peacetime footing and of coping with demobilization. The returning peasant soldiers expected and demanded land reform and the question of property redistribution was one of the most important to be faced by post-war governments. It was an extremely complex issue. To ensure an equitable distribution detailed surveys were needed; there was the question of whether compensation should be paid to the previous owners and if so how much, in what form, and, not least, from what source. Frequently the process of land redistribution had ethnic and political dimensions; most of the landlords of Croatia and Transylvania had been Magyars who had supported the old regime, whilst those who received the land were predominantly Slavs and Romanians. In Slovenia the former landlords had been mostly German, whilst in Bosnia and Macedonia it was frequently the Muslims who were dispossessed to the benefit of Christians. In most cases compensation was paid, usually in the form of government bonds.

For the urban population conditions were even more difficult. With agricultural production dislocated by mobilization and then by land redistribution food supplies were frequently inadequate. Housing, too, would be in short supply if the town or city had been in a war zone. With shortages came price inflation, a problem which was compounded in some cases by the need to create new currencies. Industrial unrest was the consequence and was widespread throughout the area in the first two or three years after the war.

Uncertainty and insecurity also stemmed from a lack of territorial definition. The general lines of the settlement were soon clear but demarcation on the ground could be painstakingly slow. In some of the more turbulent regions it could be almost impossible. Romania's new north-western border with Bolshevik Russia was hard to define, whilst Yugoslavia's frontier with Italy, threatened by D'Annunzio's antics in Fiume, was not finally settled until 1924. But it was Greece which suffered the most uncertainty. The Treaty of Sèvres with the Ottoman Empire was vitiated by the collapse of that empire, after which Greece launched an ultimately disastrous attempt to incorporate part of Asia Minor and its large Greek population into the Hellenic Kingdom.

Uncertainty over future borders and dislike for new political systems produced a further problem: refugees. Tens of thousands of Macedonians did not wish to live under Serbian domination and therefore fled to Bulgaria where they placed a tremendous strain on the exiguous welfare budget. There were also significant numbers of White Russian refugees in both Bulgaria and Serbia, and a number of ethnic Albanians fled from Kosovo to Albania. It was Greece, however, which faced the largest problem. The military adventure in Asia Minor ended in defeat and the slaughter of thousands of ethnic Greek civilians and therefore, to prevent further massacres, the Treaty of Lausanne in 1923 arranged for an exchange of populations. Over a million Orthodox Christians, some of them not ethnic Greeks, were moved from Asia Minor to Greece, and in return 380,000 Muslims left Greece for Turkey. The incoming Christians were for the most part destitute and discontented and their absorption was a long, painful, and expensive process.

When frontiers had finally been settled and social unrest contained, the first priority was the search, never entirely successful, for political stability. There were a number of factors which helped in the search, not the least important being that once the new frontiers had been established, the new currencies introduced, and the shock waves of post-war inflation absorbed, the area's economy stabilized and, in some areas, even prospered for a while in the mid-1920s.

A second reason was to be found in the international system. Peace was preserved not so much because the Balkan states were living in blissful harmony and good neighbourliness, but more because no international sponsor could be found for any adventurist, anti-treaty policies. Russia was an international pariah, primarily concerned with its own internal reconstruction; so too was Germany until the Locarno agreements of 1925 after which it was keen to stress its own international good conduct; and France stood full-square behind the territorial status quo. Furthermore, there was only one potential revisionist state, Bulgaria, and it was too weak to pose a threat to the settlement.

A third reason was to be found in the weaknesses of the settlement's most radical domestic opponents. At the end of the war, much extreme left-wing opinion had gravitated towards the communists and, given the widespread social unrest in the region in the first few years of peace, it was they who presented the greatest internal threat to the governments of the region. Yet the communists soon showed themselves to be a busted flush. They arrogantly refused to cooperate with other left-wing forces and in Béla Kun's Hungary they made the critical mistake of not handing the land to the land-hungry peasants. But if the Communist International corrected this mistake it soon made another. In rejecting the Versailles settlement and in calling for the break-up of states such as Yugoslavia the communists enabled governments to suppress them on grounds of national security. In Greece the International's insistence upon the creation of a separate Macedonian state did huge damage to the Greek Communist Party (KKE). In Romania the communists suffered from the fact that the world communist movement was dominated by Russia and included in its leadership a number of Jews, both of which were disadvantages in Romania. In both Romania and Yugoslavia the party was banned in the early 1920s and did not present any threat to the established order until the Second World War.

An important reason for the weakness of the communists was the strength of their main rivals, the agrarians. This was the case in all the Balkan states where the peasants remained the largest element of the population, but ironically it was particularly so in Bulgaria, the one country where the communists did have a large popular following. Agrarianism had emerged in south-eastern Europe in the pre-war years and was closely associated with the co-operatives, which provided cheap credit and frequently also organized the marketing of the peasants' crops. Agrarianism confounded Marxist theories and was the means by which the square peg of capitalized and commercialized agriculture was to be fitted into the round hole of small-scale peasant proprietorship. The agrarians' calls for land redistribution, for tariff policies geared to the protection of the peasant producer, for indulgent credit regimes, and for investment policies which favoured the farmer as opposed to business and industry enjoyed support throughout the region. But although they were radical the agrarians were not a threat to the international status quo. They were little interested in militarism and if the Croat agrarians spearheaded the Croatian demands for decentralization in Yugoslavia they did not advocate external adventure.

If the communists were weakened by the strength of agrarianism, so too was the extreme right. In the first place peasants in most of the region in the 1920s were not facing economic difficulties and were therefore not susceptible to populist propaganda. The nationalist appeal could be made in Croatia where extreme nationalists demanded secession from Yugoslavia, and in Bulgaria, where the loss of Macedonia still hurt. The international order could, however, contain these dangers as was proved in 1925 when the League of Nations defused tension between Bulgaria and Greece, the Greek army having moved into part of southern Bulgaria in retaliation for incursions into Greece by dissident Macedonians operating from that area.

If these factors favoured political stability, there were others which did not. Representative systems were well-established in the area before the First World War but the reality of parliamentary democracy was different to the theory. In all pre-war states political clientalism had become deeply entrenched. Enormous patronage, in terms of jobs, contracts, etc., was exercised by governments of whatever party and there was little evidence of a professional, non-political civil service. A change of government was usually not the result but the cause of a general election, a newly appointed administration securing electoral backing through the machinery of patronage.

A further weakness lay in the structure of parties. The communists and the agrarians, and to a lesser degree the social democrats, did establish national parties with local branches and a recognizable ideological identity, but the majority of the older parties were small factions grouped around particular figures rather than organizations united by a common programme. Parties were unstable with individuals shifting allegiance, frequently for pecuniary reasons. Furthermore, governments were frequently coalitions and the instability of the constituent parties could make for governmental insecurity. These shortcomings weakened the constitutional structures, and bred widespread cynicism and apathy amongst the population at large. In the wings stood other traditional actors in the Balkan political drama: the army and the monarchy.

Cynicism and apathy were not dangerous as long as there was a general sense of security. This was the case in the mid-1920s. These were good years for agriculture and as the overwhelming majority of the population of the area depended on the land for their livelihood; this meant, if not prosperity, then no fear of penury. Capital for those who wanted it was cheap and easy to come by, and for peasants involved in commercial agriculture there were stable markets in local towns or further afield in the centre of Europe or in the Middle East.

This changed with the onset of the Great Depression. Some peasants were so little connected with the international market that they suffered very little but many had taken out loans in the 1920s and when the banks demanded payment found they could no longer generate the requisite income. The strains imposed by the Depression highlighted a number of structural weaknesses. In some cases peasants had borrowed not for productive purposes but to spend on family or religious festivals. At the height of the Depression most governments in the region made efforts to help the most indebted but this could not overcome the further structural problem that, although alleviation of existing debts eased the symptoms, the disease afflicting peasant agriculture could not be cured without the modernization and the improvement of agricultural techniques. This could only be achieved by further borrowing which was now much more difficult because the government-enacted suspension or slowing down of previous debt-payments produced a shortage of credit because few would lend when repayment seemed slow or insecure.

A political consequence of the Depression was the advance of authoritarianism, and in particular the assertion of royal authority. This had previously appeared in Albania and Yugoslavia for non-economic reasons, but it was soon to be seen in Romania, Bulgaria, and to a lesser degree in Greece. The increase in the power

Figure 11.1. The old and the new: a young boy tends his family cattle in the time-honoured fashion, alongside the newly constructed Bucharest to Czernowitz highway, 1934

of the crown meant that, with the notable exception of Romania, the extreme, populist right did not become a major player.

Escape from the depths of the Depression was difficult and slow but for most Balkan states it was helped by the blocked-mark agreements concluded with Germany, both before and after 1933. The Germans agreed to buy Balkan agricultural products but the money so earned could be spent only by purchasing German goods. The Germans did extremely well out of these deals, but so too did the Balkan states because no one else was prepared to buy their primary produce.

Germany, of course, came to dominate the Balkans in the political as well as the economic sector in the late 1930s. The advent of the Nazis and Hitler's successful chipping away at the Versailles edifice made revisionism a viable option and made war more likely. For much of the period from 1936 to 1941 the monarchical governments of the area were preoccupied with containing this threat. The need for greater internal cohesion in the face of rising external dangers was another reason for the rise and consolidation of authoritarianism.

ALBANIA

Born in 1913 the Albanian state had been a sickly child. Before the First World War efforts to create a functioning state had failed in the face of fierce tribal and regional loyalties.

At the end of the war, Albania was partitioned and occupied by Serbian, Greek, French, British, and Italian troops. Early in 1920 a number of Albanian intellectuals met in Lushnje and drew up a constitution. It did not enjoy prolonged success. Political stability was elusive in a land where loyalties, or more importantly enmities, were based less on ideology than on personal relationships, and where the interference, real or alleged, of external powers always had to be considered; between early 1920 and December 1922 there were seven governments.

There was a fundamental division in Albanian political circles. It was neither ethnic nor religious. It was between reformists and traditionalists, with Fran Noli, an Orthodox bishop, leading the reformists in the Populist Party, and Ahmed Zogolli, a clan chief from northern Albania at the head of the traditionalists; he soon changed his name to Zogu, the original sounding too Turkish. Both leaders, in fact, acknowledged the need for modernization, as well they might in a country in which 80 per cent of the population were illiterate, where in 1914 the major export commodity was reported to be live tortoises, and which at the end of the war contained only three working motor vehicles.

Elections were held at the end of 1923 but produced no definite result. On 24 February 1924, the reformists staged an attempted coup when Zogu was shot at as he entered the parliament building. As all the deputies were armed a gun fight rapidly developed, which ended with the would-be assassin locked in the lavatory firing through the door. Soon thereafter a prominent reformist was murdered, it was generally believed with Zogu's connivance, and Noli and his allies decamped to set up an anti-parliament in Vlora. In June the latter, with Italian backing, staged a coup of their own and Noli set up a new government.

Once in office Noli moved cautiously, no doubt wishing to avoid the fate which the traditionalists had visited upon the Bulgarian agrarian leader in the previous year. He issued a proclamation which was full of good intent, but there was little real action. The landless and small peasants were bitterly disappointed at the lack of any move towards land redistribution, though they were gratified by a promise that the government would put an end to tithe payments. In fact Noli did little more than frighten the landlords without winning over the peasantry. His was deposed by a traditionalist alliance led by Zogu in December 1924.

Zogu set out to impose order on his disordered and disorderly domain. He revised what was left of the constitution, replacing the former supreme council with a president elected for a seven-year term of office. In January 1925, a constituent assembly ratified these changes and elected Zogu as president. Zogu was determined to begin modernization from above, introducing a new gendarmerie, organized by a British officer, and a new civil code which ended customs such as the automatic shooting of adulterous wives.

Zogu ruled with a firm hand, primarily because he needed to. The reformists were angered by his increasingly autocratic rule whilst the traditionalists were enraged by its modernizing content, particularly taxation and conscription. In November 1926 they organized a rising in the traditionalist, tribal strongholds in northern Albania. It was the most serious internal threat Zogu faced in all his years in power and to bolster his regime he concluded the Pact of Tirana with Italy in November 1927; closer association with Italy would at least deter the Yugoslav and Greek governments from backing discontented elements within Albania. There were still plenty of these; Zogu had become involved in up to six hundred blood feuds and was so circumspect that he seldom left his palace and would eat only meals prepared and brought to him by his mother. In September 1928 he introduced yet another constitutional change, turning Albania into an hereditary monarchy in which the King was to enjoy extensive powers. He also introduced yet another change to his own name. Ahmed Zogu was not considered a fitting appellation for a European monarch and he therefore became King Zog of the Albanians.

Zog's basic aims were to fashion a modern state and to create a sense of national identity to sustain it. He attempted to overcome tribal and regional customs by introducing another new legal code in 1929. In 1933 came a new national education system. Some progress was made in overcoming illiteracy, especially amongst women, and Zog was generous in his provision of scholarships for bright young Albanians to study abroad, there being no university in Albania. In 1930 Zog tackled the land question, decreeing that each peasant family was to have at least 40 hectares of arable land, although existing owners were allowed to retain two-thirds of their property as long as they introduced modern methods of cultivation and did not leave land fallow. It was a well-intentioned measure but it had little effect because not enough land could be surveyed and because the primitive banking system could not cope with the sophisticated transactions the reforms demanded.

The drive towards modernization was inevitably affected by the Depression. Official salaries had to be reduced and by 1935 almost all public works had come to a standstill. Improvement came in subsequent years primarily because of help from Italy.

Relations between Zog and Italy were critical. Since the late 1920s, Italy had provided non-governmental loans and thousands of Italian advisers had been posted to Albania. Even the headquarters of the Bank of Albania was in Rome. The Italians' money and patronage in employment meant that they could control almost every official in Albania and this power bred a colonial mentality. It also bred a determination on the part of Zog to defend Albania against this arrogance, but he failed. By 1936, his need for money was such that he had to make

Table 11.1. Ethnic composition of Bulgaria (%)

	1920	1934
Bulgarian	83.4	86.8
Turkish	11.2	10.2
Roma	1.3	1.3
Greek	1.0	0.1
Jewish	0.8	0.5
Others	2.3	1.1
Total	100.0	100.0

Source: Joseph Rothschild, *East-Central Europe between the Two World Wars* (Seattle, 1974), 328.

Table 11.2. Religious affiliation in Bulgaria (%)

	1920	1934
Orthodox Christian	83.8	84.4
Muslim	14.3	13.5
Jewish	0.9	0.8
Roman Catholic	0.7	0.8
Others	0.3	0.5
Total	100.0	100.0

Source: Joseph Rothschild, *East-Central Europe between the Two World Wars* (Seattle, 1974), 327.

concessions to the Italians on a number of issues, including granting the Roman Catholic Church more rights in Albanian education.

In 1938 Zog married the Hungarian beauty Geraldine Apponyi. In political terms a dynasty was more secure against foreign intrigue than an upstart monarchy. And Zog needed protection more than ever. Hitler's aggression whetted Mussolini's appetite and with the Spanish Civil War drawing to its close Italy had more freedom of military manœuvre. On 25 March 1939, a few days after Hitler had marched into Prague, Mussolini issued an ultimatum demanding that Albania become an Italian protectorate garrisoned by Italian troops. The ultimatum was rejected and on 7 April, Good Friday, the Italian invasion began. Albania had no forces to match the Italian army and Zog fled, taking with him his queen and their two-day-old son.

BULGARIA

Despite being the only defeated state in the region, Bulgaria avoided descent into disorder. This was in part because there were two strong radical forces, the agrarians and the communists, which could assume power after the failure of the established order.

The communists enjoyed considerable backing and used their power in the towns and the trade unions to wield the strike weapon. But the agrarians, under the charismatic leadership of Aleksandŭr Stamboliiski, were stronger. Their social base was wider and their command of electoral tactics better. After the first post-war elections in 1919 Stamboliiski secured a parliamentary majority by disqualifying the requisite number of communist deputies on the grounds of electoral irregularities. Stamboliiski was to be in power for four years.

His first task was to ensure national acceptance of the Treaty of Neuilly of November 1919. This was naturally not popular but most Bulgarians recognized that they had little choice but to accept the Allies' terms. What was more difficult for many to swallow was Stamboliiski's subsequent foreign policy. This was based on peasant internationalism. He would have liked to see a peasant confederation throughout the Balkans and Eastern Europe and this being the case he was anxious to come to agreements with his neighbours, the most powerful of which was Yugoslavia, with whom he concluded an agreement at Nish in March 1923. This provided for cooperation on border security and in Bulgaria prompted an attempted clampdown on Macedonian dissidents.

In domestic affairs Stamboliiski's Bulgarian Agrarian National Union (BANU) pursued a radical agenda. But in one respect this was difficult. Bulgaria was already a nation of peasant proprietors and therefore there were few large landholdings for a radical agrarian government to redistribute. Nevertheless, Stamboliiski's administration declared a maximum holding of 30 hectares, with more for larger families. This enabled the government to confiscate land from the Church, local authorities, and the state, but by 1923 only 82,000 out of a projected 230,000 hectares had been placed in the state land fund. There were measures, however, to intensify the agrarian nature of the country. Education was reformed to include more on the subject of agriculture, whilst in the villages the local branches of BANU became virtual parallel administrative units and frequently took responsibility for the organization of cultural and welfare facilities.

The agrarians also introduced the concept of maximum property holdings into urban life, the basic nuclear family being allotted two rooms and a kitchen. An equally unpopular act was the introduction of the Compulsory Labour Service which required all males between 20 and 60 to serve a year and all females over 16 six months on projects such as road construction and the building of schools.

Stamboliiski's government was rapidly making enemies. Its foreign policy outraged the Macedonians, still a powerful and disruptive lobby in Bulgarian affairs. The military were angered by the regime's apparent disdain for the traditional military establishment and were also concerned at the growth of the Orange Guard, BANU's paramilitary organization. The traditional political parties, discredited by their performance in the war, found renewed purpose and credibility in their opposition to the increasing indications that BANU wished to set up a one-party state. Even the usually docile Bulgarian Orthodox Church had been offended by the loss of some of its property, by reforms in education, and by proposed changes in the Bulgarian alphabet.

All important opposing elements except the communists came together after the government had banned opposition rallies and had secured a massive BANU parliamentary majority by abolishing proportional representation for the elections of April 1923. The conspirators struck on 9 June 1923, destroying the agrarian government and murdering its leader, though few of them had envisaged that the deposition of the Stamboliiski government would be so violent.

Violence was to remain endemic in Bulgarian political life for the remainder of the 1920s. The communists, who had sat on their hands in June, were ordered by Moscow to redeem their honour. This produced an abortive rising in September 1923 which provoked increased repression on the part of the government. This was massively intensified after 16 April 1925, when the communists detonated a bomb in the roof of Sofia's Sveta Nedelya cathedral during a public service, killing over 130 people. The terror abated somewhat in the second half of the 1920s, not least because international donors insisted that if Bulgaria were to receive a loan to support welfare payments to Macedonian refugees then the prime minister must step down. But when he had done so political violence continued, particularly between the competing Macedonian factions. The Macedonian extremists also caused embarrassment abroad. One faction had established a virtual state within the state in south-western Bulgaria whence it conducted incursions into Greek and Yugoslav Macedonia. After one such incident in October 1925, the Greek army moved into parts of southern Bulgaria and remained there until the League of Nations had engineered a conclusion to the crisis.

The second half of the 1920s, with its problems of endemic violence, showed the weakness of the Bulgarian political system. After the end of the BANU regime there was no strong force. The political parties, particularly the agrarians, splintered and in so doing hobbled the parliamentary system; the new King Boris III, who had come to the throne when his father abdicated in 1918, had not yet entered the political arena; the communists' terror tactics had placed them beyond the pale; and the army remained on the sidelines.

The Great Depression broke the deadlock. In the elections of June 1931, which were relatively free, the largest share of the vote went to a new alliance of traditional parliamentary parties and some agrarians. The alliance formed a government and immediately set about tackling the effects of the Depression. The powers of the government grain-purchasing monopoly, set up in 1930, were extended to cover other crops and a series of measures was enacted to alleviate peasant indebtedness. But government ministers could not resist the age-old temptation to enrich themselves, and the agrarians were amongst the most culpable.

This depressingly predictable development meant that government efforts to contain discontent failed. On the right a fascist movement led by Tsankov, the prime minister ejected because of the terror in the 1920s, grew in strength whilst on the left the communists, legally operating as the Bulgarian Workers' Party (BWP), recaptured much of its urban support and in February 1932 secured a majority of seats on Sofia City Council. The Council was dissolved in the following year. There was another opposition force: Zveno (link). Zveno was elitist, drawing its strength from a section of the intelligentsia and anti-royalist army officers. It demanded a cleansing of the political system, and better relations with France, Britain, and Yugoslavia, which made it an enemy of the Macedonian extremists.

On 19 May 1934, Zveno executed an efficient coup. The new regime's most important act was to liquidate the Macedonian extremists' stronghold in south-western Bulgaria, and although the Macedonian question was not solved the extremists never again played a major role in internal Bulgarian affairs. The new government also abolished political parties and the existing trade unions, centralized the administration, and made ready to introduce a corporate state. It also encouraged the Bulgarianization of placenames. One question the *zvenari* did not address was that of the powers of the crown. They soon regretted this omission. In January 1935, they were manœuvred out of office and in November Georgi Kioseivanov, who was totally obedient to the King, was made prime minister.

Kioseivanov's main task was to devise a new constitution, one which would provide a 'tidy and disciplined democracy', that is one which allowed some freedom but not too much leeway to Tsankov on the right or the communists on the left, the latter having been encouraged by the performance of the Bulgarian Georgi Dimitrov at the Reichstag trial in 1934 and by the growing power of their comrades in Greece. In fact, Kioseivanov was never able to find an adequate formula and though the existing constitution was modified Bulgaria was the only Balkan state in the inter-war period which did not enact a new constitution.

By the second half of the decade, foreign policy had become as important as domestic affairs. In the 1920s Bulgaria had adopted 'peaceful revisionism', whereby it looked to the League of Nations and to Italy for help in its quest for the access to the Aegean it had been promised. In the late 1930s the League was enfeebled and Italy increasingly hostile. Boris attempted to keep Bulgaria out of any entanglement with a great power and to rely instead on regional pacts, and in 1937 and 1938 concluded agreements with Yugoslavia. But after the Munich settlement and the first Vienna award in 1938, Bulgaria was the only defeated power which had not benefited from territorial revision and this increased the vociferousness of the pro-Axis lobby. Bulgaria did recover some territory in September 1940, when the treaty of Craiova forced Romania to hand back the southern Dobrudja. Even then, Boris did not yield to blandishments from Berlin but in the spring of 1941, with France defeated, the Soviet Union still allied to Hitler, and Britain distant and embattled, Boris decided that voluntary cooperation with was better than forcible subjection to Hitler's Germany.

GREECE

For Greece, the First World War ended not in Paris in 1919 but with the collapse of the Anatolian campaign and the Treaty of Lausanne in 1923. The Anatolian disaster divided yet further a nation already deeply riven by the feud between Venizelos and the monarch. The disaster also greatly increased the need for welfare spending which the government could scarce afford. The inter-war period was to see a bewildering succession of coups, referenda, and constitutional changes.

After the war King Constantine had gone into exile but the royalists who remained behind questioned Venizelist policies in Asia Minor and though they continued the war after defeating Venizelos in the elections of November 1920, their changes in military leadership did not improve the effectiveness of the Greek army. With the defeat of that army a group of Venizelist officers seized power in Athens and tried eight prominent military men and politicians on charges of high treason. The execution of six of them intensified even further the feud between the Venizelists and the royalists.

Most of the Christians who arrived in Greece as a result of the population exchanges were settled in Macedonia, greatly increasing the proportion of ethnic Greeks in that region. But the resettlement brought many social problems. A disproportionate number of the arrivals were women and children, and most of them totally destitute. A surprising number did not speak Greek, the population transplants being determined by religion not ethnicity, and many others spoke difficult dialects or only the formalized literary language taught in schools. Work was difficult to find and many new Greeks ended living in destitution. International loans did something to ease the burden but could not meet the full costs of providing welfare.

Domestic politics in Greece in the 1920s saw the struggle continue between the royalists and the Venizelist Liberal Party, with the army also playing a role, usually on the side of the latter. The royalists had emerged victorious in the elections of 1923, not least because their opponents had boycotted the poll. In 1924 a referendum was staged on the question of the monarchy, a substantial proportion of the country deciding that the institution should be abolished. This did not mean, however, that political stability had been achieved. The government was dominated by the vainglorious General Pangalos who was removed in a coup in 1926. Elections were held under proportional representation after which an administration of Venizelists and anti-Venizelists was formed. This provided a period of calm long enough to enact a new, republican constitution in 1927, after which Venizelos returned to the premiership in 1928. One of his first acts was to abolish proportional representation. This was only one of the signs that Venizelos, now in his sixties, was moving towards authoritarianism.

At the end of the 1920s, the main concentration of the Venizelos government was on foreign affairs where Venizelos had more experience and faced less opposition than on the domestic front. He concluded agreements with Yugoslavia, improved relations with Bulgaria and Romania, and came to an accommodation with Italy with whom relations had been difficult since the Italians had 'temporarily' occupied the Dodecanese islands in 1913. Most important of all, however, was the agreement with Turkey in 1930 which enabled Venizelos to become the first Greek premier to visit the Ecumenical Patriachate in Istanbul. Venizelos's administration was the only one in inter-war Greece to complete its constitutional four-year term of office.

In 1932 elections were held, once again under PR. They resulted in deadlock and ushered in four years of chaos. Further elections, this time under the majoritarian system, were held in 1933 producing victory for the Populist Party. In March disaffected Venizelist army officers staged an unsuccessful attempt to remove the Populist prime minister and the confusion was increased in June when Venizelos's car was machine-gunned; he was unhurt. In March 1935 Venizelist officers sought their revenge in yet another attempted coup, after which Venizelos himself was forced into exile. Later in the year further elections were held, despite the fact that the country had been placed under martial law. The Venizelists boycotted the poll and the Populists secured almost a third of the votes and 95 per cent of the seats in parliament. Still the army was not content. In October a group of royalist officers told the prime minister to restore the monarchy or go. He went; and George II returned.

The restoration of the monarchy did not mean a return to the relative political stability of the 1926–32 period. A faked plebiscite was supposed to give legitimacy to the restoration but it did not swing public opinion behind the King or the Populists. In elections held shortly after the restoration, and conducted once more under PR, the Populists and Liberals emerged with almost an equal number of seats. The balance was held by the communists, the KKE having secured 6 per cent of the vote which gave them fifteen seats; in 1935 they had taken 10 per cent of the votes but the prevailing electoral system had denied them any parliamentary representation. The KKE's electoral prominence was a reflection of the industrial unrest which had been growing as a result of the Great Depression. In 1936 that unrest intensified; in the first six months of the year there were 344 strikes, the most important of which was by tobacco workers in Salonika in May in which twelve strikers were killed by police. For a while the city was out of control and only the army was able to restore order.

This was a metaphor for the country as a whole. The communists responded to the Salonika events by calling for a general strike. The threat was probably hollow, but it provided General Ion Metaxas with the excuse he needed. The leader of a small far-right party, he had for some months been calling for firm action by the central authorities to restore discipline in society. On 4 August 1936, the King agreed to abolish key sections of the constitution and the reins of power were handed to Metaxas.

Metaxas was a traditionalist, a paternalist, a disciplinarian, and an authoritarian rather than a fascist, though he did establish a number of corporate bodies, particularly the youth organization. He abolished the political parties which he regarded as the fount of most social and political evil. Civil liberties were severely restricted and police powers greatly extended. In foreign affairs, which were so important in the late 1930s, Metaxas kept Greece, despite the benefits it was deriving from economic ties with Germany, on its traditional, pro-British path. But by the end of the 1930s, Britain's ability to provide protection was

Table 11.3. Ethnic composition of Romania, 1930 (%)

Romanian	71.9
Magyar	7.9
German	4.1
Jewish	4.0
Ukrainian	3.2
Russian	2.3
Bulgarian	2.0
Roma	1.5
Turkish and Tatar	1.0
Others	2.1
Total	100.0

Source: Joseph Rothschild, *East-Central Europe between the Two World Wars* (Seattle, 1974), 284.

Table 11.4. Religious affiliation in Romania, 1930 (%)

Orthodox Christian	72.6
Greek Catholic (Uniate)	7.9
Roman Catholic	6.8
Jewish	4.2
Calvinist	3.9
Lutheran	2.2
Muslim	1.0
Others	1.4
Total	100.0

Source: Joseph Rothschild, *East-Central Europe between the Two World Wars* (Seattle, 1974), 284.

diminishing just as the Axis Powers' predilection for expansion was increasing. In October 1940, Mussolini, anxious to prove his fascist regime the equal of its German ally, decided upon expansion and used his bases in southern Albania to launch an invasion of Greece which thereby became the first Balkan state to become a combatant in the Second World War.

ROMANIA

Before the First World War, Romanian party politics had been dominated by two large factions, the Conservatives and the Liberals. The former, being pro-German, had lost credibility and the vast majority of the population was almost equally suspicious of the Liberals because their economic policy of stimulating industrialization by taxing agriculture hit the peasant hard. Two new parties now dominated the political scene. In the Regat the newly formed Peasant Party (PP), which included many former Conservatives, received widespread popular support. The PP's main demand, for the break-up of the large estates in the Regat, was not contested; it had already been promised by a regime frightened by the massive 1907 outbreak of rural violence and anxious during the war to retain or recover peasant loyalty. This left the PP to argue for economic policies which were less harmful to peasant interests, for an increase in support for the co-operative movement, and for greater representation of peasant interests in local and central government. Of the newly acquired territories, only Transylvania was politically sophisticated and organized, but its Transylvanian Nationalist Party (TNP) was a formidable machine. It had come to maturity in the tough political world of the former Hungarian Kingdom, and it was now as watchful of Bucharest's power as it had recently been of Budapest's. It was also as assiduous as the PP in its campaign against corruption.

The PP was popular but not anxious to rule. It believed a strong man was needed to contain the communists and to push through policies which the Liberals might find offensive, above all the redistribution of property in the acquired territories. The PP therefore boycotted the elections of October 1919 and in March 1920 welcomed the advent to power of war hero General Averescu. Averescu did contain the communists and having done so made way in January 1922 for the Liberals who were to remain in office until December 1928.

The Liberals' most important enactment was the new constitution of 1923. It bore many Liberal trademarks, particularly in the limitations it imposed on foreign ownership of Romanian property. In 1926 a new law, borrowed from fascist Italy to contain the problems which the plethora of political parties was causing, provided that any party which received 40 per cent of the votes in an election would be granted 50 per cent of the seats in the lower house. In fact, the operation of this system was seldom needed. Romanian political managers had long since perfected the art of electoral management and could engineer the desired result.

The Liberals used their years in office to reinforce their policies of state-sponsored industrialization paid for by taxing agriculture. Peasant resentment at these policies inevitably grew and peasant power was considerably increased in 1926 when the PP merged with the TNP to form the National Peasant Party (NPP). The Transylvanians had been angered by increasing centralism as was seen, for example, in the Liberals' decision to increase Bucharest's control over local government.

By 1928, the NPP had grown massively in strength and when elections were held in December it secured 70 per cent of the votes. It was the one basically free vote in inter-war Romania. True to its programme the NPP in office reduced the role of the government in various sectors of the economy, a measure which also limited the amount of patronage and therefore of corruption. The NPP regime also fostered the cooperatives and sought to shift the balance of economic policy more in favour of the peasant, its abolition of duties on agricultural exports being particularly popular. But the NPP could not meet all its supporters' expectations and, with the advent of the Great Depression in 1929, its strategy of financing foreign loans with the profits from agricultural exports collapsed. The NPP left office the following year.

At the opening of the 1930s, the left, the old establishment, and the NPP had all failed. The Romanian army was not a political factor and therefore the two main contestants for power were the monarch and the new right.

Extreme nationalism and virulent anti-Semitism were not new features in Romanian public life but not until the 1930s did they become a major contender for power. The were represented by Corneliu Zelia Codreanu who had acquired great acclaim in the previous decade by killing an unpopular official, a crime for which he was not punished. A later offence did result in imprisonment and in gaol he claimed to have been visited by the Archangel Michael who urged him, on release, to lead Romania to a new age of discipline and purity. As soon as he could Codreanu formed the League of the Archangel Michael, otherwise known as the Iron Guard. Codreanu insisted that his organization was a 'movement', not a political party. It was closely associated with the Romanian Orthodox Church and in addition to the standard fascist notions of leadership, discipline, ethnic purity, and authoritarianism, it had bizarre characteristics such as the cults of self-sacrifice and of veneration for Romanian soil, a small bag of which most Guardists wore round their necks.

The Guard had a powerful appeal. It flattered the peasants by extolling them as the embodiment of the pure Romanian spirit; it also offered them the supposed economic security of autarky and delivered direct assistance by organizing volunteers to build roads, bridges, schools etc. The Guard also appealed to young middle-class Romanians; the francophile intelligentsia of the nineteenth century, typified by the Liberal Party, had hoped to industrialize Romania, but by 1930 this strategy seemed to have failed; in rejecting the ambitions of their fathers and grandfathers the young Romanian intelligentsia identified truculently with Romanian traditions and customs rather than those of France.

The Guard's chief opponent was the crown. In 1926 the Liberals had persuaded the heir to the throne, Carol, to renounce his right of succession. The ostensible cause was his liaison with a Madame Lupescu but in a country where sexual morality was notoriously lax everyone knew the real cause was that the Liberals feared Carol would interfere too much in politics. In 1927 the reigning monarch died and Carol kept his word—but only until June 1930 when he returned to Bucharest as King Carol II. Madame Lupescu arrived in October.

For much of the decade the King kept the Guard out of power through a series of restrictive regulations but in 1937 he hit a major obstacle. Elections in that year, which were relatively free, gave no party 40 per cent so the premium could not operate. There was also an electoral pact between the NPP and the Guard. Carol seized upon this as proof that the existing constitution was fundamentally flawed and in February 1938 introduced a new one. Romania would now have a 'guided democracy', with the King as guide. The Guard was kept at bay and on 29–30 November it suffered another blow when thirteen of its imprisoned leaders, Codreanu included, were 'shot whilst trying to escape'; in fact they were garrotted.

One of the bones of contention between the King and the pro-German Guard was foreign policy which Carol regarded as a royal preserve. The Nazis were not put out by action against the Guard; in oil-rich Romania they valued stability more than ideological compatibility. But as Europe descended into war domestic and foreign affairs became ever more closely linked. After the defeat of Poland emboldened Guardists murdered the King's chief adviser, Calinescu, but the final nail in Carol's political coffin was the defeat of France.

Carol had assured his people that he would construct an impregnable barrier around Romania. It became known as the 'Imaginot Line'. And so it proved. The fall of France enabled Stalin to cash in the cheques given to him under the Nazi–Soviet Pact. In June he took Bessarabia and northern Bukovina. It was now open season on the defenceless, isolated Romania. In August northern Transylvania was ceded to Hungary and in the following month came Craiova and the loss of the southern Dobrudja. In a few weeks Romania had lost a third of its territory and a third of its population, half of them ethnic Romanians.

Before the Craiova treaty was signed, Carol had abdicated and fled. Power passed to General Antonescu, who declared Romania a National Legionary state in which the Iron Guard was the only legal political organization.

Table 11.5. Ethnic composition of Yugoslavia, by mother tongue (%)

	1921	1931
Serbo-Croat	74.36	77.01
Slovene	8.51	8.15
German	4.22	3.59
Magyar	3.90	3.36
Albanian	3.67	3.63
Others	5.34	4.26
Total	100.00	100.00

Source: Joseph Rothschild, *East-Central Europe between the Two World Wars* (Seattle, 1974), 203.

Table 11.6. Religious affiliation in Yugoslavia (%)

	1921	1931
Orthodox Christian	46.67	48.70
Roman Catholic	39.29	37.45
Muslim	11.22	11.20
Lutheran and Calvinist	2.45	1.66
Others	0.37	0.99
Total	100.00	100.00

Source: Joseph Rothschild, *East-Central Europe between the Two World Wars* (Seattle, 1974), 203.

YUGOSLAVIA

The political structure of the newly created Kingdom of the Serbs, Croats, and Slovenes, as Yugoslavia was officially known until 1929, could not be designed until social stability had been secured and the state's borders defined. A major factor in the first problem was, as elsewhere in the region, the redistribution of land; but as ever in Yugoslavia this problem was compounded by ethnic and regional differences. In some instances, large estates were seized and divided immediately, especially when the former landlords were Hungarian, German, or Muslim, but even when the process was carried out according to the law, the beneficiaries were generally Christian Slavs. There was considerable tension in the first years of the redistribution process and here, as in other cases of unrest caused by unemployment or other social problems, order was restored and maintained by the Serbian army and Serbian police units which were sent throughout the new kingdom. They were not always appreciated.

The problem of boundaries could not be solved by internal agencies. By the autumn of 1920 the provisional government in Belgrade felt confident enough of internal order and external definition to hold elections for a constituent assembly. It convened in December and on 28 June 1921, St Vitus Day (Vidovdan), enacted a new constitution. Yugoslavia was to be a hereditary monarchy with a unicameral legislature, the skupština, elected by universal, male suffrage. Its critical provisions determined that Yugoslavia should be a centralized state with thirty-three departments which in most important matters were to be controlled from Belgrade. The anti-centralists denounced the settlement but their most powerful element, the Croatian People's Peasant Party (CPPP), had boycotted the constituent assembly and thereby gravely weakened the anti-centralist lobby.

The anti-centralists' main complaint was that the new state was an extended Serbia with Serbs dominating all the state institutions from the army to the banks and the bureaucracy. The Serbs themselves argued that Serbia alone had had a state system before the creation of Yugoslavia and therefore it made good pragmatic sense to adopt the only one that existed; and as to the widespread deployment of the Serbian army and police, who else, asked the Serbs, could protect the area from Hungarian Bolshevism or Italian aggrandizement? Many Serbs also believed that they had a natural right to dominate the new state. Serbia had made huge sacrifices during the war whilst many Croats, Bosnians, and Slovenes had fought under the Habsburg colours.

The Croats rejected such views. They resented domination by a system which they considered more backward and corrupt than their previous one. They also demanded widespread autonomy. For the Slovenes, the new system brought more benefits. Their language was much more distant from Serbian than was that in use in Croatia, and at least they now had the freedom to regulate education as they wished. The other ethnic groups and regions were much less influential. The Montenegrins were divided between those who wished to merge with Serbia and those who wanted to retain more of their former independence; the Macedonians were rigidly controlled from Belgrade; the Albanians of Kosovo were weak and divided; and the Muslims of Bosnia feared that if they complained too loudly their administrative regions would be redefined so as place all of them in units dominated by non-Muslims.

These divisions, and above all that between the Serbian and Croatian political establishments, were deep and lasting. They wrecked the fragile settlement propounded in 1921.

After the enactment of the constitution central Yugoslav affairs were dominated by Nikola Pašić of Serbia's National Radical Party which had been in office since before the war; he remained in power partly through the extensive use of patronage and also because his main opponent, the CPPP leader Stjepan Radić, adopted idiosyncratic and at times self-damaging tactics. In 1924, for example, he turned up in Moscow claiming to be in favour of the communist-dominated agrarian international, the *krestintern*, the main result of which was that Pašić could brand him as a stooge of the Bolsheviks. Radić also made such extreme demands that he was put in gaol for a short period. After elections in February 1925, however, he moderated his views. Strengthened by a vote of confidence from the Croatian electorate he dropped his call for a separate Croatian republic and accepted the Vidovdan constitution. He then joined Pašić in a grand coalition in which Radić served as minister for education. By August 1925 tension had subsided enough for King Alexander to pay his first visit to Zagreb.

It was a false dawn. In April 1926 the grand coalition collapsed not because of action by Radić but because Pašić resigned after his son had been accused of corruption. Pašić had been the dominant figure in the skupština and there being no one of equal stature to replace him the assembly fell into chaos. The denouement came on 20 June 1928 when a Montenegrin radical produced a revolver and killed two deputies; he also wounded Radić who died seven weeks later. The country seemed on the verge of dissolution. The political parties were weak and divided; there was no political figure who could command overall respect; the trade unions and the left were enfeebled; and since a purge of the officer corps in 1917 the army had remained a pliant tool of the King. The King therefore was the only factor left, and on 9 January 1929 he executed a *coup d'état*.

The short-term objective of the 1929 coup was to avoid political collapse. The King considered that the villains of the piece had been the political parties and the particularist aspirations they fed on and fuelled. He therefore dissolved all political parties, increased the powers of the police and the military, suspended the trade unions, and banned all organizations which had a regional basis. Political collapse was avoided, but the long-term objective of fostering a new Yugoslav consciousness was not achieved. It was not for want of trying. A series of measures designed to win Alexander's peoples over to the new system were enacted: a third of the bureaucracy, including its most corrupt elements, were sacked; a new Agrarian Bank was introduced because the existing ones were seen as repositories of Serbian patronage; and in October 1929 the departments were replaced by nine new regional units, the *banovine*, which were named after topographical features and which were intended to split up the old, regional/ethnic allegiances. In 1931 a new constitution codified these changes and relaxed some political controls. These reforms made little impact and the King was contemplating more when he was felled by an assassin in Marseilles on 9 October 1934. His killer was a Macedonian who had connections with extremist elements in his home area and in Croatia.

The heir to the throne, King Peter, was a minor and a regency was therefore established under his cousin, Prince Paul. The Regent insisted that there could be no further constitutional revision until the King became of age and Yugoslavia was thus given respite from the fraught process of political redefinition. This was as well, given that the major issue facing the majority of the country was now the impact of the Great Depression. The government attempted to alleviate peasant sufferings by guaranteeing their households and a minimum of land against restraint for debt, and in 1936 halved pre-1932 debts. It also sought to encourage the development of agrarian co-operatives. By the second half of the decade some relief was felt, primarily as a result of trade agreements with Germany in 1933 and 1934.

In January 1935 Milan Stojadinović became prime minister and was to remain in office until February 1939. Stojadinović's main tasks were to increase internal cohesion, primarily by easing the Serb-Croat problem, and to secure Yugoslavia's position in the international arena. He made a number of concessions to the Croats, including granting permission for the erection in Zagreb of a statue to Radić. His major effort, however, was to regularize relations between Yugoslavia and the Vatican, a move which would obviously please the Catholic Croats but which might also alarm the Orthodox Serbs. In 1935 he negotiated a Concordat and in the summer of 1938 seemed about to persuade the Orthodox Serbs in the skupština to endorse it. The night before they were due to do so, the head of the Orthodox Church in Serbia died—of natural causes. The agreement collapsed. So too, in February 1939, did Stojadinović's government. Stojadinović's successor was impelled to continue to seek an accommodation with the Croats and this he achieved in the so-called *sporazum*, or agreement, of 20 August 1939. The *sporazum* made huge concessions to the Croats. The old *banovine* were redrawn to the great advantage of the Croats who were now to have their own assembly and were to be governed by a Ban who was to be responsible not to the skupština but directly to the monarch.

The *sporazum* was as much the result of external as internal pressures. In the 1920s Yugoslavia had found security in the Little Entente which had given it protection against Hungary. A treaty with France in 1927 gave it increased security against Italy. In the mid-1930s Belgrade sought to bolster regional security through the Balkan entente of 1934 and more significantly via an agreement with Bulgaria in January 1937. But by then revisionism was rampant in Europe and it increasingly threatened Yugoslavia. The Anschluss in March 1938 had brought the Nazi imperium to the very borders of Yugoslavia and in March 1939 the creation, under Nazi aegis, of an independent Slovakia set an example of which the Slovenes and even more so the Croats took notice. Immediately afterwards Italy, which had designs on Dalmatia, seized Albania. Yugoslavia was now caught in an Axis vice. This naturally intensified Belgrade's anxiety to secure an agreement with Zagreb, but not even the *sporazum* could overcome the besetting difficulty of inter-war Yugoslavia, the division between Serbs and Croats.

THE SECOND WORLD WAR

During the Second World War two Balkan states, Bulgaria and Romania, aligned with the Axis; two, Albania and Greece, were occupied by the Axis, though Greece lost territory whereas Albania gained it; and one, Yugoslavia, was dismembered. The major changes were effected when German forces entered the area in the spring of 1941. Resistance movements appeared in all occupied states but those movements were bitterly divided. There were differences over tactics: should sabotage operations be carried out or should the resistance effort be saved until the approach of the liberating Allied armies when diversionary and disruptive activities would do most damage to the enemy and most good to the Allies? But the largest divide was over what was to happen after liberation and here there was an abyss between the communists and the non-communists. Despite these divisions the resistance forces of Greece, Albania, and Yugoslavia remained a thorn in the side of the occupiers.

The first of the Balkan states to be invaded had been Greece but the Italian forces who surged into the country from Albania in October 1940 were soon repulsed. The Greek army and nation had resisted heroically but there was nothing they could do when the Wehrmacht poured into Greece in April 1941. By the end of the month the country was occupied and a government in exile established in London and then in Cairo. Most of Greece was placed under Italian occupation, with the Germans taking Athens, Salonika, Crete, and the border with Turkey; Bulgaria was given administration of Greek Macedonia and western Thrace.

The first winter of the occupation produced an appalling famine, in large measure a consequence of the plundering of Greek food reserves by the occupiers. Over a hundred thousand Greeks starved to death. Death came too to the vast majority of Jews living in Greece, who were deported to the extermination camps in the spring of 1943.

By the spring of 1942, armed resistance units had appeared in the mountains and were soon being supplied and guided by officers from Britain's Special Operations Executive (SOE). In November 1942 the guerrillas succeeded in blowing up the Gorgopotamos viaduct which carried the vital Salonika to Athens railway line. The Gorgopotamos operation was a combined effort by the two main Greek resistance Organizations, the National People's Liberation Army (ELAS) and the National Republican Greek League (EDES). ELAS, an acronym which conveniently sounded like the Greek word for Greece, was the military wing of the National Liberation Front (EAM). Most members of EAM and ELAS were not communists but the leadership of both organizations was dominated by communists and it was fear of communist domination after the war which led to suspicion on the part of EDES. The British, who played a major role in Greek affairs, were probably even more suspicious of EAM/ELAS and unwisely insisted upon the return of the King as soon as the war was over; EDES was determinedly anti-royalist.

Relations between the two resistance groups deteriorated and there was sporadic fighting between them from October 1943 to February 1944. A solution was found only after George Papandreou, an anti-communist and anti-royalist, was made head of the government in exile in the spring of 1944. That the communists accepted the terms he offered them probably came as a result of orders from Moscow. Churchill had approached the Soviets in May 1944 with a request for an agreement over the future of Greece and to this the Soviets had proved receptive. It culminated in the per centages agreement in Moscow in October 1944 when Churchill and Stalin divided south-eastern Europe: the West was to have a 90 per cent 'of the say' in Greece and the Soviet Union 90 per cent in Romania; in Bulgaria the Soviets were to have 75 per cent influence and Yugoslavia was to be shared equally. Albania was not mentioned.

In the same month that this agreement was signed Papandreou entered a liberated Athens. But if Greece was soon to leave the Second World War, it had by no means found peace.

The resistance in Albania was as divided as that in Greece. The first force to be established was that of Abas Kupi, a royalist, but he could do little without external help, which was not forthcoming. A further impediment to resistance came with the Axis conquest of Yugoslavia in 1941 because Kosovo was incorporated into Albania. The communists, however, were not influenced by nationalism. The Albanian Communist Party (ACP) was established in November 1941 under Yugoslav patronage, much of the work being done by ethnic Albanians from Kosovo. In September 1942, at Peza, a National Liberation Committee (NLC) was set up in which both Kupi and the ACP participated. Shortly thereafter a third force emerged, National Union or Balli Kombetar (BK).

In the early autumn of 1943, the Italian surrender meant that Albania came under German occupation. Under it the fragmentation of the resistance forces increased. BK decided it had no great objections to the regency council established by the Germans and therefore its resistance activity decreased. That of the communists increased, not least because they had acquired many of the arms laid down by the Italians, and these they used against BK as much as against the Germans. The communists' aggression towards BK persuaded Kupi that they would not make congenial post-war political bed-fellows and he therefore cut his links with the NLC and demanded the restoration of King Zog. This did little to stem the growth of communist power, and when the Germans left Albania in October 1944 Enver Hoxha's forces were the strongest in the country.

Of all the resistance movements in the Balkans that in Yugoslavia was the most divided. When the Second World War began in September 1939 Yugoslavia was still in a febrile condition. The *sporazum* of August had failed to satisfy the extreme elements amongst the Croatian nationalists but had mightily angered the Serbs. When the government announced in March 1941 that it would sign the tripartite pact a group of angry Serbian airforce officers staged a coup in defiance of this unpopular move but also in the hope that they might redress the internal balance of power in Serbia's favour. There was no opportunity to do so. Hitler's forces invaded Yugoslavia on 6 April and met little opposition. Yugoslavia was then dismembered. A rump Serbia was placed under a German-dominated quisling regime with other parts of it going to Hungary, Albania, and Bulgaria; an independent Croatia, which included Bosnia and Hercegovina, was created; Serbian Macedonia was put under Bulgarian administration, though its western border area went to Italian-occupied Albania; the Italians also took control of Montenegro and Dalmatia, and Slovenia was partitioned between them and their German allies. A Yugoslav government in exile was established in London.

Resistance began with Serbian pro-royalist forces taking to the hills immediately after the invasion. Initially the communists did nothing, and only became organized as an effective resistance force after the German invasion of the Soviet Union had cleared the ideological air. The first efforts at communist action, a rising in Montenegro, was easily and bloodily repressed. In Serbia the royalist leader, Mihailović, made attempts to cooperate with the communists under Tito but the differences on tactics and ultimate political objectives were too great. At the end of 1941 Tito, finding little support amongst the traditionally royalist Serbian peasants, moved his partisan forces to the mountains of Bosnia. Here he found much more support primarily because of the vicious anti-Serb policies of the Croatian government under Ante Pavelić who was living up to his promise to solve the 'Serbian problem' by converting a third of them to Catholicism, expelling a third, and killing a third. The appalling atrocities committed by the Croatian regime persuaded Tito that his propaganda must stress above all the need to create a new Yugoslavia in which ethnic rights would be respected.

Tito's forces gathered strength and in the areas under their control applied reformist policies. The communist nature of the partisan movement was not emphasized, not least because Stalin insisted that to do so might frighten the Allies into a separate peace. At the end of 1943, Tito's partisans had impressed British SOE observers sufficiently for British support to be switched from Mihailović to the partisans. This was despite the fact that in November 1943 Tito had established a virtual provisional government in Yugoslavia with a blueprint for a future, federal state. It was a direct challenge to the government in exile but that by now commanded little respect, not least because of the behaviour of the King, particularly his marrying whilst his country was under foreign occupation.

The internal conflict in Yugoslavia was every bit as fierce as that with the Germans, and sometimes took precedence over it. Tito was not above negotiating with the Germans and might have concluded a temporary armistice had Hitler not insisted there could be no negotiating with rebels. All sides in the conflict committed acts of gross barbarity, not least the occupiers who exacted horrible revenge for the killing of their own troops. As in Greece and Albania, it was the communists who benefited from the Italian surrender as they picked up most of the weaponry the Italians had abandoned. Again as in Greece and Albania, it was the communists who emerged the strongest from the occupation, but unlike in Greece the British were not on the ground nor had the per centage agreements allotted Yugoslavia to the Western sphere of influence. The way was open for a communist take-over.

The two states which cooperated with the Axis pursued individual policies. In Romania when General Antonescu inherited power from King Carol in September 1940 he was prepared to work with the Iron Guard but at the end of November the Guardists indulged in an orgy of anti-Semitism and political revenge so violent that the country was brought to the edge of anarchy. In January 1941 hotheads amongst the Guardists attempted to oust Antonescu who thereupon suppressed the Guard and instituted military rule. The Germans, more than ever requiring stability in Romania so as to import its oil, did not object.

The German invasion of the Soviet Union was welcomed by Antonescu who joined in the attack and secured the return to Romania of the northern Bukovina and of Bessarabia, and also the cession of Transnistria. The military adventure came to grief at Stalingrad where 150,000 Romanian soldiers died. With them went the fighting spirit of the Romanian army and the political credibility of Antonescu. He now concentrated on trying to extricate Romania from the war before the Red Army advanced and occupied the country. He did not succeed. In August 1944, Soviet forces advanced rapidly towards and into Romania and the young King Michael took matters into his own hands. On 23 August, he removed the general from office, the disbelieving Antonescu being locked into a commodious safe housing the royal stamp collection. Romania then switched sides and joined the Soviet forces in the war against Germany.

In internal affairs the Antonescu dictatorship had been rigid and had imposed numerous restrictions on the Jews. The Jews of Romania itself suffered indignities and discrimination but they were not killed in large numbers. This was not the case in the occupied territories, and especially Transnistria.

Bulgaria joined the Axis in March 1941 and after the German invasion of the Balkans was allowed to administer most of Macedonia and western Thrace; the Nazis did not confer outright possession in case the Bulgarians took their gains and ran. Bulgarian policy during the Second World War was singular. Britain declared war on Bulgaria when it joined the Axis and King Boris joined Hitler in declaring war on the United States in December 1941. But Boris refused to join the war against the Soviet Union, arguing that the Bulgarian army was not modernized enough to fight such a war. Instead Bulgarian forces helped the Germans control parts of north-eastern Serbia.

Bulgaria, like Romania, did not deport the Jews from the pre-war state. In Bulgaria, however, there were plans, drawn up by the Germans and the minister of the interior, to do so, but when these leaked there was a furious popular outcry amongst most sections of the nation. The King recognized the national mood and refused to implement the deportation plans. The Jews, however, were placed under a separate regime; they were forced to wear the yellow star and most of them were moved to camps outside the cities. Tragically, the Jews from Bulgarian-occupied areas were not saved. Both the Bulgarian and Romanian authorities saved their Jews by arguing that they were Bulgarian or Romanian citizens and subject only to Bulgarian or Romanian law.

In August 1943 King Boris died suddenly and, his heir being a minor, power passed to a pro-German regency. Boris had described Bulgaria as being at 'symbolic war' but after Stalingrad real war approached ever closer. At the end of 1943 and early in 1944 British and US planes blasted Sofia and other cities in an attempt to persuade the Regency to abandon the Germans. It was, however, reluctant to do so without guarantees that Bulgaria should keep its occupied territories and a series of negotiations with the Allies in the summer came to naught. The dilatoriness of the government in these negotiations encouraged the growth of a resistance movement. This, however, had little effect until September 1944. By then Romania's sudden exit from the German alliance had brought the Red Army to the Danube, and on 9 September 1944 a coup by the resistance and the army installed a new government under the communist-dominated Fatherland Front. Like Romania, Bulgaria now changed sides and joined the Red Army in the war against Germany. At home the communists and their allies began a ruthless removal of their political opponents.

EPILOGUE

The First World War ended with the large-scale redrawing of the boundaries of the Balkan states but with surprisingly few shifts in the balance of social and political power. The Second World War ended with very few changes in the pre-1939 borders but with the total elimination of what remained of the pre-war social and political elites.

The Second World War had seen the dismantling of the international settlement of 1919–21 which had been replaced by one based, at least in Yugoslavia, on the claims of the minorities. After 1945 the communist rulers of most of the peninsula began by believing that the nationalism which had caused so much friction in the past would disappear as a new socialist system bred a new socialist and internationalist morality. It was not long before this remained little more than fine-sounding theory as nationalist rhetoric and policies became standard practice in Albania, Bulgaria, and Romania. And Greece and the Greeks, never strangers to national self-assertion, found their own nationalist cause in Cyprus. At the same time nationalist pressures grew in the multi-ethnic Yugoslavia until the explosion of the 1990s produced a map more akin to that of 1943 than that of 1934 or 1954. Nationalism had survived and strengthened despite the huge social and economic changes introduced between 1945 and 1990. Those changes were initially imposed by force and violence but the changes themselves were by no means all detrimental. Literacy levels rose, women were, in theory at least, released from social subjugation, and living standards rose. By the middle of the first decade of the twenty-first century, with one south-east European state within the EU and two at least on its doorstep perhaps it was time for the term 'the Balkans' to revert to its purely geographic meaning.

Before the First World War, the political evolution of the Balkans had ultimately been dependent on the devices and desires of the great powers. In the eyes of those powers the area itself, in Bismarck's oft-quoted quip, was not worth the bones of a single Pomeranian grenadier. This did not change. The Balkans were always, and have perhaps remained, second-class states in the European polity. 'I hate the Balkans', wrote Sir Eyre Crowe in the early 1920s, and attitudes in the Foreign Office were little changed almost twenty years later when his successor as permanent under-secretary, Sir Alexander Cadogan, confided to his diary on 10 July 1940, 'Not much work. Only a stream of telegrams about Turkey and the Balkans, which I can *not* understand. These esoteric speculations as to the backstairs intrigues of that deplorable part of the world are quite beyond my comprehension, and I'm afraid I ignore them.' Churchill did not ignore the Balkans; he used them as bargaining counters. The purpose of the percentages agreement was not to settle the Balkans but to ease the path towards an agreement with the Soviet Union over Poland; its allocation of Greece to the Western sphere of influence was one motive but it was not the main one. Sixty years later, when two victims of the percentages agreement, Bulgaria and Romania, signed accession agreements with the EU, the conditions imposed on them were harsher than those imposed on any previous entrants.

FURTHER READING

Allcock, John B., *Explaining Yugoslavia* (New York, 2000).

Clogg, Richard, *A Concise History of Greece* (Cambridge, 1992).

Crampton, R. J., *A Concise History of Bulgaria* (Cambridge, 1987).

Fischer, Bernd Jürgen, *King Zog and the Struggle for Stability in Albania* (New York and Boulder, Colo., 1984).

Glenny, Misha, *The Balkans 1804–1999: Nationalism, War and the Great Powers* (London, 1999).

Hitchins, Keith, *Romania, 1866–1947* (Oxford, 1994).

Jelavich, Barbara, *History of the Balkans*, ii. *The Twentieth Century* (Cambridge, 1983).

Lampe, John R., *Yugoslavia as History: Twice There Was a Country* (Cambridge, 1996).

—— and Marvin R. Jackson, *Balkan Economic History, 1550–1950: From Imperial Borderlands to Developing Nations* (Bloomington: Ind., 1982).

Malcolm, Noel, *Kosovo: A Short History* (London, 1998).

Mazower, Mark, *The Balkans* (New York, 2000).

Pavlowitch, St K., *A History of the Balkans, 1804–1945* (London and New York, 1999).

Stoianovich, Traian, *Balkan Worlds: The First and Last Europe* (Armonk, NY, and London, 1994).

Todorova, Maria, *Imagining the Balkans* (Oxford, 1997).

12

Finland and the Baltic States

Kristina Spohr Readman

INTRODUCTION

Discussing Finland together with the Baltic States of Estonia, Latvia, and Lithuania may seem surprising. Indeed, there are good reasons why Finland could have been included in the chapter on 'Scandinavia'. Its cultural and historical bonds with Sweden, its membership in the Nordic Council after 1955, and its extensive welfare system established after the Second World War are all reasons why Finland tends to be linked to the Scandinavian countries. The majority of Finns, however, are not Scandinavian. Rather, in ethno-linguistic terms, they are related to Estonians.

More importantly, Finland shared a common fate with the three Baltic States (and Poland) in 1917–20 and the two decades that followed. All five states gained independence from Russia in the context of her defeat in the Great War and the October Revolution, and together they formed the Soviet Russian north-western 'border-states'. As such, they were united in their fear of Soviet expansionism. Security issues thus dominated their interaction and their foreign policies up until 1939, when the Baltic States (and Poland) disappeared from Europe's map as a result of the Hitler–Stalin Pact; and Finland, attacked by the Soviet Union, opted for war to defend her independence.

It would, however, be wrong to assume that the inter-war period was simply a prehistory to the Second World War. And it was not just geo-politics and security concerns that united these new border-states after the Great War. The central challenge was to establish independent, stable, prosperous, and viable democracies. Yet, despite these affinities, there was much that divided Finland from the three Baltic States and the Baltic States from each other.

When Europe went to war in 1914, the Grand Duchy of Finland, and the provinces of Estonia, Latvia, and Lithuania were part of the Russian Empire.

When the war on Germany's Eastern Front ended in 1917, they emerged as independent, democratic nation-states. What had happened?

In the context of the upheavals of the First World War and the October Revolution, the Finns realized that 'national self-determination *within* Russia' (which had been central to the late nineteenth-century Finnish national discourse) was no longer an option, and on 6 December 1917 independence was declared. By the end of the month Prime Minister Pehr Evind Svinhufvud received a letter of recognition of Finnish independence from the Russian Council of People's Commissars.

Meanwhile within Finland the breach between the parties of the pro-Russian left and the pro-independence right became irreconcilable, and in late January 1918 the left-wing parties staged a coup. The government was forced to flee Helsinki. A bloody civil war between the 'Reds' (supported by Russian troops still stationed in Finland) and the 'Whites' ensued. It ended in May with victory for the White government troops, led by General Gustaf Mannerheim who was to become a hero in independent Finland. Initially, the monarchists among the Whites had their way and as a counterweight to Russia a German prince was chosen to be king of Finland. The Reich's end in sight, the prince however renounced the nomination, without setting foot in Finland. Svinhufvud and then Mannerheim governed the state in their capacity as state protectors for the first eighteen months. In May 1919, Finland became a republic, and in July Kaarlo Juho Ståhlberg was elected first president.

As for the Baltic nations, it would have been impossible at the outbreak of the First World War to predict if or when Baltic nationalist demands for cultural independence from especially German dominance would be translated into a call for political autonomy within or even full independence from the Tsarist empire. Political activity in these provinces was kickstarted in earnest during the February Revolution of 1917. Estonians, Latvians, and Lithuanians suddenly saw the chance to fight for their nations' independence from Russia. The Bolshevik Revolution forced matters. Following in Poland's footsteps, Lithuania with German agreement declared independence on 16 February 1918—although in practice the country remained under German occupation. In Estonia and northern Latvia local Bolsheviks managed to seize power in late 1917, but Germany's attack on the northern Baltic provinces caused the Bolsheviks' flight from Tallinn. This allowed Estonia to declare her independence on 24 February 1918, while Latvia followed suit on 18 November after the German Reich's capitulation. Two years of independence wars against the Red Army (and also against the Germans)—in which both sought to establish 'their' governmental regimes—followed. Finally, in 1920 peace treaties between Soviet Russia and the Baltic States (as well as Finland) were signed.

Thus 1920 was the first year in which the Baltic countries and Finland enjoyed full control over their own affairs. The challenges these new, independent countries faced in the political, economic, social, and cultural realms were formidable.

Figure 12.1. The Border-states' Conference, Tallinn, Deccember 1921.

THE INDUSTRIALIZATION AND MODERNIZATION OF AGRICULTURAL SOCIETIES

One of the most pressing socio-economic questions faced by the first governments of these predominantly rural nations was the 'land question', as the majority of people who earned their living in the agricultural sector were landless. Indeed, the radical land reforms undertaken in Finland, Estonia, Latvia, and Lithuania were to serve as much as a social equalizer as a means of nation-building.

The reforms tilted the balance strongly in favour of small farmers. In Finland, according to laws of 1918 and 1922, tenant farmers could redeem their farms on favourable terms (up to a size of 20 ha for agriculture and 20–75 ha for forestry), and by 1930 almost 90 per cent of all rented farms and plots had been purchased by their tenants. The number of independent farms increased by 100,000. These were smallholdings catering mainly for a family's own needs—the extra income from forestry often being vital. Measures promoting cultivation of marginal land and new settlements increased farmland from 2.015 million hectares in 1920, to 2.631 million in 1940 (Karelia included). Alongside the structural social changes in the agricultural sector—the decline of the number of agricultural labourers (from 38 per cent of those working in the agricultural sector in 1920 to 27 per cent in 1940), and the rise of the number of independent farmers—Finland saw significant population shifts from rural to urban areas. In 1920, 16.1 per cent of the population lived in cities and townships; by 1940 the figure had risen to 26.8 per cent. Such shrinkage of the agrarian population was primarily a sign of agricultural workers looking for a better life as workers in factories. This development was mirrored in more general occupational statistics: 66 per cent of Finns lived off income from agriculture and forestry in 1920, 61 per cent in 1930, and 54 per cent in 1940. The figures for industry, handicrafts, and building industry were 13, 15, and 18 per cent respectively and in the sectors of transport, trade, and services 10, 13, and 16 per cent. Despite these changes, three out of four Finns still lived rural lives in the 1930s.

In the Baltic States the land reforms—involving a whole-scale redistribution of land owned by a minority of large and ethnically foreign landowners (in Estonia and Latvia, Baltic German landed aristocracy; in Lithuania, Polish gentry) and what had been owned by the Russian state—were much more sweeping than in Finland and had a much bigger impact on society. It was a problem that most landowners were members of the old ruling elites, some of whom had tried to subvert the developments towards national independence in the final stages of the First World War. While in Estonia all landed estates were expropriated with little compensation, in Latvia landowners were allowed to keep 50 ha of land, some livestock, and equipment, without further compensation. Lithuania was most lenient, granting the landowners *c*.150 ha of land and some compensation. Consequently, the number of new, independent landowning farmers went up by 56,000 in Estonia, 125,000 in Latvia, and 38,700 in Lithuania.

The radical nature of these land reforms must be seen against the background that the elites who had held some 58 per cent of all cultivated land in Estonia, 48 per cent in Latvia, and 40 per cent in Lithuania were perceived as oppressors by native Balts who had mostly worked as agricultural labourers for them. The first Baltic governments feared that, if the land was not redistributed in the spirit of a strong peasantist and patriotic ethos, agricultural labourers might fall under the spell of Russian Communism, which could destabilize the young nation-states. Generally, the land reforms established a satisfied agrarian sector with small, individual farmsteads.

As in Finland, agriculture remained in the Baltic States the most important livelihood throughout the inter-war period. A great emphasis was placed on national self-sufficiency. With mechanization and the establishment of co-operatives, yields of cereals rose significantly by the 1930s, so becoming one of the Baltics' export products. Apart from grain, timber and flax, as well as butter, meat, and livestock, became important export commodities. The only problem was that Estonia, Latvia, and Lithuania competed with each other in selling these goods on world markets, which was not particularly conducive to good relations with each other.

There were however some notable national differences in industrial output. Estonia had a well-developed chemical industry thanks to its large deposits of oil shale in the north-east of the country; and Latvia had a larger and more diverse production of machinery than elsewhere in the Baltic. Lithuania's industrial sector by contrast remained rather underdeveloped and inefficient, mostly because the economic policy of Antanas Smetona's government after 1926 was influenced by nationalist principles. While it supported the ethnically Lithuanian agricultural sector, it had no great interest in promoting what were primarily German or Jewish-owned industries. These national differences were also reflected in the figure for employment in industry, which in late 1930s Lithuania was only 7 per cent, and in Latvia and Estonia closer to 20 per cent.

In general, the destructive impact of the Great War on 'imperial institutions'—banks and trading links with Russia—in the Baltics must not be overlooked. While Germany filled the post-war banking void, Tsarist Russia's huge factories in Estonia and Latvia were lost. The Baltic States had to build new industries of their own, and with their new national currencies reorientated towards the Western markets. Estonia and Latvia, after an initial period of gradual but steady growth in the early 1920s, underwent a period of rapid industrial expansion and modernization in the mid to late 1930s under the authoritarian regimes of Konstantin Päts and Kaarlis Ulmanis. It was especially for these economic successes that both leaders were to be favourably remembered by their peoples.

If we turn our attention again to Baltic trade, it is not surprising that (given the similarity of Baltic exports), their most important trading partners were also the same: Great Britain and Germany, both importers of foodstuffs and timber. This new Anglo-German-Baltic triangle of trade then reflected European interdependence and underlined how much the Baltic States were part of the European system. It demonstrated their ability to survive economically without Russia/USSR.

Finland, in terms of economic and industrial development, was much closer to the Scandinavian states, especially Sweden, than the Balts. Indeed, despite being still predominantly an agrarian society in the 1930s, Finland had entered a growth curve of industrial development that would take the country to its post-1945 affluence. Industrial production reached pre-war levels by 1922, and during the inter-war period the growth rate of Finnish industry averaged 8 per cent, higher than in other Nordic states, possibly even than elsewhere in Europe. The volume of industrial production rose in particular in 1924–8 and 1933–7 (during the latter period by 15 per cent), with the Depression years being overcome both in Finland and the Baltic States (as well as Scandinavia) faster than in most other countries, as they were less burdened with debts, and their food and timber industries were so significant for importer nations. This is not to deny that in Estonia and Latvia the economic crisis, either directly or indirectly, brought about serious political repercussions, as will be explained further below.

During the 1920s, Finland emerged as the world's greatest exporter of sawn and planed softwoods. The timber industry dominated Finland's domestic industry during this decade with a stake of 20 per cent of gross GNP. Yet after the Depression, it was the paper and pulp industry that became the major industrial branch, with a 15 per cent stake (and timber at 13 per cent). Together the

timber and paper industry made up 80–90 per cent of Finnish exports, with
the rest being mostly agricultural goods. Like the Baltic States Finland's sold
the largest amounts to Britain and Germany. Although a trade agreement was
discussed with the Soviet leadership from 1922 onwards, Finnish–Soviet trade
was minimal. Indeed, apart from political reasons, Finnish passivity *vis-à-vis* the
USSR was largely due to the fact that the new Western markets were so much
better than Russia's.

If we are then to compare the success of Finnish and Baltic economies to the
other European inter-war economies in terms of GDP per capita, it emerges
that in 1938 Finland (as well as Estonia and Latvia) were about equal with
France and the Netherlands, and not far behind Denmark and Belgium. Sweden,
Germany, and Britain in turn were as much ahead of Finland, as Finland was
ahead of Europe's average. Below average were among others Austria, Italy,
Czechoslovakia, and Lithuania. Important contributing factors to such economic
success and the ensuing social stability as Finland, Estonia, and Latvia experienced
were the significant increase of women in the workforce and the widely developed
system of social welfare. In contrast to 26.8 per cent of women working in Britain
in 1931 and *c*.36 per cent in Germany, in Finland the figure was closer to 40 per
cent and in Latvia 57.2 per cent—the highest in Europe.

EDUCATION, HIGH AND POPULAR CULTURE: BUILDING A NATION

Though relatively little research has been done on the cultural life and society in
the Baltic States, this can nevertheless be identified as one of these new states'
key areas of focus, as it was considered bringing to fruition the goals enunciated
during 'national awakening': the creation of modern, independent and viable
Estonian, Latvian, and Lithuanian cultures. Gaining official recognition of the
Baltic peoples' cultures was believed to eliminate the threat of loss of national
identity. In Finland too, the inter-war period was seen as a time when Finland's
'body and soul' was built, though the formation of the Finnish nation had its
roots in the nineteenth century. Following international trends, the nation's
cultural history has been at the centre of recent Finnish research.

Estonians, Latvians, and Lithuanians sought during the inter-war years to
consolidate their national (high) culture by a number of measures. Teaching in
mother tongue was introduced at all levels of the education system, and universal
access to schooling was granted. The principle of compulsory primary education
was introduced. Education levels thus rapidly rose to Western European standards. If illiteracy rates in Lithuania were about 33 per cent in the early 1920s
(in Latvia 14 per cent and Estonia only 6 per cent) this deficiency was largely
rectified by the late 1930s. Under the Päts, Ulmanis, and Smetona regimes,
in the three Baltic States education underwent further reform, with vocational

training in particular being encouraged and promoted as an ideal of the future. This was comparable to educational reforms in Mussolini's Italy. Consequently, in Estonia for instance, the numbers of pupils in secondary schools declined from 18,721 (1924–5) to 16,600 (1939–40), while the number of pupils in vocational training went up from 1,521 (1922–3) to 13,032 (1939–40).

Despite this emphasis on vocational training in the 1930s, universities (Tartu University in Estonia, the University of Latvia, and Kaunas University in Lithuania) and other institutions of higher education that had sprung up in the early 1920s continued to be considered important *national* institutions. There was a great interest in promoting scientific research as well as research into native culture, history, and philology. Indeed, these new nation-states were keen to propel themselves onto the global map of scholarship and, domestically, to see their existence justified and their identities strengthened by knowledge about their peoples' histories.

The introduction of the use of the native language alone in education was not undertaken for solely symbolic reasons, but to strengthen Estonian, Latvian, and Lithuanian as languages of academe and of the nation and nation-state. It is hence not surprising that these languages underwent serious modernization. The written language was standardized, which meant sidelining language related to the old folk cultures (as well as leaving behind the oral folk tradition), the creation of neologisms, and the borrowing of foreign words.

In Finland, already in 1910 the parliament (*Eduskunta*) had accepted the idea of compulsory primary education and most children had been educated in some way. But it was only in 1921 that it was introduced by law. As primary education spread across the country, the number of secondary/grammar schools grew too (though mostly in urban areas). In the early 1920s, Finland had 164 grammar schools with some 32,000 pupils; by 1950 the figures were 338 and 90,000 respectively. In 1921, only 1 in 10 moved from primary school to secondary/grammar school, whereas in 1950 the ratio was 1 in 3. In 1921, 1,200 students gained the university entry/school-leaving certificate, in 1930 c.2,000 and in 1950 c.4,000. Although the figures seem small, the proportion of university students in relation to the population was higher than anywhere else on the continent. In contrast to their Baltic colleagues, Finland's students early on had a choice of old and new, Finnish or Swedish universities, as well as other specialized institutes of higher education in Helsinki and Turku.

As elsewhere in Europe, in Finland and the Baltic States most grammar school pupils and thus university students were from cities, though the majority of children grew up in rural areas. Farmers (but also factory workers in cities) wanted their children to earn their living rather than spend the family's income by staying in education. Yet, as expanding industrialization and urbanization brought about new job opportunities and as the number of schools increased, the advantages of education became more palpable. Education became seen as the path of upward social mobility.

Education was also crucial for the forming of a *national* consciousness and a unified nation. As Finnish historian Raimo Salokangas has explained, Finnish primary school teachers from the period of Finnish autonomy onwards saw it as their duty to pass on their thinking to the next generation. In contrast to teachers in Western Europe, who considered themselves closer to the left of the political spectrum, Finnish teachers were typically on the right—keen to play an active part in building a 'White' Finnish nation. It was important not just to teach children to read, write, and count, but to help them gain a sense of Finnish national identity, of Finnish independence, and of the fatherland's position in the world.

The same nationalist trend also emerged in Finnish and Baltic writing which underwent a huge expansion in the 1920s and 1930s. To be sure, in the Baltic States in particular this was tied to the new opportunities of independence and the excitement of writing in the native language. But both here and in Finland, much of this wave of inter-war writing was history oriented. This seemed to grow out of the need to offer justification for these new states' existence. In Finland, the most popular theme during the inter-war years was the so-called 'war of independence' of 1918. This was 'White' Finnish history; and for decades to come, given the developments of Finnish–Soviet relations in the Second World War, Finnish historical literature was to become dominated by what could be called the grand narrative of nationalist liberation. The same could be said about Estonian and Latvian histories of the 1920s and 1930s, though Soviet annexation of the Baltic States in 1939 meant that very little was published during the cold war decades.

Fiction was dominated during the first few years after independence by the national romantic approach of the nineteenth century. Yet, in the 1920s many new influences came from abroad. In Estonia, Latvia, and Lithuania Western European literary trends were increasingly followed and elements of impressionism, symbolism, and expressionism were soon fused with the national romantic style. Under the nationalist regimes of the 1930s, realism became the leading direction. The same stylistic trends could also be witnessed in Baltic theatre, and in the fine arts, where Cubism and Constructivism as well as the new realistic trend (popular in France) and modernism held sway. The prevailing late art deco style of architecture gradually gave way to European-style functionalism—a development that in the Baltic was fostered by the authoritarian regimes which wanted to strengthen national identity and create the image of strong, viable nations-states by preserving neo-classical and Jugend architecture while pouring money into new modernist buildings.

In Finland, much of the late 1920s, and early 1930s, literary output was realist prose. New modernist trends were introduced by Swedish-speaking authors. Significantly, the works by the first generation of writers of independent Finland focused on national unity and the true Finnish spirit, and displayed an aggressive outward nationalism (reflected in the expressed hatred for the

Russians and estrangement from Sweden). In Finnish music and the fine arts the national romantic trend of the late nineteenth century was continued after 1917. Sculpture became central to the inter-war fine arts, as independence memorials and sculptures portraying national heroes and great men were commissioned. Although this agrarian nation preferred traditional themes and styles, by the late 1930s, the Finnish art scene finally warmed to modernity. Developments included new methods of teaching art in Helsinki, and the opening of the now-famous Artek shop in 1935, which promoted foreign art and sold functionalist furniture by architect Alvar Aalto.

As education and prosperity levels increased, urbanization advanced, and technology progressed, the press and communications gained a position of ever growing importance in the newly independent states. In Finland, newspapers had a circulation of 1.6 million in the late 1930s compared to 600,000 in the early 1920s. With the growing number of different weekly or monthly magazines added to this, the 1920s and 1930s emerge as a golden age of the printed media.

If the media in the form of printed press was central to the 1920s modern capitalist world, it also acted as a national unifier. This was intensified by the arrival of the radio and the founding of national broadcasting houses in 1925/6 (Yleisradio in Finland, Raadio Ringhäling in Estonia, Latvijas Radio in Latvia, and Lietuvos Nationalinis Radijas in Lithuania). While there has so far been no historical research on the impact of mass-communication and media on the Baltic nations, Finnish research shows that radio broadcasts helped create a unitary sense of national belonging. The radio was the first truly national tool of mass-communication, and governments soon realized the potential of national broadcasters as a means of communicating to their citizens. The aim was to civilize the nation and to bring the views of higher echelons of society that ran the country closer to the rural population.

Furthermore, the radio in the 1930s also became a distributor of popular/mass culture to all levels of society, as light music was given airtime next to classical music. Light music was a big hit. That jazz bands and dance orchestras came to the Baltic area with American cruise ships and that Hollywood films as well as Anglo-American pulp fiction in translation became ever more popular reinforced the growing global influence of US popular culture. Indeed, even if Russian plays and operas remained among the favourites, it was evident that the average person's daily life was more and more informed by *Western* (if not to say American) culture.

One of the truly *national* areas of leisure in the period of growing cultural exchange was sport, as 'the health and strength of the new nation' stood at the forefront. Sport received substantial support from the state, and participation in international championships was strongly encouraged. In comparison to the size of other nations, Finland and the Baltic States were remarkably successful. Finland's Paavo Nurmi became the runners' king with nine gold and three silver medals in the Olympic Games between 1920 and 1928, while Estonia and Latvia produced champions most notably in wrestling, speed skating, and weightlifting,

Figure 12.2. Poster for the (postponed) 1940 Olympic Games—depicting Finnish gold medallist Paavo Nurmi in front of a globe showing Finland in its 1920 borders.

and Lithuania in basketball. The governments saw sport as a national unifier, and sporting success in international competition as a means of putting the new nation-states on the world map, proving the nation's strength. At home, the media facilitated the creation of national sporting heroes.

The development of the Baltic states' culture, society, and economy in the inter-war period reveals that, as they sought to come out of Russia's shadow, they moved ever closer to Western Europe and the Western world. It was for these new, multinational states a difficult tightrope walk between promoting the national while seeking to match it with the modern trends from and cultural affinities with the West (and rejecting the East). To be sure, international developments did dictate to some extent which forms the small Baltic States' own developments took.

Finland—geo-politically further to the periphery, with a longer history of autonomy and a more coherent nation—had more control over its own development. This is not to say that were no divisions in Finland. On the contrary, they did exist: along linguistic, political, class lines; between urban and rural, religious and secular Finns, and others. Yet by the late 1930s, the Finnish people had truly grown together into one Finland or, following Benedict Anderson's lines, one imagined Finnish national community. Surprisingly, this national coherence was first reflected in domestic politics, as the rift between left and right was overcome in a coalition government, the so-called red–earth coalition of

Figure 12.3. The newly built Finnish Parliament (*Eduskunta*) in the early 1930s.

1937. Significantly, in what were by the mid-1930s seemingly uniform (Baltic) States, many differences continued to lurk underneath the surface.

NATION-STATES AND MINORITY QUESTIONS

After the First World War, the area of Lithuania, Latvia and Estonia—like most of East-Central Europe—was multi-ethnic and multicultural. Borders had to be defined, and often the international community as well as domestic plebiscites played an important role in defining territory. The territorial problems were all too visible in the German–Lithuanian tensions over Memel (Klaipeida), and the Polish–Lithuanian territorial dispute over Vilnius which after Poland's annexation of the region in 1920 was to poison Polish–Lithuanian relations over the entire inter-war period. Latvia in turn suffered from being a merger of three culturally different regions: Livland, Courland, and Latgale.

Apart from settling boundary questions, however, the new ruling elites were concerned with proving that their new nation-states were viable entities, able to defend themselves against external and internal threats. The heritage of the Russian Empire loomed large in an international discourse in which the three Baltic states, Poland, and Finland were bundled together as the 'Russian successor states'. As a corollary to this, the idea of a Baltic group of fellow sufferers as Russia's 'border-states' was part of the 'Baltic' discourses in all five states. The question as to which states formed the nucleus of a regional 'Baltic' group (of cooperation to ensure survival) was a matter of opinion. Estonians thought more of a Finnish–Estonian–Latvian group, while Latvians and probably Lithuanians more of an Estonian–Latvian–Lithuanian group. What tended to unify the small young states of Estonia, Latvia, and Lithuania was that all three felt the squeeze between Russia and Germany, while Poland and Finland did less so. Though bordering both Germany and Russia, as heirs of the former Polish kingdom, the Poles had greater confidence in their strength. Poland was bigger and had a very large army. Indeed, Lithuanians and Latvians looked with suspicion at Poland as they feared Polish ambitions. Finland, without an exclusive 'border' against the Germans and on the northern periphery of Europe, saw itself and was seen by the Balts more as part of the Scandinavian group of states. In domestic politics too, Finland was a political, cultural, and economic entity of its own, and its population rather homogeneous.

The most significant minority in Finland were the Swedish-speaking Finns. Unlike their German Baltic, Polish, or Russian counterparts, they never constituted an oppressive landowning elite. Swedish-speaking Finns were mostly small farmers and fishermen in the southern and western coastal provinces, though they also represented large parts of the affluent and well-educated elites in Helsinki and Turku. Still, the shift from the four-estate Diet to the *Eduskunta* in 1906 had destroyed the principal bastions of the old aristocratic and burgher elites, and the

Table 12.1. Ethnic composition of the Baltic States

	Population	Natives	Ger.	Rus.	Pol.	Jews	Swe.	Lit.
1922 census in Estonia	1,107,059	87.7%	1.7%	8.2%		0.4%	0.7%	
1934	1,126,413	88.2%	1.5%	8.2%		0.4%	0.7%	
1945	845,000	97.3%						
1920 census in Latvia	1,596,131	72.8%	3.6%	7.8%	3.4%	5.0%		1.6%
1935	1,950,502	75.5%	3.2%	10.6%	2.5%	4.8%		1.2%
1943	1,760,162	82.9%	1.0%	9.5%	2.2%			
1923 census in Lithuania*	2,170,616	80.6%	4.1%	2.3%	3.0%	7.2%		
1938	2,549,668	80.6%		2.3%		2.3%		
1945	2,400,000	80%						

* including Memel

creation of the Swedish People's Party (SFP) was, as David Kirby has written, 'the Swedish-speakers' tacit and intelligent acceptance of their new status as a *linguistic minority* whose only home was Finland'. Indeed, they considered themselves as Finns, even if there existed (unfruitful) campaigns for a regional autonomy in the first years after 1917. Finnish nationalists' pressure for a monolingual state in the 1930s also came to nothing. To be sure, never was the position of the minority within the state of Finland seriously under threat. The mutual acknowledgement that the Swedish-speakers' well-being was tightly bound to Finland's well-being was a bond strong enough to ensure that the rights of this minority anchored in an officially bilingual state have continued until today.

The impact and position of national minorities in the Baltic nation-states was rather different (see Table 12.1). While a general growth of the Baltic states' populations can be detected in the period, interestingly, the size of the minorities dwindled. Indeed, many Germans moved to Germany and Poles to Poland, and in towns especially, the minorities became increasingly integrated into the titular nations.

Relationships between majority population and minorities fluctuated during the 1920s and 1930s. Their nature depended quite a lot on the minority in question. Baltic German and Jewish communities continued to flourish culturally and economically in Estonia and Latvia, and this despite the tough agrarian reforms that had hit the German landed aristocracy. Indeed, the dwindling German communities were quite united and effective in sending members to the Estonian and Latvian parliaments. While the Germans were thus rather influential in politics, the much larger Russian community was not.

Bearing in mind, that in Estonia and Latvia the formerly ruling German minorities had demanded between 1918 and 1920 a historical right to exist as a second Staatsvolk next to the titular nations, the new leaders of those nation-states—who first and foremost wanted to satisfy the wishes of their national majorities—were wise to seek accommodation with the numerous minorities within their borders. There could be no doubt that the constitution makers of the Baltic republics were keen to ensure loyalty of the minorities.

In the 1920s, the quest for cultural autonomy in the newly independent Baltic states was driven largely by the minorities themselves, and its implementation depended upon goodwill and real interest on the part of the political leaders. As Smith and Hiden have explained, the early advocacy of minority rights in the Baltic parliaments was partly driven by a desire to gain international support for statehood and legal recognition, as well as membership in the League of Nations, which strongly promoted minority rights. Baltic interest inevitably fell away as these goals were achieved. Still, apart from finding expression in the systems of proportional representation for parliamentary elections that were introduced, more enlightened attempts were made to enshrine rights of minorities. Baltic constitutions stated that all citizens, irrespective of their nationalities, were equal before the law; and education in their mother tongues and the use of native languages in public offices was guaranteed to them.

However, in Lithuania (where Poles and Jews in particular were subject to discrimination from early on) the constitutional provisions of 1922 that included cultural autonomy and a nationalities minister were never properly realized due to the country's early drift towards nationalist authoritarian rule. In the constitution of 1936 minority rights were dropped altogether. To be sure, apart from Lithuania's nationalist right-wing turn, the Vilnius and Memel disputes also played their part in the country's changes in minorities policies.

In Latvia, the minorities issue was most acute with 27.8 per cent of the population in 1920 being non-Latvians. Independent Latvia's citizens included seven larger foreign nationalities, in particular an initially disenchanted German community expelled from political leadership. Latvia's minority rights were anchored in the 1919 Law on Schooling for Minorities. This was diminished in 1934 under the Ulmanis regime when the minorities' cultural establishments and societies were expropriated and dissolved. Latvia's German minority, with its financial links to the Nazi Reich, was the subject of particular suspicion; even more so once national socialism had gained control over the German community in Latvia. There was fear of a state within a state.

It is ironic that a German-Balt from Riga emerged as one of the most progressive thinkers and leading theorists of minority rights of his time. A prominent political figure at the European Congress of Nationalities as well as leader of the Latvian German-Balt Democratic Party, Paul Schiemann kept canvassing for minorities' cultural autonomy *and* loyalty for newly independent Latvia. His ideas included the move away from the purely territorial view of nation-states and nation, and he imagined a European Union founded on co-national groups and peoples.

In Estonia the relevant provisions of the constitution for minorities of August 1920 were formalized by the 1925 Law on Cultural Autonomy for National Minorities. This legislation was a model of its kind. It stated that any minority of over 3,000 persons had the right to become a corporation in public law and to administer its educational, cultural, and charitable affairs—even to the extent of being able to raise 'culture taxes', which were supplemented by funds from central and local authorities. Since Swedes and Russians tended to live in close communities, they were able to secure their rights through regional or municipal governments, and thus did not choose to take advantage of the autonomy legislation. Germans and Jews however did and established cultural self-governments that were to remain in place until 1940.

Despite both the Baltic States and Finland taking liberal stands *vis-à-vis* their minorities, it is mostly true that, as David Kirby has argued, the much 'more diverse national minorities of the three Baltic states were too disunited, and too much distrusted by the autochtonomous majority to have played any effective or constructive role in nation-building'. Yet, there was more to Baltic internal weaknesses than just issues of territory and nationality. Given the lack of historical precedents or viable existing institutions on which to build a political system as well as the lack of democratic experience, the creation of constitutional and institutional frameworks and the running of parliamentary politics (in a period marked by difficult economic circumstances) were to prove a major challenge; a challenge and experience that was to differ enormously between each Baltic state and even more altogether from Finland.

PARTY POLITICS AND NATIONAL UNITY

Regarding the form of their states, Estonia, Latvia, and Lithuania as well as Finland followed a general post-First World War trend in establishing republics founded on parliamentary democracies. A common feature of the Baltic constitutions was their emphasis on parliamentary supremacy at the expense of the executive. Baltic parliamentarianism was similar to that of the Weimar Republic: a single chamber parliament was elected by proportional representation. Significantly, the parliamentary representatives of the minorities considerably increased the already high number of political parties represented in the rather small legislatures of the Baltic Republics. With their highly fissiparous multi-party systems and unstable coalitions, the Baltic States were mirror-images of Weimar.

In Finland, as a result of social developments before independence, conservative desires to counter revolutionary pressures, and compromises between conservative and liberal politicians concerning the division of power between different state organs, a semi-presidential system was established. One peculiar feature of the 1919 constitution was the strongly guaranteed rights of minorities in government: a one-third minority could effectively block legislation in the *Eduskunta*. The intention was to prevent potential radical socialist reforms and revolution being effected by a simple majority in parliament.

Governments in the Baltic states and Finland were invariably coalitions of short duration. Lithuania had thirteen governments between 1918 and 1926, Latvia and Estonia had eighteen and twenty-four respectively between 1918 and 1934, and Finland twenty-nine between 1918 and 1945. Unsurprisingly, most governments were coalitions, and broke up due to internal disagreement.

During the period of parliamentarianism, there was a normal multi-party system in the Baltics. In Estonia and Latvia the conservative farmers' parties tended to be central pillars of government, providing ten out of eighteen state elders in Estonia (1920–34) and thirteen of eighteen prime ministers in Latvia (1918–34). These agrarian parties drew their electorate from the more prosperous sections of the farming community, rather than the poor smallholders or landless labourers. The interests of the small farmers were represented by the Settlers' Parties of Estonia and Latvia, which started off as centre parties and shifted over time to the right. The agrarian ethnic minority communities had their own (farmers') parties. Significantly, in Finland too, the Agrarian Union—the largest non-socialist party in the *Eduskunta*—was rarely absent from government. Yet, there was no smallholders' party as such and Swedish speakers of all walks of life tended to vote for the SFP.

The dominance of the farmers' parties can be explained by the strongly agrarian character of the countries as well as by the fact that they epitomized popular nationalist sentiment in a way that none of the centrist parties of nationalist intellectuals could match. In Finland, the latter included the National Coalition and National Progressive Party; in Estonia the People's Party; in Latvia the Democratic Centre. Still, even if they failed to win seats, these parties played an important role in government in Estonia and Finland. The Finnish Progressives headed two coalition governments 1932–6 and 1937–43.

The Finnish Social Democratic Party (SDP), which had recovered quickly after the civil war, won eighty seats in the elections of March 1919 making them the largest bloc in the *Eduskunta*. This remained unchanged even after they lost up to a third of their members and seats to the communist front party in 1922. Yet, despite being the largest party, the SDP (with the exception of 1926/7) remained outside government for nearly two decades, because of anti-left coalitions. Only in 1937, did the SDP form a majority coalition government with the Progressives and Agrarian Union. This was a milestone not just for Social Democrats but for Finnish politics, as this coalition epitomized the overcoming of the country's left–right divide that had persisted since the civil war.

In neither Finland nor the Baltic states were Soviet-backed communist parties allowed to operate freely, and their front organizations were under constant police surveillance. Against the background of the independence wars, this was not really surprising. Yet, the real potential of the communist left to disrupt or subvert the existing order was probably smaller than was feared at the time, and their only real success was their influence in a number of trade unions.

A wave of anti-communism was unleashed in Finland in 1929 after strained relations in the labour market had led to widespread disturbances in 1927–8 and made the communists' presence more visible. An attempt to subdue the radical left began in late November 1929 when nationalists clashed with communist youths in Lapua. This soon led to the creation of the ultranationalist Lapua movement (comparable to the Danish Farmers Union, see Scandinavia chapter), with its core support in rural Ostrobothnia. 'Lapua' sought to continue the defence of White Finland. Yet, among its leaders were right-wing extremists with leanings towards Italian fascism, whose target was Finnish democracy not communism. In 1932 the organization tried armed revolt against the government, but was forced to back down and its activity ended.

In Estonia and Latvia, politics evolved somewhat differently. The large number of parties represented in parliament (in Latvia up to twenty-eight) brought about very unstable and constantly changing multi-party coalitions. Infighting was serious and frequent, and politics tended to be guided with party-political advantages in mind. Parliamentarianism became tainted with corruption, and there were soon calls to change the constitutions to concentrate greater power in one man's or party's hands. The immediate impetus for a turn to the right appears to have been the impact of the world economic crisis that caused the fall of living standards. As a result new forces which disparaged pluralism appeared: in Latvia the Thunder Cross youth organization and in Estonia the proto-fascist League of Veterans of the Estonian Independence War, both of whose members advocated authoritarian rule and national unity. Alarmed by the prospect of these organizations gaining power, the political executive and the army staged coups, and opened the road for authoritarian presidential rule.

In Lithuania, the political situation looked initially much more stable. The most influential party by far, the Christian Democratic Party (LKDP), tended to get 50 per cent of the votes in most of the early parliamentary elections. The Catholic bond blurred the classic rural–urban class division, which was reflected in Lithuania's much smaller party spectrum. The LKDP stressed the role of the Catholic Church in national life and pressed for the religious rights of the faithful. Moreover, the party was strongly anti-Polish. Supported by the Catholic Church, the LKDP organized a multitude of Catholic societies and labour organizations, including the Labour Federation and the Lithuanian Farmers Union, which always formed a coalition with the LKDP despite nominating their own candidates.

Other parties included the liberal Populists (Liaudininkai, LVLS)—who opposed the Catholic Church's influence in education and state adminis-tration—the high-brow Lithuanian Social Democrats, the Moscow-directed Labour group, as well as the right-wing National Progress Party, later Lithua-nian National Union (Tautininkai). To the LKDP's shock, the 1926 elections brought a coalition government of Social Democrats and Populists to power, which almost immediately began a process of democratization of society and took fiercely anti-clerical measures. This caused great dissatisfaction among conservative circles and led to the Smetona coup. After the collapse of an initial LKDP–Tautininkai coalition in November 1927, Smetona and the Tautininkai were to govern on their own.

In May 1928, a new constitution was promulgated, strengthening the institution of the presidency. Political parties and organizations not affiliated with Tautininkai were shut down, together with cultural organizations, and freedom of press and assembly rights severely restricted. It is significant that, as Smetona emphasized himself, Lithuania's regime was not a direct copy of Italian fascism: neither was corporatism instituted (indeed the emphasis was on a nationalist agricultural policy), nor did Smetona follow any specific political long-term plan.

Importantly, Päts, Ulmanis, as well as Smetona—men who had played key roles in the wars of independence and in state-building—sold themselves as the 'fathers of the nation'. Indeed, they saw themselves as coming to rescue the weak democracies of their countries. As Hiden and Salmon have pointed out, an idealized image of patriotic peasantry were the Baltic presidents' political leitmotifs. Though Smetona's regime was quite similar to that of Päts and Ulmanis, it is noteworthy that the former's got closest to becoming a classic one-party state, with the Tautininkai's firm grip of society and politics. Also, Smetona went furthest in establishing a unifying nationalist ideology with distinctly totalitarian overtones and strong emphasis on the youth movement. Latvia's Ulmanis was probably the most tolerant. He neither set up a one-party system nor was a new constitution introduced—though the constitution of 1922 was largely ignored.

Konstantin Päts's distinctive political agenda merits particular scrutiny. Throughout the Cold War and even thereafter, Päts tended to be seen by historians—often Baltic *émigrés*—in a positive light. This is only being questioned today, as a new generation of scholars has gained access to papers that the governments of the restored Baltic states have released. The positive portrayal of Päts was founded on the view that (1) Estonia's 1938 constitution *in theory* returned to more democracy; and that (2) this was the constitution to which Estonians could hang onto during the USSR's occupation between 1940 and 1991 as they hoped to regain independence. But defenders of Päts now stand on relatively weak ground. His regime's affinity with fascism must not be overlooked. In concert with the army, Päts ruled by decree virtually without interruption until 1940. He sought to restructure the economy around the model of Italian corporatism, and in 1935 all political organizations were replaced by his Fatherland League (Isämaa Liit, IL). Despite tentative liberalization with the election of a constituent assembly and the adoption of a new constitution in 1938, political parties remained suspended, except for Päts's IL. Päts was re-elected president and continued to reserve many powers for himself, the ban on parties and press censorship not being lifted.

The establishment of nationalist authoritarian regimes in the Baltic States harmed the previously progressive relations with minorities. Yet, ironically, the influence and long historical existence of German-Balt communities in the Baltic states was not ended by nationalist policies, but by Nazi Germany's policies of resettlement implemented in 1939.

In general, it is significant to note that the survival of the democratic system in Finland in contrast to the Baltic states owed a lot to the country's much stronger foundations. Rooted in the era of the Grand Duchy of Finland as well as its even older (Swedish) constitutionalist tradition, its institutions had by the 1920s and 1930s become deeply engrained in a united Finnish national consciousness. In post-civil-war Finland, the constitutional system and parliamentary democracy were never seriously threatened—by neither the left nor the right—and despite the Great Depression and 'Lapua', the nation steadily unified, which was ultimately reflected in the red—earth coalition government. National unity thus was not achieved on the terms of the right, by forcing the labour movement to conform; rather the Social Democrats won recognition as a legitimate element of the democratic system.

The Baltic states lacked democratic experience, and the negative experience they had (partly inflicted by the international circumstances) made them more willing to accept nationalist, right-wing authoritarianism. Crucially, there were few strong defenders of the parliamentary system. The Baltic states' constitutional systems were undermined from within by established national leaders who rode the tide of patriotism and nationalism, and who colluded with the military to establish their new power bases. Political opposition was weak if not fully stifled. In this shift to the right, the Baltic states followed the same path as many other Central and Eastern European states. This does not mean that there was an environmental determinism that brought about fascism or rather right-wing authoritarianism. Finland, after all, did not turn its back on parliamentary democracy.

To understand the causes of this shift towards authoritarianism, it is important to focus on the social, economic, and political developments of each individual state. Indeed, Robert Paxton in his recent book *Anatomy of Fascism* has underlined the importance of identifying and studying the national differences rather than seeking the 'fascist' common denominator. In this vein, the Baltic States' period of independence and their experiment with parliamentary democracy must not be seen as an unsuccessful 'pre-war history' but as an era full of challenges; a period during which the young nation-states sought for ways to catch up with Western modernizing trends while consolidating their national identities. Why then did the Baltic states, but not Finland, disappear in 1940?

FINNISH AND BALTIC FOREIGN POLICY ORIENTATIONS

Historical analyses of the international relations of the eastern Baltic during the inter-war period have tended to be heavily influenced by the fact that the Baltic states were swallowed by the Soviet Union in the context of the Second World War, while Finland survived sovereign and free. As a consequence, debate in Baltic historiography has centred on two interpretations: (1) that the Baltic states were hostage to international developments; and as pawns of the great powers they were eventually sacrificed at an opportune moment; (2) that the Baltic states could have survived, if only they had cooperated better with each other. Both interpretations are tied to the fundamental question of the Baltic states' viability as independent entities.

Our aim being to avoid the teleological trap of treating inter-war years as pre-war history, the key foreign policy questions, based on the assumption that three fully functioning sovereign states had been created after the First World War, are the following. What were Baltic foreign policy initiatives? How did the West react to Baltic fears of losing independence? Why did Estonia, Latvia, and Lithuania opt for capitulation in 1939/40, and why did Finland choose the military option? Baltic and Finnish decisions had far-reaching consequences for their states' future. Following Ilmjärv's ground-breaking new research, Baltic and Finnish foreign policy (choices) will be examined against the background of international *and* domestic developments.

Once sovereign statehood had been established, Finland and the Baltic states had to find a formula for survival, which in geo-political terms meant survival among much larger powers. The single overwhelming theme that dominated Estonian, Latvian, and Finnish foreign policy considerations in the 1920s and 1930s was the issue of security. Though this was true also for Lithuania, its disputes with Poland over Vilnius and with Germany over Memel were high on the agenda too, leaving Lithuania somewhat separate from Estonia and Latvia.

In important ways the security situation for Finland was quite different from Estonia and Latvia (and Lithuania). Located in the north-eastern periphery of Europe, with Sweden as its western neighbour, the USSR in the east was seen as its only real threat. Indeed, the foreign political discourse in the immediate aftermath of 1918 tended to the view that Finland was somewhat separate from the *cordon sanitaire* between Germany and Soviet Russia, which included the Baltic states. While it was understood that some kind of grouping (against Bolshevism) of small nations was needed, Finns were cautious about defining new regional entities. They did not want to endanger or challenge their own national identity, which was based on the tradition of the Grand Duchy. By contrast, Estonians and Latvians did not have this tradition, and thus were much keener on a regional security organization.

Apart from contemplating the Baltic option, Finland also looked north-west to the Scandinavian states, which could offer membership in an established Western state group of the North. Finland was torn between these alternatives, and many placed Helsinki between the two. Indeed, aside from geo-political orientations, in foreign policy Finnish–Estonian cultural links had to be considered; a multifaceted relationship that had grown in the era of national awakening.

The difference between the two main competing discourses—Baltic and Nordic—was significant, and the direction of Finnish foreign policy depended on which circles dominated the foreign policy leadership. Finland's first foreign minister Rudolf Holsti of the Progressives was keen for Finland to be part of the 'Baltic group'; and soon joint conferences, mostly between Poland, Finland, Estonia and Latvia, began.

With joint conferences a new and popular tool in post-war diplomacy, what was unusual about the 'Baltic group' was the intensity with which the practice was adopted. It owed much to Latvian and Estonian initiative—the foreign ministers of both soon advocating a more formal Baltic League. This initiative for multilateral cooperation reflected the political enthusiasm of the new states and the high hopes for regional peace, stability, and cooperation in the first inter-war decade.

Yet towards the late 1920s, multilateralism began to stagnate. The Poles in particular were keener on bilateral cooperation, while the Finns objected to a military alliance that might include a Poland they did not trust. Mutual conflicts arose, many of which had their root in Poland's policies, as well as in the fact that the original common emphasis on sovereignty shifted towards specific national interests and realpolitik calculations as states became more established. Without true common ground, the efforts to create a mutual security community ended in failure. This made further political cooperation difficult, too.

Finland hence tied itself in 1926–7 to the League of Nations' collective security arrangements, while rejecting a Soviet security pact initiative, which Moscow had been seeking with the Baltic group. Still, to improve relations with the USSR, Helsinki as part of its own realpolitik signed a non-aggression pact with Moscow in 1932; at the same time, Finland secretly engaged in military cooperation with Estonia. As international tensions increased during the 1930s, Finland for fear of the Soviet Union which became ever more active in the League began to doubt the strength of the latter and increasingly oriented its foreign policy towards Scandinavia.

If Holsti through much of the 1930s treated the Scandinavian orientation as a tool to get security back-up from the West, namely France and Britain, his ideas soon lost their potential foundation (and he his job) after the British government changed its mind on the League's ability to protect small countries, and once the Austrian *Anschluss* had occurred. The Finnish leadership now sought an all-encompassing solution that included the improvement of Finland's own defences as well as considering a potential last-minute option of seeking a military alliance with Sweden. The Swedish card, however, quickly lost its appeal over the question of common defence of the Åland islands, as Sweden indicated in spring 1939 its unwillingness to commit to these islands' defence.

With the Hitler–Stalin Pact of 23 August 1939, the international haggling over alliances, security guarantees, and non-aggression pacts that had taken place during spring suddenly seemed like the distant past. The immediate reality of the

German–Soviet Pact changed life in north-eastern Europe instantly—and for the worse. But before I address these post-Pact events, let us consider the Baltic states' foreign policies during the inter-war period, which were far more complex than Finland's.

Estonia and Latvia having gained independence were status quo powers, while Lithuania—due to territorial problems with Poland—sought change, which greatly affected the other Baltic states' foreign policies. Lithuania first annoyed Estonia and Latvia with its unilateral Soviet–Lithuanian non-aggression pact in 1922, and thus excluded itself from the above-mentioned 'Baltic group' negotiations. Indeed, until 1934, Lithuania remained politically oriented towards the USSR and to a lesser degree to Germany, which were both enemies of Poland. Yet, the increasingly strained situation in Memel in the 1930s and the German–Polish non-aggression declaration changed Lithuania's foreign policy direction. In 1934–8, Kaunas looked to Moscow and Paris and supported the collective security policies of the League of Nations. Also during the 1930s, Lithuania began to more actively seek limited foreign policy cooperation with Latvia and Estonia. The Treaty of Friendship and Cooperation was signed by the three Baltic states in 1934. It failed, however, to lead to a common security system. The differences over their common enemy were too great.

Estonia and Latvia (like Finland) viewed the Soviet Union as the only hostile power in the region, and both countries until the mid-1930s looked for guarantees from Poland and Great Britain, which were not forthcoming. They knew that the Estonian–Latvian defence pact of 1923 lacked teeth, and were deeply suspicious of relations between Lithuania and the USSR—which explains their interest in a regional alliance with Poland and Finland in the 1920s. As we know, nothing came of this, and with the Nazis' rise to power in Germany and Germany's growing military strength, Estonian and Latvian foreign-policy shifted too. Towards the late 1930s, Latvia's governing circles split as the foreign-policy elites continued to view the USSR as Latvia's arch enemy, while the military began to see Germany as the principal danger and considered potential readiness to fight on the side of the Soviets. If until the Munich crisis the Latvian foreign policy leadership believed in the power of the League of Nations and collective security to ultimately guarantee their independence, they (like their Estonian counterparts) moved in 1939 to discussions of 'unconditional neutrality'. In Estonia, this rhetoric went hand in hand with the Päts regime's continued fear of the USSR, whereas interestingly large parts of the Estonian population tended to be mostly worried about German ambition and were more sympathetic to the USSR—probably due to alienation from their authoritarian leadership as Ilmjärv suggests. According to his findings the Baltic 'neutrality rhetoric' was not genuinely concerned with neutrality, but implied in truth an orientation towards Germany. At the same time few (certainly not the Soviets) seriously respected Baltic neutrality anyway.

With few holding the monopoly over foreign policy-making in the Baltic and ties between Estonian and Latvian leaders and the Germans getting closer in 1939, the ability to make free choices was lost. To be sure, the rhetoric of neutrality served national interests in so far as Estonia, Latvia, and Lithuania all eventually pinned their hopes on German determination to overpower Bolshevism. The irony is that this option instead pushed the Baltic states into the hands of a Germany that in truth was the enemy of their sovereignty, too. This is not to say that, if the Baltic leaders had acted differently, the Soviet occupation that ensued after 1939 could have been avoided. But maybe the relatively calm Baltic surrender to the new realities made it ultimately, as Ilmjärv has speculated, much easier for the Soviets to annex rather than just to occupy.

That said, there can be no doubt that international relations, and especially the role played by Germany, the Soviet Union, and Poland, greatly influenced Baltic policies. They disrupted Baltic efforts to cooperate and undermined their relations with other democratic countries. There can also be no doubt about how crucial the failure of Anglo-French-Soviet alliance talks in spring/summer 1939, and the signing of the Hitler–Stalin Pact were for Estonia's, Latvia's, and Lithuania's loss of independence. Yet, while these external developments were most likely crucial for the Baltic fate (and with this point I beg to differ from Ilmjärv's emphasis on the impact of Baltic leaders' own actions), we should not ignore that the Baltic leaders were as much actors as pawns. The actions of Päts, Ulmanis, and Smetona probably pushed their countries closer to the abyss, closer to annexation than to occupation. Yet the root causes for these actions lay in the early years of independence which allowed the rise of the Päts, Ulmanis, and Smetona regimes in the first place—and in the most unfortunate international context.

Although great bloodshed was avoided in 1940, the Baltic's 'silent submission' to the USSR in the summer of 1940 stood in sharp contrast to Finland's vigorous defence of independence in the Winter War in 1939/40. And this submission might have sealed the Baltics' fate of disappearing from the European map faster than under other circumstances. At the same time, given the international circumstances there was little chance for Estonia, Latvia, and Lithuania to have avoided Soviet annexation without Western aid.

Finland, in response to Soviet demands in the wake of the Nazi–Soviet Pact, refused to allow the USSR to build military bases on its territory, which led Moscow to revoke the non-aggression pact of 1932 and attack Finland on 30 November 1939. The Winter War that followed saw stiff Finnish resistance, but sheer Soviet weight of numbers forced the government to sue for peace. The peace treaty drawn up in Moscow on 13 March 1940 ceded Finnish Karelia (where 12 per cent of Finnish citizens had lived) to the USSR. Population resettlement and war damages meant significant economic and social problems, but for the Finns the most important issue was safeguarding independence. Indeed, in the long run this defence of the country's sovereignty was to prove significant.

Much research has focused on the Winter War and the factors that brought about the preservation of Finnish sovereignty: clever diplomacy or the Finnish people's united effort to safeguard their independence in the face of Soviet territorial ambitions and overwhelming military might. To be sure, the strength of a national identity that had been built in nearly all spheres of life must have played an important part as did diplomacy.

Hitler invaded the Soviet Union in the summer of 1941, and Finland, hoping to regain the lost Karelian territories, entered the war as a cobelligerent with Germany. Given their collaboration with Nazi Germany, the Finns' military campaigns beyond the borders of 1920 in eastern Karelia put their war aims and effort (to unite *all* of Karelia within Finnish territory) in a negative light, and even forced Britain to declare war on Finland. This 'Continuation War' ended in armistice in September 1944, after Finland was able to stop the Soviet army's massive summer offensive and Stalin decided to transfer his troops from the Finnish front to the 'race to Berlin'. In addition to the areas already lost to Russia in 1940, Finland at the end of the Second World War also ceded Petsamo on the Arctic Ocean. The terms of the armistice were confirmed in the Paris Peace Treaty of 1947. Crucially, Finland, among the countries on the losing side in the Second World War, was the only one to avoid foreign occupation. During the Continuation War of 1941–4, civic society in Finland held its ground. The free, civic organizations that worked in various capacities on the home front were to prove important also for Finnish post-war developments. After 1945, it was the determined resistance of civic society that helped defeat the Finnish Communist Party's efforts to take power. As a result, Finland held onto its independence and democracy and could thus continue its development towards what was to become a prosperous and stable Nordic welfare state.

CONCLUSIONS

The inter-war years for Estonians, Latvians, Lithuanians, and Finns were a period not only of independent statehood from Russia, but economic and social modernization and progress. They also greatly benefited from the new intellectual and cultural influences and transfers from Western/Northern Europe and the USA to which they were now strongly orientated. At the same time, they experienced how difficult it was to build stable democracies in a politically and economically unstable international context. Indeed, in the three Baltic states the eventual authoritarian turns to the right seemed to reflect patterns in much of the rest of Europe, though technically the Baltic regimes were not directly comparable to other European fascist regimes. This path away from democracy, as well as their eventual annexation by the USSR in 1940, has often been related to their smallness and heterogeneity as nations. And furthermore this fate has often served as an example for those who have put forward the 'dark years' or 'pre-war' interpretation of the inter-war era. Yet the idea that the 1920s and 1930s were merely a gloomy prologue for worse years to come is in the Baltic case in part linked to lack of historical research into their existence as sovereign republics.

Baltic historiography (in contrast to the rather well-developed Finnish historiography) is still in its infancy: the bulk of works on inter-war Estonian, Latvian, and Lithuanian politics, culture, society, and economics are of their time, that is, contemporary histories. Apart from a few works by Baltic *émigré* historians written during the Cold War, which idealize the years of independence, we are only now beginning to see the first results of research based on declassified archival materials. And here, with the exception of the field of minority rights and German-Balt activities, so far the focus has primarily been on foreign policy in the late 1930s and Soviet occupation policies in the 1940s.

It is important to note that, despite the predictable difficulties the Baltic governments—as governments of new states in this era—encountered in their foreign and domestic policies, their disappearance from Europe's map was not inevitable; just as Finland's survival as an independent and democratic nation during and after the Second World War was not inevitable either. While the Baltic nations were stifled under Soviet rule, post-war Finland continued to pursue the highly beneficial political cooperation with its Scandinavian neighbours that had its roots in the 1930s. To be sure, Finland had certain advantages over the Baltics, but its survival in Soviet Russia's shadow and its ability to build one of the most homogeneous, modern, highly educated, and prosperous societies in Europe during the Cold War could not have been foreseen.

FURTHER READING

Eidintas, Alfonsas, and Vytautas Zalys, *Lithuania in European Politics: The Years of the First Republic, 1918–1940* (Basingstoke, 1997).

Fewster, Derek, *Visions of Past Glory: Nationalism and the Construction of Early Finnish History* (Helsinki, 2006).

Hiden, John, *Defender of Minorities: Paul Schiemann, 1876–1944* (London, 2004).

——and Thomas Lane, *The Baltic and the Outbreak of the Second World War* (2nd edn., Cambridge, 2004).

——and Patrick Salmon, *The Baltic Nations and Europe: Estonia, Latvia and Lithuania in the Twentieth Century* (London, 1994).

——and David J. Smith, 'Looking Beyond the Nation-State: A Baltic Vision for National Minorities between the Wars', *Journal of Contemporary History*, 41 (2006), 387–99.

Ilmjärv, Magnus, *Silent Submission: Formation of Foreign Policy of Estonia, Latvia and Lithuania* (Stockholm, 2004).

Jussila, Osmo, Seppo Hentilä, and Jukka Nevakivi, *From Grand Duchy to Modern State: A Political History of Finland since 1809* (London, 1999).

Kirby, David, *The Baltic World 1772–1993: Europe's Northern Periphery in an Age of Change* (London, 1995).

Lehti, Marko, *A Baltic League as a Construct of the New Europe: Envisioning a Baltic Region and Small State Sovereignty in the Aftermath of the First World War* (Bern, 1999).

Plakans, Andrejs, *The Latvians: A Short History* (Stanford, Calif., 1991).

Raun, Toivo U., *Estonia and the Estonians* (Stanford, Calif., 1991).

Spekke, Arnolds, *History of Latvia: An Outline* (Stockholm, 1951).

Upton, Antony F., and Fred Singleton, *A Short History of Finland* (2nd edn., Cambridge, 1998).

13

Russia

Hubertus F. Jahn

INTRODUCTION

Europe is a matter of perspective. Much more than simply a geographical denomination, it is a vision, an idea of civilization and culture, peculiar religious traditions, and common historical experience. People living at the geographical margins have always been particularly sensitive to these intangible qualities of Europe, to what it meant to be European. Since the eighteenth century, conceptions of Europeanness and Russia's position in Europe have been at the heart of discussions among educated Russians. Under the influence of Enlightenment and Romanticism, that is, essential European phenomena, questions of socio-economic progress, cultural development, and national character in Russia have generally been debated in relation to Europe. In the eyes of many Russians, Europe meant modernity. As a consequence, modernity in Russia was much more accentuated as something alien than elsewhere, both in its positive and negative connotations. Everything, it seems, was a bit more intense in Russia: industrialization happened faster and with more dramatic results; Tsarist autocracy was more reactionary and despotic than other European monarchies; revolutionaries were more fanatic (and successful) than their European counterparts; Russian artists were more radical in their projects than the rest of the European avant-garde; Stalinist modernization projects were more grandiose, yet also more destructive than anything else in the world. The list goes on.

The rifts between civilization and barbarity, between the benefits and the pitfalls of modernity, appear to be particularly wide in Russia between 1914 and 1945. This makes these years so fascinating and challenging for historians. While specialists of Russian history have already for some time looked at this period not just as one of inevitable decline into the abyss, but also of utopian visions, creative experiments, and new beginnings, general textbooks still tend to focus mostly on the horrors associated with revolutions and wars. Without doubt, these years were terrible for many Russians, and more people died in Russia from war, revolution, famine, and state terror than anywhere else in the world. Yet even more people survived, lived their daily lives, worked, dreamt, and engaged in all kinds of leisure activities. Very few of them, if any, were able to grasp the full complexity of what was going on around them at the time, the chaos and the whirlwind of changes, so neatly pressed into categories by historians later on. In this respect, the Russian experience was similar to that of many other European countries, just a bit more intense.

THE FIRST WORLD WAR

'God Save the Tsar' was a tune which Russian workers would not usually have on their lips. Since hundreds of their comrades had been killed by troops on 'Bloody Sunday' in St Petersburg during a peaceful attempt to deliver a petition to Nicholas II in January 1905, the traditional belief in a good and benevolent Tsar, so popular for many centuries among the Russian people, was steadily withering away. Moreover, another massacre among protesting workers in 1912 at the Lena goldfields in Siberia as well as worsening working conditions in factories throughout the country led to a broad movement of strikes, which reached its peak in the summer of 1914. Yet in August of that year, the strikes suddenly stopped, workers returned to their factories, and now many of them sang the Tsarist anthem before starting their workday. Just as in other European countries, the outbreak of the First World War triggered a wave of patriotism in Russia, which encompassed even staunch opponents of the autocratic regime. Large crowds gathered in the streets of major cities to vent their anger at the German and the Austro-Hungarian Empires. Germans, and in particular their ruler, Kaiser Wilhelm II, became the target of cartoons in the print media and were lampooned on stage and in film, while shops owned by Germans, who often had lived in Russia for generations, were looted and German businesses nationalized. Even the name of the capital was changed: the German-sounding Sankt Peterburg became Petrograd.

Yet unlike in other European countries, patriotism in Russia was relatively short-lived. By mid-1915, much of it had disappeared to make way for social criticism, fear, and escapist tendencies. Military and economic failures were behind these changes, as were serious political blunders. Initially, the Russian armies were quite successful. Under the command of Paul von Rennenkampfrd, they advanced quickly in the north-west and took East Prussia from the Germans. In the south-west, they pushed back Austrian forces and occupied the city of Przemysl after a long siege. However, already by the end of August the tide began to turn when General Samzonov's army was encircled and beaten at Tannenberg. This cataclysmic defeat with some 170,000 casualties marked the beginning of the end of Tsarist rule. In May 1915, the Germans and Austrians together launched a massive offensive and pushed the Russians back on all fronts. When this 'great retreat' came to a halt in autumn 1915, the Russian Empire had lost vast territories, including all of Poland, Lithuania, and White Russia. While the front line remained relatively static from late 1915 onwards, extending roughly along a line from Riga south to the Danube, all these defeats were having a highly destabilizing effect on morale. With many soldiers sent into battle without sufficient ammunition and weapons—they were supposed to get them from fallen comrades or the enemy—and with a casualty ratio of seven Russians to one German, it had become quite obvious that the average Russian soldier was little more than cannon fodder. Consequently, cases of desertion, disobedience, and open contempt for officers increased, as soldiers were angry at those who spoke of dying for Tsar and fatherland and then left them do the dying. In the end, of nearly 15 million soldiers serving during the war, over 5 million were taken prisoner, 5.2 million were wounded or fell sick, and 1.8 million were killed.

The disasters at the front were matched by events behind the lines. As a result of the 'great retreat', some 3.3 million people had become refugees, a number that increased to roughly 6 million by the beginning of 1917. Under the circumstances, transport was stretched to the limits, hampering the supply of the army. Moreover, the railways were unable to ensure sufficient delivery of raw materials to factories and food to urban centres, many of which were already overrun by refugees. Nevertheless, war-related industrial production more than doubled between 1914 and 1916, leading to an influx of many young, politically volatile new workers into the cities. Reacting to increasing food shortages and miserable working conditions and easily incited by radical socialist agitation, they made up the backbone of a strike wave, which by early 1917 reached proportions similar to that of summer 1914.

FIN-DE-SIÈCLE CULTURE AND THE AVANT-GARDE

While social tension, economic pressure, and geographic dislocation affected many in the Russian Empire, particularly in its European parts, the war and its repercussions were only one part of people's everyday experience. By 1914, Russia was a fast-changing country, with rapidly expanding cities and industrial towns, increasing literacy rates, an emerging middle class, a vibrant art scene, and a flourishing consumer culture, which began to have an impact even in more remote rural areas. These long-term changes shaped the lives of Russians just as much as political and military events. Depending on income, people enjoyed all kinds of different entertainments, from taverns to posh restaurants, from circus to fairground, variety show (or *estrada*), and opera. They were concerned about the latest fashions, whistled the latest tunes they might have heard on a gramophone (a popular and widespread technical innovation), and dreamt about a better future. They met friends, got married, discussed politics, made love, and worried about the harvest. In other words, normal life, so essential for the human condition (and so elusive to the historian), continued during the war.

Like other countries, Russia was in the grip of a dance craze. The tango made its first appearance then. Clowns in the circuses poked fun at the Kaiser, and later in the war attacked speculators and profiteers, some of whom might well be sitting in the front row. Balalaika troupes and peasant choirs were core fixtures in the *estrada*, while concerts with classical music, now usually for a charitable cause, continued to attract huge audiences. Opera was still a rather elitist entertainment. However, the long-time favourite, Richard Wagner, had been purged from the programmes in 1914 and was replaced by more works by Glinka and Rimsky-Korsakov. Cinema was the most popular and democratic entertainment during the war. Cut off from Western competition, the nascent Russian film industry experienced a boom, producing on average one film a day in these years. Twenty-five cinemas operated on Petrograd's main street the Nevsky Prospect alone, and movies were shown in provincial towns and even in villages on mobile projectors. The quality of the films varied widely, from crude shorts to the elaborate masterpieces of Evgeny Bauer. Set in plush lounges, palm-studded winter gardens, nightclubs, and similar luxurious surroundings, Bauer's films captured all the drama and bliss of Russian fin-de-siècle society, the social climbing and falling, decadence, murder, and madness. In an ominous way, their unhappy endings became a trademark, a premonition of the end of an era.

Long before the political and social upheavals of 1917, some avant-garde artists had already sensed the spirit of the time, broken with the past, and initiated a revolution in the arts, which was to last well into the twentieth century and reach far beyond Russia's borders. The emergence of modern art was indeed a pan-European phenomenon, and Russians played an important role in it, before, during, and after the First World War. Around 1900, and following French examples, symbolist writers attempted to separate literature from the social demands of realism, turn it into a transcendental experience and create art for art's sake. In 1912, futurists, like their Italian counterparts, went even further, promised to 'liberate the word' and to 'throw Pushkin, Dostoevsky, Tolstoy, etc., overboard from the Ship of Modernity'. Their poetry rejected all stylistic conventions, took words apart and played with sounds. Similarly, the composer Alexander Scriabin ignored classic rules of tempo and melodic development in his highly introspective works, while Igor Stravinsky destroyed harmony altogether in his ballet *The Rites of Spring*, which caused a huge scandal including fist fights in the audience when it was premiered in Paris in 1913. Around the same time, the painter Vasily Kandinsky moved away from representational art and produced his first purely abstract works, while his colleague Kazimir Malevich founded the so-called suprematist movement and exhibited his famous 'black square' painting in a Petrograd exhibition in 1915. Many of these artists reacted in one way or the other to the war. Some futurists drew funny cartoons of the

Kaiser, and later wrote pacifist stanzas, while some symbolist poets welcomed the war as a potentially new spiritual beginning. But these are minor aspects in light of the eminent contributions these artists made to the European avant-garde.

THE FEBRUARY REVOLUTION AND DUAL POWER

In stark contrast to the social and artistic ferment in the country, the Tsar and his government proved to be unimaginative and largely incompetent in face of the war. Indeed, they often made matters worse. When Nicholas took over the supreme command at the front in September 1915, he became personally associated with the defeats of the army. Furthermore, in his absence from Petrograd political decisions were left to the whims of his wife and her dubious confidant Gregory Rasputin, a Siberian charlatan turned healer and a notorious womanizer and nightclub habitué, whose presence at court was causing serious moral damage. The lack of political and moral leadership was confounded by inadequate economic policies. Even worse, voluntary relief initiatives and civilian support for the war effort were widely hampered by state bureaucrats. Mutual distrust between the rulers and the ruled grew fast. Even the Fourth Duma, or parliament, with its conservative majority became alienated from the government. Most of its parties formed the so-called Progressive Bloc in August 1915, demanding a government of popular confidence. Its leader, the liberal Pavel Miliukov, made the point most eloquently in November 1916, when he listed the blunders of the regime and then asked: 'Is this stupidity, or is this treason?'

The utter loss of trust in the government was soon followed by the collapse of the regime. When striking workers in Petrograd were locked out and joined women from the numerous bread queues for a demonstration on international women's day on 23 February, clashes between the demonstrators and troops triggered a general strike and more demonstrations in the centre of the capital. On 27 February, some 70,000 troops of the Petrograd garrison, upset about the violence against hungry people and afraid of being sent to the front, mutinied and joined the demonstrators. The whole city was in turmoil. Tsarist symbols were attacked everywhere, double-headed eagles were torn down from official buildings, police were chased through the streets, and some houses of high-ranking officials were ransacked or burnt down.

The total implosion of Tsarist power became complete with the abdication of Nicholas II on 2 March. In the mean time, two new political bodies emerged, a Provisional Government and a Soviet, or Council, of Workers' and Soldiers' Deputies. The Provisional Government was formed by members of the major parties in the Duma and some prominent politicians. It proclaimed civil liberties, an amnesty for all political prisoners, and, for the future, the convocation of an assembly in charge of drafting a new constitution for the country. The Soviet was a body elected from factory workshops and military units, with a moderate social-ist leadership. Its main aim was the protection of the interests of workers, soldiers, and peasants in this time of transition. The appearance of these two centres of power meant that Russia now had effectively two governments, although with rather different qualities and aspirations. While the Provisional Government was generally seen as the official government of Russia and recognized as such by the Allied states (who hoped to gain a more committed partner in the fight against Germany), it had a mostly upper-class constituency, was distrusted by the popular masses, and, most importantly, had not been elected into office. Without democratic legitimization it was effectively a caretaker government, postponing all major reforms until after a new constitution had been passed. The Soviet, however, was a democratically elected body and thus had legitimacy and power. Yet it refused to accept this power. Following Marx's ideas of historical progress, its socialist leaders believed that before they could take power and create socialism, a bourgeois revolution and the development of a capitalist system would have to take place first. In their eyes, the events of February 1917 repre-sented this bourgeois revolution. They consequently recognized the Provisional Government, but refused to join it. Instead they adopted a principle of oversight and control, to ensure that the Provisional Government would not act against the interests of the masses. Its first decree, Order Number 1, made this abundantly clear. It declared that no governmental order to the army would be considered legal without the approval of the Soviet. Initially meant only for the Petrograd garrison, it was mistaken as valid for the rest of the country, where meanwhile other Soviets began to emerge in factories, military units, villages, and cities.

The February Revolution and the subsequent system of dual power did not resolve any of Russia's problems; it rather led to a process of further dissolution. It also highlighted two conflicting understandings of revolution. While the Provisional Government and its moderate, liberal leadership stood for a democratic revolution, which would above all turn Russia's political system into a Western-style republic and a *Rechtsstaat* based on a constitution, the Soviet and its moderate socialist executive represented the hopes for a social revolution which would eventually destroy the traditional structures of Russian society and empower the lower classes. To make matters more complicated, from February onwards, these two centres of power had to contend with at least two more political players: the volatile mood of the masses and the Bolshevik Party. The areas of contention were manifold. First of all there was the question of the war. The Provisional Government wanted to honour Russia's obligations to the Allies and continue fighting alongside such respected democracies as France and Britain. The moderate socialists in the Soviet reluctantly favoured a continuation of the war to defend the Revolution and defeat German militarism. Popular opinion was mostly against the war, and the Bolsheviks rejected it altogether. The issue first came to the fore in the co-called April crisis, when foreign minister Miliukov had to resign under public pressure after having sent a note to the Allies, expressing Russia's willingness to fight on and reiterating old Tsarist annexationist war aims. As a result of this governmental crisis, some socialists from the Soviet joined the Provisional Government in a coalition, thereby discrediting the Soviet in the eyes of the masses and setting in motion a process of polarization from which mostly the Bolsheviks were to benefit.

In addition to the war, the lack of fundamental social reforms, mainly in the areas of labour policy and land redistribution, increasingly alienated the population from the government and the ruling elites. Clearly, the jubilant days of early March, when everyone together celebrated the Revolution and when Russia was the 'freest country in the world' were over. Instead, society and the political system rapidly disintegrated, helped along by some key events. When in June the socialist minister of war, Alexander Kerensky, ordered an offensive on the south-western front, the army suffered heavy casualties and began to fall apart. Hundreds of thousands of troops deserted, went back to their villages, and joined other peasants who were seizing land in a rural revolution, which had already been under way for some time. In early July, an angry crowd of armed workers and soldiers in Petrograd demanded unsuccessfully that the Soviet take power. Blamed on the Bolsheviks, who only joined reluctantly some time after the demonstrations had started, the July Days revealed the high level of agitation and radicalization among the masses. They also gave the government a pretext to raid the offices of the Bolshevik Party and arrest some of its leaders. In late August, finally, the supreme commander of the Russian troops, General Kornilov, attempted but failed to seize power from a government which, since Kerensky had become prime minister in July, had drifted more and more to the left. The Kornilov affair essentially turned into a catalyst for the political consciousness of the lower classes. They rallied to protect the Revolution, and in September ensured Bolshevik victories in elections to the Soviets in Petrograd and Moscow, where the Bolsheviks gained absolute majorities.

THE OCTOBER REVOLUTION

How was it possible, that a tiny fringe party, the result of a split in Russia's Social Democratic Workers' Party in 1903, gained so much support so quickly? Most of its leaders had been abroad or underground for extended periods of time. Its head, Vladimir Ulianov, called Lenin, had come back to Russia from exile only in April 1917. Yet it was he who more shrewdly than other politicians sensed the opportunities of the current situation. On his return, he formulated what became known as the April Theses. They were effectively a political platform, which, unlike the programmes of other socialist parties, was plainly responsive to the demands of the masses and largely ignored Marxist ideological constraints. Apart from calling for a handover of all power to the Soviets, the April Theses included the highly popular demands for peace, bread, and land for the peasants.

On this basis, the Bolsheviks were able to substantially broaden their support base, as reflected in the elections to the Soviets in the autumn, and to almost treble their party membership between April and October.

In accordance with Lenin's 'What is to be Done', a programmatic tract from 1902, in which he had elaborated his ideas of a rigid party organization, the Bolsheviks had developed into a centrally organized vanguard party of professional revolutionaries. What mattered was not so much the law of historical process, but rather the guidance of the proletariat by a determined political leader with the will to power at the right moment. Lenin saw this moment coming in September 1917. By 10 October, he had secured a majority for his idea of an armed insurrection in the Party's Central Committee. Lev Bronshtein, or Trotsky, was in charge with the military planning, and in the night of 24/25 October, armed workers' militias, or 'Red Guards', loyal soldiers and sailors occupied strategic installations in Petrograd. The Provisional Government retreated into the Winter Palace, the former Tsar's residence, defended only by young cadets and members of a women's battalion. After a short struggle, they were arrested in the night of 25/26 October, although without the prime minister. Kerensky had already left the city. What was portrayed later by Soviet propaganda and most notably in Sergey Eisenstein's famous film *October* as the heroic 'Storming of the Winter Palace' by thousands of proletarians was in effect a rather low-key affair. Altogether six people died in the event. Hardly anybody in Petrograd noticed what was going on. The theatres were playing as usual, restaurants were busy as ever, and public transport continued uninterrupted.

Inconspicuous as it appeared at the time, the October Revolution soon turned into one of the key historical events of the twentieth century. Already a few years later, it served as a model for revolutions and short-lived Soviet republics in places such as Munich and Budapest; throughout the century it captivated the hopes and fantasies of workers and intellectuals, inspired liberation movements, and fuelled socialist regimes all over the world. Crucially, it also became the main legitimization for the existence of the USSR until its demise in 1991. Historians have consequently debated its causes and effects, mostly in political terms. For Soviet historiography, the 'Great October Socialist Revolution', as it was called, was the inevitable result of socio-economic changes in Russia. It was part of a teleological historical process, as described by Marx, and represented the victory of the proletariat over a capitalist system. Western historiography presented a number of more complex interpretations, which, simply put, largely revolved around the question whether Russia before 1917 was on her way to becoming a liberal democratic state or caught in a free fall towards a class-based revolution. More specifically, the question was whether the popular masses supported the Bolsheviks' revolution in October or whether the Bolsheviks simply staged a *coup d'état* and then suppressed the legitimate aspirations of the Russian people. The latter is largely the view of the so-called 'liberal' school of historians, who tend to focus mainly on the immediate causes of the Revolution, in particular the First World War and its economic and military disasters. In their view, the war disrupted Russia's democratic development and allowed Lenin to mastermind and succeed in his *coup d'état*. Opposed to this interpretation is the so-called 'revisionist' school of historians. While conceding that October was a skilfully executed seizure of power by the Bolsheviks, they also look at long-term structural reasons and social causes for the Revolution, in particular Russia's pre-1917 agrarian order, her rapid industrialization in the late nineteenth century, and the plight of the urban workers. In their view, Lenin's coup could only have succeeded with at least some kind of support from the popular masses.

In the end, no single line of interpretation can sufficiently explain all the causes and the outcome of an event as multifaceted and complex as the Russian Revolution. Was it driven by individual people or by broad historical processes, or both? Was it progress and the beginning of a bright future? Or was it the end of civilization and a descent into barbarity? Is there any linear, teleological progression of history in any direction, of which it would have been a constituent part? Already some contemporaries were struggling to grasp its meaning. It may thus help to broaden our imagination and further our understanding of the Revolution if we consider how a famous artist at the time attempted to interpret and mythologize it. The Russian avant-garde by 1917 had already long broken with traditional notions of style, form, and content. Many of its members welcomed and supported the Revolution as an apparent extension of their artistic experiments into real life. When Vladimir Tatlin was asked in 1920 to create a monument to the Third International or Comintern (the new international organization of communist parties), he had a quite original idea. In a synthesis of architecture and sculpture, he envisioned a high, leaning tower, made of steel and glass, with different platforms, revolving like a spiral. In many ways, Tatlin's tower became symbolic of the Revolution. For him and his contemporaries, it represented modernity *per se*: planned in the latest constructivist style, employing the latest technology and materials, and functioning like a machine. It reflected progress in the forward-moving spiral. Yet Tatlin had probably not taken into consideration that a spiral only gives the appearance of moving forward, while in reality it remains in its place. Moreover, Tatlin's tower could never be built. There was simply not enough money and know-how available for such an extravagant construction. It remained a small, plain wooden model, which fascinated art connoisseurs in Russia and abroad, but eventually went up in flames in an accident.

Like Tatlin's tower, the Bolshevik project often appeared to make big progress, where there was little or none. Many initial plans were not realized due to a lack of means, or they remained grand utopian designs with great propagandistic value, but collapsed once exposed to reality. The Bolsheviks had promised quite fundamental changes in April 1917, most notably a handover of power to the Soviets, peace, bread, and land. And indeed, already one day after taking power they issued a decree on land and one on peace. The former nationalized all private land without compensation, the latter contained the offer of immediate

Figure 13.1. Model of Vladimir Tatlin's Tower, (Monument to the Third International, 1920).

peace without annexations, which was eventually accomplished after difficult and protracted negotiations with Germany, Austria-Hungary, and Turkey in the Treaty of Brest-Litovsk in March 1918. A decree on workers' control followed in November 1917, effectively placing the running of factories into the hands of the workers, who were, after all, the people in whose name the Revolution had been carried out. While these early decrees were clearly in line with earlier Bolshevik promises, others were less so and already foreshadowed a development towards authoritarianism and centralized state-building, in other words, a regression into old Tsarist traditions.

Two days after coming to power, the Bolsheviks published a decree restricting severely the 'bourgeois' press. On 7 December, they created the Cheka, the infamous secret police in charge with suppressing counter-revolutionary activities, which was later renamed into GPU (1922) and NKVD (1934) and which eventually became the KGB. Moreover, the notion that all power should go to the Soviets, who were in principle democratically elected bodies, was not really taken seriously. Instead, all power went de facto to the Bolsheviks, who on Lenin's behest refused to join coalitions with other socialist parties in the Soviets and who were the only members of a newly formed government, the so-called Soviet of Peoples' Commissars (Sovnarkom). Although elections to a Constituent Assembly, which was supposed to draft a new constitution, were still held in November, the Bolsheviks managed to dissolve this body, in which they had gained only a minority of seats, as soon as it met in January 1918. It was only a matter of time before they banned all other political parties. By 1918 the Bolsheviks had thus satisfied some of the demands of the masses, while others were already being suppressed. They began to build a new bureaucratic state structure, which was highly authoritarian and centralized, with the power of the party increasing and the importance of the Soviets diminishing. While this development was partly to blame on the ideology and the political style of the Bolshevik leaders, it was also a result of the national and international situation in which the new regime had to survive. More specifically, Lenin and his comrades had to deal with the secession of numerous nationalities, had to fight a bloody civil war, and they had to face a complete economic breakdown and a devastating famine.

NATIONALITIES IN REVOLUTION

Tsarist Russia, like Austria-Hungary, had been a multi-ethnic empire in which some 130 languages were spoken. Most of the non-Russian nationalities had been exposed to a rigid Russification policy since the late nineteenth century. When Tsarist power collapsed in February 1917, many local elites saw an opportunity to improve their status within the empire or even become independent. Ukraine thus achieved a limited autonomy in July 1917, while Finland, which had been part of the empire since 1809, declared independence in December 1917. Among the first decrees of the Bolsheviks was a declaration of the rights of the peoples of Russia. In it, they solemnly proclaimed that, after liberating peasants and workers, they also wanted to free suppressed nationalities from the imperial yoke. They granted them the right to decide their own future and offered them the opportunity to join as equals in a voluntary union with Russia. Yet much of this declaration turned out to be pure rhetoric. Whenever they could, the Bolsheviks tried to get back lost territories, and only the countries that managed to successfully fight off the Red Army did eventually stay independent. Among those were Finland, Poland, and the Baltic States of Latvia, Lithuania, and Estonia, whose independence had been part of the Treaty of Brest-Litovsk, but was subsequently challenged by Soviet intervention or, in the case of Poland, by a bold military reaction against a foolhardy Polish offensive in 1920. In any case, with the Western border now so much closer to Petrograd, the Bolsheviks decided to relocate their capital to a safer place further inland. They chose to move it to Moscow in March 1918.

Ukraine presented a particular problem to the Bolsheviks. Traditionally the bread basket of Russia and, with the Donbass region, one of the important industrial centres as well, its loss meant serious economic trouble. Since its autonomy in 1917, Ukraine was plagued by internal disunity and foreign intervention. Until 1922, it experienced multiple occupations by Germans, Poles, and various armies fighting in the Civil War as well as a peasant partisan or 'green' movement, led by the legendary anarchist Nestor Makhno. After a series of puppet regimes installed by the different occupants, the Bolsheviks eventually managed to create a more stable Ukrainian Socialist Soviet Republic. It was slightly easier for them to regain possession of the Caucasus, which had also broken away in the Revolution. In its northern part, local Russians, Cossacks, and a multitude of mountain tribes were more concerned with fighting each other than resisting a Bolshevik take-over. In Transcaucasia, the traditional enmity between Armenia and Azerbaidzhan erupted in several pogroms after 1917, killing thousands of people. Combined with widespread economic decline, these conflicts quickly led into anarchy and chaos, making it easy for the Bolsheviks to gradually consolidate their power over these regions. Only Georgia was more difficult to win back. Since May 1918 it had developed into an independent and relatively prosperous state, first under German, then under British protection, and as such was officially recognized by the Bolsheviks in 1920. A year later, however, in a blatant violation of international law, the Red Army made an end to Georgian independence and forced the country to join a new Transcaucasian Soviet Republic together with Armenia and Azerbaidzhan. In 1924, this republic, together with the Russian Socialist Federal Soviet Republic (RSFSR), which included several more or less autonomous regions, the Ukrainian Soviet Republic, and the Byelorussian Soviet Republic, formed the Union of Socialist Soviet Republics (USSR), which, until 1936, was further enlarged by five Central Asian republics. With the exception of the areas lost in the West, the Bolsheviks had thus regained much of the Tsarist Empire's territories. Like its predecessor, the new Soviet Empire, while paying lip service to national self-determination, engaged in an intense Russification policy and set up a highly centralized state administration.

CIVIL WAR AND WAR COMMUNISM

Territorial consolidation was closely interlinked with the consolidation of power in general. As the elections to the Constituent Assembly had shown, the Bolsheviks were by far not the strongest political force in Russia. Yet nor were their opponents particularly powerful. The Civil War, which broke out in the spring of 1918, was thus in many ways a war of the weak against the weaker. It pitched the Bolshevik 'Reds' against the 'Whites', that is, a variety of Tsarist generals and their troops, Cossack detachments, and interventionist forces from Britain, France, Japan, and the United States, who resented the Bolsheviks for making a separate peace with Germany, rejecting Russia's foreign debt, and nationalizing Allied property. Military activity initially centred around the so-called Czech Legion, a well-trained military unit consisting mostly of former prisoners of war, who wanted to leave for Europe via Vladivostok to fight for the liberation of their country from Austro-Hungarian rule. When Soviet officials wanted to disarm them, they swiftly took hold of the Transsiberian Railroad, thereby gaining control over Russia's most important communication line. Encouraged by this Czech success, White armies attacked mostly in the south, along the Volga, and in Siberia. Unlike in the First World War, frontlines moved quickly and vast territories changed hands, often several times. It was during one of these offensives, on 16 July 1918, when the Czechs approached Yekaterinburg, that the Bolsheviks murdered the former Tsar and his family, whom they had kept under arrest in that city.

The Civil War was fought with extreme brutality. In many ways, it was a war against the people in the name of the people. Both sides were convinced that they represented the best form of government for the Russian population. The latter, however, remained largely passive and tried to avoid the war whenever possible. Hundreds of thousands of soldiers, who were pressed into service, deserted on both sides; peasants hid in forests and tried to save their grain and cattle from forced requisitioning. In the end, victory depended on a few strategic and ideological factors. The Bolsheviks had the advantage of holding the centre of the country around Moscow, from where most of Russia's train lines radiate out into the rest of the country. They were thus relatively flexible in transporting troops to and from the different fronts. The various White armies, in turn, were operating from the margins. Although logistically supported by the interventionist forces, they were often unable to coordinate their actions. Moreover, under the charismatic leadership of Trotsky, the Red Army, which had been founded in February 1918, quickly turned into a highly efficient fighting force, which was able to survive even heavy defeats. One of its particular features were political commissars, stalwart Bolsheviks, who would enforce the loyalty of former Tsarist officers now made to serve in the Red Army. The figure of the dedicated and ruthless commissar, dressed in a leather jacket and carrying a Mauser pistol, would remain the classical image of a Bolshevik for years to come.

It was certainly an image that would upset many of those people who had emigrated from Russia as a result of Revolution and Civil War. This 'first wave' of *émigrés* (two more were to follow over the twentieth century) numbered around one million people. It consisted not only of supporters of the monarchy and, after their defeat in the Civil War, troops and officers of the White armies, but also of political figures from the Provisional Government, artists and intellectuals, and numerous ordinary citizens. Most of them went to Central and Western Europe, where large Russian communities formed in cities like Paris, Prague, Belgrade, and Berlin. Paris quickly became the centre of this emigration, with its own Orthodox church, theological seminary, Russian publishing houses, libraries, and periodicals. In Prague, a Russian university was opened, which provided a refuge for academics who had left their country, while many Russian artists thrived on the vibrant cultural scene in Berlin during the Weimar Republic.

Back in Russia, it was evident that victory in the Civil War depended not only on military success, but also on winning over the hearts and minds of the Russian population. In their majority peasants, they hated both the Reds and the Whites, who only brought terror and destruction. But the Bolsheviks had two important assets. They would certainly not re-establish the former landlords, who had been chased away in the Revolution, and they were much better than the Whites in spreading their message through graphic art, posters, and direct agitation by party members. Taking advantage of the train network, for example, they would not only send troops back and forth, but also numerous agitators, actors, and musicians on special agitational trains. Equipped with a printing press for the production of leaflets, a screen to show short agitational films (so-called *agitki*), and a car for motorcycles with which outlying villages could be reached, these trains were painted in bright colours and covered with political graffiti. They were often the first sight that peasants had of the new regime, and their arrival was usually celebrated in a festive atmosphere. Moreover, the Bolsheviks understood the importance of mass organizations to bring their ideas closer to the people. They were particularly keen on enrolling the enthusiasm of young people, for whom they founded the Communist Youth League or Komsomol in October 1918. The Komsomol was supposed to keep youngsters away from the bad influence of politically backward parents and to shape them into new socialist men and women. It soon became one of the main suppliers of political agitators and an important tool to spread Bolshevism in the country. It opened clubs and communist cells, organized communist holidays and 'communist Saturdays' or *Subbotniki,* when voluntary communal work would be carried out. During a major campaign against illiteracy, it also opened reading huts in villages, where the latest political brochures would be read. The Bolsheviks quite correctly saw literacy as one of the preconditions for the success of their ideological message.

For the time being, however, most people had other worries than overcoming illiteracy. The Civil War caused major economic havoc. In order to secure supplies for the Red Army, the Bolsheviks introduced what became known as War Communism. This was a system of centralized, state-planned production and distribution of all goods, a veritable dictatorship over the whole economy. It failed abysmally. Peasants, who had their grain requisitioned by force, stopped sowing new crops. Combined with a severe drought in 1921, this led to a major famine in 1921/2, which cost the lives of some five million people. Moreover, workers in the cities went hungry and lost their jobs, as sufficient fuel and raw materials did not reach the factories. In Petrograd, for example, the sixty-four biggest factories had to shut down. Life in the former capital generally came to a standstill. Two-thirds of the population had left the city or died in the war, and numerous houses dilapidated as pipes froze and walls collapsed. Those people who remained had to burn furniture, wooden fences, or abandoned frame-houses to heat their flats. By 1920, over 5,000 such houses had disappeared in Petrograd as fuel for the now popular small cast-iron stove, called *burzhuika*. These little stoves with their long pipes sticking out of windows were the new social gathering places in a magnificent ghost-town of baroque and classicist façades.

People reacted in different ways to the harsh conditions of War Communism. Disgruntled peasants often joined 'green' movements or lynched those who came to take their grain. Workers, the constituents of the Revolution, went on strike to demand the right to trade for food directly with peasants, but also to protest against privileges such as better housing and exclusive supplies which some Bolshevik Party officials enjoyed. While these protests spoilt the ideal picture of a workers' and peasants' state, they did not really threaten the position of the regime. This changed, however, when sailors at the Kronstadt naval base near Petrograd, who had been the vanguard of the Revolution, declared their sympathy with striking workers in February 1921. In their resolutions, the sailors challenged the monopoly of the Bolshevik party and demanded a return to such achievements of the Revolution as basic democracy, that is, new, equal, and secret elections to the Soviets, freedom for political parties and free disposal of the land by the peasants. Lenin reacted swiftly to these demands. 50,000 Red Army troops were sent over the frozen Gulf of Finland and, after ten days of fierce fighting, the Kronstadt sailors were defeated. Only very few escaped over the ice to Finland.

The Kronstadt uprising, for all its symbolic significance, was not the only sign of disillusionment with the policies of the Bolsheviks. Even within the Party itself, opposition against the autocratic leadership of its Central Committee was voiced. However, as with the sailors, Lenin responded promptly. At the 10th Party Congress in March 1921, with the impact of Kronstadt still fresh, he attacked all 'independent platforms' within the Party. Eventually, a resolution 'On Party Unity' was passed, effectively silencing all differing opinions for decades to come and paving the way for the dictatorial rule of the Central Committee already one year before Iosif Dzhugashvili, or Stalin, became its omnipotent secretary. A perfect administrator and meticulous bureaucrat, who never forgot anything about anybody, he was soon able to turn this body into an efficient tool of his own paranoid power politics.

NEW ECONOMIC POLICY AND REVOLUTIONARY EXPERIMENTALISM

The difficult economic situation of the country was another major issue at the 10th Party Congress. Lenin understood that a major change was needed after the Civil War and War Communism. Particularly the disastrous food situation caused concern. He thus promoted what became known as New Economic Policy (NEP). NEP brought capitalism back to Russia, at least to some extent. The idea of a union between cities and countryside (*smychka*) was actively promoted. Instead of requisitioning, peasants were given incentives to produce grain to feed the urban population. They had to pay a legally fixed tax and were allowed to sell excess goods on newly opened markets. Moreover, internal trade was permitted again, and entrepreneurs could open small businesses. The so-called 'commanding heights', however, that is heavy industry, banking, and foreign trade remained nationalized. Clearly, NEP did not mean an all-out negation of Bolshevik principles; it rather was seen as a temporary measure, a way to reach communism on a slower pace and with the help of persuasion rather than violent action. People were meant to voluntarily build a communist state. As a consequence, NEP became a time of major pedagogical efforts and propaganda campaigns.

With the help of Komsomol enthusiasts, the Bolsheviks not only attacked illiteracy. They also lashed out against alcoholism and hooliganism, moral depravity, and all kinds of deviant behaviour. At the same time, they promoted anything from industrialization and large-scale co-operative agriculture to paying taxes on time and joining workers' clubs. During such campaigns, reading huts in the villages, of which over 20,000 existed in the mid-1920s, clubs in factories, and educational institutions were flooded with posters and pamphlets. Particularly prominent campaigns were run to propagate electrification—according to Lenin, communism was Soviet power plus electrification—and personal health and hygiene. The light bulb illuminating a remote peasant hut and the attacks on head lice in outlying villages, like all the other campaigns, reflected both the Bolsheviks' vision of modernity, that is, of socialist order, enlightenment, technological, and scientific progress, and Western civilization, and their condescending attitude towards ordinary Russian people, which they had inherited from the nineteenth-century intelligentsia.

Religion and the Church posed a peculiar problem to the Bolsheviks. Orthodox rituals and holidays had been part of everyday life in Russia for many centuries.

Now they were stigmatized as backward and superstitious. A 'League of the Militant Godless' was founded, organizing lectures about the non-existence of God and the superiority of communist science over religious tradition. To prove the point, it was shown to peasants, for example, that insecticides, not prayers, kill pests. However, it was soon realized that mocking religion in this way was not achieving the expected results, that people still needed some kind of spiritual sustenance. Instead of abolishing religious ceremonies altogether, the Bolsheviks therefore began to replace them with their own rituals. Holidays marking anniversaries of revolutionary history or the international labour movement, like 7 November and 1 May, were introduced. On such days, huge street festivals and mass spectacles took place, presenting, for example, a re-enactment of the storming of the Winter Palace. On a more personal level, religious family rituals were changed as well, although most people, especially in the countryside still adhered to old traditions. 'Red Weddings' were held in which fidelity was vowed not just to the partner, but to communism as well. On such occasions, the guests might well intone the 'Internationale', the new national anthem, and present the couple with the works of Lenin. Once a child had been born, 'Octobering' took the place of baptisms. Instead of a priest, comrades from the factory would come over, inspect the newborn child, perhaps bring a picture of baby Lenin, and then celebrate together with the parents. Children were now often given names that related to the new times, for example, Elektrifikatsiya, Traktorina, or, after Lenin had died on 21 January 1924, Ninel (Lenin read backwards) or Arlen (Army of Lenin). Lenin quickly became a god-like figure after his death. Only five days later, the old capital was renamed Leningrad in his honour, while 'Lenin corners' were introduced in clubs and reading huts, with pictures of him taking the place which formerly religious icons had occupied.

Campaigns of the 'propaganda state', as one historian called it, were not the only attempts to implement radical change in the USSR. The Revolution set free a vast reservoir of utopian ideas and triggered numerous experiments in social life. All kinds of revolutionary dreamers, avant-garde artists, and architects quite practically went about building a 'new world'. This new world was above all modern, just, and equal. Equality was expressed, for example, in plans to erect huge communal housing projects and in a movement to form communes, both for living and/or for working together. Tens of thousands of such communes sprang up both in the countryside and in cities. They helped to ease economic problems, but above all served as a laboratory for a new socialist life. In the more extreme cases, everything from kitchen duties, cleaning, food, and money to even underwear was shared (the desire to wear one's own was declared a 'bourgeois' deviation). Drawing on the ideas of Frederick Winslow Taylor, which were then widely popular in Russian factories, attempts were made in some communes to introduce rational time management into daily life and turn entertainment into a purposeful experience. In one commune in Moscow, for example, in order not to waste time, some members played classical music while others did the ironing. In other communes, families were dissolved, the women freed from household work, and the children raised together and apart from their parents. As the poet Vladimir Maiakovsky put it: 'Communism: it's not only on the land, in the mill, in the sweat of your toil. It's at home, at table, in family life and daily round.' It even influenced the world of music and fashion. In a move to eradicate old symbols of hierarchy, a conductorless orchestra was founded (seriously extending rehearsal times, as everything had to be discussed by the whole ensemble), while avant-garde artists like Alexandra Exter designed highly functional unisex costumes with clear lines like military uniforms, and without any unnecessary embellishments. Exter also created the extravagant sets for one of the most ingenious films of the NEP years: Yakov Protazanov's *Aelita* posed the ultimate modern utopia—life on Mars—against the oddities and twists of contemporary Russian reality.

Life during NEP was indeed quite different from any modern utopia, let alone from the preceding years of civil strife. Although not a time of abundance for all (as a result of war and dislocation, millions of homeless children and countless beggars were still roaming the country), NEP at least brought some level of prosperity. Most importantly, the food supply increased and goods were back in the stores. Cities began to look different. Moscow in particular became a buzzing metropolis, with thriving theatres and cinemas, art shows, streets full with automobiles and trams, and with NEP men, or *nepmeny*, as the newly rich entrepreneurs were called, frequenting posh restaurants and nightclubs. In a way, these years of accelerated urban dynamism were Russia's 'Roaring Twenties', with old 'bourgeois' entertainments enjoying a comeback next to the experiments of revolutionary art. Gypsy romances were as popular as before 1917, while jazz became increasingly trendy, feeding a revived obsession with ballroom dances, in particular the tango and the foxtrot. In the cinemas, costume dramas, adventure films, and melodramas by far outnumbered the much better-known masterpieces of the Soviet avant-garde. Eisenstein's *Battleship Potemkin*, for example, was successful mostly abroad, but hardly popular at home, where audiences preferred entertainment and the products of Hollywood over moralizing politics and cinematographic experiments.

With some semblance of normality returning to the internal life of the country, foreign relations also began to move towards realpolitik. They had been essentially defunct during the Civil War and, in anticipation of a world revolution, had been deemed unnecessary by Trotsky, Soviet Russia's first foreign secretary. An exception was the Comintern, which had seen supporting communists abroad since 1919, conducting essentially a foreign policy of the Bolshevik Party and, in later years, often hampering the much more pragmatic government diplomacy of Trotsky's successors, Georgy Chicherin and, after 1930, Maxim Litvinov. As the country urgently needed industrial goods, Chicherin promoted a number of trade agreements, starting in 1921 with the United Kingdom. Under its first Labour government, the UK also led the way among the Western powers in recognizing the Soviet state in 1924, followed soon by other nations, and eventually bringing the USSR into the League of Nations in 1934. Soviet relations with Germany were of a peculiar nature. Internationally isolated since World War and Revolution, the two countries had much to gain from closer ties. Already since 1920, top-secret military contacts led to exchanges of officers and the training of Reichswehr troops in Russia, blatantly undercutting demilitarization clauses of the Versailles Treaty. In 1922, at the first international conference, to which they had been invited, the two countries signed a treaty in the Italian town of Rapallo, agreeing on full diplomatic relations and favourable trading conditions. The 'ghost of Rapallo', of a special relationship between Germany and Russia, from then on haunted European diplomacy, making Western politicians deeply suspicious of Germany's strategic intentions and, within Germany, nourishing dreams of an autonomous foreign policy oscillating between East and West. Eventually, and after a break during the Spanish Civil War, the special relationship, in the hands of two paranoid dictators, would lead to the Hitler–Stalin Pact of 1939, cutting up Eastern Europe into spheres of interest, resulting in occupations of Poland, the end of independence of the Baltic States, and the Winter War of 1939/40 between the USSR and Finland. More immediately, however, Rapallo led to a sizeable increase in trade, with almost 75 per cent of German machine tool production exported to the USSR by 1928.

INDUSTRIALIZATION AND COLLECTIVIZATION

The import of machinery shows that one of the Bolsheviks' main goals, extensive industrialization, had not been achieved during NEP. Indeed, while agricultural production increased, industry hardly expanded. By 1924, its output was still only one-third of that in 1913. Yet for the Bolsheviks, industrialization was crucial to the building of communism. It was part of their utopia of technological progress, leading to abundance of everything for everyone, and their fascination with planning and machine culture; quite practically, it was also a precondition for national strength and military might. The latter became increasingly important issues, as revolutions elsewhere, that might have helped to secure the Soviet state, did not occur. By the mid-1920s, the notion of 'Socialism in one country' was thus pushed through in the Party by Stalin and Nikolai Bukharin against the 'leftist oppositionists' around Trotsky, who still counted on a world revolution. It meant that all efforts should be made to consolidate the power of the Soviet state from within. Consequently, the question how to industrialize was fiercely debated, closely interlinked with inner-party power struggles. The accumulation of investment capital was obviously a prerequisite for industrialization. Since it was hardly forthcoming from abroad, it had to come from internal sources. As under Tsarism, industrialization therefore ultimately meant squeezing the peasants, the vast majority of the population. The question was only whether to do this by incentive or by force. While Bukharin favoured a slower, evolutionary path, calling on the peasants to enrich themselves and trigger industrial development through their demands for goods, others followed Trotsky's ideas and promoted high taxes, even if this would cause resistance. The debate was eventually resolved at the 15th Party Congress in 1927, when Stalin, by then safely in power, sided with the advocates of fast and forceful industrialization.

Industrialization and the subsequent collectivization of agriculture started what historians have called Stalin's 'revolution from above'. This was a massive push to modernize the country, which would eventually enable the USSR to withstand the onslaught of Nazi Germany in the Second World War. However, it was also one of the greatest crimes in modern history, a veritable 'war against the nation', causing the lives of millions of people. In order to industrialize, the economy was organized in Five-Year Plans. The first one foresaw an increase of industrial production by 230 per cent. Carried out in four years between 1929 and 1933, it focused predominantly on the production of steel and iron. To become independent from imports, machine tool production was given high priority, as were tractor plants, which were meant to prop up the modernization of agriculture, but could also easily be converted into tank factories. Other parts of the economy and infrastructure were inevitably neglected, causing disruptions of transport and fuel supply and often leading to frantic struggles for raw materials. At times, trains were ambushed and their freight commandeered by desperate factory directors who lacked the necessary supplies to fulfil the norms set out in the Plan. Yet despite the confusion, several gigantic projects got under way: the autoworks in Gorky, the tractor factories in Stalingrad and Kharkov, the coal mines in the Kuzbass, and the metallurgical industries of Magnitogorsk. The latter was a completely new town, built from scratch in the Southern Urals in a feat of socialist construction and mass mobilization, which soon became the biggest steel plant in the USSR. Incidentally, the concentration on heavy industry during the First Five-Year Plan also had a deeply symbolic side, apart from its importance for national defence. It gave rise to a cult of steel, with the tractor as harbinger of a bright future, which perfectly complemented the emerging cult of Stalin, the 'man of steel'.

The social impact of industrialization was enormous. In the First Five-Year Plan, the number of non-agricultural workers increased from 15 to 24 million, the urban population rose from 27 to 40 million. In face of this rapid change, housing, medical services, education, and basic infrastructures in the cities were completely overwhelmed. In new towns, like Magnitogorsk, they hardly existed at all. Here people often lived in sheds without running water, surrounded by open cesspits. Working conditions were hardly better. Workers were mostly not used to strict time discipline and the rigid demands put on them. They reacted with a high level of mobility, leaving backbreaking jobs in search for better ones. As a consequence, an internal passport system was set up in 1932, tying everyone to their employment and place of residence. Harsh punishments, including loss of housing and even execution, were introduced for absenteeism, lateness, and breaking of machines. Terror clearly was meant to offset the widespread lack of skilled and motivated workers. Moreover, in order to improve work ethic and productivity, the Stakhanovite movement was launched in 1935, named after the miner Aleksei Stakhanov, who overfulfilled his norm by a record 1,300 per cent, serving as a model for similarly heroic feats of labour.

Industrialization could only succeed if a sufficient and reliable grain supply was secured to feed the workers. From an economic point of view, and as the Tsarist gentry had shown, large agricultural producers were better suited to generate a surplus of grain than individual smallholders. For ideological reasons the Bolsheviks also favoured the large collective farm (*kolkhoz*) over private peasant economies, which still constituted 97 per cent of agriculture in 1928. As a serious grain procurement crisis in 1927–8 showed, something had to be done urgently in order not to endanger industrialization. After initial attempts failed to make peasants join collective farms voluntarily, the Party decided on all-out collectivization in early 1930 by unleashing a 'class war' in the villages. GPU agents and 'workers' brigades', that is, armed urban mobs recruited by the Party, went out to villages to stir up poorer peasants against their better-off neighbours, the so-called *kulaks*. Although these were anything but rich compared to Western standards, they were to be liquidated as 'class enemies'. As a consequence, more than half a million *kulaks*, that is, the most diligent and innovative elements among Russia's peasantry, had their property confiscated and were deported to deserted areas in the middle of the winter, where many of them died. The remaining villagers were made to join newly created *kolkhozy*. The result of these policies was utter chaos and violence, causing millions of lives to be lost. Many *kulaks* fled or committed suicide. Peasants rushed to sell their animals or slaughtered them rather then handing them over to the *kolkhoz*. By 1933, half of the horses, cows, and pigs were gone. As fields were not cultivated in time, a famine led to the death of over five million people between 1932 and 1934. By 1937, most of the arable land was under control of collective or state farms, and Stalin and the Party had successfully imposed their power over the countryside.

CULTURAL REVOLUTION AND THE JOYS OF STALINISM

Stalin's revolution from above consisted not only of industrialization and collectivization. It also entailed a cultural revolution. At its end, pre-revolutionary 'bourgeois' specialists—for example, doctors, engineers, and teachers—whose expertise had still been needed during NEP and industrialization, had often been purged and replaced by a new 'proletarian' intelligentsia. Moreover, utopianism in social life and experimentalism in the arts had disappeared and made way for more conservative values, petit-bourgeois taste and the style of socialist realism. Starting in 1928, when mining engineers from the Shakhty area in the

Donbass were charged with sabotage and put on a show trial, members of the old intelligentsia, like *kulaks* in the villages, were labelled as 'class enemies' and made responsible for the failures of industrialization. In their place, a new elite of communist-educated proletarians, wholly dedicated to Stalin, was promoted. These people, moving up from lower class backgrounds, were, however, anything but radical revolutionaries or intellectuals. They generally espoused middle-class tastes and aspired to traditional notions of hierarchy, order, and stability. They became the carriers and beneficiaries of what some historians have called the 'great retreat' of the 1930s, a revival of traditional Russian values. Other historians, however, have shown that this 'retreat' was actually a major step forward in the establishment of a Soviet civilization. As a result of the upheavals of industrialization and collectivization, traditional forms of social control and public order had largely broken down and widespread hooliganism, deviant behaviour, and crime had become serious threats to the regime. In order to cope with these problems, 'culturedness' (*kul'turnost'*) was now promoted. To be a respected member of Soviet society, one had to dress, live, behave, and speak in a certain way. Most importantly, however, one also had to internalize the new values and develop a Bolshevik consciousness by moulding one's own personality in accordance with communist ideals.

The new values were particularly evident in the area of social policy. Instead of women's equality, for example, which had been proclaimed as achieved by 1930, 'family responsibility' was now promoted. Abortion was outlawed in 1936 and divorce was made more difficult, while femininity was emphasized and more elaborate wedding ceremonies were established. In schools, uniforms, rigid schedules, examinations, and other old forms of authority were restored, promoting ideas of discipline and order from an early age. With paternalism thus (re)introduced as the main building block of society, it was only logical that Stalin was portrayed as the caring father-figure benevolently leading the country.

'Life has become better, comrades, life has become more joyous'—with this notorious quote from 1935, Stalin provided the official interpretation for what had happened in the previous years and gave out the line for what was going to come. Indeed, life was getting better on a quite practical level. After a good harvest in 1934, food rationing was abolished in early 1935. In 1936, the Central Committee of the Party decreed an expansion of champagne production from 300,000 bottles to four million by 1939. Chocolate and candy, produced by the Moscow 'Red October' factory, became available in ever growing varieties, while the output of cosmetics manufacturers rose dramatically in these years, with perfumes like 'Crimean violet' and 'Red Moscow' in fancy crystal-glass bottles providing the latest sensual kick. Gastronom, a chain of high-quality food shops, opened in 1933, often in beautiful pre-revolutionary delicatessen stores. These were showcases of Soviet luxury, temples of a new communist consumer culture, which, in place of money, was largely regulated through privilege, position, and personal connections. Despite the new commercial shops, goods were still mostly distributed through the workplace or professional associations (for example, the writers' union), with privileged groups like politicians, factory directors, famous artists, or Stakhanovite workers receiving anything from large flats to summer cottages and chauffeur-driven limousines while ordinary citizens had recourse to the flourishing black market.

That life was now 'more joyous' was also becoming evident in the arts and in mass culture. Since 'socialist realism' had been declared the official style in 1934, playful experimentalism and avant-garde art rapidly declined. Under the new aesthetic rules, reality was to be presented as it was supposed to be, not as it actually was. In an attack on Dmitry Shostakovich's opera, *Lady Macbeth of the Mtsensk District*, the Party newspaper *Pravda* in 1936 lashed out against 'formalism' in the arts and modernism in general. According to the article, healthy people have a 'biological need' for harmonious forms; they 'love melodically organized sounds and bright colours' and they 'want art to make their life happier and more beautiful, not complex and depressing.' Accordingly, painters, writers, and musicians now had to focus on optimistic and heroic motives, depicting happy scenes from factory or *kolkhoz* life, in simplistic and easily recognizable forms. This thematic emphasis was particularly widespread in mass culture, where uplifting songs and films had huge success. These were the heydays of schmaltzy, Hollywood-style musicals, jazzy and folksy comedies, factory love stories, and *kolkhoz* operettas of the 'boy meets girl meets tractor' genre. At the end of one of the most fascinating films, *Circus* from 1936, happy people in white suits march over Red Square, singing joyfully what for its popularity became almost an unofficial national anthem, the 'Song of the Motherland': 'O, vast country of mine . . . There is no other land the whole world over, where man walks the earth so proud and free.'

Obviously, this 'iconography of happiness' had nothing to do with actual reality. Like the new Soviet constitution of 1936, which was proclaimed to be the only thoroughly democratic constitution in the world, *Circus* and other products of art and mass culture were part of an ideological *Gesamtkunstwerk*, a utopian 'fantasy state' led by a ruler whose cult was all-pervasive. Unlike the many social utopias of the 1920s, Stalin's utopia presented a homogeneous picture of wholeness and clarity, of a society based on heroic achievements and joyful solidarity with Stalin as the mentor to whom everyone is grateful. He was the real hero behind all the little heroes, of whom quite a few existed in the 1930s. Apart from the Stakhanovites, these were above all polar explorers and aviators. The first and most famous were the flyers coming to the rescue of the icebreaker *Cheliushkin*, trapped in Arctic ice in 1933. Stalin himself supervised the rescue operation, kept in contact with the pilots, and personally welcomed them back. He acted like a father caring for his sons. Yet it was obvious that his family was the whole country, and as the example of another hero, Pavlik Morozov, showed, it was this national, not one's biological family, to which everyone had to be loyal. Pavlik had denounced his father for hoarding grain and was subsequently

Figure 13.2. The Russian actress Lyubov Orlova in *Circus* (1936), directed by Grigory Alexandrov.

killed by relatives. His heroism consisted of rejecting his blood ties in favour of the higher ties of the political community.

THE GREAT TERROR AND THE SECOND WORLD WAR

Stalin's Russia was a place of clear distinctions between good and bad, friend and foe. It was a place where euphoria alternated with fear, where the joy over historic achievements of socialist construction and heroic victories over nature was tempered by the terror of the dictator's 'paternal' authority and quest for total control. While this all-pervasive 'democracy of fear' cannot be blamed only on Stalin himself—traditions of collective control in the Russian village and of Tsarist autocracy certainly played into his hands—the dictator's personality undoubtedly did have a major impact on the Great Terror of the 1930s. Coming from a cultural background where trust was regarded as highly as honour and socialized in the secretive world of small circles of friends in a priesthood seminary in Tiflis and later in the underground Bolshevik Party, Stalin had developed a keen sense for loyalty. He consequently was extremely distrustful and suspected conspiracies everywhere. When the popular Leningrad

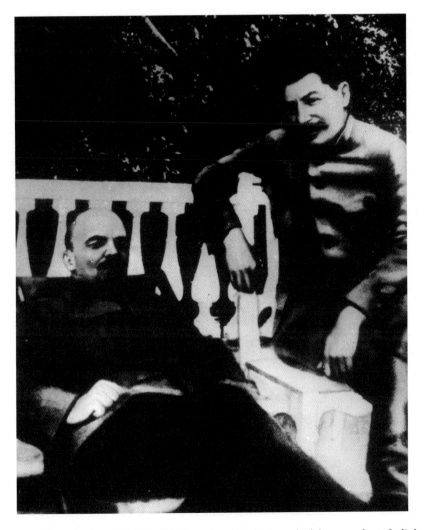

Figure 13.3. Lenin and Stalin (1922)—photograph retouched later to show Stalin's closeness to Lenin.

Party leader Sergey Kirov was murdered in 1934—with or without Stalin's approval is still not known—the dictator used the opportunity to get rid of countless old Bolsheviks and purge the Party of potential future rivals. They were put on elaborate show trials and accused of treason and the most bizarre crimes. Well rehearsed beforehand and with the desired confessions secured through torture, these trials were meant to intimidate the Party and catered to Stalin's paranoia. They set off an unprecedented wave of terror, which affected almost all levels of society and state and which was driven on through denunciations and guilt by implication or association.

During the Great Terror, approximately 700,000 people were executed and well over two million were sent to prison camps (exact figures are still unknown). The Terror started with the show trial of Grigory Zinoviev, Lev Kamenev, and some other high-ranking Bolsheviks in August 1936. They were all executed, after confessing to murdering Kirov and intending to kill Stalin as members of a so-called Trotskyite–Zinovievite centre (Trotsky had been expelled from the USSR in 1929; he was assassinated by a Soviet agent in Mexico in 1940). Two more show trials of eminent Party members followed, in January 1937 and March 1938, the latter leading to the execution of, among others, Nikolai Bukharin and Aleksey Rykov, the former president of the Soviet of Peoples' Commissars. But lower ranks of the Party were also heavily affected by the purges: 110 out of 139 members of the Central Committee were either executed or sent to labour camps; of 1,966 delegates to the 17th Party Congress, 1,108 were caught up in the purges. Soon the Terror reached beyond the Party and spread to other parts of society and the state as well—artists, intellectuals, factory managers, *kolkhoz* directors, the secret police, or just ordinary citizens. By 1937, it led to a major purge of the army, in which over 30,000 officers were arrested and in which 2 out of 5 marshals, 13 out of 15 generals, and 62 out of 85 corps commanders were killed. The army was thus effectively in a state of paralysis when the German Wehrmacht started Operation Barbarossa and invaded the USSR in the dawn of 22 June 1941.

The attack came as an utter shock for Stalin, who had expected Hitler to adhere to their mutual pact from 1939. The Germans and their allies invaded with over five million troops, taking Soviet forces completely by surprise. They quickly advanced in three directions—north towards the Baltic and Leningrad, east towards Moscow, and south towards Kiev. By September, Kiev had fallen and Leningrad been put under siege. The cradle of the Bolshevik regime was supposed to be destroyed through a blockade, which eventually lasted for 900 days, starving and freezing to death over a million people under the most unimaginable circumstances. Moscow escaped occupation, when the first German advance was exhausted in December 1941 just a few miles away from the city's defences. In 1942, the Wehrmacht pushed further south towards the Volga and the Caucasus. It was stopped at Stalingrad and, after a fierce battle, which lasted from August until January 1943, was utterly defeated. The Soviet triumph at Stalingrad marked the beginning of the end of Hitler's regime. From 1943 onwards, the Red Army persistently moved west, taking all of Eastern Europe and occupying Berlin in April 1945. These military victories and the huge human toll which the USSR had paid—some twenty-eight million Soviet citizens were killed, almost half of all the victims of the Second World War—gave Stalin a strong position in the negotiations with the Allies about a European post-war order and eventually allowed him to extend the Soviet sphere of influence considerably.

Soviet victory in the 'Great Patriotic War', as it was called in reference to the 'Patriotic War' against Napoleon in 1812, was achieved through truly heroic efforts. In face of a foreign aggressor, the people united behind Stalin, who presented himself as successor of great Russian military leaders of past centuries. Resistance against the invaders gathered in the form of a partisan movement operating behind German lines. The economy was put on a war footing, with about 1,000 factories relocated further east and tank and ammunition production increased dramatically. Under the Lend-Lease programme, thousands of US planes, trucks, and jeeps came into the country, increasing the mobility of the Red Army. Morale was boosted by a revival of Russian patriotism and by enlisting the support of the Orthodox Church. Musicians, artists, and writers produced numerous works glorifying the defence of the motherland. They created a myth of heroic struggle and selfless sacrifice, which lasted for many decades and became one of the main focal points of Soviet post-war identity. Incidentally, at the height of the struggle for Stalingrad, plans were made for a new national anthem, as the 'Internationale' was deemed not patriotic enough anymore. Officially adopted in 1943, the anthem proclaimed that: 'United forever in friendship and labour, our mighty republics will ever endure. The great Soviet Union will live through the ages. The dream of a people their fortress secure.' While the lyrics have changed, the solemn and uplifting tune is still used today by the Russian Federation.

CONCLUSIONS

Between 1914 and 1945, Russia went through momentous changes and upheavals. It witnessed the collapse of one and the creation of another empire, both under extremely violent conditions. Building the Soviet Union and turning it from a political outcast in 1917 into a world power by 1945 entailed social engineering and human suffering on an unprecedented scale. New elites emerged as entire segments of society were purged, and millions had to change their ways of life. For those who survived, the gigantic projects of the Soviet state and the events of the Second World War often meant profound social, economic, and cultural adaptation. Yet the first socialist state in history was also an experimental stage on which ideas and dreams of social justice and equality as well as new forms of government and, indeed, civilization were enacted. As such, it provided an alternative model that was attractive to scores of underprivileged people, workers, intellectuals, and politicians all over Europe and in the rest of the world.

FURTHER READING

Acton, Edward, *Rethinking the Russian Revolution* (London, 1990).
Barber, John, and Mark Harrison, *The Soviet Home Front 1941–1945* (London and New York, 1991).

Conquest, Robert, *Harvest of Sorrow* (New York, 1986).

Figes, Orlando, *A People's Tragedy* (London, 1996).

Fitzpatrick, Sheila, *The Cultural Front* (Ithaca, NY, and London, 1992).

——, *Everyday Stalinism* (New York and Oxford, 1999).

——, *et al.* (eds.), *Russia in the Era of NEP* (Bloomington, 1991).

Gatrell, Peter, *Russia's First World War* (Harlow, 2005).

Getty, J. Arch, and Roberta Manning (eds.), *Stalinist Terror: New Perspectives* (Cambridge, 1993).

Jahn, Hubertus, *Patriotic Culture in Russia during World War I* (Ithaca, NY, and London, 1995).

Kelly, Catriona, and David Shepherd (eds.), *Constructing Russian Culture in the Age of Revolution: 1881–1940* (Oxford, 1998).

Kenez, Peter, *The Birth of the Propaganda State* (Cambridge, 1985).

Kotkin, Stephen, *Magnetic Mountain. Stalinism as a Civilization* (Berkeley, Calif., 1997).

Stites, Richard, *Revolutionary Dreams* (Oxford and New York, 1989).

——, *Russian Popular Culture* (Cambridge, 1992).

Ward, Chris, *Stalin's Russia* (London, 1993).

14

Europe and the League of Nations

Patricia Clavin

INTRODUCTION

'For days and weeks they have been crossing the oceans, and have covered hundreds and thousands of miles of the railways of Europe. The ports of the open seas and of the Mediterranean, the capitals of Western and Central Europe were their first gathering points. And now they are hastening towards Switzerland.' Published in 1932, these words from Max Beer's dramatic *A Journey to Geneva*, an account of the work of the League of Nations, demonstrates how the League provided the opportunity for its members to get to know the landscape of Europe as well as its people and the social, political, and economic challenges before it. The League of Nations was an international organization created after the First World War, intended 'to promote international co-operation and to achieve international peace and security', and was intimately associated with the foreign policy of US President Woodrow Wilson. It has been studied primarily within the context of international or global history.

Despite its global pretensions, in many ways the League was a very European institution located at the heart of Europe. Although sixty-one countries eventually joined (but not the United States), the League was dominated by European powers and their preoccupations: Britain and France provided its leadership while many of the permanent and non-permanent members of the Council of the League of Nations were European. Much of the League's work in the 1920s and 1930s was focused on Europe: the reconstruction of Central and Eastern Europe and its concern to protect ethnic minorities left vulnerable after the collapse of European Empires, and the redrawing of Central and Eastern European borders. Its work in the field of disarmament was, again, directed primarily by, and at, European powers. Even the League's social and physical space was European, meeting first in a series of converted hotels and after 1936 in the purpose-built Palais des

Nations in Geneva. So, too, were the League's official languages (French and English) as well as the habits that governed its diplomacy.

THE ORIGINS OF THE LEAGUE OF NATIONS

There was nothing inherently new in Wilson's proposal to form a 'general association of nations under specific covenants for the purpose of affording mutual guarantees of political independence and territorial integrity' as part of his 'Fourteen Points' that provided the basis for peace negotiations in the First World War. A variety of scholars, statesmen, and artists had got there before him, including the thirteenth-century Italian poet Dante Alighieri and the sixteenth-century Dutch humanist scholar Desiderius Erasmus. But it took the First World War and the pivotal role played by the United States in negotiating an end to the conflict to bring to fruition the plan for an organization 'to promote international co-operation and to achieve international peace and security', in the words of the League's founding charter. These high ideals were born of bitter experience of world war, and this 'international parliament' aspired to represent and to shape the interests of the whole world.

In the age of 'total war', generating war aims and presenting them to the general public was far more important than it had been in earlier conflicts. Of the combatants' leaders, it was Wilson alone who placed the creation of a League of Nations at the heart of war aims and his efforts to shape the peace settlement. In his imagination, such an organization would offer the opportunity for a flexible and healing peace settlement that the negotiating rooms of the Palace of Versailles could not.

The ideal which brought Wilson praise and damnation in equal measure was, first and foremost, his determination to create a new world order in which a 'peace of justice' could be fashioned. Wilson, like many of his countrymen and women, believed the war had revealed the bankruptcy of a European-style diplomacy centred on maintaining a balance of power through the use of bilateral alliances and secret treaties. The US President reasoned that agreements that focused on, in his words, 'mutual guarantees of political independence and territorial integrity' by all states and for all states were the best way to safeguard international peace. This was to become known as the principle of 'collective security'. At no point, however, did Wilson set out how such a system should be organized. He was even less specific as to what he meant by a further concept he believed should shape the peace settlements: 'self-determination', the right of nations (not, as it was widely interpreted, 'people') to choose their own government. The Fourteen Points made no mention of it, and it became a notion to be honoured more in the breach than in the observance in, for example, the German and Eastern peace settlements in 1919. Even darker episodes were to follow. Self-determination became the means by which Nazi Germany could claim *Lebensraum* in Czechoslovakia and

Poland in the 1930s, and by the start of the twenty-first century, its role in the African and Middle Eastern politics prompted critics of American foreign policy to call self-determination not so much a concept as a disease.

Ironically, the American Congress was less swayed by Wilsonianism during Wilson's presidency than in the time of Presidents Franklin Roosevelt, Harry Truman, or George W. Bush. In November 1919, the Senate refused to ratify the Covenant (constitution) of the League of Nations. Without American support the plans for collective security collapsed and, in rejecting the League, the USA also failed to ratify the Peace of Versailles.

There were other notable absentees from the League, most obviously Germany (which joined in 1926) and the USSR, which did not become a full member until 1934 but participated in its work in a number of ways before then. Leadership of the organization fell to the Europeans, notably to Great Britain and France, who also provided the lion's share of its financial and administrative resources: in 1928 Britain contributed over 10 per cent to the entire budget of the League (a third more than anyone else), with France paying just under 7 per cent of the total. Of its fifty-five members, the twenty-six European countries contributed around 65 per cent of the League's total budget. Among the smaller European powers, the Scandinavian countries made the largest payment, while beyond the European continent, India, China, and Japan were also significant contributors.

When it was inaugurated in 1920, three enormous tasks lay before the League: to build an institution that reflected the wide-ranging commitment to international cooperation articulated in the Covenant, and to provide aid and succour to the devastated European continent. The third task was to prove the most challenging: to preserve the peace treaties of Versailles with Germany, Saint-Germain-en-Laye with Austria, Neuilly with Bulgaria, Trianon with Hungary, and Sèvres with Turkey. While the original Covenant of the League of Nations aspired to 'elasticity and security' in international relations, without collective security France, in particular, resolutely maintained that the Paris deliberations had determined the status quo which could not and should not be changed. Although the League of Nations had not generated the peace treaties, it was now charged with upholding them. This was not a responsibility that could be wished away. As the Oxford Professor of Greek Studies and Chairman of the British wing of the League of Nations Union (an international supporters' club for the League) Gilbert Murray put it, to talk of 'an absolutely clean slate was mere moonshine. You cannot ever in human affairs have a clean slate. The work of the League will be to make the slate gradually cleaner.'

The problem was dramatically illustrated by the humanitarian crisis unfolding in Central and Eastern Europe in 1919. The colourful figure whose tanned, creased face with melancholy eyes came to represent the League's humanitarian mission was the Norwegian Arctic explorer Fridtjof Nansen. The 'Polar Bear', as he was affectionately called, was appointed the organization's High Commissioner for the repatriation of prisoners of war in 1920. By 1921, he and his three

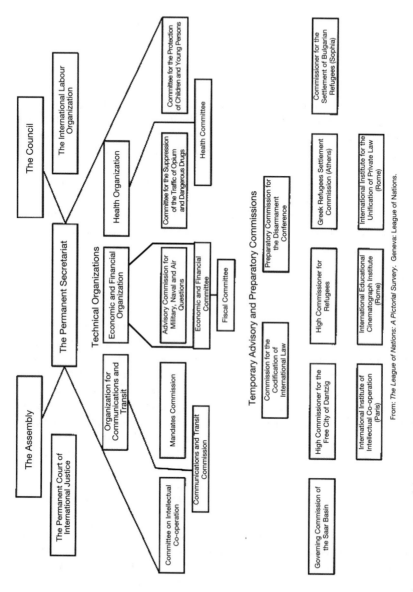

The Council

The Assembly

The Permanent Secretariat

The International Labour Organization

The Permanent Court of International Justice

Technical Organizations

Organization for Communications and Transit

Economic and Financial Organization

Health Organization

Committee on Intellectual Co-operation

Communications and Transit Commission

Mandates Commission

Advisory Commission for Military, Naval and Air Questions

Economic and Financial Committee

Fiscal Committee

Committee for the Suppression of the Traffic of Opium and Dangerous Drugs

Health Committee

Committee for the Protection of Children and Young Persons

Temporary Advisory and Preparatory Commissions

Commission for the Codification of International Law

Preparatory Commission for the Disarmament Conference

Governing Commission of the Saar Basin

High Commissioner for the Free City of Danzig

High Commissioner for Refugees

Greek Refugees Settlement Commission (Athens)

Commissioner for the Settlement of Bulgarian Refugees (Sophia)

International Institute of Intellectual Co-operation (Paris)

International Educational Cinematograph Institute (Rome)

International Institute for the Unification of Private Law (Rome)

From: *The League of Nations: A Pictorial Survey.* Geneva: League of Nations.

Figure 14.1. Organization of the League of Nations.

assistants, had returned 430,000 men from Russia back to their original homes in twenty-six countries (at the approximate cost of £1 per POW). The complexity of Nansen's legacy for the League is underlined by recent research which draws out, contrary to the League's enthusiastic publicity machine, Nansen's heavy dependence on other agencies for his relief work, notably the Red Cross, for the return of POWs.

Between 1921 and 1923, the Nansenhilfe (Nansen-aid) project supplied food first to POWs and then to starving Russians. Other agencies provided invaluable assistance, notably the Save the Children Fund, the Red Cross, and the Quaker Friends Committee. Everyone benefited from the arrangement. The charities provided vital in-field expertise, while Nansen and the League had important political contacts, notably links with the new Soviet government, that significantly facilitated the aid programme. Both sides contributed financial resources, although in their entirety the sums granted were dwarfed by the contribution of the American Relief Administration that made up around 80 per cent of the total aid programme.

The Norwegian also inaugurated the 'Nansen Passport' to enable 90,000 or so stateless refugees moving across Europe to have some claim to an identity. The multifaceted cooperation between League member states, officials of the League, non-governmental organizations, such as the Red Cross, and non-member states, like the USA and the USSR, that characterized the League's humanitarian intervention was also an important marker of how the League would operate once it was fully established.

In the 1930s, a series of League agencies continued Nansen's work. Between 1931 and 1938, the Nansen International Office served as the principal organization charged with refugee assistance and protection. Particular measures were taken to help German refugees after 1933, when the League appointed an Independent High Commissioner for Refugees coming from Germany. There were shortcomings in its humanitarian work, but the League, more than any other single international institution in the twentieth century, founded an international system to deal with the challenge posed to nation-states by refugees. It created a regime based on asylum, assistance, and burden-sharing that continues to this day.

THE INSTITUTION AND ITS LOCATION

There had never been a world body like the League before, although it gathered within it many practices from the past. In French, the League's title was the 'Société des Nations', and 'society' goes some way to capturing the diffuse structure of an institution which proved to be more creative and flexible in the face of the enormous challenges before it than its early critics recognized. By 1920, it had a constitution, a membership, and some notion of the items on its agenda. The institution itself, however, remained to be built. The task was put into the capable if unimaginative hands of Sir Eric Drummond, an Eton-and Oxford-educated British civil servant. Sharp of mind, but gentle in demeanour, Drummond's responsibility was generating and coordinating the organs of the League. This was no easy task. He was confronted by serious practical problems, such as trying to secure large enough financial contributions from the member states, appointing quality personnel to work for the League, and finding sufficient and appropriate office space in Geneva. The League's first home in 1920 was the drafty Victorian Hotel National in Geneva. As the number of its personnel grew and its coffers swelled, it finally moved in 1936 to a purpose-built Palais des Nations, set in a 45-hectare park with peacocks allowed to roam freely within the grounds. The sumptuous building and its magnificent setting in the Alps, complete with a view of Lake Geneva, and on a clear day the peak of Mont Blanc, perfectly matched the League's intention to build itself a home 'where statesmen could hold discussions, independently and easily in a calm atmosphere'. To socialist critics, however, the League's decorative setting was more appropriate for the lid of a biscuit tin than the environment in which to build a new world order. It confirmed their view that the League, as one British trade unionist put it, 'was built on a capitalist basis that reflected the accumulated power of militarism, nationalism and economics . . . it was a new Entente not a League of Peoples'.

While the League's finances and personnel had to be brought together from scratch, ideas about how to run an international organization were borrowed from both national governments and from the unofficial worldwide organizations, such as the Universal Postal Union, that had sprung up during the nineteenth century. The two main governing institutions of the League were the Council and the Assembly. Much like the Security Council and the General Assembly of today's United Nations, the Council was a much smaller body than the Assembly, meeting four times a year while the Assembly, notionally a parliament of the world's people, met once. While the world's 'great powers' dominated meetings of the Council and, to an extent, the Assembly, all member countries made an important contribution to the work of the secretariat, the international civil service that supported the work of the League.

It is hard to overestimate the importance of the secretariat. It sustained the League's work in five key areas: healthcare, economic and financial cooperation, the care and settlement of refugees, the treatment of minorities, and disarmament. It was made up of around 600 or so men and women from around the world whose work provided a continuity of expertise (many of its members worked for the League for at least a decade); and who served as powerful advocates for the League in its contacts with member governments, businesses, and financial institutions, and a whole host of other non-governmental agencies who were interested in questions of peace, healthcare, and economic stability. The secretariat also gave men and women from smaller countries the chance to have a louder international voice, and it is here, too, that significant numbers of women could be found. Typically impressive was the formidable Briton, Dame Rachel Crowdy, a veteran of the battlefields of France and Belgium, who was in charge of the League's work on 'Social Problems', particularly the illegal traffic of drugs and women.

Appreciating the work of the secretariat and the huge number of international experts it drafted in to support its work holds the key to recognizing the scale and variety of the League's contribution to European history. Not only did the League, for the first time, encourage sustained international debate on topics like children's welfare and international law between countries large and small, it also facilitated a host of new social and intellectual connections between governments and experts who worked in universities, charities, and a variety of other 'think-tanks'. E. H. Carr, author of the seminal *The Twenty-Years Crisis, 1919–1939* and no great fan of the League, believed that its experts were the only people who commanded genuine respect in the corridors of the League because 'diplomats were long regarded with suspicion in League of Nations circles, and it was considered the League would contribute greatly to the solution of international problems by taking them out of the hands of reactionary foreign offices'.

In its desire to be publicly accountable to the whole world, the League presented its civil servant representatives with an impossible circle to square. All its debates had to be held in public and the decisions taken by the Assembly and the Council had to be unanimously agreed. This became a serious handicap in many areas. On major issues, like disarmament, of course, large countries could ignore the League even if the Council and the Assembly were united in condemning their actions—as when Germany decided to rearm and leave the League in 1933—while the requirement for unanimity meant it was very difficult to put anything sensitive or contentious on the agenda. Pressing issues, like the causes of poverty, currency stabilization, or what to do when a serious infectious disease gripped a part of the world, often did not make it onto the League's public agenda for fear of the public repercussions. (All the reports published by the League also had to be agreed by their authors, which made for some spectacular fights in private.) It is hardly surprising that Drummond, alongside many other high-ranking League officials, became extremely fond of 'off-the-record' diplomacy.

PEACE: THE PRIMARY GOAL

The peace-keeping activities of the League followed three principal paths: acting as guardian over nominated regions and cities whose ownership was contested (the mandate territories and the Free City of Danzig); facilitating negotiations when national tempers flared to prevent countries from resorting to war; and facilitating disarmament that would ultimately rid the world of weapons that had brought such carnage and destruction in the First World War.

We still do not know too much about the history of the League's mandate system. What we do know is that the Mandates Commission was set up in

February 1921 with the expressed responsibility of studying annual reports from provinces placed in the 'mandated care' of nominated governments in the post-war treaties, and advising the Council as to conditions within the territories. We also know that, in keeping with the League's agenda as a whole, it was the League's, largely failing, efforts at direct peace-keeping, in mandate territories like Palestine, that most interested both the general public at the time and historians since. Far less studied is what would now be labelled the humanitarian agency of the League—the League, borrowing from the language of European imperialism, called it 'a sacred trust of civilization'. Yet it was precisely the enhancement and well-being of these less developed territories that the League cared most about.

A related concern was the League's protection of the Free City of Danzig which, in conceptual terms at least, came under the auspices of the Mandates and the League's Minorities Commission. This predominately German city was not incorporated into the nation of Poland that surrounded it after 1919. Danzig's citizens were assured protection under the League against discriminatory treatment. This provision of the Treaty of Versailles left the League caught between the danger of encouraging discontent and disloyalty by these minority groups, on the one hand, and the risk of permitting injustice, on the other hand. The League did not have sufficient power to manage the dilemma, for it could do little more than exert moral pressure on governments to ensure that the groups for which they were responsible were treated fairly. The only threat in the commission's arsenal was that any offending majority would be held up before the Council and the Assembly for criticism.

The problems for the League were amply illustrated in the case of Danzig where, in the 1920s, the League was called in to mediate disputes between the city's German majority and the Polish majority in the country as a whole. There was a League High Commissioner on the spot to help resolve fairly routine disputes about water management, for example. But his job took on an altogether more challenging and sinister dimension when the Nazi Party became the ruling majority in the city parliament, the Danzig Volkstag, which it then, matching the party's treatment of Germany's democratic institutions, dissolved in February 1935. The actions of the Nazi Party divided the city, and Sean Lester, the Irish High Commissioner and future General Secretary of the League, found himself inundated with petitions from Germans who were not Nazis and who were now being discriminated against—Jews, Catholics, Socialists, and Communists. Lester's presence in the city did give these groups the opportunity to voice their complaints about the Nazis internationally, and he was able to offer them some protection. The problem was that he had no power to force the Nazi Party to act constitutionally. This became crucial after 1936 when the political authority of the League was severely dented by events in Abyssinia. In 1919, the faith in democratic institutions that accompanied the creation of the League, the successor states in Europe, and the Free City of Danzig, meant that no one had anticipated it might be necessary to grant the High Commissioner special powers to act. After 1936 relations within the city and between the German and Polish governments rapidly began to deteriorate; the situation reflected the wider problems that were infecting European diplomatic relations. In the end, though, the increasingly belligerent tenor of European relations was more down to the behaviour of nation-states than shortcomings in the machinery of the League.

The covenant of the League contained a number of complex and detailed articles about how conflicts should be resolved through voluntary or forced arbitration between League members, as well as between a member and a non-member of the League. But these same articles were vague about how arbitration and agreements would be enforced; and this, of course, was the difficult bit. Early League successes in the field also gave little indication of the trouble that was to come in the crisis-ridden decade of the 1930s.

In the early years, the League chalked up some notable achievements in European peace-keeping. It succeeded in preventing war breaking out between Yugoslavia and Albania in 1921, and between Greece and Bulgaria in 1925. It also acted as mediator in a dispute over the Åland islands between Sweden and Lithuania, as well as resolving a quarrel over the city of Vilnius that was occupied by Poland after 1920 but claimed by Lithuania. These might sound like small beer, but in the past such squabbles often had culminated in war. From the beginning, frustrations with the post-war peace settlement dominated the League's work, but it did arbitrate a number of non-European disputes, notably the outbreak of hostilities between Bolivia and Paraguay in 1928.

The League was an uncomfortable international policeman, partly because it could only *recommend* a course of action, and partly because it responded to crises when hostilities were imminent or had already broken out. This responsive mode of peace-keeping brought some successes in the 1920s, but the record came to a dramatic end with the Japanese invasion of the Chinese province of Manchuria in 1931. This was a real shock for the League. Japan was a permanent member of the Council. Its foreign policy had been conciliatory in the 1920s and it had cooperated in the naval disarmament conferences of 1921 and 1930. While the Japanese military had opened hostilities against China without the direct support of the political authorities, the Japanese government went along with the military action and ultimately so did the League. It was only in February 1933, almost two years after military intervention, that the members of the League offered a unified response condemning the Japanese action, at which point the Japanese just walked out. (Although, interestingly, Japan retained representation on the League's committees and within the secretariat for a number of years afterwards.)

The fact that it was a non-European nation was the first to step out of line so dramatically, however, blinded no one to the fact that divisions within Europe were becoming the most serious threat to world peace. With Adolf Hitler as German Chancellor, German foreign policy became more openly revisionist, and German determination to revise the terms of the Versailles peace treaty, notably with the remilitarization of the Rhineland in 1936, posed a serious challenge to the League against which it appeared powerless. But it was Italian aggression in Abyssinia (Ethiopia) in 1935–6 that marked the League's most decisive failure in the field of international arbitration. Italy, another long-standing council member whose nationals were found widely employed in a number of League committees (including the leadership of the Economic Committee), ignored the vociferous protests against its illegal invasion and conquest. Trading sanctions were instituted by the League but were widely flouted by non-members, including the United States, and then even abandoned by the British, who initially had been the driving force behind them. By July 1936, sanctions had been dropped. The Ethiopian Emperor Hailie Selassie became the first head of state to address members of the League Assembly in person in a desperate and forlorn appeal for help to save his 'soldiers, women, children, cattle, rivers, lakes and pastures' from the 'deadly rain' of poison gas and conventional weapons showered upon them by Italian troops. Selassie's warning that 'it is us now, it will be you next' was soon borne out in German predatory behaviour in Central and Eastern Europe, and the escalation of Japanese military actions in China. By then, efforts at peace-keeping had moved away from the League altogether, returning to the bartering of great power diplomacy that had characterized the origins of the First World War.

Events in Abyssinia demonstrated that the League lacked the necessary power to defend the peace treaties on which the institution was founded; more crucially, in the wider context of the diplomacy of the period, it demonstrated that the leadership from Britain and France on which the League had relied since 1919 was lacking and there was no prospect of the other 'great' democratic power, the United States, stepping in any time soon to assist nations under increasing threat from the world's aggressors. It was clear that when it came to national security, the great powers sought to rely on their own resources to protect themselves rather than to develop a coherent notion of shared security. This left smaller countries especially vulnerable. Although they recognized that their national security depended as much on the actions of others as on themselves, regional and international cooperation here was patchy: whereas the Scandinavian countries worked together effectively, Central and Eastern European countries failed to cooperate on security issues both within and beyond the framework of the League.

The third prong of the League's peace-keeping efforts was in the field of disarmament. Here, too, the League was deprived of political support from key nation-states and, of course, the rising level of international armament in the inter-war period reflected both rising international tensions and, at the same time, gave the League a rising number of disputes to arbitrate. Disarmament offered the opportunity for the League to be proactive: it could seize the initiative for peace and prove its determination to fulfil the task set out in Article 8 of the Covenant, which stated that 'the maintenance of peace requires the reduction of national armaments to the lowest point consistent with safety', a responsibility echoed in all the arms reduction clauses of the European peace treaties.

Figure 14.2. League of Nations' Disarmament Conference, Geneva, 1932.

Disarmament was one of the most technically difficult and politically complex problems of the inter-war period. Between 1920 and 1925, the League adopted a broad approach to the issue, including attempts to regulate the global arms trade, to limit national military budgets and to link disarmament to new security regimes. By the early 1930s, generating a political will to disarm had turned into the altogether more difficult and urgent challenge of containing the burgeoning arms race in the heart of Europe. The problems were amply highlighted in the failure of the World Disarmament Conference, which finally opened in Geneva after ten years of preparation, on 2 February 1932. The first twelve months of its life were spent discussing trivialities; the second twelve months were given over to a painful death at the hands of 'great' power indifference, the inability and unwillingness of smaller countries to develop a united front, and most damaging of all, Nazi withdrawal from the Conference and the League in October 1933. The failure of the Disarmament Conference by June 1934 is the best studied of all the League's activities, and historians are largely united that the two most potent reasons for its failure were, first, that all countries adopted a very rigid approach to the negotiations. Given the number of countries involved, and the fact that each state advanced only its own national interest, reaching agreement was always likely to be extremely difficult. Secondly, and more damaging, was that no country involved in the process believed it had credible security guarantees, and it was precisely a sense of security that was needed to facilitate disarmament.

All the League's efforts met with very limited success. It failed to achieve either quantitative disarmament through substantial reductions in the military forces of nation-states, or qualitative disarmament, through the production and regulation of certain types of weapons. Average levels of military expenditure in the years between 1920 and 1938 remained at much the same level they had been in the period from 1870 to 1913. A lower than average level of spending on armaments in the 1920s was cancelled out by the significant increase in military expenditure from the mid-1930s onwards. In short, the League of Nations failed to contain the arms race of the 1930s after having only a limited impact on developments in the 1920s.

But it is possible to recast the League's record on disarmament, arguably the weakest aspect of its performance, as something more than a story of irredeemable failure. In subsequent decades, the disarmament negotiations were studied extensively, and in that process new approaches to peace-keeping emerged. Cooperation always operates in a historical context; the roots of any agreement lie in an earlier history of disagreement, and the very negative assessments of its work written between 1940 and 1980 became a prescriptive history widely consulted during disarmament negotiations in the Cold War.

The failure of disarmament negotiations also caused the League to think creatively about the underlying causes of international tension. It re-emphasized the importance of the League's economic, financial, social, and cultural work as a means to reshape the broader context in which debates about national security were framed. It is also worth reiterating that even the more recent historiography on the League's work on European disarmament often reads as a history of the international relations of nation-states; the League of Nations is treated merely as the venue in which they met. But these meetings generated a social and intellectual space in which social contacts were made and ideas exchanged. The task of implementing disarmament drew in representatives from every single member of the League of Nations, as well as from the most important non-member states. Significantly, for most of these countries, the same people tended to be assigned to deal with disarmament year after year. As a result, a group of individuals set themselves apart over time as the chief experts on disarmament. While some held very high public profiles, many remained almost unknown outside the committee rooms of Geneva. Prominent among them were a core of delegates from the European states, the most powerful and influential of whom were those representing the major powers.

For Britain, there was first and foremost the irrepressible Lord Robert Cecil, a Conservative cabinet minister, and one of the founders of the League itself. France was represented by the flamboyant Joseph Paul-Boncour, a socialist minister and president of the 'study commission' of the Conseil Superieur de la Défense Nationale. For Italy, there was the senator Carlo Schanzer and General Alberto de Marinis, who was first soldier and then senator and a member of almost every League disarmament committee. Germany was represented by the dour Reichstag deputy Count Johann von Bernstorff and the USSR the chubby and clever deputy commissar of foreign affairs Maxim Litvinoff. Equally, if not more, important to the intellectual vitality and credibility of the disarmament committees were representatives from smaller states. Two of the most prominent were the foreign minister of Czechoslovakia, Dr Edouard Beneš, and the Greek foreign minister, Nicolas Politis. Most forceful of all in pressing for action on disarmament were the Scandinavians, who were represented by the Swedish prime minister Karl Branting (until his death in 1925), and Christian Lange, the secretary general of the Inter-Parliamentary Union who represented Norway almost consistently from 1920 until his death in 1938. In recognition of their work for the League in support of disarmament and pacifism, they were awarded the 1921 Nobel Peace Prize.

Over the years, all these men acquired a deeper understanding of the challenges before Europe and the wider world when it came to disarmament, and the compromises and concessions that were needed if success was to be achieved. Their expertise was communicated to their respective governments as well as to the wider international community. But each delegate was powerfully constrained by the primary goal: to safeguard the security of their nation-state, at the expense of (rather than in conjunction with) others, an attitude that was a powerful manifestation of nationalist attitudes that were already strong in the 1920s and became overwhelming by the 1930s. Few men were able to distance themselves from the positions adopted by their governments. Lord Cecil was a witty exception, once retorting to an exasperated Foreign Office in London, 'had you desired merely a gramophone mouthpiece [in Geneva], you ought to have sent somebody else'.

The division of the secretariat concerned with disarmament similarly enjoyed a continuity of personnel and experience. It also became crucial to the collection and dissemination of information on armaments. This proved to be a deeply sensitive matter and the League was forced to abandon its plans to collect military data by a mandatory submission compiled annually by each country and, instead, resort to collecting information independently on each country from a variety of official and public sources. From 1924 onwards, the League published an *Armaments Year-Book*, regularly examining some sixty countries, as well as the *Statistical Year-Book of the Trade in Arms and Ammunition*, which contained information on the global arms trade. These series were essential, and sometimes the sole source of information to monitor changes in national armament levels, and the data on the military establishments of most countries (excluding on Germany) were fairly reliable.

This type of technical work was characteristic of League methods across all of its activities. In many ways it is a mistake to distinguish, as some writers have, between the 'political' and 'technical' aspects of the League's work, for each agency of the League, be it the Disarmament Organization, the Economic and Financial Organization, or the Health Organization, housed its own secretariat (or section) which coordinated the collection and dissemination of information, liaised with governments and non-governmental organizations, and sought to influence the overall agenda of the League. The League of Nation's Health Organization and the International Labour Organization are the best known of these technical agencies. They were also distinguished, like the Permanent Court of International Justice, by being largely independent of the intergovernmental work of the League, because they lacked an overarching intergovernmental committee.

The court is among the least known of the League's achievements; its foundation is usually credited to the United Nations, which absorbed it in 1946. In January 1922, nine judges and four deputy-judges, elected by the Assembly, convened in the Peace Palace at The Hague, the headquarters of the court. Its size, reputation, and authority grew, serving first as a source of legal advice for the League, but increasingly on cases presented to it by individual governments. Its judgement and impartiality were rarely questioned, and by 1939 nearly 600 international agreements contained a clause that referred to its jurisdiction, marking a considerable advance in the character and composition of international law.

The desire for wider intellectual exchange and cooperation was embodied in one of the most studied but least influential League institutions, the Committee of Intellectual Co-operation. Prior to and during the First World War, two pioneering Belgians, Henri Lafontaine and Paul Otlet, founded and maintained a Union of International Associations with the intent of fostering the culture of 'internationalism'. This organization, strongly supported by its government and by the powerful French Federation of Intellectual Workers, concerned with improving the condition of the 'intellectual workers' of the professions, demanded and secured League support for an intellectual agency designed to bring together teachers in schools and universities, and to exploit the hitherto untapped skills of historians, poets, scientists, and authors in the service of the League.

Significantly smaller than most divisions of the League and bereft of the funds necessary to have premises in Geneva (it was based in Paris), the Committee on Intellectual Co-operation's work comprised trying to foster international links between cultural and scientific institutes, between particular cultural industries, notably Europe's burgeoning film industries (institutes were set up in Paris and Rome) and between leading high-profile intellectuals. Figures as eminent and diverse as Marie Curie, Béla Bartók, Albert Einstein, and Thomas Mann were brought together under its aegis, in the Committee's words, to forge 'a true rapprochement between peoples'. The Committee's emphasis on the value of intellectual work to society and on selling the benefits of international cooperation to young people in particular, offered valuable lessons, especially to the project of European integration after the Second World War, but was insufficient to counter the potent political ideologies that came to dominate European history in the inter-war period. Ultimately, the League's contribution to European history lay in more concrete issues: promoting peace, health, and social and economic stability.

ECONOMIC AND FINANCIAL COOPERATION

What the Economic and Financial Organization (EFO) of the League lacked in glitz and glamour, it made up for in ambition and impact. EFO was the fastest growing, and largest, element of the League during the 1930s. It sought to improve people's lives through economic, social, and health initiatives, which were also seen as a means to promote political stability and peace in the longer term. Until recently, very little of its pioneering work was known, which is a pity given that EFO was the world's first intergovernmental organization dedicated to promoting economic and monetary cooperation.

When the League was founded in 1919, no real thought was given to economic and financial questions. This was not so much an oversight as a reflection of continued international tensions between the former Allied powers with regard to reparations and war debts. It reflected also the widespread conviction that there would be a quick return to the pre-war world economy, a world in which national governments played but the most minimal role. Where international cooperation was necessary, it was believed the lead should be taken by independent central banks of the world's major economies. Statesmen, bankers, and economists all feared the potential anarchy that might be unleashed by allowing the polyglot League into such a sensitive area of policy-making where one false move, so the reasoning went, had the potential to trigger financial and economic instability around the world.

But by 1920 the difficult economic environment in which nation-states found themselves quickly challenged these assumptions. In particular, the continued economic dislocation of Central Europe, the infectious problem of rising inflation, and the end of the wartime boom starkly illustrated that the European economy was not likely to right itself after the war without some kind of international cooperation. The League's response was to set up an Economic and Financial Section within the Secretariat of the League. The section's initial remit seemed innocuous enough: to collate economic statistics. In this form, the Economic and Financial Section had neither the authority nor the power to formulate policy recommendations (although its data often informed the policy choices of governments), it had little direct contact with governments, and certainly posed no threat to nation-states' determination to formulate and to implement economic and monetary policy as they saw fit.

Early on, however, officials of the Economic and Financial Section sought to extend their powers, pressing for the creation of an independent expert advisory committee on economic and financial questions to help the Assembly and Council and to fortify the role of the League in the world economy. Officials in EFO, one of the most proactive groups in the secretariat, argued for an expanded technical institution that would have the power to develop and to advocate particular policies to member and non-member states.

Events on the ground in Central and Eastern Europe supported this ambition. By 1922, the financial pressures of the First World War and post-war reconstruction-triggered inflationary pressures in Austria and Hungary had blown into a full hyper-inflationary crisis, with inflation running at a breathtaking 3,000 per cent. The states' financial and political resources were insufficient to cope and, faced with national bankruptcy, the Austrian Chancellor Ignaz Seipel approached the League for help. Austria received a loan equivalent to £26 million and, shortly afterwards, Hungary a loan of £10 million. In an unprecedented step, the League appointed a commissioner general to both nations, whose budgets effectively were placed under international control. Through the League's assistance, both currencies were stabilized, the countries' national budgets balanced, and their economies reconstructed. This was an impressive achievement. International confidence in Austria and Hungary returned and their economies subsequently grew. The League's aid had come at a price, however. The ethos of the gold standard, which underpinned the currencies' stabilization, meant that both countries endured high levels of taxation, low wages for public employees, and comparatively low levels of economic growth, so that during the 1920s they began to experience serious deflationary pressures. That said, the blame for these economic pressures should not be laid at the door of the League. The same 'gold standard' ethos dominated economic policy around the world in the 1920s, and to catastrophic effect during the Great Depression. Indeed, while in 1922–3 the League reflected current economic thinking, by the 1930s it had fostered new, creative approaches to the questions of economic cooperation.

The apparent success of its Central and Eastern European venture meant that by 1923 the League had established two separate elements that formed the heart of EFO: the Economic Committee and the Financial Committee. The most significant sign of the committees' growing importance, however, came in 1927 when the United States of America, the world's economic powerhouse, agreed to participate in its work. In 1927 and 1933 the Economic and Financial Organization supported two huge World Economic Conferences with participants from over sixty countries, alongside key non-governmental organizations (NGOs) like trade unions, employers' organizations, and economic think-tanks, attending to discuss an agenda that exceeded twenty-five pages. From a political perspective the conferences failed to produce any lasting commitment to, for example, reduce the rising levels of international protectionism. But the conferences did serve as important opportunities for nation-states, NGOs, big business, and financiers to develop an appreciation of the challenges before other nations and, more importantly in the long run, formulate ideas as to the value of, and the best means to effect, international cooperation.

EFO was guided by a number of particularly energetic, committed, and able civil servants. These included the first director of EFO until 1931, the Briton Arthur Salter, his compatriot Alexander Loveday, who became Director of the Financial Section in 1931, and the Italian Director of the Economic Section,

Pietro Stoppani, who defied Mussolini's demand in 1936 that he return to Rome. By the mid-1930s these two sections were by far the largest of any section of the League Secretariat, and they were supported by the path-breaking Economic Intelligence Service (EIS). This generated economic and financial data that to this day remain the most reliable source of material on the performance of the international economy in the inter-war period. It was the first time that statistics on this great a range of economic and financial materials were collated. EFO's publications included the *Statistical Yearbook of the League of Nations*, the *Monthly Bulletin of Statistics, Money and Banking*, the *Review of World Trade*, and the *World Economic Survey*, and many of these series were taken up after 1946 by the United Nations.

These compilations were supplemented by annual reports on the general economic situation published under the name of the general-secretary, many of which demonstrated EFO's growing preoccupation with the condition of European and world trade, as well as the health of the international economy more generally in the wake of the Great Depression. A further layer to EFO's work came from the special subcommittees. These examined a huge variety of issues and consisted of members from both the Economic and Financial Committees as well as specially appointed experts from universities, central banks, and assorted other financial and economic institutions. The list of officials and experts who worked for EFO at various points in its life reads like a 'Who Was Who' of the leading economists in the twentieth century. It includes highly respected contemporary economists, like the Austrian Gottfried Haberler (whose pioneering study on *Prosperity and Depression* was published under the auspices of the League in 1937), as well as men who were to become famous in later years, including the Dutch economists Jan Tinbergen and Tjalling Koopmans, and the Briton James Edward Meade (all three were awarded the Noble Prize for Economics), as well as future leaders of important economic institutions, including Per Jacobsen (a future director of the International Monetary Fund), and Jean Monnet, the architect of European Unity after the Second World War.

It is easy to dismiss the Economic and Financial Organization as a boring outfit, dedicated to producing weighty research tomes when a driven, hands-on approach to economic diplomacy was what was needed. But the political limits imposed on its work meant that EFO had to use 'technical' issues to encourage the nation-states to address contentious topics of foreign policy. During the 1930s, EFO sought to advance international cooperation on a range of pressing economic and financial issues—including the character and impact of clearing agreements, the viability of the gold standard, the ever-rising levels of international protectionism, the causes of the Great Depression, and the means by which another economic collapse might be averted. In EFO's mind, analysis was not divorced from practice. Rather it believed the better its analysis, the greater the chance of policy coordination between the world's great democracies. Its attitude was a statement of faith in the ultimate rationality of mankind.

In the wake of EFO's failed attempts to facilitate international cooperation on monetary questions, notably the operation of the gold standard in the Great Depression, the organization became particularly concerned with the condition of European and world trade. It was a preoccupation that came to shape the discourse on European reconstruction and unity after the Second World War. The topic was of more than academic interest. Trade offered a way to bridge three key areas of the League's work: first, it offered an economic route to tackle the growing tensions in European relations following the breakdown of the Disarmament Conference. Secondly, poor levels of international trade in the 1930s (having fallen by around 65 per cent of its value in 1929 and 25 per cent of its volume) were part of the reason why the world was struggling still to recover from the impact of the Great Depression. Thirdly, it offered a way of luring the United States into closer cooperation with the League of Nations. Loveday and Stoppani took their lead on trade protectionism from the overtures of US Secretary of State Cordell Hull regarding the planned Reciprocal Tariff Agreement Act (RTAA) made at the League-sponsored World Economic Conference of 1933. In 1934 the RTAA passed into law and by 1945 the United States had signed trade deals with twenty-nine countries, reducing the US tariff by nearly three-quarters. The RTAA is associated with the development of US trade with Latin America, but Hull had first hoped to use the RTAA to secure agreements with the European powers (the earliest target was Britain). It was only when these early hopes were dashed that Hull and the Departments of State and Commerce turned their attention to Latin and South America.

Between 1933 and 1936, EFO drafted a series of reports that explored the essential policy differences between countries still on the gold standard, some of which owed a lot of money to the United States in particular (France, Germany, the Benelux states, Switzerland, Poland, and other Eastern European states), on the one hand, and the countries who had left gold (notably Britain, the Dominions, the Scandinavian states, and the USA) on the other. Central to the initiative was Washington's new commitment to bilateral and ultimately multilateral trade reductions based on the most-favoured-nation clause and 10 per cent tariff reductions.

The initiative went to the heart of much current thinking about the relationship between the Great Depression and rising tensions in international relations after 1931. The economic collapse had underlined the importance of economic stability to democracy in Central and Eastern Europe and the interdependence of nations. Economic bargains and deals entered diplomacy in a more calculated fashion than ever before as Britain and the United States came to believe that some form of 'economic appeasement'—providing Germany with economic concessions and economic satellites of its own—might work to assuage Hitler's expansionism. (It was a strategy particularly favoured by those bankers and industrialists who invested and traded with the 'Axis' Powers.) The problem was that Hitler, Mussolini, and the Japanese nationalists had yoked their economies to the service of their war ambitions. No matter how profitable the trading concessions on offer, Hitler and his cohorts were pledged to political annexation. Opening up their economies to the outside ran counter to this aim.

In 1936 and 1937, the League proposed a five-power conference (Britain, France, the United States, Germany, and Italy) to negotiate an ambitious, all-embracing economic and financial agreement as a prelude to a political settlement. Britain and the USA, the countries with the most powerful currencies and the least economic and financial (but not political) constraints, should take the first step by agreeing to stabilize their currencies for a fixed period of time, while the Gold Bloc countries (Germany and Italy) would devalue their currencies to relieve the deflationary pressures on their economies. The next step was for Britain and the United States to extend debt, credit, and trade concessions to Germany, Italy, and the smaller countries of Central and South-Eastern Europe to encourage them to abandon their extensive network of currency and trade controls, thereby reintegrating them into the international economy.

EFO argued it was the ideal body to carry through such an initiative for, if it were unsuccessful, the governments in Paris, London, and Washington would not be held responsible, thereby avoiding any unnecessary embarrassment or domestic opposition that might result. Older, negative assessments of the League's attempts at economic appeasement have failed to appreciate the organization's trenchant condemnation of German economic nationalism in particular and that a key element in the League's strategy was an attempt to reconcile the differences in British, French, and American monetary and commercial policies.

Much to the League and America's frustration, however, Britain, France, and, less surprisingly, Germany and Italy rejected the League's proposals. EFO officials knew it was always unlikely that Germany and Italy would abandon their economic nationalism, but British and French refusal to lower their tariffs came as a huge disappointment. (Signs of disunity among the leading democracies, by contrast, hugely encouraged the Axis Powers.) It was not all doom and gloom, however. In 1936 there was a new currency agreement signed between France, Britain, and the United States, which helped France to manage the devaluation of the franc and to which, behind the scenes, EFO had made an important contribution. But that was all. Mere cajoling by the secretariat simply was not enough to effect progress. The EFO secretariat had no power other than reason to secure cooperation, and American support at this stage was not enough in the face of French indifference and strong British opposition—an opposition that throws into question the dominance with which Britain is usually credited over the League. The British government certainly were in no doubt as to US support for the League initiative. But, as a Foreign Office memorandum put it in 1938, trade liberalization 'is not a promising line of advance . . . although its [the League's] economic activities receives a considerable measure of collaboration from some non-member states' (i.e. the United States). Britain was strongly of the opinion that trade liberalization would bring neither economic gain for

Britain nor do much to meet the demands of the Germans and Italians. Although EFO's efforts did not revolutionize the situation of the League in the 1930s, they did make a contribution to the creation of organizations intended to coordinate economic and financial policy, independently of the United Nations, in the Bretton Woods agreements of 1944. This time economic and financial concerns were put top of the agenda for post-war planning, rather than developed as an afterthought.

These obstacles left EFO feeling deeply frustrated by the failure of nation-states to support its work. It was a sentiment widely shared in the League. In EFO, it prompted attempts after 1937 to reform and uncouple itself from the League and become an independent body for the coordination of economic and financial policy. The Bruce Report of 1939 called for an independent EFO Central Committee and, although the outbreak of war put paid to this initiative, its findings were echoed in the Bretton Woods agreement that established new independent financial and economic organizations.

THE 'WELFARE' AGENDA

As we have seen from the work of EFO, the practical or, as the League called it, technical aspects of its agenda were part and parcel of efforts to shape the wider social, economic, and cultural context of human affairs in the cause of peace. It was also in these areas that some nations assumed greater independence in international relations. Poland, for example, took a leading role in the Health Organization (LNHO), while Canada was a driving force in the Child Welfare Committee. The League marked a coming of age for countries that were formerly part of empires. The Dominion powers were initially viewed with resentment by other nations who saw them as adjuncts of Britain. In the technical committees, this perspective soon changed. Ireland, too, cut its foreign-policy teeth at the League, and by the end of its history provided the final general secretary, the former journalist and enthusiastic angler Sean Lester.

The work of the Health Organization and the ILO also illustrated the wider tendencies in European healthcare in the inter-war period towards the rigorous application of scientific principles, shared standards, and the professionalization of health and social care. A dynamic and imaginative medical health director, the Polish bacteriologist and public health administrator Ludwik Rajachman, led the Health Organization from 1921 to 1938. His leadership was not free from controversy thanks to his links with the USSR in the 1930s, his anti-fascism, and his ties to the Spanish Popular Front, all of which infuriated the right-wing French Secretary General Joseph Avenol who took office in June 1933. But in the LNHO, Rajachman was an inspirational figure. He generated an *esprit de corps* which enabled the organization's work far to exceed the resources at its disposal.

It is naïve to assume that the LNHO's work in the field of international healthcare in the inter-war period was uncontested. But the LNHO, more than any other of its rivals in the field of international healthcare in the inter-war period, notably the International Committee of the Red Cross, generated, coordinated, and sustained an elite network of biomedical and healthcare specialists who wanted to alleviate human suffering by reducing, if not eliminating, disease. Their perspective reflected the new confidence in an agreed body of scientific research about aetiology (the causes and origin of diseases) and epidemiology (the treatment of epidemics), and the physiological conditions and socio-economic factors contributing to human illness. In this latter respect, of course, the Health Organization's work dovetailed with programmes launched and administered by other elements of the League, notably the Economic and Financial Organization and the International Labour Organization.

Summarizing the LNHO's achievements can mask the rich variety of the League's work, the degree to which each of its technical organizations had a distinct ethos, and its varied ties to different non-governmental and governmental organizations where culture and national preoccupations still played a role. That said, a crude listing of the LNHO's achievements draws out its path-breaking and positive contribution to European history both in the inter-war period and to the World Health Organization, which it effectively became in 1948 by merging with a number of more specialized health organizations like the Office International d'Hygiene Publique. Like EFO, the LNHO pioneered the generation and circulation of systematically generated data: it created the Service of Epidemiology Intelligence and Public Health Statistics in Geneva, and developed a system to communicate reports of epidemic diseases by telegraph and radio. A particularly significant achievement was the establishment of an epidemiological database more or less from scratch because it required health officials in different countries to employ a standard nomenclature, agree to uniform reporting methods, and a standardized report form. The database covered Europe first, although, in time, it came to cover the whole world.

The LNHO set up and directed a series of expert committees, technical commissions, and specialized conferences that studied specific diseases. At an LNHO conference held in 1926 countries agreed to report outbreaks of typhus, small pox, cholera, and yellow fever. The Health Organization also acted on scientific discoveries, establishing international cooperation on a host of topics relating to biomedical and health administration, research, and education. League health officials were keen not just to set the standards for good science and circulate their findings; they also wanted to get their hands dirty and created a laboratory-based programme that established international standards for numerous biological agents, including antitoxins, sera, vaccines, hormones, and vitamins. Laboratories in Copenhagen and London, directed by Thorvald Madsen and Henry Dale respectively, coordinated trials and evaluations of drugs around the world. By 1935, an international convention had been signed and several vaccines for diphtheria, tetanus, and tuberculosis were standardized. By the late 1930s, when its international reputation was at its lowest ebb, at its own expense the League was supplying sample standards to many countries around the world. It also furnished technical assistance to governments who needed help in suppressing epidemics, evaluating their nations' health, training personnel, and reorganizing and developing their healthcare administrations. The Balkans were among the first and most consistent recipients of this aid. In the immediate aftermath of the First World War, the League's Epidemic Commission's work in Greece, Austria, Romania, Hungary, Czechoslovakia, the Ukraine, Latvia, Poland, and the USSR (under LNHO's auspices the latter two countries signed a series of sanitary conventions in 1922) helped to contain a serious typhus epidemic in Eastern Europe. Despite widespread fears, Western Europe remained largely unaffected by the outbreak, thanks to the League's efforts at containment.

Countries also drew on the LNHO's expertise as to how best to construct sewerage systems and the League, in general, did a great deal to expand the boundaries of social medicine by initiating more studies than ever before on how social and natural environments affect public health. Its work included studies of nutrition, physical education, the purity of water and milk supplies, housing, rural hygiene, and medical insurance. Indeed, its interpretation of rural hygiene was a broad one, and in the 1930s the Health Organization organized several pan-European conferences on the topic. As in other aspects of the League's work, communication was central to its effectiveness: it sought to socialize health officials into a shared value system and to diffuse modern practice from advanced to less advanced healthcare administrations. It was an ambition that underpinned so much of the League's work and, perhaps, was easier to realize in the field of healthcare than elsewhere because political and cultural concerns were less apparent; they were by no means absent, however, as was clear by the LNHO's careful avoidance of issues such as birth control. The religious and political persuasions of the League's directors undoubtedly shaped its stance: although European Roman Catholics were only beginning to formulate a hostile position towards contraception in the 1930s, Drummond's conversion to Catholicism and the conservative sympathies of his successor Avenol and others like him acted as a brake on any discussion as to whether condoms should be promoted as an effective barrier to sexually transmitted disease.

The International Labour Organization (ILO), a similarly semi-detached organization from the League to the LNHO, also had an interest in birth control: the French director of the ILO, Albert Thomas, took a prominent role at the World Population Congress held in Geneva in 1927 which inaugurated the International Union on Population. But this meeting failed to endorse birth control, opting instead to promote welfare benefits and selective immigration controls. Like the LNHO, the ILO, too, remained enigmatically silent on birth control and, as a whole, the League's position on the issue was closer to the pro-natalist ethos of the French government than that of (largely Protestant) European countries where eugenic ideas made a greater impact.

The League was comparatively untouched by eugenic thinking, which is somewhat surprising given that its policies were strongly influenced by the same trends that promoted eugenics: positivist notions of scientific expertise supporting the notion the world could be reshaped by biologically trained experts dictating the 'right' social policy. Where the League differed, however, was in its conviction that environment, rather than crude genetics, was the key to society's growth and well-being.

In the 1930s, the LNHO and the ILO joined forces in a series of studies and conferences exploring how health was shaped by diet, housing, and economic conditions, and the relationship between public health and sickness insurance, and for both agencies nutrition was an important focus. They were also concerned with the impact of economic depression and unemployment on public health, and poverty's especially harmful effects on children and young people. The *Nutrition Report of the League of Nations* (1937) was a considerable public success. The semi-detached status of the ILO enabled it to have a broader membership than the League: Germany and Austria were members as early as 1920, it had considerable informal contacts to the USSR throughout the 1920s, and the United States joined officially in 1934, although it had been collaborating with the ILO before then. As in other agencies of the League, the ILO's work was highly technocratic, with a great deal of effort going into the collection of economic and labour statistics that would provide the basis for conventions on industrial and welfare legislation.

The initial concerns of the ILO were the protection of women and children, and securing an eight-hour working day. It also campaigned for women to have six weeks of paid maternity leave before and after birth, and a further three months' paid leave in case of illness. In keeping with the gendered policies that shaped welfare legislation in advanced industrial countries in Europe, the ILO fought for women to be excluded from dangerous work, especially when they were pregnant. The ILO also launched industry-specific campaigns, such as its efforts to ban the use of highly toxic white phosphorous in the manufacturing of matches and pottery. By 1935, the ILO had produced an accessible compendium of technical diseases which was, and has remained, an international standard work of reference, *The Encyclopaedia of Occupational Health* (currently in its fourth edition). By 1939, this work had facilitated agreement on sixty-seven different conventions and made an additional sixty-six recommendations to member states and, once a convention had been agreed, member states were obliged to consider acting on it within a year. The idea was that all countries would develop standard welfare legislation so that no unfair economic competition would result from members flouting the conventions. This was easier said than done, especially given the trying economic conditions of the inter-war period. For the new states of Central and Eastern Europe, the ILO's work offered useful guidelines for framing their social legislation, but the conventions were not so easily translated into legislation in European countries with more established welfare states. Britain, for example, refused to ratify the convention on the eight-hour working day and became the excuse for other countries, notably Italy and Latvia, also to delay ratification.

There were limits to the ILO's success. First, its recommendations were indeed Eurocentric: many of its policies were inappropriate for non-European and non-industrial states, reflecting the interest of its principal authors. Secondly, as with other elements of the League's work, the emphasis on consensus and a scientific, technical approach to every problem meant the pace of work was deliberate and could be frustrated by technical as well as political obstacles. The scientific burden of proof is a demanding one, and the ILO was slow to respond to new occupational diseases like asbestosis. Potential political objections to its agenda meant the ILO shied away from drawing out the broader socio-economic perspective of its research and publications on occupational hygiene that were such a striking feature of nineteenth-century studies of the topic, and neglected new advances in the field of the industrial psychology of the time that emphasized the dangers of fatigue and stress at work. It is possible, however, to view some of these limitations in a positive light given the damaging intrusion of biological and interventionist forms of social medicine on civil society in some European countries, notably Germany, which became subordinated to medicalized control.

A wider failure of the League was its inability to move the discussion of welfare on to a broader consideration of the causes of poverty and disease. But this was not so much a failing of the Health Organization and the ILO as of the Economic and Financial Organization, which had attempted to address the problem (Weindling's otherwise excellent work on the League's health programme has failed to consider EFO's role), and, more significantly, national governments which did not want the League to encroach into this area.

The Social Committe of the League found itself more confined by the national priorities of member governments than the ILO and the LNHO. Its 1919 remit was tightly focused: the welfare of women and children and the traffic of opium and other dangerous drugs. Led by Dame Rachel Crowdy, women almost exclusively staffed the Social Section, a decision taken very consciously by the League's founders in keeping with the notion that women had a special capacity as actors in the social field. (The trend was mirrored in the gendered construction of European welfare states in the inter-war period.) Prominent European feminists and social reformers were among the politicians and civil servants who came to work with the Social Section and the Assembly's Fifth Committee responsible for social questions. Among the most influential in their home countries as well as in the Social Committee were the German socialist politician and feminist journalist Dr Gertrud Baümer, Alexandra Kollantai, the commissar for social welfare in the USSR, the feminist French war heroine and leading pacifist, Germaine Malaterre-Sellier, and the feminist social reformer and university MP Eleanor Rathbone from Britain.

The Social Section was entrusted with monitoring and building on agreements signed before the First World War regarding the 'traffic in women and children'. Its first achievement was to agree traffickers should be punished and to raise the age of consent to marriage to 21. It also promoted policies intended to protect women and child migrants, including the supervision of 'employment agencies' recruiting women. As in the early twenty-first century, this meant primarily attempting to monitor the procurement of women in Central and Eastern Europe to be shipped as 'white slaves' to Western Europe. Although the League was initially nervous of addressing the topic of state regulation of prostitution and its treatment in law more generally, by the end of the 1930s it had drafted a convention for the punishment of persons who exploited the prostitution of others. The measure was very important in the field of international law for it marked the shift away from the control of traffic across borders to punitive measures to be taken against those exploiting prostitutes in their own countries. The Convention on White Slavery was a landmark step in European history, helping to reshape the legal treatment of prostitutes within European countries. It demonstrated the international community was concerned about the treatment of prostitutes within their own countries as well as their movement across national frontiers.

In many ways, the Social Section's work was conceived as an issue of human rights. It focused on measures to protect women from exploitation that, in certain instances, could take on a strongly moral tone, with some campaigners lobbying the League about the need to 'protect innocent girls' and to 'reclaim fallen women'. But it also meant that one of the important roles of the Social Section and the intergovernmental committee was to ensure that the member states did not go so far in their efforts to 'protect' women as to unduly restrict the rights of women and prostitutes. Proposals quashed by the League included calls that women alone be allowed to travel only in specified circumstances, and that underage girls travelling alone should carry certificates attesting to their good conduct and moral character.

The issue of child welfare proved more problematic for the Social Section as it overlapped with the concerns of the LNHO with healthcare and the ILO with employment. But the issue also ran foul of powerful nation-states, notably Britain, who argued, as British foreign secretary Austen Chamberlain put it in 1926, that 'child welfare is not primarily a matter for international action'. As in other areas of the League's work, the Social Section found it difficult to move on to the constructive side of child welfare and focused primarily on the rights and protection of vulnerable groups. It commissioned various studies on fostering (then called boarding out), juvenile offenders, and child neglect. The Child Welfare Committee, at the urging of Eleanor Rathbone, investigated the relationship between family allowances and the birth rate, child mortality, and the physical and moral well-being of children. It came out in favour of family allowances as a means of making it possible for 'parents adequately to discharge their responsibilities towards their families'. But as with the Health Organization and the ILO, the shadow of pro-natalism also hung over its work on child welfare and it fought shy of any direct discussion of sex education.

In keeping with the general reorientation of the League's work after 1936, the Social Section, too, was brought into a general reconsideration of the League's technical organs. There was a new demand for integrative health programmes that fostered collaborative projects between the LNHO, the ILO, and the Social Committee. There was a keen interest in linking social work to the wider economic sphere and to focus on the needs of the 'normal' child, but as political interest in the League's social work increased, the important expert (usually female) voices that had been so valuable in the 1920s were gradually silenced. A broader approach to social welfare finally was also apparent in the way that all three agencies now worked more closely together. Equally striking was these organizations' emphasis on the need to involve government social services in their work; the cooperation with voluntary organizations was no longer considered sufficient. At the same time, rising nationalism and the rhetoric of war reinforced the view of many member states that child welfare was a matter primarily of domestic concern. As a result the League's work in this area remained largely confined to the exchange of information and expertise that shaped national policy by indirect routes. Its more measurable achievement lay in the field of international law, where many of the LN social committee's findings on the treatment of juvenile offenders, the age of consent and marriage, and foster placement all became the subjects of human rights conventions.

Of all the technical committees of the League, the Committee on Transport produced the most measurable and tangible outcomes. As in other aspects of the League's technical work, international cooperation on this topic had begun prior to the First World War, but the coordination of international conventions governing transport was greatly facilitated and eased by the advent of the League. Under League auspices, major conferences were held in Barcelona in 1921 and Geneva in 1923 that agreed conventions for the International Regime governing Maritime Ports and Railways. As modes of transport changed, so too did the League's focus: in 1931 it drew up a Convention on the Unification of Road Signals. Other aspects of the Transport Section's work, under the direction of Frenchman Robert Hass, were more low-key, but no less effective. Further agreements were signed as to the procedures governing the issue of passports and visas, and regulations on the passage of road traffic and electric power across national frontiers. These were achievements which would be appreciated only in their absence: chaos on the railways, on the roads, and in the ports; disputes over power supplies; and frustration in embassies and legations that, likely as not, would have led to military engagement of some kind.

THE LEAGUE OF NATIONS AT WAR AND IN PIECES

In the inter-war period, the League of Nations served as both an actor and a stage for the drama of international relations. With the outbreak of the war in Europe in 1939, it found itself confined to the wings but was not, contrary to Avenol's wish, consigned to the role of audience. These were the darkest days of the League. It had failed to avert war and bitter infighting broke out over what it should do next. Avenol declared publicly his anxiety that the League retain its neutrality in the war. But this publicly stated conviction was undermined by some highly contentious actions, including the expulsion of the USSR from the League after the invasion of Finland (neither Germany nor Italy had been expelled), and Avenol's attempts to build bridges to the new Vichy government in France. His Greek deputy, Thanassis Aghides, branded him a 'crook'. There was no love lost, either, between Avenol and his successor as general secretary in August 1940, Sean Lester, who described him as 'a pompous self-opinionated creature' who was plotting with France's enemies before the country had accepted defeat 'and the blood of his massacred countrymen was cold'.

Although Avenol was banished in disgrace, the League's sense of intellectual isolation and physical diminution—in December 1939 the 'Axe Committee' sacked over 50 per cent of the League's staff—was reinforced in July 1940 when Italy declared war on Britain and France. Geneva was now almost entirely cut off from the free world. The only way out was through the unoccupied zone of France, and then through Spain to Lisbon, a route which the Axis Powers could bring under their control at any moment. They did so one month later, forcing back one League delegation that was trying to leave the continent. Support from many member states also evaporated, and Switzerland, too, did its best to ignore the League to safeguard its badge as a neutral. In 1940, Britain was rare in urging the institution to keep its flag flying for 'its moral and political significance'.

Ironically, rescue came from the nation that had abandoned the League at its birth: the United States. In 1940, America and Canada took in what became the League's greatest legacy, its technical institutions. The economic and social organizations were of particular interest. The Economic and Financial Organization was quartered in the Institute for Advanced Study in Princeton, a portion of the Social Section was based in Washington, DC, while the International Labour Organization moved lock, stock, and barrel to Montreal.

The key to the League's impact on the post-war order was the range of its personal contacts, and its emphasis on the primacy of social and economic considerations in post-war reconstruction. In 1941, the ILO published the details of these codes in a weighty tome (two kilos in weight to be precise), along with a lengthy appendix addressing the appropriate standards of social policy, with the explicit intention of shaping debate on post-war reconstruction. The book's opening words chimed precisely with the central motif of President Roosevelt's post-war planning: that 'the most striking contrast between the discussion of post-war reconstruction which is taking place today and the discussions on the same subject which took place a quarter of a century ago is the shift of emphasis from a mainly political conception of the problem of world order to an essentially social and economic conception'.

The League's influence on the planning for the post-war world remained largely hidden from view, primarily because no one wanted to associate the new United Nations with the 'failed' League of Nations: when well-known League officials met with American planners at large, public gatherings, they were urged to enter the building through the tradesmen's entrance to avoid unwanted attention from the press. The problem was less acute for the semi-detached technical organizations, such as the International Labour Organization and the League's Health Organization. Their expertise was absorbed directly into the United Nations Economic and Social Council (UNESCO) and the World Health Organization. It was more acute for members of the Economic and Financial Organization, who were more intimately connected with the political work of the League. However, it was precisely the range of EFO's governmental and non-governmental contacts that gave it the opportunity to pass on its expertise on economic and financial policy. Internationalism (in other words intergovernmentalism) and transnationalism provided the locus for change in the *longue durée*.

Two themes stand out in the widely circulated and consulted EFO publications that shaped both European reconstruction and European economic integration. They were clearly articulated in two of the most important reports written by EFO during the war: *Economic Stability in the Post-War World* (1945) and *The Transition from War to Peace Economy* (1943). The first theme was that it was crucial for nations to exchange information on economic, financial, and social issues, and the second was that planning and coordination should be conducted with the long term in mind. These elements had been noticeably and catastrophically absent during the hyper-inflation of the 1920s and the Great Depression. True, the Economic and Financial Organization's statistical work on the contribution of business cycles to economic stability was out of step with the appeal of Keynesian economics, which suggested ways in which shocks to the economy could be neutralized nationally by a government taking appropriate fiscal measures. But the League's emphasis on the importance of international cooperation on trade as a means to foster political reconciliation and economic growth was enshrined in both the General Agreement on Tariffs and Trade signed in 1947, and, much more significantly from Europe's perspective, in ideas underpinning European unity enshrined in institutions of which the European Coal and Steel Community was but the first.

When it came to the challenges facing those charged with effecting European reconstruction in the short term, the European economic elite employed by EFO also made an important contribution. They played a crucial role in determining the agenda and materials for the United Nations Relief and Rehabilitation Administration and in the creation of the United Nations Food and Agriculture Organization. A key theme of the League's work here was that the only means by which European reconstruction could be successfully effected at the end of the war was through a real and substantial transfer of resources from the United States to Europe. The League was ahead of its time, for this transfer to Europe came only with the European Recovery Programme of 1947. Interestingly, the argument was made on moral as well as practical grounds for, as *The Transition from War to Peace Economy* put it, peace-makers should make 'the fullest possible use . . . of the resources of production, human and material, of the skill and enterprise of the individual . . . so as to attain and maintain in all countries a stable economy and rising standards of living'.

The rhetoric demonstrated the League had come of age, reflecting a truly universal and genuinely global perspective. Its concern that the world's 'productive resources are used to meet the physiological needs of all classes of population, that men and women's education needs are met, and that society distribute the risk to the individual of any economic as far as possible' was loudly and resoundingly echoed in the plethora of international and regional organizations that emerged after the Second World War. While the League slid into oblivion, these objectives were articulated as the central goals of national and international efforts of European reconstruction and integration. The network created by the League lived on into the period of European reconstruction and beyond.

FURTHER READING

Burns, Michael, 'Disturbed Spirits: Minority Rights and New World Orders, 1919 and the 1990s', in S. F. Wells, Jr., and P. B. Smith (eds.), *New European Orders, 1919 and 1991* (Washington, DC, 1996)

Clavin, Patricia, and Jens-Wilhelm Wessels, 'Understanding the Work of the Economic and Financial Organisation of the League of Nations', *Contemporary European History*, 14/4 (2005), 465–92.

Cooper, John Milton, *Breaking the Heart of the World: Woodrow Wilson and the Fight for the League of Nations* (Cambridge, 2001).

Crozier, Andrew J., 'The Establishment of the Mandates System, 1919–1925: Some Problems Created by the Paris Peace Conference', *Journal of Contemporary History*, 14 (1979), 483–514.

Dinstein, Yoram (ed.), *The Protection of Minorities and Human Rights* (London, 1992).

Dunbabin, J. P., 'The League of Nations' Place in the International System', *History*, 78 (1993), 421–42.

Fink, Carole, 'The League of Nations and the Minorities Question', *World Affairs*, 157 (1995), 197–205.

Frentz, Christian Raitz von, *A Lesson Forgotten: Minority Protection under the League of Nations: The Case of the German Minority in Poland, 1920–1934* (New York, 1999).

Henig, Ruth, 'New Diplomacy and Old: A Reassessment of British Conceptions of a League of Nations, 1918–1920', in M. Dockrill and J. Fisher (eds.), *The Paris Peace Conference, 1919: Peace Without Victory?* (Basingstoke, 2001).

League of Nations, *The League of Nations: A Survey, a Directory and Who's Who* (London, 1929).

Mazower, Mark, 'Minorities and the League of Nations in Interwar Europe', *Daedalus*, 126 (1997).

Metzger, Barbara, 'The League of Nations and Human Rights: From Practice to Theory', Ph.D. thesis, Cambridge University, 2001.

Ostrower, Gary, *Collective Insecurity: The United States and the League of Nations during the Early Thirties* (Lewisburg, Penn., and London, 1979).

—— , *The League of Nations from 1919 to 1929* (Garden City Park, NY, 1995).

Scott, George, *The Rise and Fall of the League of Nations* (London, 1973).

Skran, Claudena M., *Refugees in Inter-War Europe: The Emergence of a Regime* (Oxford, 1995).

Steiner, Zara, *The Lights that Failed. European International History, 1919–1933* (Oxford, 2005).

Weindling, Paul (ed.), *International Health Organisations and Movements, 1918–1939* (Cambridge, 1995).

15

Europe and the Wider World

Nicholas Doumanis

INTRODUCTION

It could be argued that Eurocentrism, the notion that anything of historical significance has been obtained from Europe (or the West), has been one of the most insidious and distorting influences on modern historiography. Historians of Asia and Africa have long bewailed its effects, which marginalize the great bulk of humanity by privileging the stories and achievements of Britain, Western Europe, and, by extension, North America. And no phase of modern European history is more tainted by Eurocentrism than the period 1914–45.

From an international history perspective, the period is seen as the decadent aftermath of Europe's golden era of global domination. American refusal to fill the vacuum after the First World War left Europe's surviving (albeit diminished) great powers clinging precariously to global power by default. In terms of colonial or imperial history, the period witnessed colonialism's consolidation *as well as* the beginnings of its dissolution. Transitory rather than transitional, the period lacks distinction.

In most accounts of 1914–45, the rest of the world, with the important exception of Japan and the United States, is a passive realm that is routinely ignored or mentioned only in passing. Occasionally, the absence is noted and defended. In his masterly synthesis *Europe since 1870* (1976), James Joll justified his exclusive attention to European affairs for the inter-war chapters on the grounds that, as far as the ruling elites were concerned, 'Europe alone mattered in world politics'. Besides, the scramble for empires had ended. 'The confidence in the European powers' right to dispose of non-European peoples', he added, '[meant that] problems outside Europe were of secondary importance and were still thought of in European terms'. In the last volume of his landmark tetralogy on the modern world, Eric Hobsbawm claimed 'the age of extremes' can only be appreciated in geographically skewed terms: 'the fact remains that the dynamics of the greater part of the world's history during the Short Twentieth Century are derived, not original'.

And yet the very notion that Europe (or the West) wielded unfettered power is patently absurd, as is any suggestion that its history is explicable without reference to the wider world. Even a casual acquaintance with the history of the colonial empires will show that ties between the colonizers and the colonized were intensified throughout this period in significant ways. Colonial governance became much more extensive and intrusive. Colonial economies became recipients of technological transfers, of railways, modern communications, and electricity grids, if only to increase levels of colonial wealth extraction. During the Second World War, as the ascendancy of the superpowers become ever more apparent, British and French colonial administrators contemplated pooling their colonial resources in order to maintain parity.

Meanwhile, Europeans at home were negotiating the impact of US financial muscle and mass culture. The First World War allowed the United States to displace Europe as the centre of global economic power, giving Washington considerable leverage over individual European states. The period also witnessed the beginnings of 'Americanization', especially jazz, Hollywood, Fordism, and a lifestyle structured around commodity consumption. Even the Soviet Union, which had isolated itself from the wider world in order to consolidate its unique socialist experiment, was not immune to the attractions of American cultural forms. At the end of the First Five-Year Plan in 1933, the ban on jazz and its associated dance crazes was lifted, and workers were free to celebrate Stalin's triumph with a cultural form that was distinctly African American. The colonies, too, were impacting directly on Europe, especially when it came to sharpening racial categories and planning mass murder and ethnic cleansing projects. Nazi authorities took heed of the discreet genocidal operations against indigenous peoples in German African colonies and other settler societies, as they did the British Raj and its ability to control the vast Subcontinent. When it came to Nazi visions for a new Europe, the effective subordination of hundreds of millions of Indians by small numbers of Britons was a source of great inspiration.

Indeed, the closer one looks at Europe's relationships with the wider world, the more entangled, wide-ranging, and bilateral these relationships begin to appear. This period brought to a close the greatest transcontinental migration and return-migration movements in world history, which spawned large and enduring diaspora networks that continued to flourish through the inter-war years. Emigration from Europe between 1840 and 1932 saw 34.2 million people move to the United States, 12 million to Argentina, Brazil, Uruguay, and Cuba, and 8.7 million to Canada, Australia, and New Zealand. While transatlantic movements slowed to a trickle in the 1930s, Ireland, Poland, Germany, Italy, and most other parts of Europe remained intimately linked through ethnic community institutions, especially churches, and familial connections. Meanwhile, many European emigrants attained a much sharper sense of homeland national identity

天都於追傀區陰棧
天忙奔，災搶一·

Figure 15.1. 'Europeanized' Shanghai nightlife in the 1930s.

whilst living in the diaspora, while at the same time contributing to the making
of such archetypal cosmopolitan cities as Buenos Aires, São Paulo, Shanghai,
Alexandria, and New York, non-European cities that carried distinctly European
cultural baggage. It was in this period that Eastern European and Italian
immigrants changed North American eating habits. Novel renditions of the
pizza, more akin to a pie, began to permeate the Western diet via the expansion
of pizzerias across the United States and Canada.

The litany of crises that destabilized European society between 1914 to 1945
were of such a scale that they have overshadowed the continent's deep-seated

connections with the world abroad. And yet much as Europe's exceptionally dramatic interregnum was not wholly 'dark', nor was its history self-contained. Europe's complicated relationship with the wider world is not difficult to document. The real challenge is to ascertain the significance of its global interactions for our understanding of Europe's early twentieth century.

GLOBAL HEGEMONY, c.1900

At the dawn of the twentieth century, most of the Earth's surface was held captive by a handful of European states. Belgium and Portugal possessed African territories that were many times larger than the imperial state. Britain ruled 350 million overseas subjects, France 56 million, and the Netherlands 35 million. These massive colonial empires were conquered, to quote Hobsbawm again, 'with ridiculous ease'. Even China, historically wealthier and more populous than the whole of Europe combined, had been divvied into spheres of economic influence by predatory colonial powers. Germany's seizure of the Chinese port city of Jiaozhou (Kiautschou) in 1897 evokes European arrogance rather well. A latecomer to colonial expansion, Germany demanded its share of the world's surface, including its share of China. In November 1897, two German missionaries were found murdered in China's Shantung province, and Germany retaliated by sending a naval squadron to capture Jiaozhou. Tellingly, Germany's intentions regarding Jiaozhou had been an open secret for quite some time. Kaiser Wilhelm II and his ministers had deliberated upon Jiaozhou's suitability as a coal station for their projected Pacific naval force, but were forced to wait impatiently for a 'moral' pretext. In the meantime, the Chinese had tried to shore up Jiaozhou's defences, but these efforts proved ineffective.

As one Russian general famously quipped: 'Far East affairs are decided in Europe.' In the lead-up to Jiaozhou, Germany was deeply concerned about British and Russian reactions, but hardly at all about China's. In this world of secret diplomacy, Europe's great powers settled matters concerning the wider world amongst themselves, often compensating each other with overseas spoils so as to maintain balance in a global power structure that served their mutual interests. Thus an earlier agreement (1895) between the great powers awarded Germany 'concessions' in Hankow (Wuhan) and Tientsin.

Yet such hubris belied deep insecurities. The principal colonial powers, Britain, Germany, and France, looked to the future with a degree of trepidation, for they anticipated the emergence of even greater powers, namely Russia and the United States. It was only a matter of time before these two rapidly industrializing states, with their colossal manpower reserves and material resources, would acquire the means to master the planet. German strategists dreamt of creating a super-territorial state within Europe, largely at the expense of Russia, which involved strangling this would-be superpower in its adolescence. By the 1890s, the United States was ready to displace Britain as the predominant political and economic influence in the Caribbean and Latin America. Having recently assumed the mantle as the world's greatest industrial power, it now had the strength to enforce the Monroe Doctrine of 1823, which evoked American aspirations to keep the Western hemisphere free of European influence. Cuba and Puerto Rico were wrested from Spanish control in 1898 without difficulty. Despite its avowed isolationism, the United States also began to throw its weight around in the Pacific, seizing the Philippines and numerous Micronesian and Polynesian islands. Japan, another dynamic industrial force, had also come of age. Fast becoming the dominant influence in East Asia, the Japanese won a decisive war in 1905 against Russia over Manchuria. More than Italy's crushing defeat at the hands of the Ethiopians in 1896, Russia's humiliation proved to the world that Europeans were not invincible. The colonized took heart: Indian villagers named newborns after Japanese admirals who destroyed the Russian fleet.

The colonial empires were therefore put on notice well before 1914, but it was the First World War that hastened the end of Europe's global domination. The great powers had hitherto benefited greatly from a century-old inter-state system that managed a 'balance of power' and defused tensions that might lead to a destructive multilateral war on the continent. The system made it easier to channel European aggression overseas. The competition for colonial territories, however, along with the rise of militant and xenophobic nationalism at home, had greatly diminished the mutually beneficial spirit of cooperation that had sustained the power balance since 1815. By century's end, international relations were construed by most pundits as a Darwinian struggle in which only the fittest could survive. In the decade or so prior to 1914, diplomacy, especially as practised by nations with an unrequited appetite for colonies (e.g. Germany and Italy), was conducted in an increasingly aggressive mode. The war, when it finally came in 1914, surprised few observers, though hardly anyone anticipated its consequences for Europe's global mastery.

'WORLD' WAR, 1914–18

Most scholars have read the war of 1914–18 as a European affair that included some Middle Eastern 'side-shows' and very belated US intervention. The conflict therefore carries a widely accepted misnomer. Its outcome hinged on developments within Europe, particularly the Western Front and the 'home fronts' of the principal Great Power protagonists. Yet the global ramifications of this European quarrel were so extensive that what seems an inaccurate designation is actually quite apt. Somewhere between 200,000 and 250,000 Africans lost their lives for their colonial masters. France recruited 555,091 African troops, including 211,860 from Madagascar, and 49,000 from Indochina. British India enlisted

877,068 combatants and another 563,369 in non-combatant roles, and the death toll was as high as 60,000. British dominions dispatched a high proportion of their male populations (New Zealand 20 per cent, Australia 13 per cent). Each played key operational roles on the Western Front and in the Middle East, and suffered severe casualties as a consequence. (Indeed, it was dominion troops that broke the Ludendorff Offensive, which forced Germany to seek an armistice.) For Australia, the disastrous Gallipoli campaign of 1915 was particularly traumatic, so much so that it was quickly memorialized as Australia's rite of passage to nationhood.

For the two million Africans conscripted as soldiers and carriers, the war proffered no redemptive meaning. More Africans had been mobilized for this European conflict than for any war in sub-Saharan African history. Colonial officials initially received ample numbers of volunteers hoping to gain citizenship, or reclaim lost warrior status, but most were recruited by force, often through means that involved deception and entrapment. The bulk of the Africans who served the French army were recruited against their will, as were the quarter of a million Congolese serving Belgium. The wars in Africa over German colonies were wide-scale and wrought extensive economic damage and social dislocation. The death toll among East African carriers recruited by the British alone has been estimated at roughly 120,000.

On balance, the economic consequences of Europe's war on the colonized were also severe. The usual wartime labour shortages made available a range of blue- and white-collar opportunities for indigenous workers, but most wartime economic opportunities were exploited by the colonizers themselves, especially white settlers. For indigenous Kenyans the period was an unmitigated disaster. A crisis in colonial governance allowed white settlers to radically appropriate native land: so whereas in 1913, 70 per cent of exports came from indigenous producers, by 1919 that share was held by white settlers. As many as 80 per cent of indigenous males were mobilized in British East Africa to serve as carriers and other war-related activities.

When it came to financing the war, the colonies paid heavily, and none more so than India. The Indian government delivered a 'gift' of £100 million to its British 'counterpart', as well as two massive war loans amounting to £75 million. At the same time, India was responsible for recruiting, supplying, and maintaining its own army, which was supported by massive hikes in income taxes and customs duties. Prices for staple commodities such as coarse grains greatly affected India's working poor, for whom even the slightest price rise could induce great social distress. Food prices rose by 31 per cent during the war, and by 1917 food riots had become endemic.

Needless to say, Europe's conflict had a deleterious impact on the world economy. It effectively reversed economic trends that had characterized the long nineteenth century: global economic growth, the expansion of transcontinental trade and capital flows, and mass migration. The war inevitably stimulated sectors that fed the needs of wartime Europe, thereby promoting industrialization in

Latin America, the British dominions, and parts of Asia, especially Japan. However, the collapse of transoceanic shipping, the drying up of credit, and skyrocketing food prices had more comprehensively damaging effects. Latin American governments, which were heavily reliant on import duties for income, were almost bankrupted by the massive contraction in global commercial activity. Inflation and rising food prices made labour conflict and food riots commonplace throughout Latin America.

Germany and its allies had no choice but to milk domestic sources to finance the war, whereas Britain and France, their access to colonial territories and other overseas markets notwithstanding, went cap in hand to Washington. In global history terms, the ramifications of this humbling option were revolutionary. The war transformed the United States from the world's greatest debtor nation to its ultimate creditor. At war's end the governments of Britain and France owed $9.6 billion, while Europe generally owed $12.6 billion. In the meantime, the United States raced ahead of all rivals as an industrial power. US industries fed the Entente's insatiable demand for munitions, machinery, steel, and other raw materials. Between July 1914 and January 1916, stock prices for American Locomotive jumped by 130 per cent, and Bethlehem Steel had skyrocketed by 1,115 per cent. At the same time, while Europe's own industrial production capacities neglected their overseas markets to focus on wartime needs, American interests filled the vacuum. It was during the First World War that the United States completed its usurpation of Britain's position as the dominant economic influence in Latin America.

As the centre of global economic power shifted decisively across the Atlantic, Japan used the war to enhance its economic and political profile in the Pacific. Europe's war saved the Japanese economy from fiscal and balance of payments difficulties that it inherited from the Russo-Japanese war, and converted Japan from debtor to creditor nation. The period was a boon for Japanese shipping and shipbuilding, for finance and manufacturing—manufacturing output rose by 72 per cent. Japan opportunely extended its influence over China and acquired German possessions in the Pacific. Immediately after the war, Japan was to be recognized as one of five 'great' powers when it took a permanent seat on the Council of the League of Nations.

THE UNITED STATES AND RECASTING EUROPE, 1917–23

Europe's self-immolating war gave the United States the opportunity to assume global leadership. Traditionally unwilling to entangle itself in Old World political conflicts, the United States entered the fray in April 1917 essentially to secure its lucrative economic connections with the Entente powers. Intervention proved decisive, not so much in direct military terms, but in breaking the military stalemate via the threat of prolonged economic attrition. Backed by American industrial strength and manpower reserves, the US–Entente alliance could in theory fight on indefinitely. The Central Powers, which had no such option, invested all hope in a quick military solution. Impressive territorial gains along the Western Front during the Spring Offensive of 1918 were all but relinquished by August. For the remaining months of war, Germany's political elites were focused on securing an armistice that least damaged their interests.

The United States emerged with enough political clout to influence the resolution of Europe's calamitous war. President Woodrow Wilson believed Europe's unprincipled approach to foreign policy was responsible for the catastrophe of 1914–18. Diplomacy guided purely by national self-interest and conducted in secrecy made for an anarchic international environment that jeopardized peace and (more to the point) global commerce. Wilson proposed replacing Europe's failed 'balance of power' system with an international order based explicitly on civic values that were enshrined in law, and were monitored by international bodies such as his projected 'League of Nations'. This new order was to be made functional through open diplomacy, public accountability, and the elimination of secret deals. More revolutionary still were the implications of American ideals for state formation. Wilson envisaged a world of liberal democracies engaged in free trade, of nation-states working explicitly to maximize opportunities for commercial exchanges, whether domestic or transnational. In essence, the United States was promoting a peculiarly market-oriented vision of state and society that entailed an overhaul of Europe's *ancien régimes* and the break-up of its colonial empires.

Although greatly diminished, Europe's surviving regimes were resilient enough to thwart much of the Wilsonian agenda. Attempts to recast European high politics were stoutly resisted. After all, in demanding an end to imperialism and irredentism, Wilsonianism threatened what for many Europeans was the *raison d'être* of the nation-state. Nor was the strident advocacy of internationalist values enough to dissuade British and French determination to punish Germany. The war had certainly generated powerful anti-war sentiments among soldiers and civilians alike, and in 1918, Wilson was confident that national self-interest had 'fallen more and more into the background and the common purpose of enlightened mankind [had] taken [its] place'. In reality, European society was deeply polarized. Powerful reactionary sentiments were just as commonplace, especially among the middling classes. If the war bred internationalism in some, it bred a more zealous nationalism among others. National elections in Britain and France at the end of 1918 made clear that public opinion wanted Germany severely punished. In any case, David Lloyd George and Georges Clemenceau were far more concerned about restoring British and French power than promoting Wilson's lofty ideals. Wilson succeeded in curbing French territorial claims over the Saarland, but Clemenceau (along with Lloyd George) secured other territorial concessions as well as reparations, which certainly did make Germany look very much the defeated nation. In the meantime, US society was deeply divided over the international responsibilities entailed in Wilson's agenda. His failure to secure domestic acceptance of the League severely hampered its ability to broker inter-state relations and solve conflicts.

The US-led attempt to recast post-war Europe was not a complete failure, however. The defunct empires of East-Central Europe (Hohenzollern, Habsburg, and Ottoman realms) were reconstituted into a series of nation-states with (albeit short-lived) liberal democratic systems. Although Britain and France were not compelled to apply principles of national self-determination to their colonial empires, weaker European nations were easily disabused of their imperial aspirations. Britain and France had recruited Italy in 1915 with promises of imperial spoils, but none were honoured. Italy emerged from the war empty-handed. Britain and France divided most of Germany's colonies and Ottoman Arab provinces amongst themselves—the latter this time under mandates from the League of Nations, meaning they were technically custodians of such territories as Syria, Iraq, and Cameroon until such time as they were ready for national self-determination. Wilson was unable to stop punitive reparations imposed on Germany, but he was influential in reducing the sums owed from $320 billion to $66 billion. Other achievements included the orderly (albeit distressing) population exchange and settlement programme that was arranged between Turkey and Greece in 1923, and the workings of the Dawes Committee, which overrode certain sectional interests in Eastern Europe to stabilize local currencies in the late 1920s. And while the League failed to prevent Italy's conquest of Ethiopia in 1935, it generated loud global condemnation of at least one colonial aggressor.

US hopes for a global civic order, consisting of liberal democratic states committed to the free market, faded gradually through the 1920s. Europe's continental democracies were displaced successively by authoritarian regimes that championed protectionist economic policies, and which were openly contemptuous of international bodies such as the League and the International Labour Organization (ILO). Fascist Italy, which celebrated autarchy with a major exhibition in 1938, espoused unashamedly a foreign policy guided by 'sacro egoismo'. With the support of Nazi Germany and Europe's other authoritarian governments, Mussolini's regime sought a lawless international environment that would accommodate its naked imperial ambitions. By the late 1930s, it was the ultranationalists, especially the Nazis, who were setting the agenda for Europe's future: one defined by national self-interest, ethnic/racial exclusivity, and wars of conquest.

AMERICANIZATION: THE MARKET EMPIRE

Whereas some Europeans sought to realize national dreams and recast civilization by reverting to imperialism, the United States hoped to conquer Europe and execute its own civilizing mission by more subtle means. Frederick W. Taylor's ideas on labour rationalization and productivity maximization had already engaged the interest of European big business before the First World War. 'Taylorism' entailed close management of factory-floor time usage, optimal utilization of workers' skills, and the application of appropriate motivational techniques, such as the indexation of pay to productivity rates. After the First World War, it was Henry Ford and his Detroit-based motor company that captivated European big business and political elites. 'Fordism' extended scientific rationalization as applied to the factory floor to include all aspects of business and consumption practices. In seeking to promote mass consumption of mass-produced goods, Fordism entailed a significant measure of social engineering. Americanization, as far as the great Italian Marxist thinker Antonio Gramsci was concerned, was akin to recasting society according to an American factory model.

The implications of Fordism for European society were wide-ranging. To maximize profits, Ford sought to make his automobiles affordable to Ford workers, who were paid high wages on the strict proviso that they maintained high rates of productivity. The 'virtuous circle' of mass production driven by mass consumption, and sustained by high wages on the basis of high productivity levels, entailed nothing less than a societal transformation. Whereas European thinking assumed economic benefits accrued by one social category came at the expense of another, in other words a zero-sum equation, the American vision overcame this impasse by demonstrating the mutually enriching outcomes of economic growth. The most appealing aspect of Taylorism and Fordism for many European observers was that as corporatist ideas they offered a solution to class tensions. Workers enjoying greater purchasing power, and hence better living standards, were expected to be less receptive to radical political ideas, and more committed to the existing socio-economic order.

Fordism was but one feature of a much broader transatlantic cultural offensive that sought to make European society more conducive to American capital and consumption practices. Americanization in this case was about making product-purchasing part of the '*habitus*' or dispositional practice in everyday life. The inter-war years saw the penetration and expansion of Woolworth's and other US chain stores that were keen to promote a mass-consumption *habitus*. Whereas classic department stores such as Bon Marché and Harrods were located in the city centre and pandered mainly to an up-market clientele, chain stores had branches embedded near residential areas, were conveniently open for business during lunchtimes, displayed their wide range of merchandise in inviting ways, and extended a high level of service to all customers regardless of social class. In contrast to the department stores that went through regular cycles of price discounting, the chain stores offered something significantly more attractive: fixed low prices. Americans also refined marketing strategies that could make brand names instinctively recognizable, such as 'Singer', rather than 'sewing machine', and 'Hoover' rather than 'vacuum cleaner'.

Inter-war Europe was besieged by what historian Victoria de Grazia has aptly labelled the 'Market Empire'. Typically American, given that it was an informal empire that sought voluntary recruitment rather than involuntary duress, the 'Market Empire' applied scientific rationalization and 'best practice' from production through to retail. Woolworth's offered an exemplary model at the retail end, as each outlet shared an identical management structure, service standards, product range, and advertising and discounting strategies. The first Woolworth's store was opened in Liverpool in 1909, but by 1930 there were four hundred stores in Britain. The first German branch opened in 1927, with another twenty-three opening the following year. A further eighty-two branches had opened for business by 1932.

For all that, the Market Empire found Europe difficult to conquer. Fordism required sustained economic growth and governments subscribing earnestly to free-market values. The inter-war years provided neither. As it happened, European governments focused on those aspects of Fordism relating to labour discipline, and little else. In any case, the Great Depression destroyed any chances of generating an American-style consumer cuture. Much as Hitler would have liked every German family to possess an automobile, ownership remained a privilege, and hence a striking symbol of class distinction. In any case, there were aspects of Americanization that grated with European sensibilities. Rotary International, which promoted outwardly American ways for conducting business and rendering customer services, and which at an organizational level overlooked class and national divisions, found it difficult to replicate the organization in Europe. In Britain, Rotary became yet another exclusive social club, while elsewhere Rotarians found their patriotism scrutinized and questioned by menacing state authorities. Many Germans left the organization when the Nazis denounced Rotarians as Freemasons and internationalists in disguise. Moreover, autarchy and the imperative of US enterprises were clearly incompatible. The Nazi regime's determination to supervise national consumption through rationing and 'buy German' campaigns was antithetical to the values of the Market Empire. Later, its bid to extend its own economic order of command consumption across Europe would be an important reason why the United States went to war in December 1941. In the meantime, foreign interests were left vulnerable to harassment, particularly once the regime contrived a link between firms like Woolworth's and 'Judeo-capitalism'.

It was only after the Second World War, and especially during the long period of sustained economic growth that persisted into the early 1970s, that Western Europe would emerge as a fully fledged consumer society. Only then did Volkswagen truly become a 'people's car'. In the inter-war years, 'Americanization' was more a promise: a paradigm of modernity in which ordinary Europeans sought a stake.

AMERICANIZATION: HOLLYWOOD AND JAZZ

The most vivid imagery of this propitious 'America' came to Europeans via the medium of Hollywood film. Hollywood flooded European markets during the

First World War with its distinctive brand of motion picture that Europeans consumed ravenously. As a perfect case study of American-styled capitalist enterprise, the Hollywood film industry was more than capable of feeding Europe's growing addiction. The dominant studios, of which five formed an impregnable oligopoly (Warner Brothers, Paramount, 20th Century Fox, MGM, and RKO), controlled all aspects of the business, from production to distribution and marketing, including the primary cinemas (picture palaces), growing rich on a massive domestic market before conquering Europe. The system settled on a standardized product of proven popularity: a 90-minute feature film, prefaced by a 10-minute newsreel. Each studio produced a rapid succession of films and supplied each of its cinema outlets with something new almost weekly. The intention was to make movie-going a routine rather than a special outing. European cinema had begun to claw back its share of ticket sales by 1927, only to be overwhelmed yet again when Hollywood introduced sound films.

Hollywood films were popular because they were tailored specifically to meet popular tastes. The big studios were essentially interested in maximizing ticket sales rather than promoting film as an art form. They gave audiences what they wanted: well-produced, uncomplicated, and fluently delivered story lines. Audiences were treated to genres of proven popularity, from romantic and slapstick comedies to westerns and gangster flicks, from history epics to science fiction. Crucially, the success or failure of each movie depended on the appeal of its stars, a factor that could make or break a film. For the studios, stars such as Rudolph Valentino, Charlie Chaplin, and Bette Davis, the world's most recognizable faces, were cash cows. Each star, of course, was tied contractually to one of these studios, which assumed responsibility for cultivating public image and protecting personal privacy. Hollywood also had the power to appropriate and assimilate European stars, such as Greta Garbo and Marlene Dietrich, with the effect of drawing even bigger European audiences to Hollywood films.

Via the medium of film and the phenomenal appeal of these stars, American modernity attained a purchase on the European popular mind, for many Hollywood films served as benign advertisements for a bourgeois, consumption-focused 'American way of life'. Romantic comedies such as *The Gay Divorcee* (1934), with Fred Astaire and Ginger Rogers, or *The Philadelphia Story* (1940), with Katherine Hepburn and Cary Grant, worked against backdrops of Cadillacs, refrigerators, and consumer-related daily routines that suggested a level of material life to which Europeans might wish to aspire. The studios were all too aware of their role in marketing US culture abroad. In 1927, the president of the Motion Picture Producers and Distributors of America lobbied for a subdepartment dedicated to the film industry within the Department of Commerce, arguing that movies were the silent salesmen of US goods around the world.

Jazz was a cultural import that represented a very different 'America'. An African American art form that could not conform easily to the normative imperatives of the Market Empire, jazz became a force in European nightlife from

1917, becoming an obsession within avant-garde circles and among the fashion-conscious more broadly. Jean-Paul Sartre fantasized about being a jazz musician, while the bob-haired, short-skirted 'modern woman' who frequented nightclubs was also, according to the stereotype, a jazz fan. African American musicians, who found Parisians relatively tolerant and polite compared to whites back home, formed an expatriate colony in the bohemian Montmartre district in the inter-war years. It was in France that someone like Josephine Baker, whose sensual dancing and stage nudity was not tolerated in the United States, could enjoy the trappings of real celebrity status. Along with the tango, mambo, and rumba from Latin America, jazz figured at the cutting edge of urban popular music, and found a natural constituency among European youth. Considered too depraved by parents, community leaders, and politicians, jazz was an apposite symbol of youth subversion. German youth circles such as the *Edelweisspiraten* consciously resisted Nazi authorities by identifying closely with 'swing', an offshoot of jazz.

The dynamic efflorescence of American culture was the most distinctive feature of global transmission in the inter-war years, but Europe, specifically Paris and Berlin, remained the arbiters of high culture. When it came to the latest fashions in apparel and accessories, social elites around the world took their cues from Paris rather than New York, while Weimar Berlin was the trend-setter in the high arts. Weimar Germany, which had been most receptive to American influence, in turn exercised a disproportionate influence on American cultural production. The Bauhaus movement had a profound impact on the Chicago School, Harvard, and other centres of architectural design, particularly when leading lights of the movement were forced to emigrate across the Atlantic by the Nazis. Indeed, it was American universities and scientific programmes such as the Manhattan Project that capitalized most on the Nazi-induced brain drain.

FORMAL COLONIALISM

As the United States radically expanded its Market Empire around the globe, the Europeans persisted with the more traditional modes of global domination. Britain, France, Belgium, the Netherlands, Portugal, and Italy continued to exercise their unwelcome hegemony over millions of overseas subjects, but whereas the period 1870–1914 featured a feverish scramble by European colonial powers to lay claim to most of Asia and Africa, the new age saw these territorial claims brought under tighter formal control. Railway construction and modern communications made it easier for the colonizers to wield direct and indirect power over vast hinterlands that were hitherto out of reach, thus bringing many more Africans and Asians under effective European supervision.

The costs associated with the expansion of government were offset to a considerable degree by indigenous collaboration. Even the French, who dreamt of a culturally assimilated global empire that was managed by a highly centralized

Figure 15.2. Greek immigrant shopkeepers in North Queensland, Australia, 1917.

administrative system, had by the 1890s recognized the expediency of integrating West Africa's chiefs, for example, within the system. There were also particular communities, such as the *priyayis* in the Dutch East Indies, the *principalia* of the American-ruled Philippines, or the Sikhs and Parsis in India, who were prepared to support the imperial order if cherished privileges could be retained, or new ones were granted. In sub-Saharan Africa, the colonial state enlisted local chiefs who, by virtue of their legitimate power status and their mastery of local knowledge, could take a reliable census and collect taxes. During the First World War, the chiefs were crucial when it came to supplying the colonial state with soldiers and labourers for wartime service. To be sure, these elites were at the disposal of the colonial state. Between 1917 and 1938, for example, chieftaincies were abolished, amalgamated, or created anew in Belgian Congo: their number reduced from 6,095 to 1,212.

In making greater demands on the colonized and their resources, the colonizers inevitably generated strong indigenous demands for power, and as the Europeans would not countenance any real power-sharing arrangements with African and Asian elites, the situation was likely to stimulate anti-colonial agitation. In any case, the new intimacy between ruler and ruled meant the latter could see the contradictions and hypocrisies of European colonialism at closer range. The 'civilizing' pretences of colonial rhetoric were more likely to enrage than enthral. It was difficult for Indian elites, for example, to stomach the British pontificating about the virtues of parliamentary democracy and participatory government. Similarly, educated subjects of the French Empire found it insulting that the universal values that the republic symbolized did not extend to people of colour. The hypocrisy generated acrid responses. In the 1921 publication *Batouala*, a landmark in the history of the African novel, the Martinique-born writer René Maran cast the French *mission civilizatrice* as a form of barbarity: 'You are not a torch, but a fire. Whatever you touch you-devour.'

As a consequence, colonialism found its pool of potential collaborators contracting during the inter-war years. In Asia and the Middle East, and more belatedly in sub-Saharan Africa, educated opinion was increasingly convinced of the need for political self-determination, though most anti-colonial movements were incapable of pursuing such aims openly until after the Second World War. There were some exceptions. In Egypt, for example, where traditional elites managed to mobilize mass support for national self-determination, the British relinquished formal control while securing some vital interests, including the Suez Canal. For Suez remained Britain's gateway to India, which was the hub of its empire, and the colony it was most desperate to keep. Here, the 'Raj' had to contend with formidable elites that were increasingly impatient for political participation and self-government. Piecemeal gestures, such as the Montagu–Chelmsford reforms of 1919, gave Indians limited provincial government powers while the British retained complete control of the central government. The reforms supposedly made India a dyarchy, a term that signified an Anglo-Indian partnership. But such disingenuous and miserly attempts to assuage local aspirations generated more obdurate opposition. So too did the brutal repression of dissidents allowed for under the Rowlatt Acts, and the Amritsar Massacre in April 1919, when the slaying of unarmed protesters exposed the violent and racist undercurrent of British rule. In the inter-war years, the Indian National Congress, led by Mohandas Gandhi, was able to rally the disparate discontented groups across India into a coherent national movement, while also mobilizing the 'teeming millions' of peasants and working poor. The British managed to contain the movement until the Second World War, but by that point the vast majority of Indians had been politicized. British India's days were numbered.

COLONIAL DEVELOPMENT

In the meantime, the Europeans had settled on what appeared an incontrovertible justification for colonialism. The keynote of colonialism in the inter-war years was economic development. Wartime mobilization did much to demonstrate the economic potential of colonialism. The challenge after the war was to realize that potential through capital investment, infrastructure development, and technology transfers. In theory, economic development addressed the backwardness of the darker races. Leading imperial thinkers such as Frederick Lugard and Albert Sarraut argued that rulers and subjects would each reap the rewards of realizing the full economic potential of empire. Development therefore solved any moral and economic dilemmas regarding the efficacy of colonialism.

On the surface, European investment seemed exceptionally generous. The new civilizing mission brought with it electricity grids, modern town planning, aircraft, upgraded port facilities, irrigation channels, and steel bridges. Colonial cities such as New Delhi, with its monumental buildings and wide boulevards, or smaller but equally striking examples of modern town planning, such as Rabat (French Morocco) and Tripoli (Italian Libya), were perhaps the most stunning symbolic projections of European modernity. Indeed, the colonizers appeared to be competing against each other to see which European civilization was more deserving of imperial responsibility. The complex environmental challenges encountered in Africa and Asia put European technical ingenuity and economic power to the test. The most celebrated road-building achievement of the 1930s was Italy's *Litoranea Libica*, a 1,822 km highway running along the Mediterranean coastline between Tunisia and Egypt. Roadworks throughout the African continent made possible the ascendancy of automobile transport. The period saw the triumph of the lorry, which dramatically cut transportation costs and made remote territories viable for commercial farming. The Dutch produced 60,000 km of roads in the East Indies by 1930, half of which were asphalt. More striking in terms of scale and advanced technology was colonial railway construction. In 1898, Indochina had a mere 178 km of track, but forty years later 2,908 km of track linked every major population and economic hub. Taking just under forty years to complete, the Trans-Indochinese railway link (1,735 km) was the most expensive in the colonial world. Other important long-haul links were the Congo–Ocean and Dakar–Bamako lines. India had the world's largest rail network: between 1870 and 1936, the network was extended from 7,250 km of track to just under 70,000 km.

However, European science and technology could not meet every challenge. Quite often the colonizers overcame technical difficulties by seeking local knowledge, as happened when it came to Indian railway construction. British engineers adopted Indian building techniques to produce the long bridges that spanned the massive rivers of the Ganges Basin. The extent to which the colonized contributed to colonial science and engineering is only just beginning to be appreciated by historians, suffice it to say it was a contribution that the colonizers rarely acknowledged. Europeans preferred to assume that, when it came to science and technology, Africa and Asia had nothing to offer.

The colonized, no doubt, did not read colonial development in the same way as their masters, although they were sometimes impressed by the schools, hospitals, mechanized transport, urban development, and other facilities, especially if they enjoyed sufficient access. On the Aegean island of Rhodes, locals would later remember Italian rule as having transformed this one-time Ottoman backwater into a modern tourist centre. Italian buildings and roadworks gave locals an intense sense of parochial pride. Yet Rhodians were also keenly aware that public investment was designed to serve Italian military interests, private enterprises, and farming settlements. Any benefits forthcoming to indigenous businesses and labourers were incidental. There is little doubt that colonial subjects worldwide recognized Europe's new 'civilizing mission' to be a ruse for implementing a more efficient system of plundering, for they could hardly fail to notice that Europeans monopolized development contracts, as well as mining and plantation leases. Colonial development was especially geared to support European big business; companies such as Lever Brothers, Dutch Royal Shell, and Banque de l'Indochine, and the United Africa Company, which by 1930 handled almost half of West Africa's export trade. Belgian Congo was held hostage by a handful of big mining companies that produced two-thirds of the colony's revenue. Moreover, the costs of development in Africa weighed heavily on subject populations, for colonial development required extensive land acquisitions that inevitably displaced local producers, demanded widespread use of forced labour, and it was financed partially by hikes in direct taxation.

If anything, the economic order imposed by colonialism was its ultimate source of destabilization. Asian and African producers, sometimes voluntarily or under compulsion from colonial authorities, made the switch to cash crop cultivation. By the 1920s, specific colonial territories were specializing in a small repertoire of goods, such as palm oils, palm kernels, ground nuts in Nigeria, cotton in the East African colonies, and rubber in Malaya. The dependence on cash crops rendered most of these colonial economies vulnerable to global price fluctuations. The impact of the Great Depression was therefore exceptionally hard on the colonial world. Africa's export prices fell by about 60 per cent, while India's cash-crop prices dropped by 50 per cent. When the price of rubber collapsed, Malayan peasants were forced to revert to subsistence farming. Needless to say, social protest and rioting were endemic at the height of the Depression, but of greater consequence was the fact that any trust that the colonized had in the colonial system had been broken. As R. F. Holland puts it: 'The geyser bursts of anti-westernism after 1945. . . are explicable only as the delayed aftermath of the 1930s experience in which the political understanding between rulers and ruled had been crucially undermined.'

Inter-war discontent provided a fillip to Asian nationalist movements and the genesis of counterpart movements in Africa, but nowhere did such movements threaten the overthrow of the colonial system. The Europeans retained overwhelming military superiority, even during the Second World War when Britain was fighting a desperate war back home, and when France, Belgium, and the Netherlands were under German occupation. In the few cases where independence was conceded early, such as Egypt (1922) and Iraq (1930), the British negotiated from a position of strength: they retained control of Iraq's army and foreign policy, and a major interest in Iraqi oil production. Most attempts at armed struggle were easily quashed, as in the Yen Bay uprising in Vietnam in 1930, when thirteen of the eighty-three insurgents captured were guillotined, and villages suspected of collusion were devastated by air-bombing. The most audacious but foolhardy anti-colonial struggle of the period was the Rif War of the mid-1920s, when Berber tribes in northern Morocco established a republic until French and Spanish troops subdued it in 1926. Even in India, where Gandhi's non-violent campaigns went a long way towards wearing down British resolve, the Raj was able to crush the Quit India movement of 1942 and incarcerate the Indian National Congress (INC) leadership.

European colonialism never looked stronger or more tenuous in the inter-war years. The INC might have been put out of action in 1942, but it had more or less appropriated the social base that was vital to the Raj in terms of political support and revenue. Throughout the inter-war years, it was becoming more apparent that the future maintenance of empire would require much greater recourse to force, as the colonized became less and less receptive to colonial overtures and legitimacy claims. One attains a vivid sense of this erosion of symbolic authority in George Orwell's oft-quoted essay 'Shooting an Elephant', in which he reports the experience of shooting a rampaging elephant while stationed in Burma during the 1920s:

I could feel their thousand wills pressing me forward, irresistibly. And yet, at this moment, as I stood there with a rifle in my hands, that I grasped the hollowness, the futility of the white man's dominion in the East. Here I was, the white man with his gun, standing in front of the unarmed crowd, seemingly the leading actor of the piece; but in reality I was an absurd puppet pushed to and fro by the will of those yellow faces behind.

For Orwell, empire was an 'evil thing' that corrupted colonizer and colonized alike. Historians and anthropologists have only just begun to recognize the ways in which the colonial experience might have impacted upon European life itself, particularly with regards to notions of domesticity and constructions of gender. Most such work demonstrates how negative images of exotic Africa and Asia were used to shore up positive European self-perceptions. More direct forms of governance that defined inter-war colonialism, and which required greater colonizer–colonized collaboration, had the effect of fostering renewed European interest in questions of race. Within metropolitan France, racial exclusivity was an imperative that featured heavily in public debate on citizenship, immigration, eugenics, and the nation's low population growth. Even in Germany, which formally lost its colonies in 1919, memories of ruling Cameroon, Tanganyika, and Namibia were vivid enough to inform racial theory. Nazi Germany sought to reorganize Europe along racial lines and, within its short-lived empire, 'non-Aryans' were shocked to find themselves being treated as Europeans had treated the 'darker' races. Within colonial dependencies, race was reaffirmed as a secure marker of social differentiation. Regulations inhibiting miscegenation or inter-racial cohabitation were more stridently espoused across the colonial world in this period, although much to Mussolini's annoyance Italian troops in East Africa ignored orders by continuing to liaise with local *madamas*.

Figure 15.3. Greek Orthodox Church Wedding in Sydney, 1938. Community declare loyalties to homeland, new country, and empire.

MIGRATION AND DIASPORA

Italians were far more prolific builders of a more benign form of overseas empire. Created by families rather than armed forces, the Italian diaspora was a more powerful and enduring projection of metropolitan culture. While only a handful of European states had overseas empires, even the poorest ethnic groups could boast expatriate communities in the Americas, Africa, and in the Antipodes. Despite the drop in migration flows from Europe, the period 1914 to 1945 witnessed the consolidation of emigrant communities across urban North America, as seen in the establishment of more immigrant churches, educational institutions, newspapers, regional fraternities, welfare groups, and other associations.

The First World War halted the massive flows of Europeans across the Atlantic and the Urals. Transatlantic movement resumed temporarily during the 1920s, only to dry up again by 1930, just as mass movement into Siberia and Central Asia had recommenced. Between 1926 and 1939, roughly five million Soviet citizens moved eastwards. The great majority were labourers, many transplanted by force. What distinguished the Soviet experience was the fact that migration was shaped by the imperatives of a command economy. The Soviet state imposed tight controls on migration from 1928 so as to determine precisely the movement and distribution of labour. The movement eastwards was accelerated during the Second World War, when Siberia became the Soviet Union's industrial heartland. Between 1939 and 1959, the population of Soviet Union's Asian territories expanded by a further ten million.

Government intervention also played a role in conditioning the nature of transatlantic movements. Immigrant receiving nations, fearing domestic disorder and cultural disunity, placed heavier restrictions on immigrant intake. Brazil and Argentina continued to receive huge numbers of Italian immigrants from 1924, just when the United States decided it no longer wanted Southern and Eastern Europeans. A strict quota system reduced the US annual intake to about 150,000 immigrants per year, of which Italians made up a mere 3,600. The Great Depression ended mass migration movements across the globe (except in the Soviet Union), as governments sought to shield their economies and their own labour markets with tariff walls and prohibitive immigration laws.

In the meantime, migrant-emitting nations began to see emigration as a stain on national pride, or in the Soviet case, as repudiation of the Revolution. Those who fled and remained abroad were denationalized. Confiscating passports was also a means by which Europe's authoritarian regimes restricted the activities of political opponents, especially those operating from abroad. The commonplace obsession with pro-natalism also had implications for European migration. In an age when a large population supposedly reflected virility, by the same token, population loss, whether through low birth rates or emigration, was deemed a threat to national security. Mussolini tried unsuccessfully to channel emigration flows towards Italy's semi-arid African colonies. In Fascist eyes, Italy's vast diaspora symbolized national failure, although the regime believed it could exploit the diaspora's global reach for political ends. Fascists used Italian consulates and infiltrated cultural institutions, such as the Dante Alighieri Society. After the Lateran Pact of 1926, Mussolini's regime could also work through the tacit auspices of the Catholic Church, the most global of all institutions. Fascism did find support within the diaspora among politically active expatriates such as Italian-language newspaper owners, journalists, and businessmen, but in the diaspora they were faced by as many vocal anti-Fascists who were free to express open dissent. The Nazis were also active among the German communities abroad. In Australia, for example, the Nazis infiltrated the German-Australian Chamber of Commerce and attained intelligence about Australia's northern coastal defences from a retired postal worker of German descent. Of course, fascist activity in the diaspora came to nought with the outbreak of the Second World War.

THE GLOBAL RAMIFICATIONS OF HITLER'S WAR

In the 1930s, Europe's major powers were unclear as to the roles the United States and the Soviet Union might play in an international environment rendered increasingly unstable by imperial Japan, Germany, and Italy. The 'superpowers' seemed content to remain detached—in the case of the Soviet Union, an ideological pariah, its involvement in international crisis resolutions was rarely welcomed. The mere fact that the US and Stalin's Russia were greater powers, however, weighed heavily on the minds of European statesmen. Britain and France remained mindful of America's anti-colonial convictions, while Germany's traditional fear of the Russians running roughshod over Germany and the rest of 'civilized' Europe remained as vivid as ever. The Nazi solution was to crush the 'Judeo-Bolshevik' regime, and to conquer and colonize the vast expanses of the Ukraine and European Russia. In doing so, Germany expected to attain the material resources to dominate Europe and compete with the United States and Japan at the global level.

The Nazi regime's bid for superpower status started in June 1941. For the US President, Franklin Roosevelt, the attack on Russia merely confirmed in his mind that Nazi Germany was a greater threat in global terms than imperial Japan, even though the latter presented a more direct and imminent threat to US interests. Roosevelt was convinced that Nazi Germany would not be content with European hegemony, given the naked imperial aggression it had displayed since Munich. Roosevelt expected the Nazis to channel their aggression more directly at the United States, perhaps by prying in Latin American affairs. The president's main challenge was to win over a country that as late as 1940 remained overwhelmingly in favour of neutrality, and to induce Hitler into giving him *casus belli* like the Zimmerman telegram in 1917, which helped to swing Congress and the public behind intervention.

While the Soviet–German war of 1941–5 was conceived as an ideological struggle, the United States also regarded its war against Hitler as a clash between contrasting civilizations. Roosevelt harboured a heartfelt repugnance for Nazi barbarities, but along with many other Americans he also sensed that the fascist disposition to extend political controls over the market posed a direct challenge to the Market Empire. The Nazi economic vision for Europe was to place the continent's human and material resources at the complete disposal of German military and political exigencies. Japan had also imposed its own highly regulated system of resource acquisition in East and South-East Asia. In controlling Europe, however, Germany threatened access to America's most vital external market. Furthermore, an economic stranglehold on Europe could also give Germany leverage over parts of the world where Europeans already exercised domination, such as Latin America and the colonies. Roosevelt, among others, feared the Nazis might engineer America's economic isolation by exploiting these networks.

Before the American-led forces could land on European soil, however, Germany's dreams were already ruined by the Soviet Union. The excessively brutal subjugation of Soviet territory between 1941 and 1943 forced the Soviet Union to realize its superpower potential virtually overnight. During the second half of 1941, 1,523 large factories, and between twenty-five and thirty million workers, were transferred across the Ural Mountains to the relative safety of Siberia. By the middle of 1943, the Soviet Union had the industrial capacity to overwhelm

Germany, whose resources in turn were fast diminishing. The United States, Britain, and France were party to the defeat of Germany in May 1945, but Soviet military and industrial might did most of the hard work. Whether the Soviet Union was already a fully fledged superpower by this stage is a moot point; suffice it to say that along with the United States it determined the continent's immediate political future.

Alexis de Tocqueville's prognostications of a world dominated by superpowers had arrived. For its part, the United States heeded the mistakes of the first post-war era and supervised the creation of a more civic-minded international system, monitored by the United Nations, which from 1952 had its permanent headquarters in New York. To secure post-war political stability in Europe and make its Western half less vulnerable to Communism, the Truman administration in 1948 also granted financial assistance for economic reconstruction. The Marshall Plan, which made available $13 billion, helped trigger a post-war economic boom that was sustained until the early 1970s, during which time Western Europe became much more conducive to the influence of the Market Empire. American capital would finally enjoy access to an array of advanced consumer societies.

For European colonialism, the war determined the fate of another ambiguous feature of inter-war global politics. In some senses colonialism had been revitalized. The British were able to bring South Asia, Africa, and the Middle East under firmer control, and colonial resource extraction was more extensive and efficient than it was during 1914–18. This time, Britain could count on more than just raw materials and manpower. Indian industries went a long way towards supplementing British production in such areas as munitions, machine tools, chemicals, and drugs. The war also stimulated mining, manufacturing, and infrastructure development in Africa and the Middle East. For a moment it seemed as though the British Empire was functioning as an economic unit, much like a superpower.

These economic changes, however, had social ramifications that were to make the future of colonialism untenable. Inevitably, colonial subjects responded to the colonizer's greater demands on resources by making even more strident demands for power. Many indigenous elites profited immensely from industrial expansion and rising commodity prices, which meant greater political influence and leverage *vis-à-vis* the colonial state. Wartime privations among the working poor, whose numbers expanded as a result of wartime economic opportunities, meant that independence movements could count on a much broader popular base. India's extremely generous support for Britain's war effort would come at the ultimate price. The Indian population endured higher direct taxes, price inflation, which was partially responsible for the Bengal famine that killed 3.8 million people, and numerous other privations, so much so that neither political leaders nor Indian society in general would tolerate the continuation of British rule beyond the war. Besides, Britain this time had to foot the bill for India's military forces, which meant that by war's end the colonizing power was indebted to its colony by a massive £1.3 billion. Faced by the future prospect of widespread social unrest, if not open rebellion, the British had no choice but to begin negotiations for independence as early as June 1945.

In South-East Asia, the war's impact on colonialism was more dramatic still. The Japanese had completely dismantled European colonial administration throughout the region, with the significant exception of French Indochina. The Japanese could be as brutal as the Europeans, but they were somewhat more accommodating of indigenous political interests, and gave promises of national self-determination. In Malaya and Indochina, the Japanese showed (initially at least) respect for traditional authorities, while in the East Indies, nationalist dissidents were released from gaol and allowed to fly the Indonesian flag. The Japanese advanced the careers of nationalists such as Achmed Sukarno and Mohammad Hatta (Indonesia), and Ba Maw (Burma). In Vietnam, where the French operated a puppet regime, the Vietnamese Independence and Brother-hood League (Viet Minh), formed by Ho Chi Minh in 1941, worked diligently through the war to cultivate mass support. In both Indonesia and Vietnam, nationalist movements that already enjoyed popular support were ready to fill the power vacuum immediately after the Japanese withdrawal.

The most telling effect of the Japanese interregnum, however, came at a symbolic level. The Japanese inverted the old racial hierarchy by parading Western POWs before locals and by placing European colonial officials and their families in internment camps, in full view of indigenous eyes. After 1945, the returning colonial powers found it almost impossible to reconstitute an image of imperial mastery. In 1949, the Dutch were forced to give up the East Indies after much fighting and international criticism. The French managed to hang on longer in Indochina. In the Viet Minh, however, they faced the region's most indomitable anti-colonial movement, and after a long and costly campaign the French, at a loss as to how to deal with guerrilla warfare, were effectively driven out by 1954.

Colonialism persisted after the war, particularly in Africa, where the social preconditions for nationalism were essentially formed during the Second World War, and where the largely successful push for independence ensued over the next two decades. In 1945 many Europeans, including Winston Churchill and Charles de Gaulle, were steadfastly resolved to keeping their colonial empires intact, especially as colonial resources could be used to fund post-war reconstruction. It took time to disabuse Europe's remaining imperial enthusiasts of such fantasies. The humiliating Suez Crisis of 1956, France's costly attempts to hang on to Vietnam and Algeria, and the sudden, albeit delayed, demise of Portugal's ramshackle empire, apart from showing that old habits die hard, demonstrated that the age of formal overseas empires had long gone. The anti-colonial geysers had burst. Thereafter, European powers were to find more lucrative the informal type of colonialism that could be practised via the International Monetary Fund, World Bank, and especially through multinationals such as Dutch Royal Shell and British Petroleum. 'Third World' dependency and debt traps created highly lucrative empires at minimal expense.

DARK CONTINENTS

Since the beginnings of decolonization, the moral legitimacy of colonialism and 'neo-colonialism' has been a recurring issue within Western academic and political circles. In *Lords of Humankind* (1967), a highly critical survey of European attitudes towards colonial subjects, the Marxist historian Victor Kiernan reflected regretfully that the colonized did not have 'the capability to find their way forward towards a new kind of life, either one resembling Europe's or some other form of their own'. Hence, the forward march of progress made imperialism a necessary evil. In 2002, the conservative historian Niall Ferguson argued a similar line, albeit unashamedly. Ferguson claimed rather provocatively that, on balance, the British Empire was 'a good thing', for Britain and the wider world, and that the United States should follow in its footsteps. One need not go so far, however, to make the simple point that colonialism had its benefits. Within Italy's post-colonial dependencies, some of which had been subjected to vicious pacification campaigns, memories of the former masters remain ambivalent. Recollections of property expropriations and fascist bastardry continue to be weighed up against the impressive material legacies (model towns, roads) and the kindness of individual Italians. On balance, colonialism was not a good thing, but even the colonized could sometimes concede that it was not wholly bad either. For many individual Libyans, Ethiopians, and Rhodians, Italian colonialism was good *and* bad.

Such ambivalences have wide-ranging implications for historians seeking to make sense of such general phenomena as colonialism, or the epoch covered in this volume. The maelstrom that started when Gavrilo Princip assassinated Archduke Ferdinand in Sarajevo, and which ended when Russian troops raised the Soviet flag over the Reichstag, affected Europeans and societies across the globe in radically different ways. The eminent British historian Lawrence Stone, who spent much of the Second World War on a British naval vessel, summed up the war as follows: 'As anyone who experienced it knows, war is 99.9 per cent boredom and discomfort, and 0.1 per cent sheer panic.' One wonders what Eastern Europeans who endured the terror of the Nazi New Order, who were caught in the middle of vicious anti-partisan campaigns, and spent the duration of the war malnourished and at death's door, might have made of this wistful and seemingly implausible summation. And yet Stone's comments would have resonated with more than enough of his contemporaries.

It remains incumbent upon historians to define any given epoch with temporal boundaries, and justify the characterizations that they ascribe to an age. There is much to be said for grouping the ideological struggles, catastrophic wars, and the genocides that blighted Europe between 1914 and 1945 as components of a more integral malaise; a 'Thirty Years War of the twentieth century' if you will. The foregoing chapters have nevertheless shown that no ascription, however well conceived, is an essential guide to a given epoch. Europe's early twentieth century was characterized by twisted paths and featured phenomena that seem misplaced when set beside trench warfare, Hitler's regime, and Auschwitz, but some of these phenomena (international bodies, written constitutional systems, welfare state policies, minority legal rights) had a more enduring influence on how European society was recast after 1945. The better times that followed were based on the achievements or innovations that took root in the earlier half of the century.

FURTHER READING

Abernethy, David, *The Dynamics of Global Dominance: European Overseas Empires, 1415–1980* (New Haven, Conn., 2000).

Aldrich, Robert, *Greater France: A History of French Overseas Expansion* (London, 1996).

Arnold, David 'Europe, Technology, and Colonialism in the 20th Century', *History and Technology*, 21 (2005), 85–106.

Betts, Raymond, *Uncertain Dimensions: Western Overseas Empires in the Twentieth Century* (Minneapolis, 1985).

Chandavarkar, Rajnarayan, 'Imperialism and the European Empires', in Julian Jackson (ed.), *Europe 1900–1914* (Oxford, 2002), 138–72.

Doumanis, Nicholas, *Myth and Memory in the Mediterranean: Remembering Fascism's Empire* (London, 1997).

Eckes, Alfred E., and Thomas W. Zeiler, *Globalization and the American Century* (New York, 2003).

Ferguson, Niall, *Empire: The Rise and Demise of the British World Order and the Lessons for Global Power* (London, 2002).

Gabaccia, Donna, *Italy's Many Diasporas* (London, 2000).

Grazia, Victoria de, *Irresistible Empire: America's Advance through 20th Century Europe* (Cambridge, Mass., 2005).

Hobsbawm, Eric J., *The Age of Extremes: The Short History of the Twentieth Century, 1914–1991* (London, 1994).

Hoerder, Dirk, *Cultures in Contact: World Migrations in the Second Millennium* (Durham, NC, 2002).

Holland, R. F., *European Decolonization 1918–1981: An Introductory Survey* (London, 1985).

Kennedy, Paul, *The Rise and Fall of the Great Powers: Economic Change and Military Conflict from 1500 to 2000* (London, 1988).

—— and William I. Hitchcock (eds.), *From War to Peace: Altered Strategic Landscapes in the Twentieth Century* (New Haven, Conn., 2000).

Maier, Charles S., *In Search of Stability: Explorations in Historical Political Economy* (Cambridge, 1987).

Mayer, Arno J., *Why Did the Heavens Not Darken?: The 'Final Solution' in History* (New York, 1988).

Mazower, Mark, *Dark Continent: Europe's Twentieth Century* (London, 1998).

Perkins, John, 'The Swastika Down Under: Nazi Activities in Australia, 1933–39', *Journal of Contemporary History*, 26 (1991), 111–29.

Europe in 1914

Europe between the Wars

Europe after 1945

SWEDEN

FINLAND

● Helsinki
● Leningrad

● Stockholm

Tallinn

Gotland

ESTONIA

● Riga

LATVIA

Dvina

BALTIC SEA

LITHUANIA

Niemen

● Vilnius

Gdansk

Vistula

● Warsaw

POLAND

Oder

● Prague

CZECHOSLOVAKIA

Vienna ●

RIA

● Budapest

HUNGARY

Belgrade ●

YUGOSLAVIA

Adriatic Sea

Tirana ●

ALBANIA

GREECE

Aegean
Sea

Athens ●

SEA

Crete

RUMANIA

Bucharest ●

Danube

BULGARIA

● Sofia

UNION OF SOVIET

● Moscow

SOCIALIST

REPUBLICS

Dnieper

Dniester

BLACK SEA

Istanbul ●

TURKEY

Rhodes

Cyprus

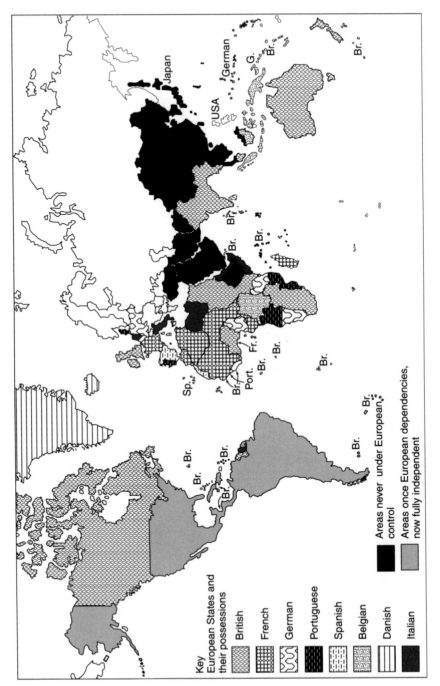

European Colonial Empires in 1914

Key
European States and
their possessions

British

French

German

Portuguese

Spanish

Belgian

Danish

Italian

Areas never under European control

Areas once European dependencies, now fully independent

Japan

German

G.

Br.

Br.

USA

Br.

Br.

Br.

Fr.

Br.

Port.

Br.

Br.

Sp.

Br.

Br.

Br.

Br.

Br.

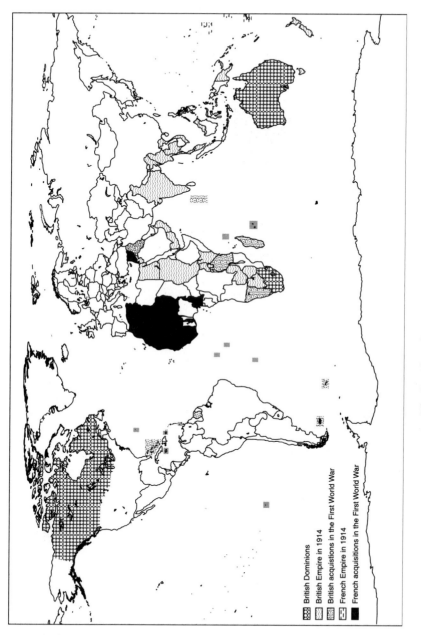

British Dominions
British Empire in 1914
British acquisitions in the First World War
French Empire in 1914
French acquisitions in the First World War

The British and French Empires in 1930

Select Chronology of International Events

1914

28 June	Assassination of Archduke Franz Ferdinand in Sarajevo
28 July	Austrian declaration of war on Serbia
1 August	German declaration of war on Russia
3 August	French declaration of war on Germany
4 August	German invasion of Belgium and British declaration of war on Germany
26–8 August	Battle of Tannenberg
6–10 September	Battle of the Marne
18 September	Third Irish Home Rule Bill enacted

1915

23 April	Treaty of London between France, Great Britain, and Italy signed
23 May	Italy declares war on Austria-Hungary

1916

21 February	German offensive against Verdun begins
24 April	Irish Easter Rising begins
1 June	Russian offensive in Galicia
1 July	British offensive on the Somme
27 August	Romania declares war on Austria-Hungary

1917

14 March	Formation of Provisional Government in Russia under Prince Lvov
15 March	Abdication of Tsar Nicholas II
6 April	United States declares war on Germany
16 April	Lenin returns to Russia
19 July	German Reichstag votes Peace Resolution

24 October	Italian defeat at Caporetto
8 November	Russian People's Council of Commissars established (October revolution)
6 December	Finland declares independence

1918

8 January	Woodrow Wilson presents the Fourteen Points
28 January	Civil War between Whites and Reds in Finland breaks out
24 February	Estonia declares independence
1 March	Peace Treaty between Finland and Soviet Russia
3 March	Soviet–German Treaty of Brest-Litovsk
21 March	Ludendorff offensive on Western Front
16 July	Tsar Nicholas II and his family murdered
8 August	'Black day' of the German army
29 September	Bulgaria concludes armistice
30 October	Ottoman Empire concludes armistice
3 November	Austria–Hungary concludes armistice
5 November	Independent Polish state proclaimed
9 November	Proclamation of German Republic and abdication of Kaiser Wilhelm II
11 November	Armistice signed between Germany and Allied Powers
12 November	Austrian Republic proclaimed
14 November	Czechoslovak Republic proclaimed
16 November	Hungarian Republic proclaimed
18 November	Latvia declares independence
4 December	Foundation of Kingdom of Serbs, Croats, and Slovenes

1919

18 January	Opening of Paris Peace Conference
2–6 March	First Congress of the Communist International in Moscow (Comintern founded)
28 April	Adoption of the Convenant of the League of Nations
15 May	Greek forces occupy Smyrna
21 June	Finland adopts a republican form of government
28 June	Treaty of Versailles (Germany) signed
4 August–13 November	Romanian forces occupy Budapest

10 September	Treaty of Saint-Germain (Austria) signed
12 September	D'Annunzio seizes Fiume
19 November	US Senate fails to ratify Treaty of Versailles
27 November	Treaty of Neuilly (Bulgaria) signed

1920

15–22 January	Helsingfors conference: Poland, Finland, Estonia, Latvia, and Lithuania discuss common policy towards Soviet Russia
16 January	First meeting of the League of Nations' Council in Paris
2 February	Soviet–Estonian peace treaty of Tartu
9 February	Allied troops enter Danzig
19 March	US Senate rejects Treaty of Versailles
5 May	Supreme Council assigns 'A' mandates: Syria to France; Mesopotamia and Palestine to Britain
4 June	Treaty of Trianon (Hungary) signed
6 July	Soviet offensive against Poland begins
10 July	Northern Slesvig formally reclaimed as part of Denmark
12 July	Soviet–Lithuanian peace treaty of Moscow
19 July– 7 August	Second conference of Communist International; establishes Twenty-One Conditions (6 August)
10 August	Treaty of Sèvres (Turkey) signed
11 August	Latvia and Soviet Russia sign the peace treaty of Riga
14 August	Czech–Yugoslav alliance formed
14–16 August	Soviet army defeated at Warsaw
1–8 September	Baku Congress of the Peoples of the East
7 September	Franco–Belgian military convention
20 September	Eupen and Malmédy assigned to Belgium
9 October	Poland occupies Vilnius
12 October	Soviet Russian–Polish armistice
14 October	Soviet Russian–Finnish peace treaty of Tartu signed
27 October	Headquarters of the League of Nations established in Geneva
15 November	Danzig formally becomes a 'Free City'
15 November– 18 December	League of Nations: first meeting of the Assembly in Geneva
10 December	Nobel Peace Prize awarded to Wilson (1919) and Bourgeois (1920)
15 December	Austria admitted to League of Nations

16 December	Statute of the Permanent Court of International Justice opened for signature at Geneva
16 December	Bulgaria and Finland admitted to League of Nations
23 December	Government of Ireland Act

1921

26 January	Independence of Estonia and Latvia recognized by Allied powers
19 February	Franco–Polish Treaty of mutual assistance
18 March	Polish–Soviet Treaty of Riga
20 March	Upper Silesian Plebiscite
27 March	Failed Habsburg coup in Hungary
23 April	Czechoslovak–Romanian alliance formed
27 April	Reparation Commission fixes German reparations at 132 billion gold marks
5 May	London schedule of reparations payments and Allied ultimatum to Germany
11 May	German government accepts London schedule
15 May	Italian elections: first significant breakthrough of Mussolini's fascist party
7 June	Romanian-Yugoslav alliance formed
22 August	Nansen appointed as League of Nations' high commissioner for refugees
24 August	US peace treaty with Austria concluded
25 August	US peace treaty with Germany concluded
29 August	US peace treaty with Hungary concluded
22 September	Estonia, Latvia, and Lithuania admitted to the League of Nations
12 October	League Council partitions Upper Silesia between Germany and Poland
12 November	Independence of Albania recognized by Allied powers
6 December	Anglo-Irish Treaty creates Irish Free State within the British Empire

1922

| 15 February | Opening of the Permanent Court of International Justice at The Hague |
| 16 April | Germany and Soviet Russia conclude Treaty of Rapallo, establishing diplomatic representation and renouncing financial claims |

30 June	Lithuania recognized by Allied powers
10 September	British–Soviet Russian trade agreement
18 September	Hungary admitted to League of Nations
27 September	Revolution in Greece. King Constantine abdicates
4 October	Geneva protocols for financial reconstruction of Austria adopted
8–9 October	Conference at Reval: Finland, Estonia, Latvia and Poland discuss Soviet Russian non-aggression proposal
28 October	Mussolini's 'March on Rome' leads to his appointment as Prime Minister of Italy on 30 October
30 December	Union of the Soviet Socialist Republics constituted (Russia, Belarus, Ukraine, Transcaucasian Federation)

1923

1 January	Soviet Union officially established
10 January	Lithuanians invade Memel territory
11 January	Belgian and French troops occupy Ruhr
14 June	Alexander Stamboliski killed in a *coup d'état* in Bulgaria
24 July	Treaty of Lausanne between Allied powers and Turkey
13 September	General Primo de Rivera seizes power in Spain
1 November	Estonian-Latvian Defensive Treaty
2 November	Estonian-Lithuanian Defensive Treaty
8–9 November	Failed beer hall putsch in Munich by Hitler and Ludendorff
20 December	League Council adopts scheme for financial reconstruction of Hungary

1924

21 January	Death of Lenin
24 January	Franco–Czechoslovak alliance treaty signed in Paris
25 March	Greece proclaimed a republic
16 April	Germany accepts Dawes reparation plan
18 August	Evacuation of Allied troops from Ruhr begins

1925

| 3 January | Mussolini dictator in Italy |
| 12 March | Britain formally rejects the Geneva Protocol |

23 April	Czechoslovak–Polish Treaty for conciliation and arbitration concluded despite continuing tensions over Teschen
26 April	Hindenburg elected as German Reich President
4 May–17 June	League of Nations' Conference for the Control of the International Trade in Arms, Munitions, and Implements of War; Geneva Protocol prohibiting use of gas and bacteriological weapons signed by 38 countries
5–16 October	Locarno conference
1 December	Treaty of Locarno signed in London
10 December	Dawes and Chamberlain awarded Nobel Peace Prize

1926

24 April	German-Soviet Treaty of Neutrality and Friendship (Berlin treaty)
12–14 May	*Coup d'état* of General Pilsudski in Poland
10 June	Franco-Romanian friendship and arbitration treaty signed in Paris
8 September	Germany admitted to League of Nations
11 September	Spain withdraws from League of Nations
28 September	Lithuanian-Soviet Agreement on Non-Aggression and Neutrality
30 September	International Steel Agreement between France, Germany, Belgium, and Luxembourg
3–6 October	First Pan-European Congress, Vienna
27 November	Italian–Albanian treaty of friendship signed in Tirana
10 December	Stresemann and Briand awarded Nobel Peace Prize
16 December	Smetona coup in Lithuania

1927

31 January	Inter-Allied Military Control Commission withdrawn from Germany
5 April	Italian–Hungarian friendship treaty
4–23 May	League of Nations' World Economic Conference, Geneva
17 August	Franco–German commercial treaty signed
28 September	Soviet–Lithuanian treaty of non-aggression signed in Moscow
22 November	Italian–Albanian treaty signed at Tirana

10 December   Polish–Lithuanian state of war ends

1928

27 August   Kellogg–Briand Pact to abolish war as an instrument of policy signed in Paris

1 September   Albania proclaimed a kingdom, President Zogu becomes King Zog

1929

9 February   Litvinov Protocol: non-aggression pacts between Soviet Union, Romania, Poland, Latvia, and Estonia

11 February   Lateran Accords between Italy and Vatican

25 April   Launch of first Soviet Five Year Plan at Sixteenth Party Congress

7 June   Presentation of Young reparations plan

5 September   Briand and Stresemann introduce idea of a European federal union at the tenth meeting of the League of Nations' Assembly

19 September   Britain and France sign the 'Optional Clause' of the Permanent Court of International Justice's statute

3 October   Death of Gustav Stresemann

24 October   New York stock market crash ('Black Thursday')

13 November   Bank for International Settlements established

10 December   Kellogg awarded Nobel Peace Prize

22 December   Referendum in Germany ends with crushing defeat of nationalist plans to reject the Young Plan

1930

2 March   Stalin's 'dizzy with success' speech calls temporary halt to collectivization and 'dekulakization'

12 March   German Reichstag approves Young Plan

16 May   Opening of the Stockholm Exhibition

17 May   French memorandum of proposed European federal union

30 June   Belgian and French troops leave Rhineland

23 September   League of Nations meeting on Stresemann-Briand Plan creates Commission of Enquiry for European Union (CEEU)

5–12 October   Representatives from Albania, Bulgaria, Greece, Yugoslavia, Romania, and Turkey attend first Balkan conference in Athens

1931

21 March	Austro–German customs union proposal announced
14 April	Fall of Spanish monarchy and proclamation of the Second Republic
6 May	Soviet–Lithuanian treaty of 1926 renewed for five years
11 May	Austrian Credit-Anstalt collapses, causing bank closures across Central Europe
15 June	Soviet–Polish Treaty of Friendship and Commerce
25 June	Banks of England, France, the Federal Reserve Bank of New York, and the Bank of International Settlement grant the German Reichsbank a credit of $ 100 million.
13 July	Darmstädter Bank and Deutsche Nationalbank collapse
10 August	French-Soviet non-aggression pact
26 August	'National Government' formed in Britain
3 September	Austria and Germany withdraw from their proposed customs union
18 September	Japanese troops stage incident on railways at Mukden, using it as pretext for occupation of Manchuria
3 December	Statute of Westminster passed granting full self-government to Dominions

1932

21 January	Soviet–Finnish non-aggression pact
22 January	Second Five Year Plan launched in the Soviet Union
25 January	Soviet–Polish non-aggression pact
2 February	League of Nation's World Disarmament Conference opens in Geneva
3 February	Soviet–Lithuanian non-aggression pact
5 February	Soviet Union signs non-aggression pacts with Latvia
9 March	Japanese establish puppet state of Manchukuo in Manchuria
10 March	De Valera becomes President of Executive Council in Ireland
12 March	Ivar Kreugar commits suicide: collapse of Swedish Match and financial instability in Sweden
10 April	Hindenburg wins against Hitler in German presidential elections
20 May	Austro-Fascist Dollfuss government established
16 June– 9 July	Lausanne conference on German reparations

21 July–	
21 August	Imperial Conference in Ottawa establishes preferential tariffs in British Empire
25 July	Soviet Union signs non-aggression pacts with Finland, Estonia, and Poland
31 July	Nazis emerge as strongest party from German general elections
4 October	The Hungarian Fascist Gyula Gömbös forms government in Hungary
29 November	Franco–Soviet non-aggression pact

1933

29 January	Kanslergade Agreement negotiated in Denmark between Social Democrats, Agrarians, and Liberals
30 January	Adolf Hitler appointed as German Chancellor
23 March	'Enabling Law' passed in Germany
27 March	Japan leaves League of Nations
12 June	Second World Economic Conference in London
25 July	Germany withdraws from World Disarmament Conference and
14 October	League of Nations

1934

1–16 February	Civil war in Austria, and suppression of socialists
6 February	Rightist riots in Paris
12 February	General strike in France
12 March	Päts and Laidoner coup in Estonia
15 May	Ulmanis coup in Latvia
30 June	'Night of the Long Knives' in Germany
25 July	Assassination of Austrian Chancellor Engelbert Dollfuss
12 September	Cooperation Treaty between Estonia, Latvia, and Lithuania
9 October	Assassination of King Alexander of Yugoslavia and French Foreign Minister Barthou

1935

16 March	Hitler repudiates disarmament clauses of Versailles Treaty, reintroduction of compulsory military service in Germany
2 May	Franco-Soviet Pact signed

12 May	Death of Marshal Pisludski
15 September	Nuremberg Laws against Jews in Germany
2 October	Fascist Italy invades Ethiopia
11 October	League of Nations imposes sanctions on Italy

1936

16 February	Popular Front victory in Spanish general elections and formation of Quiroga government
7 March	German troops re-enter Rhineland in defiance of Versailles Treaty and Locarno Pact
3 May	Popular Front government comes to power in France
9 May	Fascist Italian Empire proclaimed after victory in Ethiopia
17 July	Spanish Civil War begins with army revolt in Morocco under General Franco
5 August	Proclamation of martial law in Greece and establishment of dictatorship under General Metaxas
26 September	Dismissal of Yagoda and replacement by Ezhov as Soviet secret police chief marks beginning of large-scale purges
25 November	Anti-Comintern Pact signed between Nazi Germany and Japan

1937

February	League of Nations sponsored conference on white slavery
August	League of Nations sponsored conference on rural hygiene
6 November	Italy joins German–Japanese Anti-Comintern Pact

1938

12–13 March	*Anschluss* of Austria
29 September	Munich Agreement between France, Britain, Germany, and Italy leads to dismemberment of Czechoslovakia
9 November	Anti-Semitic pogroms in Germany
20 December	Saltsjöbaden agreement on collective bargaining in Sweden

1939

15 March	German invasion of Czechoslovakia
28 March	Spanish Civil War ends with surrender of republican Madrid
23 August	Hitler–Stalin Pact concluded
1 September	German invasion of Poland marks the beginning of Second World War
3 September	Britain and France declare war on Germany
17 September	Soviet attack on Poland
29 September	Germany and Soviet Union partition Poland
October	Soviet troops occupy Latvia, Lithuania, and Estonia
30 November	Soviet attack on Finland
14 December	Soviet Union expelled from League of Nations

1940

9 April	Germany invades Denmark and Norway
10 May	Germany invades Belgium, Luxembourg, and the Netherlands; Churchill becomes Prime Minister of Britain
10 June	Italy declares war on France and Britain
14 June	German troops enter Paris
16 June	Baltic States occupied by Soviet troops and puppet regimes established
22 June	France signs armistice with Germany and Italy
10 July	*État français* established
14 October	Meeting of Pétain and Hitler at Montoire, France
23 October	Meeting of Franco and Hitler at Hendaye, France
28 October	Italy invades Greece

1941

25–27 March	Coup against pro-German Regent in Yugoslavia
6 April	Germany invades Yugoslavia and Greece
22 June	German invasion of Soviet Union
June/July	Baltic States occupied by German troops
14 August	Anglo-American Atlantic Charter
7 December	Japanese attack on Pearl Harbor, Hawaii

11 December	Germany and Italy declare war on United States
13 December	Bulgaria declares war on United States

1942

18 January	Military agreement between Germany, Italy, and Japan signed in Berlin
20 January	Wannsee conference
1 July	Battle of El Alamein
24 August	First Quebec Conference (Churchill and Roosevelt)
17 December	Allied joint declaration on German extermination of Jews

1943

14–24 January	Casablanca Conference
2 February	Surrender at Stalingrad of German Sixth Army
10 July	Allied invasion of Sicily
25 July	Marshal Pietro Badoglio replaces Mussolini as head of Italian government
29 August	Germans impose direct rule in Denmark following a series of strikes
8 September	Announcement of Italian armistice
10 September	German troops occupy Rome
15 September	German paratroopers free Mussolini
14 November	Radical fascist Verona Manifesto provides base to Italian Social Republic
28 November– 1 December	Teheran conference of Churchill, Roosevelt, and Stalin

1944

22 March	German puppet regime established in Hungary; deportation of Hungarian Jews begins
4 June	Americans and British troops capture Rome
6 June	Allied landings in Normandy
1–15 July	United Nations monetary conference at Bretton Woods, New Hampshire

1 August	Warsaw Rising begins (until 2 October)
23 August	King Michael of Romania dismisses Antonescu and accepts Allied armistice
5 September	Soviet declaration of war on Bulgaria
19 September	Finland signs armistice agreement in Moscow
17 October	German soldiers arrest the Hungarian Regent, Admiral Horthy

1945

11 January	Soviet troops capture Warsaw
4–11 February	meeting of Stalin with Roosevelt and Churchill (the 'Big Three') at Yalta
16 April	Soviet offensive against Berlin begins
28 April	Execution of Mussolini by Italian partisans
30 April	Hitler commits suicide
8/9 May	Germany's unconditional surrender ends World War II in Europe
17 July– 2 August	Potsdam conference
6 August	US airforce drops nuclear bomb on Hiroshima
8 August	Soviet declaration of war on Japan
9 August	US airforce drops nuclear bomb on Nagasaki
14 August	Japan's unconditional surrender marks the end of Second World War

Index

Note: Bold entries refer to illustrations.